in Education

Courtney D. Schlosser

Philosophy Department
Worcester State College

The PERSON in Education:

A Humanistic Approach

Macmillan Publishing Co., Inc.
NEW YORK

Macmillan Publishing Co., Inc.
866 Third Avenue, New York, New York 10022

Collier Macmillan Canada, Ltd.

Library of Congress Cataloging in Publication Data

Main entry under title:

The Person in education.

  Includes bibliographies.
  1. Education, Humanistic—Addresses, essays,
lectures. 2. Humanistic ethics—Addresses, essays,
lectures. I. Schlosser, Courtney.
LC1011.P47   370.11'2   75-9717
ISBN 0-02-407680-5

Printing: 1 2 3 4 5 6 7 8   Year: 6 7 8 9 0 1 2

to learn to love oneself . . .
is of all arts the subtlest,
the most cunning, the ultimate . . .

Friedrich Nietzsche

Preface

The purpose of this anthology is to focus attention upon the ideal of the person in education. I have termed my approach to this subject as humanistic for several reasons. First, the concept and philosophy of humanism constitute a venerable tradition in human thought. Second, humanism, especially under the guise of humanistic education, possesses an almost household familiarity and currency which makes the term palatable to a wide audience. Third, and this is my main reason, philosophical humanism as it relates to educational thought and practice is supported by recent and vitally significant developments in human knowledge and experience, coming from existentialism, phenomenology, humanistic psychology, phenomenological sociology, neo-Marxism, and philosophical anthropology, as well as a renaissance of interest among Westerners in Taoism, Zen Buddhism, Sufism, Hinduism, and Confucianism. Additionally, a radically new kind of institution has emerged in the last fifteen years in the United States. Called "growth centers" and fashioned mainly after the Esalen Institute, of Big Sur, California, these institutions of learning, which number in the hundreds at this writing, offer opportunities and situations for the growth and development of the person that are truly unique and humanistic. Perhaps a fourth reason that I have called my approach humanistic, although it is assuredly related to the above reasons, is the fact that a general synthesis of viewpoints of new knowledge and old is beginning to filter down to the everyday level of humanity, to resurrect anew the historically and philosophically important ideals of happiness, health, beauty, truth, good-

ness, justice, and freedom, to name a few. Evidence of this renewed
historical quest of humanity is the appearance of various social prob-
blem-solving groups, among women, black people, and excluded minority groups of all kinds. Among the popular techniques being used
for humanistic development of the person have been consciousness-
raising groups, encounter groups, meditation, and dialogue directed
at expanding self-awareness and a more real sense of the world.

The main focus of this anthology is, of course, the schools, as far as
the ideal of the person in education is concerned. It is possible and
desirable, of course, to view education in the context of life as well,
for first and foremost we must strive to understand the world in
which we live if we are to cope meaningfully and effectively with it
for humanistic purposes. Thus, although this anthology clearly and
explicitly recognizes the importance of the meaning of life to humanistic education, it focuses considerable attention toward the world
that we all must live in, like it or not.

By way of an introduction to the ideal of the person in education, I
have written a brief, personal essay that appears before Part I. The
essay is certainly more suggestive than it is scholarly and prescriptive. Implicit, however, at a subliminal level in my thoughts throughout the essay is the feeling that existential philosophy, phenomenology, humanistic psychology, and the Eastern religious
philosophies of Taoism and Zen Buddhism are relevant to an adequate view of the person in education. At another time and place, I
may make these viewpoints explicit. But for now, my essay will have
to stand on its own merits, for better or for worse.

Part I is concerned with four "foundations" or disciplinary grounds
upon which to view the meaning of humanistic education. In order
of their appearance, they are the historical, the philosophical, the
psychological, and the sociological. As I strive to make clear in the
introductions to each of these sections, the problem of the wholeness
of man, his spiritual, intellectual, aesthetic, emotional, sexual, and
physical being, is foremost in the philosophy of humanistic education. And, as I hope emerges in Part I and Part II, the historical and
sociological problem of the wholeness of man can be solved through
the ideal of the person, in a philosophical and psychological framework.

Part II focuses upon the educational contexts of humanistic education, specifically teaching and learning, the curriculum, and the
schools. These "contexts," of course, are relevant to any other
scheme of education, although their meaning as humanistic—i.e.,
holistic and integrative—will emerge more fully through the writings. At the same time, I have intended that Part II make more explicit what is sometimes merely implicit in Part I, namely implica-

tions for change—in the schools, the curriculum, and teaching and learning. As Karl Marx has said, "It is not enough to merely interpret the world, the point is to change it."

There is no easy or fully adequate way to sum up my feelings, expectations, or vision of this book. In a few cases, limitations of space and even financial considerations prohibited the inclusion of certain selections, but I have put my heart and soul into the design of this book even though I know that deep down, there are no words to express the experience. Perhaps, in the end, after all has been said and written about the person or humanistic education or any profoundly philosophical ideal, *the truth remains wordless,* in the spirit of Taoism. I believe that this must be so about the deepest experiences of education and life.

There are also no adequate ways to express my feelings of gratitude to the many persons—teachers, students, and friends—who have helped me to realize myself as a person. But I would like to thank Albert Kahn, Gene Phillips, Theodore Brameld, Kenneth Benne, and Paul Nash, who were among my professors when I was a student at Boston University. Also, I would like to thank Professor Donald Traub, the head of the Philosophy Department at Worcester State College, for his support of my academic role in that department, as well as Professor Neil Brophy for his friendship and penetrating philosophical reading of and suggestions for my manuscript, and finally Professor Donald Read, the head of the Health Education Department at Worcester State College, whose friendship and professional support have helped me to realize myself through this book. As for students, I know no way to start or end a list of those to whom I have been closest over the years. It is perhaps enough to say that my experiences with students have been among the most deeply meaningful experiences of my own quest to become a person.

I also want to give special thanks to Barbara McSheey and Debbie Perotto for helping me to prepare the manuscript for publication.

C. D. S.

Contents

The Person in Education

The day outside is warm and beautiful. It is September, and the leaves are beginning to turn. I wonder what it really means to be a person. Books crowd me at my elbows on the subject; but my head and my heart turn irresistibly back toward the sunlight, the warm air, the unseasonable sounds of birds, through my open window. I wonder if anybody will ever know for sure.

The greatest certainty to me is what is happening here-and-now, in my surroundings and in the sensations of my body and the objects of my consciousness. Thus, somewhere in my logical and reasonable self, I conclude that to be and to feel like a person mean to be in touch with reality, with what is really happening, at this instant. Yet always there is abstraction, which we need to become fully human. For we are not just sensing, feeling, here-and-now beings, we are capable of thinking and remembering and imagining too. Thus, we need to see ourselves and to experience ourselves in time as well as space. But first and foremost we need to remain as fully as possible in the present, alert, alive, feeling, sensing, being.

While I am writing, I know that there are a million events going on, beyond my immediate view of the world, that I will never know about. Yet, somehow, all of them—and who knows how many more?—may imperceptibly affect me as a person. What I am saying, with a voice that only I can hear and feel, is that being a person is such an incredibly complex experience that there does not yet appear to be any way that we can definitely establish, once and for all, what it means to be one.

1

It is something beyond the adequacy of words, thought, feelings, or sensations that I want to try to communicate about being a person. Describing or analyzing what it means to be a person is inadequate because it is too general, at an intellectual level; furthermore, when someone is always describing or analyzing a particular subject, in this case a person, the observer's viewpoint of the problem imperceptibly changes and becomes something more, much like the very experience of being a person. And unless we focus upon a particular person, existing totally as his or her own subjective being in an objective, here-and-now world, as *I* and much more, we reduce the person to an abstraction, in our attempt to understand what it means to be one. And on existential grounds, if none other, reducing a person to an abstraction is a horrendous crime, against the person as well as humanity. And yet this is what we are faced with daily in society and in man's relationship with the cosmos.

Life experienced as a person is meaningful, provided that you are orienting your whole self toward the world. Furthermore, it is potentially happy and wonderful, even when the worst is happening. To live means to have courage and to remain strong in the face of adversity and suffering, as well as to have the illusion of complete happiness. Remaining a person when things are bad is not easy; but it may be the truest test of character in that it means being willing to rise above what threatens to reduce one's self to an object or an abstraction. There is no easy way to learn how to become a person except through living, and that means suffering and enjoying, despairing and hoping, hating and loving, and taking one's stand upon the conviction that we are always something more than any of the feelings, threats, or forces of existence that tend to reduce us to the status of objects and things.

2

When I begin to think about the meaning of education many things come to mind: the kind of world that we all live in, the nature of knowledge and experience, conditions for learning and teaching in schools and colleges, the meaning of life, and finally the idea of a person. These things or objects of my thinking about education do not usually appear in some systematic, cerebral order alone; they are frequently mixed with intense feelings. And sometimes, when my visionary, utopian view of education is dimmest, my feelings about the way education is usually conducted in the schools and colleges make me very depressed. But I console myself with the belief that somewhere between my lowest feelings about the reality of educational experience and the highest flights of my utopian hopes for education, the truth probably lies, for both myself and the most realistic possibilities of education. For the phenomenon of education suffers the same problem that bedevils the rest of existence: we can always imagine, hope for, and dream about a more perfect reality than actually exists in the world. The gaps between education and life, knowledge and experience, school and society, the child and the curriculum, teaching and learning, mind and body, self and other may be the unavoidable price we pay for being human and alive. Yet I know there have been times, and unforgettable times they were, when I have experienced feelings of transcendence and soared beyond everyday feelings.

One always has to cope with the real world, which also exists beyond feelings and human subjectivity. I believe, however, that the most realistic basis for education is the experience of the person. And this means that education should be oriented both toward the real world and toward the possibilities of transcendence. In the first instance education, as an institutional, public, and formal phenomenon, has great responsibilities toward the world. It should inform and awaken the person to the kind of world that he or she lives in, and that, among other things, means creating a critical, sensitive, problem-solving attitude toward the major social problems of the day. In this sense education should be meaningfully tied to other social institutions that are also educating and teaching their citizens right conduct for a humane world. Among the other great responsibilities of formal education toward the world are the goals and values of professionalism, vocationalism, and career guidance and counseling. The second major function of education, to explore the possibilities of transcendence through knowledge and feeling, has always had the greatest hold upon educational institutions, whether it is admitted or not. For what we are alluding to is, in the first instance, the historically important function of teaching and learning from the viewpoints of the arts, the sciences, and the humanities, and in the second, the hopes and dreams that many have held about the possibility of arousing both reason and passion for the wonder, beauty, and mystery that such vistas of knowledge can reveal about Being. Of course it is comparatively easy to state pessimistically, on the basis of experience, that the schools and colleges have been to some extent oriented toward promoting social conformity, docility, and even stupidity about the world and the possibilities of experience. At the same time formal education has certainly perpetuated and nurtured the social class bias implicitly present in intellectual snobbery and academic elitism. But since neither pessimism nor optimism represents an entirely viable attitude toward the world, I prefer to take, particularly toward education, the view of meliorism, which assumes that the world can be improved if man sets his mind and heart to the task, with his whole sense of personhood and feelings for what is right. In the end this may be the sole basis for a humanistic approach to education, or for actualizing the ideal of the person in education.

3

What knowledge do we really possess about being a person? Can an individual really learn or be taught how to become a person? And can education, as it is presently organized, really educate rather than train the person to an enlarged and deepened sense of himself and the world? With qualifications, I can answer in the affirmative to the second and third of these questions, on the basis of my own experience as both a teacher and a student. The first question, however, requires a philosophical reply.

There are innumerable ways to define the meaning of being a person. The idea that being a person is somehow tied to the core meaning and experience of existence itself is derived from philosophy, especially existentialism. From theology and religion comes the notion that the self or soul of the individual not only represents a basis for experiencing divinity and transcending existence, but also makes possible metaphysical knowledge about the ultimate meaning of being an individual. From psychology, particularly humanistic and existential psychology, comes the idea that to be a person requires that the individual become himself as he truly exists in the face of social goals and roles, defense mechanisms, facades, subconscious drives and impulses. From a biological viewpoint, particularly that of what Abraham Maslow has called phenomenological biology, to be a person means to learn to listen meditatively to the organic and bodily, or somatic, nature of one's being, tuning into and getting in touch with the deeper as well as higher impulses, drives, and instincts of organic being. From the perspective of sociology and anthropology, the meaning of being a person derives from one's lived-through existence as a social being both in a particular society and through the wider, and potentially deeper, identification with mankind as a whole, in culture. And lastly, from education and the human potential movement, being a person may be defined as learning to become one's self and actualizing that knowledge in the contexts of individualistic, interpersonal, and transpersonal experiences and encounters.

Theoretically, there is no knowledge that is not relevant to the problem of becoming a person, nor is there any experience that may not enlarge, deepen, and heighten one's sense of self and the world, whether the experience is counted good or bad, positive or negative. There is some question, however, whether the schools and colleges are sufficiently open to the enlarged sense of experience that one requires in order to grow as a person. Too much of what goes on in schools and colleges represents stereotypical, socially acceptable, role-playing modes of behavior, thinking, and feeling. It is indeed a rare classroom or school where the atmosphere or climate of learning encourages teachers and students, staff and administrators, to openly and authentically interact as persons, beyond the roles, facades, and masks that the social system has insidiously conditioned them to don. But in spite of the power and authority of the school system, as it appears in the behavior of those in schools and colleges, individuals do transcend their merely socialized selves and relate honestly, openly, and authentically to one another. And the willingness and the ability to relate deeply and honestly about one's self to another will always be the most radical condition for educating toward personhood.

Many questions remain to be asked and to be answered. And owing to the uncertainty and ambiguity of existence, absolutely certain and final statements about the meaning of being a person should be questioned. It is possible, however, to make some tentative assertions about the conditions under which people become more authentically and truly themselves, actualizing their deepest potentials and exploring the infinite reaches of personal consciousness, whose knowledge and experience are mysteriously and intimately connected with the deepest processes of nature and the universe. What are some of these conditions? How do individuals learn to experience themselves as something more than role-players, objects in the world, subpersonalities, or whatever?

The easiest way I know of trying to answer adequately the question of the conditions involved in the growth of the person is to explain the few things that I believe are true about the person. First, I believe that we have a free will or consciousness and that the pronoun *I* centers us in the energy field of our personal being. Second, the *I* of personal consciousness is the most real basis for our relating to a world that is both out there and in here simultaneously. And even though life or existence is a struggle for being, the most authentic and honest way we have of becoming, is through our personal sense of being, in the mode of *I am* which includes *I think* or *I feel* and *I do.* The almost constant problem of being a person is the split experienced between being and becoming; although we quest for the fullness and completeness of being, it constantly eludes us in the unhappy consciousness of mere becoming. And this, to me, is perhaps the essence of the philosophical problem of being a person.

Right now, for example, I am questing with all my powers of thought, feeling, and will to grasp the meaning of being a person; and yet nothing seems more fruitless and in vain. I would much prefer to take a walk amid the beautiful colors of autumn and view the sky streaked over from the sunset. Right now, the smell of autumn leaves seems the most real thing to me, perhaps because I can relate to the experience from the center of myself. Basically, nothing appears more true about being a person than the fact of having a body. Sometimes, I even doubt that it makes any sense to talk about a mind, a soul, or a spirit apart from the feelings, needs, and urges of the body. Rightly or wrongly, however, I do believe that the energy field of the body is our most healthy and potentially creative basis for becoming fully actualized persons.

A great deal has been made in recent years of the importance of feelings in grounding ourselves as persons. I think that feelings orient us fundamentally toward our own sense of personhood. However, the same imbalance could result from emphasis on feeling that once, perhaps, existed from emphasis on thinking. For perhaps the most basic truth or condition for growing as a person is to see and to experience ourselves as total beings, and that means inwardly and outwardly, bodily and spiritually, as feeling and thinking, existing beings. For what appears to be true for myself, over and over again, is that the moment I feel in touch with myself as a total organism, I experience what I would with humility and awe call self-actualization. And the experience of self-actualization, to me, is a feeling centered upon my personal sense of being, wherever I am, and my acceptance of the reality of it because it is me. Thus it appears that the only way to overcome the philosophical problem of being is through the acceptance of personal becoming. And unless I am very wrong, acceptance of one's self as a becoming being is the most balancing, stabilizing, and integrating attitude that we can discover for ourselves as growing persons.

4

During the unusually hot summer of 1974, I offered a course titled "The Philosophy of Human Potentiality: An Experiential Approach" at Worcester State College. It was a time of great personal anguish to me, and my most deeply held beliefs and ideas about the importance of being strong and courageous no matter what were being challenged to the quick. The course was offered on a two-week, workshop basis, and eight persons enrolled for it. Each morning, from 8:00 to 12:30, we met in an air-conditioned, windowless, carpeted room of the Learning Resources Center and encountered one another, through a variety of techniques and ideas from philosophy, and the human potential movement. And although my role was both as a group leader and a participant, it was the most intense group experience that I have ever had, either as a teacher or a person.

I am ending this essay with that experience, not only because it meant a lot to me as a person, but because it more than ever confirmed my own beliefs about the potential for human growth that is contained in interpersonal and intersubjective experiencing. The night before the course ended I wrote a poem to the members of the group that expressed how I felt at the time. When I read the poem to them the next morning, it brought out even more vividly and intensely the joy and the sorrow, the humor and the seriousness of those two weeks that we had shared together.

I am including the poem here because it expresses and gives evidence of, at least indirectly, some of my own feelings and ideas about the value of educating humanistically.

Because each of you is you
I will not forget
the way that we were

Nor will I forget how
we were together
for such a short time
in my life.

And each of you—
Linda, Paul, Cathie, Bobbie,
Doris, Liz, Jean, George—
has given something to me
that I cannot forget:

You gave to me the experience
of being alive with you
and knowing and encountering
the spirit within us
and between us.

And I gave all that I could
though I wish it had been more,
but I know and you know
what prevented and allowed
our greater giving together.
So, to each of you
I want to say thank you,
thank you for allowing me
to see into your lives
and to experience what
only those whom you love
experience and know.

I shall not forget you
since you have shown me
who you are, in such a short time,
nor can I be the less
for it.

I know no way to end this
since I have touched infinity
and the eternity of time
with each of you.

So I can only say
that I love You.

Part I

The Foundations of
Humanistic Education

The Historical Foundation: The Problem of the Wholeness of Man

Humanism, historically and philosophically, has been inseparably connected with the problem of the wholeness of man, particularly in terms of man's possible perfectibility. In education, humanism has referred to the meaning or possible meaning that the ideal of human wholeness can have in teaching and learning. The humanistic ideal of wholeness, however, in education, and elsewhere for that matter, has almost always been tempered by the recognition that our highest and deepest ideals must enable us to better cope with reality, in thought, feeling, and action. In this sense, humanism is not an entirely new way of thinking about man, but rather has deep, historical roots in human consciousness, since man has always been painfully as well as joyfully aware of the problems and possibilities of reality. What is new, however, in the history of humanistic thought is the more or less self-conscious and deliberate attempt, on the part of some, to actively engage the ideals of humanity with reality, as existence is lived from day to day in the schools and elsewhere.

The problem, or so-called problem, of man, considered as his wholeness lies precisely in the gap, and the consciousness of the gap, that exists between the ideals of humanism and the conditions of reality. And the problem, which is a source of tension, conflict, and anxiety, exists, by degree, wherever or whenever man acts, feels, and thinks as a whole being. In this sense, the problem of the wholeness of man is not solvable in any ultimate or even technically final way, since reality is constantly changing and today's solutions to yesterday's problems may be the source of tomorrow's tensions and doubts.

What, however, the consciousness of the wholeness of man leaves us with is the awareness that most of life's solutions to problems are neither final nor ultimate and that the quest for humanistic being and experience is life-long. In education this awareness is too often lost sight of behind momentary and strictly utilitarian goals and practices. Humanism, however, as it sheds light upon the history of man can enable us to better understand and appreciate what education can mean and be, in both its highest and most abysmal moments as well as all those between.

The purpose of the following group of readings is to open up this source of being and meaning for education, in the sincere hope that the process of education will become more humanized or holistic.

The first selection, entitled "Classical Humanism," is from a seminal study in the history of education, *Education in Antiquity,* by H. I. Marrou. I have chosen Marrou's chapter on classical humanism for the purpose of showing how the problem of the wholeness of man was approached during the Hellenistic Age of Greece. The "body and the soul, sense and reason, character and mind" were central to the early Greek or "classical" conception of the whole man. From the same essay it is interesting to note how many concerns, problems, and themes appeared in the humanistic education of the ancient Greeks that are present in our own times. For example, their distinction between education for the adult and education of for the child has remained, aggravatingly, with us to this day. Also their concern for educating the whole man rather than a part of him; their distinction between a literary (classical humanism) and a scientific education; their distinction also between the teacher as a role-performing technician (the ancient "schoolmaster") and the ideal of the teacher as one who has an empathic and personal relationship with the student (the ancient "pedagogue"); their ideal of the school as a community as opposed to an anonymous and alienating collectivity; their awareness of verbal as opposed to nonverbal learning—all are notions very much a part of our thinking about humanistic education today.

John E. Weakland's article, "Renaissance Paideia: Some Ideals in Italian Humanism and Their Relevance Today," focuses attention upon the humanistic concept of man as it appeared in Italy in the fourteenth and fifteenth centuries. Italian humanism, Weakland tells us, can be contrasted to medieval scholasticism. For where humanism was man-centered, scholasticism was God-centered; and whereas the former stressed the discovery of self through Socratic dialogue, the latter's approach to learning was more systematic and impersonal.

Crucial to a contemporary understanding of humanistic education is the so-called human potential movement. In "Notes Toward a History," Jane Howard vividly describes what the movement has meant particularly to one of its leading founders, Dr. Kenneth Benne. It is vital to note that consciousness of the importance of the group as an educational experience has been a potent force in the rise of humanistic education.

And lastly, Stuart Miller, the novelist and director of The Esalen Institute, the most famous of the human potential growth centers, describes his conception of what "An Education for the Whole Person" means. Emphasizing the effective, emotional, and psychological side of man, Miller asserts that humanistic education should deal with stresses that modern life exerts upon the body and how the individual can avoid the "harmful consequences of such stresses."

DISCUSSION QUESTIONS

1. According to H. I. Marrou, the ancient Greeks attached great significance to the concept of the whole man. What did they mean by the notion of the whole man, and to what extent do you think it is possible to educate for the whole man? Marrou also points out that Homer, rather than Plato, was the educator of the Greeks. What different educational traditions does this assumption point to? Finally, what is the difference between classical, or literary, humanism and scientific humanism, in terms of the subject matter of education?

2. One central point made by John Weakland in his article on Italian humanism of the Renaissance period was that it was man-centered instead of God-centered as medieval scholasticism had been. What difference, if any, do you think it would make if an educational system were centered upon the idea of man rather than the idea of God? Also, do you believe that a study of the classics, as well as rhetoric, could lead to greater self-knowledge, as the Renaissance humanists tended to think? Why?

3. Jane Howard quotes Dr. Kenneth Benne as citing three frameworks for thinking about the human potential movement: (1) the group for growth purposes, i.e., the family, classroom, and so on; (2) the scientific study of groups; and (3) the rise of growth centers designed to facilitate knowledge and experience of group encounters. To what extent have you personally been involved in any or all of these frameworks? From your own knowledge and experience of the human potential movement, what relevance do you feel it has to the humanization of education?

4. Stuart Miller examined the Greek concept *paideia*, defining it as the total, educational formation of man, in the active and passive, private and public, cognitive and affective senses. What forces or conditions do you see working against the total formation of man in

the present social and educational world, especially in view of the humanistic goals of self-knowledge, learning by discovery, affective well-being, and the sense of individual uniqueness, unity, harmony, and centeredness?

FURTHER READING

Carr, Edward Hallett. *What is History?* New York: Vintage Books, 1961.

Frankl, Viktor. *Man's Search for Meaning.* New York: Washington Square Press, 1967.

Huxley, Julian. *Man in the Modern World.* New York: A Mentor Book, 1944.

Jarrett, James L. *The Humanities and Humanistic Education.* Reading, Massachusetts: Addison-Wesley Publishing Company, Inc., 1973.

Jung, Carl. *Man and His Symbols.* New York: Dell Publishing Co., Inc., 1973.

Marcuse, Herbert. *One-Dimensional Man.* Boston: Beacon Press, 1967.

Robert, Ulich. *History of Educational Thought.* New York: American Book Company, 1950.

Scheler, Max. *Man's Place in Nature.* New York: The Noonday Press, 1962.

Classical Humanism

H . I . M A R R O U

History and Value

History is not merely a monotonous series of events, linked together one after the other throughout inexorable time. It is not enough to know that Hellenistic education took on a certain form as a result of certain antecedent happenings and as a prelude to certain further happenings. There needs to be a pause for consideration: Hellenistic education is not simply something that has passed away, it has *been*—it has *had being*—and we cannot consider ourselves to have finished with it until we have made some attempt to ponder its essence and understand its values.

And it is worth it; for this education was not merely a transitory form, one moment in a continuous evolution; it was the stable, mature Form in which the whole educational effort of antiquity was realized. The climax of seven centuries of creative effort, it was like the flat top of a curve, a long level stretch lasting many generations, during which its educational methods peacefully enjoyed undisputed authority.

It stretched through space as well as time. What is called Roman education was on the whole merely an extension of Hellenistic education to the Latin or Latin-speaking regions in the West. But we can go further and say that Hellenistic education has a significance that extends beyond antiquity and even beyond history itself. It is probably not generally realized that what we call classical culture, i.e. the culture that was handed down by tradition or rediscovered by the various "Renaissances" in the Byzantine East and in Western Europe, is the culture of Hellenistic times. And the most important point of all is that this culture does not merely belong to the past as a spent force whose greatness is over and done with: in a sense, it has not merely existed, but is ever-present and ever-living at the heart of our own thought—as an ideal transcending all its actual manifestations, a stronghold of eternal values.

This does not mean, of course, that I should claim that the classical ideal can be the standard for every possible kind of education and that we must all imitate it. In the first place, I am not at all sure about this, and secondly, any such opinion is out of place in a work of history. All I mean is that the ideal is still with us, either as a model to be copied or as an error to be avoided; it still exists, at least for educated people who have been able to appreciate and understand it, as an Idea which modern thought must be either for or against; contact with it is always rewarding, whether we accept it unquestioningly or resist the temptation to do that and subject it to our own rational analysis.

For this reason the present work will only be satisfactorily accomplished when it has managed to give a clear idea of the values that in their various ways were spread abroad by this classical Form of education. I expect the philosophical reader will want me to give a word to describe the essence of this education: I suggest that we use the old word *humanism,* however overworked it has been: properly explained, it can still be of use. For the ideal at which Hellenistic education aimed can certainly be described as humanistic from many different points of view, all of which are quite legitimate.

Man Not Child the Standard

In the first place the whole aim of this education was the formation of adults, not the development of the child. There is no point in being led astray by etymology. I know quite well that contains the word. But this needs to be translated as "the treatment to which a child should be subjected"—to turn him into a man. As we saw; the Latins happily translated as "humanitas."

Hence, as we have seen in passing, the utter absence of, the utter lack of interest in, child psychology; hence the absence of anything approximating to our infant schools; hence the abstract analytical character of all the "exercises"; hence the barbaric severity of the discipline. Nothing could be more unlike the modern "progressive school" methods than the system of education that was practised in ancient Greece.

But the moderns should not be in too much of a hurry to crow about this and dismiss the Greeks' attitude as outmoded ignorance. In a culture as refined as theirs, and which in so many other fields has given so much evidence of great creative genius, such apparent ignorance must be regarded as deliberate, the expression of an implicit, perhaps, but nevertheless a quite definite rejection of what it did not include.

One cannot feel confident that if the Greeks could have known the endeavours that psychology and education have been making ever since *Emile* was written to adapt themselves to the child and the special characteristics of his mind they would have responded with anything but amused surprise. What is the point, they seem to say, of concentrating on the child as though he were an end in himself? Apart from the few unlucky children who are condemned to a premature death, the only point of childhood is that it leads to manhood, and the proper object of education is therefore not any slobbering child or awkward adolescent or even an up-and-coming young man, but Man, and Man alone; and the only point of education is to teach the child to transcend himself.

The Whole Man

Classical Greece wanted education to concern itself with the whole man, and here for a change we find it in agreement with the modern outlook, which also insists that education and training should be "general," in reaction against the over-emphasis on "instruction," i.e. development of the intellectual faculties only. Yes, said the Greeks, the whole man, body and soul, sense and reason, character and mind.

First the body: the old ideals of chivalry had left such a profound mark on the Greek tradition that at the beginning of the Hellenistic era, at least, a liking for physical education was still the most distinctive characteristic of Greek culture as opposed to that of the barbarians. No doubt for a long time—from the time of Xenophanes of Colophon in the sixth century, at least—ancient thought had been aware of the antinomy between the contradictory and in themselves totalitarian demands of body and mind, and in actual fact such equilibrium as existed between the two was always rather precarious; but there is a difference between what is actually achieved and what remains as the essential ideal, and it is the latter than I am concerned with here. And there can be no doubt that ancient thought never renounced its ideal—which slowly became more and more unrealizable in practice—of a complete man who developed both sides of his nature equally—his bodily powers, and his mental powers.

The classical expression of this ideal was given in the words of a Latin poet who was writing as late as the second century A.D.: "We should pray for a sound mind in a sound body."

Orandum est ut sit mens sana in corpore sano.[1]

And though the emphasis on sport, as in the case of professional athlete, was sometimes severely criticized, this was not so much the result of a prejudice in favour of pure intellectualism as a consequence of the traditional ideal of a complete man whose faculties were harmoniously balanced—an ideal that was denied by specialized training, whose one aim was to produce track-champions.

This aspiration towards human wholeness was equally apparent in the school syllabuses. In theory (and here again it must be remembered that we are simply describing an ideal) Hellenistic education was never prepared to renounce its artistic side; it even tried to keep pace with the increasing specialization of culture by adding drawing to the music it had inherited from Homeric times.

In the same way, "general culture"—the ἐγχύχλιος παιδεία that aimed at supplying the intellectual basis of any really educated mind—endeavoured to combine the advantages of a grounding in both literature and mathematics.

This longing for human wholeness is nowhere more evident than in the violent conflict that went on between the two rival forms of higher culture—rhetoric and philosophy. Both derived equally and essentially from the old culture: the dialogue between the two— which could be so bitter and tense—is its chief characteristic. We must realize that Hellenistic man would hesitate before making the difficult choice: the decision would not be made without some feelings of regret and an attempt to synthesize the two.

As we have seen, each of these two hostile forms of culture was continually trying to appropriate some of its rival's undeniable pres-

---

[1] Juvenal, *Satires*, X, 356.

tige: from Plato to Themistius[2] philosophers had always insisted that Truth could not afford to dispense with the Muses, while rhetors at the time of the Later Sophists claimed like Isocrates before them that the honourable title of philosopher was the name that should be given to their ideal orator.

There was more in this than a desire for compromise, more than the selfish aim of attracting customers by adopting the good points of a rival firm. Between these two poles of the old culture there was a dialectical tension at once pathetic and fruitful; another manifestation of ἀγών—rivalry, noble discord. The orator and the philosopher could not do without each other, neither could give up what was really the other's aim and object. The Greek wanted to be both artist and sage—a man of letters, refined, charming, a maker of fine phrases, and a thinker familiar with all the secrets of man and the universe, able to establish them with geometrical accuracy and to deduce from them a rule of life. For Man included all this, and any kind of choosing meant self-mutilattion.

It has to be confessed that the realities of daily life generally gave the lie most cruelly to this paradoxical and, in a way, this desperate longing: the technical progress that went on in every branch of Greek cultural life in Hellenistic times shattered the limits that are ultimately imposed upon the human person by his nervous system and his brief span of life. The old civilization already knew something of the difficulties that confront our own monstrous civilization, whose colossal constructions no longer exist at the human but at the planetary level—where is the physicist today who can claim to know all about physics? Hellenistic man was already beginning to be torn between that aspiration towards totality which we with our bad Greek call the "encyclopaedic" tendency, and the need, no less essential to humanism, to preserve culture as something human, within the limits of some sort of personalism.

As we have seen, the only kind of Hellenistic education that succeeded in combining gymnastics, music, letters, science and art—i.e. the education that was provided by the aristocratic ephebia—only managed to do so by substituting for real knowledge a frivolous, superficial smattering of knowledge that was no more than a caricature of any genuine humanism. But the fruitfulness of any ideal is not to be judged simply by the comparative proliferation of its practical achievements: the nostalgia and disquiet and regret that remain in the depths of the heart after the perfect ideal has been glimpsed—and then so imperfectly realized in practice—are also a kind of pres-

[2] Themistius, *Speeches*, XXIV, 302d–303a, (from the Hardouin edition) Synesius of Cyrene, Dionysius Thrax, *Grammar* (the Uhlig edition), 4, 1125a.

ence. Even though Hellenistic man never in fact became a total being, nevertheless he never forgot that such was his ideal, and he never willingly gave it up.

Primacy of Moral Considerations

On one level at least this humanistic desire for an all-round education was always realized—i.e. on the all-important level of morals. Classicism was not content with producing a man of letters or an artist or a scientist: it aimed at producing a man—i.e. someone whose way of life conformed to some ideal standard. And in this respect it is a very useful model for us moderns; for our own educational system, with its increasing secularization since the time of the Reformation and the Counter-Reformation, has finally lost all sense of this.

When the Greeks spoke about "the training of the child"—τῶν παίδων ἀγωγή—what they really meant was essentially moral training.

Very significant in this respect is the semantic development whereby from the Hellenistic period onwards the word "pedagogue" gradually changed its meaning until it came to have its modern sense of "educator." The fact is that the humble slave who was known as the "pedagogue" was a more important person as regards the training of the child than the schoolmaster. The schoolmaster was simply a technician, and he only affected a limited area of the child's intelligence; but the pedagogue was with the child all day, he taught him how to behave, how to be a good boy, how to get on in life, in society—all more important things than knowing how to read. We have made the school the decisive factor in education; for the Greeks the decisive factor was the surroundings in which the child grew up—the family, with its servants and friends.

The same preoccupation with moral values can be seen in the more advanced stages of education. The grammarians who expounded Homer, the rhetors who taught the art of speaking, insisted in season and out of season on their authors' moral virtues, on the moral value of doing their exercises; not to speak of the philosophers, who at this stage of Greek culture were not so much concerned with the inmost nature of the universe and society as with the practical inculcation of an ethical ideal—a system of moral values and a way of life in conformity with it.

Hence the idea that any kind of advanced education involved a deep and absolutely personal bond between teacher and pupil, a bond in which, as we have seen, emotion, if not passion, played a considerable part. This explains why there was such a scandal when the early Sophists began to commercialize teaching; there were no real centres of higher education like those great emporiums of culture, the modern universities. School, for the Greeks, meant an enthusiastic little band of pupils centring round a well-known teacher and growing more deeply united as time went by as a result of living a more or less communal life and developing more and more intimate personal relationships.

Man As Such

The object was the whole man, but man as man, not in any special form or any special part. It is worth noting in passing that in Hellenistic schools sexual discrimination tended to disappear. In the earlier days, it will be remembered, this discrimination was very marked: Sapphic education arose in opposition to the masculine education that was so strongly characterized by pederasty. But from now on girls were normally brought up in the same way as their brothers—though not always so logically as to result in the strict coeducation that existed in Teos[3] and Chios.[4]

The Man As Opposed to the Technician

Classical teaching was chiefly interested in the man himself, not in equipping technicians for specialized jobs; and it is this, perhaps, that most sharply distinguishes it from the education of our own time, which makes it its first aim to produce the specialists required by a civilization that to a quite fantastic extent has been invaded by technology and split up into fragments.

The old civilization thus presents us with a challenge, and this cannot be explained away by glib references to its aristocratic origins. It is undoubtedly true that the Greeks' slave system enabled them to identify man—i.e. the "free" man—with the aristocratic man of leisure, who was relieved by the labour of others from performing any degrading work, and had every opportunity for indulging in a life of elegant leisure and spiritual freedom.

But, I say again, the contingent forms of history are the bearers and embodiment of values that transcend them. Let us try to "understand," rather than explain away; the more difficult this turns out to be, the more fruitful it becomes. And once again it must be insisted

[3] Dittenberg., *Sylloge Inscriptionum Graecarium*, 3rd ed., 578, 9.
[4] Athenaeus, *The Sophists' Banquet*, XIII, 566e (from the Casaubon edition).

that ancient thought deliberately refused to set out along the path that modern civilization has been rushing along so blindly.

It had no use for technique. It was not unaware of the possibility of technical development; it simply rejected it. Its one aim was to form the man himself, the kind of man who would ultimately be ready for anything but had no special bias in any particular direction.

Only medicine, because it had a more immediate social relevance, and was thus the first to split off as a separate autonomous branch of learning, managed to develop its own particular type of training. And even so the physicians seem to have been continually dogged by an inferiority complex. From Hippocrates to Galen they go on saying: "The physician is a philosopher as well." They had no desire to remain walled up within their own particular culture; they longed to join in with the general culture on a genuinely human level; and for this they did not rely on their technical training but, as can be seen in Roman times in the case of Galen, they tried to be educated men like all the others, men who knew their classics, men who could speak like rhetors and argue like philosophers.

It is from the Ancients that we have inherited our ideas of a "general culture"—which, as we have seen, is one of the meanings of the ambiguous term ἐγχύχλιος παιδεία. Classical education flattered itself that it could provide a standard training in all subjects for every type of student. It aimed at developing all his potentialities without mutilating a single one, so enabling him to fulfil to the best of his ability whatever task should later be imposed upon him by life or the demands of society or his own free choice. Ideally such an education was supposed to result in a kind of indeterminate human product of very high intrinsic quality, ready to respond to any demand made upon it by the intellect or circumstance—χαιρός. The Ancients were very much alive to the value of this kind of latent potentiality, which was never better described than in a lyrical passage by Julian the Apostate, in which the traditional "Hellenism" is contrasted with what he believed was the barbarism of the Christians. Any gifted person, he says,[5] who has received a classical education, is capable of great things in any direction: he can take the lead in science or politics, just as easily as he can become a man of war, an explorer or a hero: he comes down amongst men like a gift from the gods. . . .

This education embraced all subjects, and could be embraced by all types; since it was concerned with everything, it was suitable for all. It was thus a powerful factor in promoting unity amongst men.

[5] Julian the Apostate, *Against the Galileans*, 299 E (the Spanheim edition of Cyril of Alexandria).

Hence what seems at first sight its surprising emphasis on the idea of Speech—Λόγος: its predominantly literary tone. The Word was regarded as the prime instrument of any culture and any civilization, the best means of ensuring contact and communication between men; for it broke through the enchanted circle of solitude in which any specialist inevitably tends to be enclosed as a result of his very accomplishments.

Once again, this is the true humanism—this emphasis on the social aspect of culture, on the danger inherent in any activity that tends to be self-enclosed and aloof from the ordinary intercourse of daily life. Here we reach the really profound reason why the ancient tradition rejected Plato's great idea of making mathematics the centre of all education. No doubt mathematics was entirely a matter of reason, and reason was common to all men, and so mathematics must seem a suitable subject for everyone to learn; but as soon as it rose above the most elementary stage most minds found the barren, abstract climate in which mathematics really existed quite unbearable. Plato himself seems to have admitted this when he emphasized the great sorting-out value these difficult sciences had.

A Literary As Opposed to a Scientific Humanism

When it was not just a small group of rulers that had to be educated, but the upper section of a whole society, it was better to remain on a more modest, more concrete level, and concentrate on words and literature, on those general ideas and grand and noble sentiments that the classical tradition loved and regarded as by far the best meeting-place for the generality of good minds.

Of course it did not give up mathematics completely—it hated giving up anything—but the only side of mathematics that it took much notice of was the formal side, the early training: ideally, the four mathematical sciences only went on to secondary-school level in Hellenistic education; more advanced science was a speciality, something for which a special vocation was needed, and like every kind of specialization it needed to have a watchful eye kept on it in case it began to stray beyond the proper human bounds.

I repeat, for it is a matter of some importance: ultimately, in the eyes of posterity, it was Isocrates who carried the day, not Plato: the culture that arose out of classical education was essentially aesthetic, artistic and literary, not scientific. Homer remained the "educator of the Greeks." The philosophers had failed in their attempt to drive him out of the State, and in the end they gave up trying: it was no use trying to put Euclid in his place.

The higher levels of intellectual life were only opened by poetry. Poetry was like a marvellous instrument that could cast a spell
over men's souls, and in some unknown way give their hearts a kind
of intuitive knowledge of truth and beauty and goodness. It provided
a sort of experience that was infinitely varied, subtle, complex, something far above the strict proofs and pure concepts of geometry. It
was a product of the sensitive mind, and this, in the eyes of the
humanists, was far more important than the geometrical mind. Classicism regarded the educated man as someone whose cradle-songs
had been Hector's farewells and the tales told in Alcinous' house;
someone who had discovered the reality of human passion and the
depths of the human heart in some "chorus-ending from Euripides"
or a tale by an historian; someone who had thus had some sort of psychological experience, some refining of his sense of moral values, of
what is real and possible—of what Man is, and what the life of Man.

Value of Tradition

Poetry has its own proper power, and it matters little at the
moment that Hellenistic teachers often failed to realize that it is thus
its own best justification—they often found it difficult to explain why
Homer was so important in education, and their efforts to turn into a
model moralist or orator are pathetic. Fortunately poetry is able to do
without their well-meaning "explanations." These were often rather
comic; the essential thing is that the tradition was preserved intact.

For in the last resort classical humanism was based on tradition,
something imparted by one's teachers and handed on unquestioningly. This, incidentally, had a further advantage: it meant that
all the minds of one generation, and indeed of a whole historical
period, had a fundamental homogeneity which made communication
and genuine communion easier. This is something we can all appreciate today, when we are floundering in a cultural anarchy. In a classical culture all men have in common a wealth of things they can all
admire and emulate: the same rules; the same metaphors, images,
words—the same language. Is there anyone acquainted with modern
culture who can think of all this without feeling a certain nostalgia?

Undifferentiated Polyvalence

But to return to the technical side of the matter: the classical
ideal both preceded and transcended any specialized technical considerations. It preceded them because once the mind has been

trained it was pure power, completely free, ready for any demands that might be made on it.

Hellenistic education—as, I hope, I have made quite clear—made provision for the kind of professional training that an apprentice receives from a master who takes him on as his assistant. But the classical mind regarded such a narrow focusing of the mental powers as a handicap: it was considered self-evident that the main thing was to become a person of intelligence, someone with insight and good judgment. As for a profession, that was something to be learned as quickly as possible: anyone with any intelligence could soon learn to turn his hand to anything practical.

And the classical ideal transcended technical considerations: an educated man began by being human, and even if he became a highly qualified specialist, he had to do his best to remain human. Here again the contrast with our own attitude is instructive; for we are obviously suffering from swollen ideas about technique, and we may perhaps learn something from the Greeks' insistence that any specialized activity needs to be guided by human considerations.

There is a terrible tyranny at the heart of technology. Any particular technique tends by its own inner logic to develop exclusively along its own line, in and for itself, and thus it ends by enslaving the man whom it should serve. It is only too clear today that science can make scientists inhuman, biology can make doctors forget that it is their duty to cure people, and political science turn doctrinaire politicians into tyrants. The classics tell us again and again that no form of government, no branch of knowledge, no technique, should ever become an end in itself: since they are created by man, and supposed to serve man, they should always, no matter what their results, be subordinated in the way they are used to one supreme value: humanity.

Beyond Humanism

The effectiveness of an ideal is not a matter of logic, and it is not easy to give a blueprint of the essence of classicism, for it did not in actual fact embody a single idea—indeed one of the great merits of its "sensitive mind" was its insistence that it is dangerous to push any idea too far, that practical achievement must be hedged in by conditions.

It never, for example, actually repudiated the old totalitarian ideal that had motivated the ancient city—i.e. the absolute dedication of the individual to society—though in fact it certainly went beyond this. What remained of this ideal helped to give a certain amount of ballast to the rather nebulous idea that classical education had of man, and at the same time it served as a kind of bridge and introduction to the new totalitarian civilization which was to arise in the *Spätantike,* the Late Empire, and in Byzantium. Historians of civilization are continually coming across this curious phenomenon of superposition, whereby things left over from an earlier stage turn out to be the basis for future developments.

Nevertheless, on the whole, there was upon classical humanism a profound imprint of the personalist ideal that characterized the Hellenistic period when classicism assumed its full Form. Classical education aimed at developing men as men, not as cogs in a political machine or bees in a hive.

It was the distinctive tendency of the Hellenistic mind to make man the supreme value—the free man, of course, the wealthy, cultured man whom education had developed to his full stature and παιδεία had brought to *humanitas.* Free, utterly free, faced by the crumbling walls of his city and abandoned by his gods, faced with a world with no end to it and an empty heaven, Hellenistic man looked vainly for something to belong to, some star to guide his life—and his only solution was to turn in upon himself and look there for the principle of all his actions.

This can be regarded—and rightly—as a narrowing of perspective, and dangerous. There is something slightly alarming in the fact that the chief aim of classical humanism was to produce men of taste, men of quality, men of letters and artists; in the fact that it cultivated almost exclusively those powers of the soul that need an endless refinement of inner experience, delicate pleasures, dainty living. Undoubtedly this is what classical education led to, particularly in Hellenistic times.

But the point is that the historical conditions of the period —political, economic, social and technical conditions—did not really know what to do with the admirable human capital with which it had thus been so well provided. I must repeat that classical education supplied the *materia prima* for a higher human type than had hitherto been known, a type capable of anything—if only it could have discovered something, or someone, to devote itself to. When it failed to do this, failed to transcend itself, classical humanism turned inwards in search of an immanent perfection and became absorbed in an egoistic aesthetic contemplation, which may well seem frivolous and futile to people who belong to a more severe or more ambitious culture. And this was often the case during the Hellenistic period.

But the value of this system was not limited to its first historical achievements, which were merely empirical and contingent. Clas-

sical humanism was able to lead to—and did in fact lead to—a higher
kind of greatness, by putting itself at the service of a higher cause, to
which the human person was willing to consecrate himself and thus
find fulfilment in self transcendence. For classical humanism was not
necessarily a closed system turned in upon itself. Even in antiquity,
as we shall see in the next part of this History, there were two remarkable examples to disprove this. First, classical education put itself at the service of the State, the State of Rome in which the old
city ideals burst forth again in a civilization still Hellenistic; and
then later, when the Empire became Christian, it put itself at the service of God.

Renaissance Paideia: Some Ideals in Italian Humanism and Their Relevance Today

JOHN E. WEAKLAND

The use of the Greek term "paideia," meaning "ideals," owes much
to the work of the German intellectual historian, Werner Jaeger.[1]
Jaeger, in his disillusionment with modern civilization and its lack of
spiritual vitality, turned back to Greek culture in search of worthwhile values. In his method of analysis, Jaeger was not so much concerned with actions as he was with beliefs and how beliefs—ideals—
changed. I intend to apply this method to the study of the ideals of
the early Italian humanists, especially the educational paideia.[2] In
doing so I will in the words of Jacob Burckhardt "try to link up a
number of historical observations and inquiries to a series of half-
random trains of thought." My approach to the Renaissance is the so-
called "Italian approach" which involves an emotional participation
in the period. My judgments are thus largely influenced by my own
studies and experiences in Italy.[3]

The discipline of history is concerned with problems, but the
historian must be cautious in supplying answers; because when
something is abstracted it is simplified; it is pulled out of context and

From *Social Studies* (April 1973), pp. 153–156; Volume LXIV, No. 4. Reprinted with permission.

[1] *Paideia: The Ideals of Greek Culture,* 3 vols. (New York, 1945).
[2] A recent attempt has been made to apply Jaeger's method to the Florentine
scene. See Marvin B. Becker, *Florence in Transition* (Baltimore, 1967).
[3] For an example of the Italian approach, see Federico Chabod, *Machiavelli and
the Renaissance* (New York, 1965).

becomes distorted. The variables in any historical phenomenon are great, and unpredictable men are the central variables. The primary source material itself is vast, much of it unpublished and difficult to obtain. It is impossible to read everything and know all things. The historian is forced to rely in part upon certain carefully selected secondary works, but these are subjective. In other words, we are at the mercy of the prevailing historical climate of opinion of the time. History is not "wie es eigentlich gewesen" as Ranke held. Absolute truth escapes the historian; all generalizations are vulnerable.[4] "The most universal quality is diversity. All generalizations are loose and imperfect" (Montaigne). The most valid generalization is just one which subsumes the most facts.

With all of these limitations, why does one bother to study history? Petrarch said: "In order to forget my own times, I have constantly striven to place myself in other ages."[5] There are psychological motives for returning to the past. I have returned to the Renaissance in search of humanistic values which are often not present in our own era. Other historians have searched for and found other things. Some have found solace in Renaissance art with its beauty for beauty's sake.[6] Some historians have discovered religion,[7] while others have found only a paganism and secularism characteristic of the modern world.[8] Those attracted to an economic approach have stressed the role of capitalism.[9] The Dutch historian Jan Huizinga examined certain traits and saw rather a "waning of the Middle Ages."[10] The term "Middle Ages" is always used in relationship to the "Renaissance." The term "medium aevum" was used by a group of heretics in the thirteenth and fourteenth centuries but only in an eschatological sense in anticipation of the Second Coming.[11] The term "Middle Ages" was first used in the secular chronological sense by the seventeenth century German Protestant annalist, Cellarius, who dated the period from Constantine to the Fall of Constan-

[4] For a very sensitive analysis of these problems, see Marc Bloch, *The Historian's Craft* (New York, 1953).

[5] *Variae*, 54.

[6] Walter Pater, *The Renaissance* (New York, 1959), pp. 156–159; Bernard Berenson, *Italian Painters of the Renaissance* (New York, 1957).

[7] Giuseppe Toffanin, *Storia dell' umanesimo* (Naples, 1933), and Douglas Bush, *The Renaissance and English Humanism* (Toronto, 1939).

[8] Jacob Burckhardt, *The Civilization of the Renaissance in Italy*, 2 vols. (New York, 1958); John Addington Symonds, *The Renaissance in Italy*, 7 vols. (London, 1875–1881).

[9] Alfred von Martin, *Sociology of the Renaissance* (New York, 1963); see also the works of Gene Brucker and Marvin Becker.

[10] *The Waning of the Middle Ages* (New York, 1956).

[11] Raffaello Morghen, *Medioevo cristiano* (Bari, 1965), pp. 204–281.

tinople.[12] One can find inchoate concepts of the "Middle Ages" and "Renaissance" in the writings of Italian humanists such as Petrarch, Boccaccio, Salutati, Bruni, Palmieri, and Alberti. They spoke of their own time as one of rebirth (*rinascita*) in literature and the arts, while the period from the fall of Rome to the fourteenth century was one of darkness (*tenebrae*).[13] In the nineteenth century Georg Voight and others expanded the "rinascita" to a general conception of the world.[14] All of these elements and more can be found in the Renaissance; yet the period is more than just a total of all possible phenomena. Thus the Renaissance is almost impossible to define. There will always be a subjective element present; therefore I do not intend to make any attempt to define the era. Rather, I will limit my discussion to early Italian humanism. I will concentrate on Italian humanism as (1) a rejection of scholasticism, (2) a commitment to an active life in the community, (3) an educational reform, and (4) an interest in philology.

Scholasticism was one of the dominant themes of the late Middle Ages. It was an impersonal type of intellectual movement. No confessional element entered it. The pronoun "I" was seldom used. The thinker was less important than the thought, which was expressed in a passionless dry style. Scholastics held to the principle that faith and reason were compatible; all knowledge was subsumed under theology. Beginning in the fourteenth century, the humanists rejected the scholastic grand synthesis of theology. For Petrarch and his followers, scholasticism was vain and useless; it was too abstract and complex. Immediate problems were more important. This rejection of the canopy of theology and the consequent development of separate disciplines pursued for their own sakes was one of the most significant aspects of the Renaissance. Humanists stressed a personal theology. They sought the truths of religion by introspection. "Begin with self" was their motto. They were much attracted to the interior

[12] R. F. Drew and F. S. Lear (eds.), *Perspectives in Medieval History* (New York, 1964).

[13] W. H. Woodward, *Studies in Education During the Age of the Renaissance* (Cambridge, 1906). For Petrarch's concept see Theodor E. Mommsen, "Petrarch's Conception of the 'Dark Ages,' " *Speculum*. XVII (1942), 226–242.

[14] Georg Voigt, *Die Wiederbelebung des classichen Alterthums* (Berlin, 1859). Voigt and Burckhardt formulated the standard conception of the Renaissance as a period roughly between the early fourteenth century and the first half of the sixteenth century which witnessed the birth of modern times. This thesis has been widely criticized, but it is still held by many historians, though in a modified way. For a recent discussion of the problem, see Tinsley Helton (ed.), *The Renaissance* (Madison, 1964); see also, *Bibliographie internationale de l'Humanisme et de la Renaissance* (Geneva, 1966).

approach of St. Augustine who advised: "Recognize in thyself something within . . . ; descend into thyself; go to thy secret chamber,
thy mind. . . . For not in the body but in the mind was man made in
the image of God. In his own similitude let us seek God: in his own
image recognize the creator."[15] The early humanists were also attracted to Plato because he was unsystematic and thus nearer to reality. Humanist preference for Plato and the dialogue method meant a
preference for the conception of an open world full of contradictions
and incessantly changing.[16] Plato and the humanists were man centered and looked within, while Aquinas and the scholastics were
God centered and looked without. The humanists did not reject religion. On the contrary, they wished to accept its tenets on faith
rather than waste time in useless theological discussions. God should
be accepted on faith, and human efforts should be directed to the
solution of human problems.[17]

Early humanism was deeply committed to the active life. Virtue
was connected with participation in and improvement of the political, economic, and cultural life of the city. In other words, early
humanism was a civic humanism; and it rested upon a specific educational ideal—the formation of a complete man through the study of
the classics. Leonardo Bruni said that the only true education was
humanitas. The *litterae* were called *humanae* because they helped
to achieve the full development of *humanitas*. When one read the
classics, it was a conversation between minds across the ages; it
made the soul capable of absorbing a richer *humanitas*. The mind
unfolded and enlarged itself and learned the value of other minds.
One learned to live in human society. To humanist educators such as
Bruni, Vergerio, Guarini, and Vittorino da Feltre antiquity was not
just an authority; it was a living example. Antiquity had achieved a
wonderful fullness of life which perhaps could be revived again.[18]

These educational ideals found more concrete expression in a

[15] In *John. Evang. XXIII*, 10 St. Augustine's proof of God is in striking contrast to
the a posteriori approach of St. Thomas Aquinas.

[16] Herbert Marcuse has an interesting discussion of the dialectic of Plato and
Aristotle in *One-Dimensional Man* (Boston, 1966). pp. 122–143. Marcuse states that in
Platonic dialectic the terms are open, not completely defined; they are to be challenged in a dialogue. In Aristotle's logic the terms of the syllogism have no real meaning. In fact a letter of the alphabet could be substituted for each of the terms. For a
teaching method based upon an open concept of reality, see Neil Postman and Charles
Weingartner, *Teaching as a Subversive Activity* (New York, 1969) pp. 25–38, 59–81,
133–154.

[17] For an opposing view on the relationship between humanism and scholasticism, see Paul Oskar Kristeller, *Eight Philosophers of the Italian Renaissance* (Stanford, 1964), pp. 147–165.

[18] On early humanist education see, Eugenio Garin (ed.), *L'educazione umanis-
tica in Italia* (Bari, 1959), pp. 1–10, 29–38, 57–112, 175–192.

definite curriculum called the *studia humanitatis* which by the middle of the fifteenth century came to include: (1) classical Latin and Greek grammar, (2) rhetoric, (3) poetry, (4) history, and (5) moral philosophy.[19] With a great deal of justification, the historian, Hanna Gray, has stated that rhetoric was the identifying characteristic of Renaissance humanism.[20] Humanists distinguished between "true eloquence" and "sophistry." True eloquence was the union of wisdom and style. Its aim was to guide men toward virtue and worthwhile goals. Education should help each man lead a good life; thus the function of knowledge was not merely to demonstrate truth, but to impel each man to accept it. Man could be moulded most effectively through rhetoric because it stimulated man's will as well as instructing his reason. As stated previously, the humanists attacked scholasticism because it was too abstract and thus lacked relevance for human life. Humanists also attacked scholasticism on the grounds that it failed to communicate important truths with persuasive effect. Thus rhetoric was closely related to moral philosophy in the humanistic educational scheme.

In the Middle Ages most of those who wrote words of solace and instruction were clerics, priests, and monks who in turn gave clerical, priestly, and monkish advice advocating a life apart from the world in poverty, chastity, obedience, and contemplation. Petrarch and the other humanists were creating an *ethos* for the lay middle class of Italy through the *studia humanitatis*. The classics not only made one see virtue but also made one want to practice it. In his *De ignorantia* Petrarch said: "What is the use of knowing what virtue is if it is not loved when known?" He stated further that true moral philosophers "sow into our hearts love of the best and eager desire for it." "It is better to will the good than to know the truth." Petrarch was as much against the new philosophical skepticism as he was opposed to scholastic logic. He was fond of quoting St. Augustine to the effect that true philosophy was a moral and ethical guide to a better life. It was far better to be good than to be learned. Aristotle only explained the nature of virtue; he did not impel one to love it. "Those are much at fault who spend their time in knowing God, not in loving him." Petrarch's goal was the *docere et movere* of classical rhetoric. In his *Secretum*, Petrarch put the following words in the mouth of St. Augustine: "And what is the use of knowing many

[19] Paul Oskar Kristeller, *Renaissance Thought* (New York, 1961), pp. 3–23; Eugenio Garin, *L'educazione in Europa* (Bari, 1966), pp. 107–143.

[20] Hanna Gray, "Renaissance Humanism: The Pursuit of Eloquence," *Journal of the History of Ideas*, XXIV (1963), 497–514; see also, Jerrold E. Seigel, "Ideals of Eloquence and Silence in Petrarch," *Journal of the History of Ideas*, XXVI (1965), pp. 147–174.

things if when you have learned the dimensions of heaven and earth, the measure of the seas, the courses of the stars, the virtues of plants and stones, the secrets of nature, you still don't know yourself?" For Petrarch and the other humanists, education was a lifelong task devoted to the cultivation of the soul, to the discovery of self. Self-knowledge would result in a strengthening of the bonds of society. Love for one's neighbor, *charitas*, was the reason for and the end of the *studia humanitatis*.

History for the humanists was philosophy teaching by example, and the examples were in the inspiring prose of classical Latin. Closely related to history was a new form of reading and linguistic study, i.e., philology and textual criticism. Since the texts had become corrupted through the course of time, one must know the language to reconstruct the past. The study of history and philology gave the humanists a new approach to problems. A new and effective philosophical method emerged. The humanists broke with the static medieval vision of reality. The logic of Aristotle was not the word of God, but just a product of history. He and other thinkers were part of a certain historical age. The humanists began to understand civilization in a historical sense. They developed a sense of history, an idea of change, and a vision of a dynamic society.[21]

I have tried to present some of the highest ideals of Italian humanism. What lessons are there for us today? First of all the humanists revolted against an educational system which was not relevant, and proposed one designed to consider human problems in all their complexities. Their ideal of education was not one of withdrawal or pure contemplation. Like the figure in Plato's parable of the cave, one must return to society after catching a glimpse of truth. Education must always be connected with the active life. True education must lead to the development of our humanity; it must be for the benefit of the community. Although the humanists, following Aristotle, insisted that external goods were necessary for dignity and the good life, they did not carry this to the point of social reform; yet the principle was there. Teaching and doing was their motto. Education was not the accumulation of facts, but rather it involved the discovery of self and the discovery of others through a meaningful dialogue. The humanists can teach us the importance of a sense of history. We must realize that the patterns of the past are the products of men; they can and, in many cases, must be changed for the advancement of society. A study of the early humanists would show us that

[21] Eugenio Garin, *L'umanesimo italiano: filosofia e vita civile nel rinasamento* (Bari, 1964), pp. 7–24; Hans Baron, "Das Erwachen des historischen Denkens im Humanismus des Quattrocento," *Historische Zeitschrift*, CXLVII (1932), 5–20.

our civic virtue—our patriotism—must be a balance between the real and the ideal, that politics and science (the real) should not be separated from religion and philosophy (the ideal). Perhaps the greatest lesson we can learn from the humanists is that of human dignity, a lesson often lost in our vast, scientifically oriented and impersonal society. Petrarch said: "Many have not become what they might have because they believed they were what people mistakenly said they were."[22] The humanists such as Pico remind us of what we are: "Man is everything because he can be everything." Perhaps the poetry of St. Augustine's *Confessions* best summarizes one of the great themes and lessons of Renaissance humanism: "Man wonders over the restless sea, the flowing waters, the sight of the sky, and forgets that of all wonders, man himself is the most wonderful." The question is not whether there is life on other planets. Rather the question is whether life is possible on this planet. In this regard the humanists have something to tell us.

[22] *De remedius* I 45.

Notes Toward a History

JANE HOWARD

The genealogy of the human potential movement is as hard to trace as a foundling baby's. Foundlings have no known ancestors, but the movement is alleged to have preposterously many. One of these came to my attention one afternoon when I emerged from a dip in the swimming pool of the Chateau Marmont Hotel in Hollywood 90046, to chat with an affable young astrologer. He wondered what had brought me to California. When I told him, he said he knew all about encounters, and offered an unsolicited piece for my mosaic.

"You know who *invented* all that group stuff, don't you?" he asked. "It was Ho Chi Minh, twenty years ago."

"Really?" I said. But I filed his tip away in a folder optimistically labeled "History." The folder was already chubby with suggestions that the movement stemmed from Socrates, who after all had counseled people even as trainers do now to Know Thyself, and from ancient forms of Judaism. Another note mentioned Christ's

early followers, who assembled furtively in each other's homes before the church was made legal for what somebody said had been
"spiritual growth meetings."

I had also been advised that the movement was traceable to the
early nineteenth-century German hypnotist Friedrich Anton Mes-
mer, to the Russian vagabond-mystic Georgiu Gurdjieff, to George
Herbert Mead's idea of "social behaviorism," and to the psychiatrist
Harry Stack Sullivan, like Mead a Chicagoan. Early in this century
Sullivan conceived of psychiatry as an interpersonal rather than a
strictly individual matter. The living American psychologist B. F.
Skinner, whose theories of "operant conditioning" are applied in
many groups, is considered influential, too. A scholarly friend had
mentioned in a letter how "early Calvinist clergymen used to get
together about once a month to criticize each other's manners, morals
and deportment." He further wondered how relevant it might be that
characters in Chekhov and Dostoevosky often seemed to upbraid
each other with ruthlessly candid comments like: "Oh, Dmitri An-
dreyevitch, you're such a *bore!*"

I felt I might drown in confusion, if not in the Chateau Marmont
pool, unless I could impose some sense on all this chaos. Help finally came in the form of a wise and knowledgeable letter from Dr.
Kenneth Benne, a founder and still a prominent leader of the NTL.[1]
He suggested that I break the history of the movement down into
three different frameworks.

"The use of groups for growth purposes, at the level of folk practice, is as old as human life on earth," he wrote. "It is as silly to say
who invented groups in this sense as it is to say who 'invented' fire,
or the wheel. The *family* is a small group designed to influence,
guide and direct the growth of its younger members. The *classroom*
is a group, designed to facilitate the learning of its members. The
religious sect is a group designed to coach and influence the commitment of its members in certain beliefs and ways of behaving."

My notes abounded, in fact, with references to religions and
sects. Someone had told me that Benedictine and Trappist monas-
teries had held weekly "Chapter of Faults" seminars to discuss the
monks' shortcomings, and that eighteenth-century Methodists had
held similar "class meetings." Martin Buber's much more recent
"I-thou" idea informs nearly all manifestations of the present small
group movement. So does Søren Kierkegaard's belief that "To will to
be that self which one truly is is indeed the opposite of despair."

Benne's second framework was "the scientific study of small

---

[1] NTL stands for National Training Laboratories (for applied Behavioral Sciences). Since 1947 it has been conducting workshops and seminars similar in spirit
and substance to those at Esalen, of California, and other, newer growth centers. (ed.)

groups, how they work, how they influence their individual members, how they can be changed and altered. These relatively recent studies," he wrote, "have little focus on the use of groups in practice. Considering how important groups have been in folk practice for so long, these studies were rather late in coming." He referred me to Edward Shils' chapter on the scientific study of groups in a book edited by Lerner and Lasswell called *Policy Sciences: Recent Developments in Scope and Method* (Stanford University Press, 1951). He also mentioned a 1955 survey of scientific studies of small groups by A. Paul Hare and E. F. Bargatta. *The Encyclopedia of Social Sciences* had so many more references to scholarly treatises on groups that I decided it would be presumptuous, not to say impossible, to try to encompass them.

Suffice to say that the present movement really does stem in part from a German sociologist named Dr. Ferdinand Tönnies, who in the late 1880s first distinguished between *Gesellschaft* (an impersonal, bureaucratic hierarchy), and *Germeinschaft* (a closer, more personal community). Toward the end of the century, gropings toward *Gemeinschaft* increased. In 1905 an American physician named Joseph Pratt helped cure tuberculosis victims by assembling them in an early version of the therapeutic encounter group. Trigant Burrow, another American doctor, contributed to the same cause at about the same time. He saw mental disorder as a disturbance in communication, created largely by a patient's "privately cherished and secretly guarded" image of himself. Burrow's aim was for people to express themselves as they really were "by exposing the socially-determined basis of [their] self-image."

In 1913, in Vienna, Dr. J. L. Moreno organized a coterie of prostitutes into a trade union. ("I didn't meet them socially," he is careful to say, "I was too much of a snob or a square.") Moreno learned how unconcerned Socialists, Communists and the Roman Catholic Church all were about the prostitutes' trouble. He enlisted the help of lawyers, doctors and hospitals, and organized the women into a therapeutic weekly *kaffeeklatsch*. It struck him that "they helped each other far more than any of us could help them." Soon afterward they were acting out their problems, as encounter group members now widely do, in psychodramas.

In the 1920s an American named Frank Buchman founded what was to become a worldwide religious organization variously known as the Buchmanites, the Oxford Group and the Moral Re-Armament movement. His followers soon multiplied by the thousands in England, the Netherlands, South Africa and the United States. Like early Christian penitents before them and Park Avenue psychoanalysands after them, they regarded confession as the first step toward conversion. Candor was rampant at their meetings, which were often called "house parties," and which must have resembled some of today's encounter groups.

Philip Toynbee reminisces about such gatherings in his book *Friends Apart: A Story of the Thirties*. In his student days at Oxford, Toynbee writes, there prevailed ". . . a fluency of communication which . . . at its facile worst is simply due to a common indifference and lack of respect. It was in this . . . lamentable spirit that I and several other communists used to sit in the lounge of an Oxford hotel, titillating our stuffed, impersonal minds with the blundering personalities of the Truth game. 'What do you think of me?' we could ask each other, or, at a later point, 'Whom do you like least among us and why?' The game is detestable because it must either give real pain and embarrassment or none at all, and if it gives none at all the players must be so indifferent to each other that no confidence should have been made between them."

By the 1930s small groups had become the serious focus of scientific attention. During World War II much of humanity was involuntarily exposed—in battalions and foxholes and air-raid shelters—to "intensive group experiences" with random assemblages of strangers. Such enforced rapport on so wide a scale doubtless helped create a receptive climate for the present widespread concern with groups. Meanwhile industries were at work toward the same end. In the late 1930s the Roethlisberger and Dickson experiments were carried on at the Western Electric Company in Chicago. These experiments with factory workers led to a phenomenon popularly called the "Hawthorne Effect," which means approximately that people's behavior changes when attention is paid to them.

Dr. Kurt Lewin came to the United States from Nazi Germany intent on testing theories whereby self-help groups might learn to avoid the totalitarianism he had barely escaped. The small group struck him as the obvious link between individual and social dynamics. His theories were concerned with the social restraints imposed on groups by technology, economics, law and politics.

Many of Lewin's ideas have become important to students of group dynamics, none more so than his concept of "Forcefield Analysis," which holds that events are determined by immediate forces rather than distant ones. Behavior could be changed, he thought, if people could identify which forces restrained them from desirable action and which ones drove them on toward it. He helped found the Research Center for Group Dynamics at the Massachusetts Institute of Technology, and the Commission on Community Interrelations of the American Jewish Congress. For a state interrracial commission in Connecticut he organized what was called a Basic Skill Training

Group, designed to seek out causes of and cures for prejudice. Experiments like this were later rechristened T-groups. They convinced Lewin, as one historian writes, that "no amount of *telling* people what to do could compare with haveing them 'discover' the same information for themselves."

Along came Leland P. Bradford, an Illinoisan who had worked with the WPA and other agencies involved with adult education. Bradford also believed that laboratories could teach far more effectively than lecturers. He and his colleagues Kenneth Benne (a philosopher) and Ronald Lippitt (a social psychologist) had been experimenting with laboratory groups, which they saw as a potent means of translating scientific theory into social change. Groups, they thought, could be used to re-educate people's attitudes, values and behavior. They admired what Lippitt writes of as Lewin's "deep sensitivity to social problems and commitment to use his resources as a social scientist to do something about them." Sharing this commitment, with Lewin's guidance they founded the NTL, at first a division of the National Education Association.

At about the same time UCLA and the University of California at Berkeley were developing a joint Industrial Relations Institute to design programs for labor-management relations and community service. East met West when some NTL men were attracted to UCLA and began the Western Training Laboratories. The term "sensitivity training" was coined there in 1954 to cover programs meant to make people more effective managers and executives. Eastern T-groups, meanwhile, were being influenced by Douglas McGregor's theories of humanistic (as opposed to authoritarian) management. A tension began that still exists between groups designed for personal growth and those planned to bring about organizational change.

Several people chided me for not including a "Tavistock study group" in my itinerary. They were referring to the Group Relations Conferences, held mostly on New England college campuses in summertime. So far these Tavistock groups have affected about 1,000 mental-health professionals and others who are concerned more with groups as a whole than with interpersonal relations of group members. These groups were first transplanted to the United States (from the Tavistock Institute of Human Relations in London) in 1965, largely through the efforts of Dr. Margaret Rioch. Dr. Rioch is associated with the Washington (D.C.) School of Psychiatry and the National Institute of Mental Health.

"Tavistock groups are emotionally right wing," one of their alumni told me. "They're to the NTL what the NTL is to Esalen. But they can be terrifically powerful." They stem mostly from the wartime work of the English psychologist Dr. Wilfred Bion, who studied such concepts as mob rule and methods of selection of leaders for the British armed forces. Many consider Bion, who now lives in Los Angeles, as important an ancestor of the present group movement as Lewin.

Other ideas imported from Europe have also flourished. From Vienna Dr. Frederick S. Perls, one of the most conspicuous and controversial figures in all the movement, brought contagious enthusiasm for his Gestalt therapy. His methods, Perls believed, are best practiced in workshops "which make all individual therapy obsolete. "Trust in the group," Perls has declared, "seems to me greater than trust in the therapist. It is always a deeply moving experience for the group and for me to see the previously robotized corpses begin to return to life."

George Bach, arrived from Latvia, was meanwhile formulating his theories about intensive group psychotherapy. Aldous Huxley was conceiving of man as a multiple amphibian with vast untapped resources. Carl Rogers, then working with groups of hospitalized veterans in Chicago, was beginning to think that "well people get better the same way sick people get well," and to develop his now-famous ideas of "client-centered therapy." Abraham Maslow was carving out his theories that science should study not only the sick but also the well. Maslow suggested that human beings should go beyond adjustment and attempt to transcend—to be "self-actualizing" and to aspire to more "peak experiences." He also conceived of a "hierarchy of needs," starting with physical and going on up from security to social to ego to self-fulfillment. "A need satisfied no longer motivates," Maslow pointed out. "Our perception of what people need colors our assumptions about human behavior.

"What Freud did," Maslow also said, "was to supply us with the sick half of psychology. Now we have to fill it out with the healthy half. Freud left out the aspirations, realizable hopes, and godlike qualities. Psychologists can't keep on ducking responsibility for these things."

"Even Freud," William Schutz agrees, "wouldn't be a Freudian today. His whole career was marked by development."

Concurrently, the organization called Alcoholics Anonymous was using techniques of public confession and group support to persuade drunks to forsake liquor. "My name is Karen and I'm an alcoholic," a ritual speech would start, and thus Karens in smoke-filled auditoriums all over the United States, and later all over the world, would relate how AA had made possible their return to sobriety. One of AA's success cases was Charles Dederich, who on Wednesday nights in 1959 took to holding "free-association" discussion groups at his small apartment in Santa Monica. These boisterous, rigorously honest meetings came to attract more drug addicts than alcoholics. Holding to the idea that achknowledging a character disorder was the first step toward curing it, they led to the founding of Synanon. Some two thousand such self-help groups, all relying on group discussion and group support as a means of erasing specific problems, have since arisen, among them the recently voguish and apparently effective Weight Watchers.

In the early 1960s the movement assumed more shape. In 1959 the Western Behavioral Sciences Institute was founded in La Jolla, attracting some of the most inventive and protean innovators in the various uses of small groups. The NTL was growing fast. Followers of Maslow and Rogers founded the American Institute of Humanistic Psychology. Meanwhile Michael Murphy and his former Stanford classmate Richard Price hit on a grandiose scheme for using the sixty-two Big Sur acres Murphy had just inherited. They decided to establish there "a center to explore and expand and enhance the human potential," and call it Esalen. Described in a recent bulletin as "a forum and facility for discovery and recovery," Esalen has since grown from an occasional weekend retreat center to a year-round seminar and workshop facility, with branches and projects far removed from the Big Sur.

Because one of Murphy's most cherished hopes was to mix Eastern mysticism with Western pragmatism, Esalen became among other things a kind of *ashram*. Murphy had been a serious student of meditation for some ten years, including eighteen months spent in India. He was convinced that technological America could well use some of the benefits of Asian contemplation. Thus Esalen has become particularly hospitable to the doctrines of Zen, Hindu, Buddhist, and other Asian philosophies.[2]

The movement's infatuation with the East, which has spread far beyond Esalen, is much discussed and by no means universally applauded. Many doubt the relevance of Indian philosophy to contemporary American problems.

"The yoga system," says Stanley Keleman, "is based on an already depressed people who suffer from overwhelming heat and lack of food. Theirs is an inhalation, inspirational philosophy. It was by inhaling that they could hope to capture God and take him in. Western philosophy is more a matter of exhaling. Here the idea is to grow,

[2] The former Harvard professor Dr. Richard Alpert, who with Dr. Timothy Leary made LSD famous, has been in residence at Esalen's Big Sur headquarters, known as Baba Ram Dass, the name he acquired during his Far-Eastern travel. So have Gia-Fu Feng, a specialist in the Chinese "meditation-in-motion" method called Tai-Chi-Chuan, and the Dalai Lama's former interpreter, Sonam Kazi.

to make contact with your world. Indians don't provide a fit atmosphere and environment for their children to live in, but the whole basis of Western civilization is a strong sense of self and of the individual. It's true that we've lost our old sense of community and tribal existence. The hippies over-value this loss, not realizing that our culture has already moved, in a tremendous achievement, from emphasis on communalism to individualism. This doesn't strike me in the slightest as anything we should worry about or regret."

"The doctrines and ideas of the Far East," another student of the movement points out, "can only thrive in societies where a great segment of the population is free to, or obliged to, concentrate on something other than production. The people who have time to question what we're doing here on this earth are either terribly rich or else terribly poor—afflicted either with abject poverty or abject affluence."

(When one abjectly affluent woman wondered, during an Esalen meditation workshop, "*why* we should have to sit cross-legged for yoga when we've been trained all our lives to sit on chairs, unlike the Indians who haven't?" Murphy said he thought she might have a point there.)

Esalen was such a fast and legendary success that other "Growth Centers," similar in motive though unblessed with hot steam baths or magnificent real estate, have sprung up at the rate of one a month. The most established of the others is Kairos, outside San Diego. Dr. Benne, like many of his colleagues, is somewhat dubious about these institutions, which fall into the third framework he suggested in his letter to me: "The professional use of small groups to release and facilitate the growth of persons who participate in them . . . to make use of groups in practice more conscious, more knowledgeable, more skilled, and more professional." Such places, he wrote, "don't draw sharp lines between education and therapy, and have released all sorts of non-professional use of small groups by people with small knowledge or professional skill."

Be that as it may, the growth centers continue to grow, and so do all the other species of groups in the movement. Some followers of such matters foresee that encounter groups will eventually wane, but nobody seems to think that will happen very soon.

I much preferred discussing the movement with James and Elizabeth Heber Bugental to talking with the poolside astrologer. Bugental is one of the original humanistic psychologists, and his wife is one of a growing category of improbably radiant former nuns. I had heard enough about them to go out of my way to meet them. Having failed to track them down in California, my only chance was to catch them after a workshop outside New York and drive them in a rent-a-car to their plane at Kennedy Airport. The trip was inconvenient, but their literate good sense made it worthwhile.

"It would really be great," Elizabeth Bugental said, "if people could learn to *genuinely* encounter each other without even needing groups—if they could learn to switch gears and peel off facades when necessary, as a matter of course. It wouldn't put us out of business if that happened, either; we could then use encounter groups to heighten and deepen the growth experience, and make it really mystical. Right now, encounter groups are a kind of vestibule experience. What they do so far is help people get their feet in the door and give them a taste of how things *can* be."

An Education for the Whole Person

STUART MILLER

A NOTE ON WHOLENESS AS AN EDUCATIONAL CONCEPTION
"The schools should be helping the children to look within themselves and from this self-knowledge derive a set of values." (From Maslow, *The Farther Reaches of Human Nature*).

"We studied the history of several major courses at the general education level of college. Typically, we found that in the original state of objectives there was frequently as much emphasis given to affective objectives as to cognitive objectives . . . However . . . over a period of ten to twenty years, we found a rather rapid dropping of the affective objectives from the statements about the course and an almost complete disappearance of efforts at appraisal of student growth in this domain. It was evident to us that there is a characteristic type of *erosion* in which the original intent of a course or educational program becomes worn down to that which can be explicitly evaluated for grading purposes and that which can be taught easily through verbal methods (lectures, discussions, reading materials, etc.).
(From Krathwohl, Bloom and Masia, *Taxonomy of Educational Objectives, The Classification of Educational Goals, Handbook II: Affective Domain*).

A Brief Look at Some Larger Contents

The Historical Context

The history of education, properly so-called, is a history of the education of the whole person. But the history of American educa-

From *The Esalen Catalog* (November/December 1973). Reprinted by permission of Stuart Miller.

tion in recent decades has generally been to define education in much narrower terms: mere technical mastery, only knowledge of subject matters, just the ability to perform certain limited cognitive functions. In order to understand how our own recent notions of education have been limited by the particular circumstances of our time, it is useful to review the main line of western education.

For the Greek child, education was defined as a kind of general goal. A thousand years before Christ, Homer applauds the hero who is "a speaker of words and a doer of deeds." Such a man is a product of *paideia*, education in the sense of a total formation that has its intellectual aspects and its active ones, private and public, cognitive and affective. Hundreds of years later, for Socrates and Plato, the educational process is viewed as tending toward the harmonious and balanced development of the child. The illumined or philosophical mind is supreme in Plato's system, but it achieves supremacy by knowing and mastering the body and the passions. From these earliest times to the present the ideal of western man has been a *whole* man, a man whose person is a just combination of what is right and best. Body, emotions, mind and spirit must all be educated and formed into such a harmony. Milton's instructions to the aspirant poet were not simply that he go out and study literature in a narrowly cognitive sense (though that was obviously critical). In addition, Milton said, the aspirant poet must study and form himself: "He who would not be frustrate of his hopes to write hereafter in laudible things must *himself be a true poem;* that is, a just combination of what is right and best."

Though exact definitions of what is the fully finished character change through time, the definition of education is always an educated *person.* To take the history of higher education in this country, we see a religious emphasis in the earliest colleges—all of the great American colleges were founded by ministers. Their aim was not merely the education of the intellect but the education of man who could bring spiritual wisdom to his flock. In the nineteenth century this tradition continues, arriving at a pluralistic system of higher education spread over half a continent but one in which the education of character is considered to be the central function. So one can remember, not so long ago, when the point of a young person choosing a college was to choose what kind of a person he or she wanted to be. Thus, for example, one spoke of "a Yale man" or "a Vassar woman" and in speaking of whatever college it was that a person chose, a generalized image would come to mind of a kind of human being that typified the education provided by that college.

It is amusing to review this history because it reveals how unorthodox, how untraditional, how radical (in a deep sense) is the view that education equals mind. One could say that this current definition of education is a heresy unparalleled in the long story of western education.

Surely, however, there were complex and profound reasons that caused the over-emphasis in the last half century on cognitive training. One might list among those reasons the demands of an increasingly technical society for specialized human components, the Cold War fears that led to nations mobilizing entire populations in preparation for total war, the marvellous triumphs of physical science which required more and more intellectual training for mastery. On the other side one might also find a disillusion, already evident in the 1920's, with character models then available—at least in the colleges. The beer-drinking fraternity boy, the football functionary, the sexist smoker, the gentlemen C, the hypocritical attendant at "required Chapel," were elements of the complete "college man" that did not seem very appealing. These were debasements of a proper concern with the body, the interpersonal relations, the spiritual and emotional life of the educated person. The humanistic tradition seemed to have petered out and we began our massive experiment with cognitive education.

So American universities reconstituted themselves on new models, chief among them the model of the German graduate school. Research, publication, knowledge of fact and technique became critical. Somehow it was hoped that enough sheer knowledge would save us.

It has become increasingly clear that knowledge is not enough.

The Present Context

While the ideal of education for the whole person, to make a person whole, has been the main ideal of all liberal education down through the ages, many people in the past were denied such an education. Those who were to be petty functionaries in life's drama: the workers, the shopkeepers, the non-leaders, were to receive only enough vocational education and "morality" as would keep them producing and out of trouble. It was only the upper classes that would receive the education called "liberal" (from the Latin *liberus*, meaning free: an education suited to free men and not to slaves). But the combination of a variety of trends have made such a wholistic education a vital necessity.

First, ours is a democratic country, a country where it is hoped that more and more people will enter into full and free participation in the society. Secondly, in many ways beyond politics people have become freer than all previous generations. They have freed themselves from the ties of family, of tradition, of old definitions of sexual roles, of racial roles, of the requirements to reside in one place, and so forth. It has become a cliche to say that people will have three vocations *at least* during their work careers. And with all this freedom have come the negative sides. Deracination, alienation, physical and mental stress, divorce, psychosomatic disease, drugs and the hundred other maladies of modern life so well summarized by Alvin Toffler as "future shock."

With such freedom and such stress it becomes almost a necessity for survival that education concern itself with the whole person once more. And that means a renewed concern with the body of the child, his or her feelings, his moral and spiritual development, and the relation of these one to another and to the life of the mind. We return once again to the traditional definitions of education: self-knowledge leading to self-mastery. We see the desperate need for some inner cultivation of the child that will make him immune to the tragic escapism of drugs. We feel the need of schools and other institutions to help a person acquire that inward poise that will make bearable the wrenching changes of the future shock society. The industry of psychotherapy thrives as never before, grows portentously, as the technically successful adult realizes that he or she has an insufficiently educated personality with which to meet strain. Science conquers microbes but stressful "diseases of civilization" (heart disease, cancer, hypertension) continue to increase the number of their victims. Ironically, physicians die younger than their patients because their highly technical education has taught them only concepts about dealing with their own stresses.

A curriculum or a training program that prepares a person for life in the present context must be multidimensional. It must educate the mind so that a person can think easily and creatively while scientific innovation makes of "objective truth" only a set of temporary approximations. The educated person must be able to deal with the emotional stresses that modern life exacts. He must know how to avert the harmful consequences of such stresses on his body. He must find his free center, his self, his inner guide, his spirit—in a world where outside authority increasingly becomes distrusted. He must move from such profound self-knowledge and self-development toward contact with others and with society. And all this is necessary for simple and healthy survival.

The Future Prospect

Fortunately, along with the difficult challenges of modern life have arisen appropriate cultural responses. Ways are being found by educators, social scientists, and many others not only to revive the tradition of humanistic education but to make them relevant to our less doctrinaire time. Theoretical investigations and empirical research have combined to produce useful directions and practical techniques for humanistic education. What this amounts to is not the mere promise of survival in a difficult society but larger evolutions, a larger transcendence.

The time is full of opportunity. Freed from the trappings of particular doctrines of the past, a person living in the end of the twentieth century can go in search of the spirit underlying the letter. So perhaps for the first time in human history one can envision an education in which human values are *discovered* by most pupils, rather than forced upon them. One can envision an education in which a student is taught to find his inner authority rather than cleverly subjected to outer authority. One can imagine an education in which the body is no longer a mere tool to be used but an integral part of the human person to be harmonized.

None of this need contradict a wise and vital emphasis on content, subject matter, technical and scientific mastery. Nor should it. The "farther reaches of human nature" of which Maslow spoke in his last book are human achievements grounded in reality—in such realities as reading and writing, making a living and raising a family. The formation of one's inner life is not an end in itself, nor does it take place in a vacuum. The training of teachers, the writing of curriculum, the teaching of students must move between self and other, self and world. But unless the self is included in the educational process, unless the old traditions are revived and rejuvenated in contemporary ways, all the promise of new freedoms and opportunities will end in the hollow exercises of hollow men and hollow women.

Though there has been a primary and intuitive understanding on the part of every great philosopher of education about the need for internal wholeness in the learner, curriculum has tended in recent centuries to degrade the conception.

With the reawakening of classical learning in the Renaissance, the gigantic flash of Greek and Roman wisdom across the skies of fifteenth century Europe, wholeness came more and more to mean studying certain works. The works of these ancient masters seemed so full of significance that it was through such study that one's own significance would be found. As the centuries progressed however, knowledge increased in quantity. More and more ancient books by more and more ancient authors were unearthed. And then new books about these authors and their works were written. And then new knowledge, particularly in the form of physical sciences, came to be born. And at first a hundred and then a thousand new technologies.

And then the discovery of five hundred foreign languages. Of whole civilizations, past and present, previously unknown. Of dozens, then tens of dozens of new academic disciplines. The creation of ten thousand new vocations.

Curiously enough, the combination of this explosion of knowledge with the Renaissance idea of the whole man as a man whole because of his many skills and accomplishments, has left many highly educated people depressed. They would that they could complete their wholeness by knowing everything, by being able to do everything, by understanding everything, by being competent in everything. And, of course, they are doomed to dissatisfaction. And they know it. And they still yearn.

The wholeness they seek, however, cannot be acquired through the appropriation of skills and knowledges beyond themselves. There is not enough time. Rather a primary harmony and unity must be cultivated from within. In such a unity there will appear the recognition of one's deep individuality. The marvel and wonder of individual differences. The sense that while we must share the world in which all of us dwell, much of what we share with others will have to be our uniqueness. In such a conception, the concern with the whole child becomes a concern with the wholeness that is unique to the individual child. Because all of us are human, there will be vast similarities. Curriculum is possible, teaching is possible. But that particular freedom to find and be one's self, to play one's part in the whole is emphatic.

The Philosophical Foundation: The Phenomenon of Being

In existential philosophy the study of consciousness or mind is called phenomenology.* One of the main purposes or philosophical ideals of phenomenology is to uncover the essential meanings of existence, as existence is lived from instant to instant. Yet, according to Martin Heidegger, the most fundamental essence or meaning of existence is Being, or that which transcends strictly historical and personal existence.

Although many have attempted it, from the ancient Greek philosopher Parmenides to twentieth-century metaphysicians, there probably exists no completely adequare way to define Being. Beyond the transcendental quality of Being, or that which makes Being *more than* existence but not separate from it, the concept of Being points to the freedom and consciousness of man. Being may be likened to the universal "Way" of Taoism or the "Big Mind" of Zen Buddhism, both of which are conceived to encompass and permeate the whole of reality, without either beginning or end. However, the concept of Being probably assumes its most relevant human aspect in the form of personal consciousness and existential freedom, in the understanding that *it* is no ordinary thing in the world.

* Phenomenology, or existential phenomenology as it is sometimes called, offers, I believe, the most philosophically meaningful basis for educating humanistically. My essay and introductions to the different sections of this book express this bias. I believe that this philosophical viewpoint can be used for a great many purposes, from examining the minute-to-minute transactions of existence itself to fundamental intuitions about Being. And this approach is being taken in a number of fields other than philosophy, such as psychology and theology.

In education, particularly education that is humanistically oriented, the phenomenon or experience of Being can be the true ground upon which the practices of teaching and learning are based. Being, or the experience and knowledge of it, is always concretely and immediately in and of the world; otherwise Being becomes like any other purely idealistic phenomenon, abstract and empty of existential meaning. Existence, in this sense, points to the lived-through day to day transactions and interactions of reality with all its uncertainties.

The problem of Being points to the age-old question of the meaning of life. How can the wholeness of man's existence be comprehended, both spatially and temporally? Is it possible to understand the whole meaning of life through some magical source of knowledge? Or are we humans shipwrecked upon the rocks of existence without hope for ultimate, final knowledge, as Immanuel Kant, Karl Jaspers, Jean-Paul Sartre, and others, have asserted?

The quest for ultimate knowledge has been an alive concern for religionists and some humanists alike. Perhaps only the "hard" scientist, the naive realist, the worldly cynic, and the sensualist have altogether given up the search. For those who still have an active concern for ultimate knowledge and being, the phenomenology of Being, particularly as interpreted through existential philosophy, offers a brave hope in a world despairing of metaphysics.

Certainly the daily task of teaching and learning can be tremendously enlivened and deepened, and possibly cleared of metaphysical illusions, if one takes an existential viewpoint toward the problem of total knowing. The teacher, as a person who is free and yet destined to die, has a responsibility to have a viewpoint about ultimate matters.[1] And, for that matter, everyone else who is involved in the educational process has a responsibility not only to look deeply into existence but to attempt to experience it deeply.

In my view an education that is humanistic should take into account the whole of existence—the depths, the heights, and the surfaces—and accept whatever is disclosed as a part of Being. In this sense, Being is the most humanizing or integrating of concepts because it is the only one that embraces all others.

The selections of this section are intended to contribute to the philosophical understanding and appreciation of humanistic education. In "The Definition of Pragmatism and Humanism," for example, the English thinker F. C. S. Schiller points out the philosophically inclusive nature of

---

[1] I mean that the teacher's relationship towards the student, knowledge, and the world should not be separated from his or her philosophy of life, which should take into account ultimate (theological) matters.

humanism in that it encompasses both idealism and realism. It does this by considering the notion of pure thought, identified with idealism, and that of an external world, identified with realism, in interaction with one another.

Perhaps the most important point that Schiller makes in his comparison of pragmatism with humanism is that pragmatism is essentially concerned with the logical and epistemological dimensions of reality, whereas the philosophy of humanism is essentially and most deeply rooted in the psychological dimension of Being. And herein lies the origin of the dislike of humanism among academics, who have traditionally been preoccupied with the purely intellectual, cognitive, and scientific standards of knowing, founded chiefly upon the touchstone of dispassionate and disinterested reason. Humanism, Schiller asserts, goes beyond this limiting viewpoint of knowledge and experience, taking into account the legitimate philosophical interests of pragmatism in its quest to comprehend the whole measure of man and his experience.

In "Existentialism Is a Humanism," the famous French existentialist, Jean-Paul Sartre defends existential philosophy in the name of humanism and, in so doing, throws considerable light not only upon humanism, but upon his own position of existential humanism. Briefly, Sartre defines man's total being as (1) anguished, (2) abandoned, and (3) despairing. Asserting that existential humanism is a sternly optimistic philosophy, Sartre believes that man is more free to choose without illusions, particularly those based upon God, human nature, determinism, and absolutism. In rejecting both the scientific materialism of Communists and the theistic idealism of Christians, existential humanism believes that "man first of all exists, encounters himself, surges up in the world—and defines himself afterwards." This idea about man is the basis for Sartre's statement that "existence comes before essence." It also conditions the reality of human freedom, the most supreme and generative of phenomena, for Sartre.

The famous metaphysician, Martin Heiddegger,* perhaps makes the most direct and explicit uncovery of fundamental Being, in his "Letter on Humanism." Being, he begins, is the most important element of thought. The wholeness of man, he believes, is found through "ex-istence" or standing in the light of Being. And although language is the house of Being, it conceals as well as clears, concealing when its structures lead us to merely technical, rational concepts. Being is historical through and through, even though man simultaneously exists beyond animality and technology in his essential self. And again, Heidegger's new humanism is

* Owing to limitations of space, I am unable to include a selection from the work of Martin Heidegger. However, because of the importance of the thought of Heidegger, I have kept my interpretative remarks in their original place, in the hope that the reader will be motivated to read from the source indicated in Further Reading.

founded upon man's "ec-static dwelling in the nearness of Being"; for it is only in the speaking of Being that the real truth about man's existence will be known, and that is in the end metaphysical, or beyond the purely physical and wordly existence of reality.

Both Sartre and Heidegger, I believe, present provocative and stimulating viewpoints for considering the possible meaning of humanism in education. In Sartre we find a deep faith in the fundamental freedom of man that is in itself ethical. He believes that man, if he chooses authentically, chooses himself. And if we are to promote ethical and authentic choices in education, then we must allow the learner, teacher, or administrator to choose themselves. There can be no other way for an education that humanizes. In Heidegger, the nearness of man to Being requires that he speak from it or else succumb to the trivia and superficiality of the world. For education, Heidegger's belief that man does not matter apart from the truth of Being could cause a fundamental rethinking about what we do in the name of teaching and learning, curriculum planning, school organization, and the like. Indeed, according to Heidegger's philosophy of Being, the language, if nothing else, of education probably does more to conceal rather than to disclose Being and its truth.

I believe that Plato's theory of the Good may serve as a basis for understanding what Heidegger and others have conceived of as ultimate reality or Being. In Plato's "Allegory of the Cave," in which he describes man held prisoner in a cave, or world, of half-truths and spurious light from which few escape, the Good is a phenomenon that lies only within reach of the soul or whole being of the seeker for truth. Being or the Good, in this sense, is no ordinary, sensory object of the world, as the experience of the cave leads one to believe. For Plato, the Good or Being is the source of what is absolutely right, beautiful, and true.

It is important to realize that in Plato's theory of reality once one has seen the light, one has the responsibility to return to the world of ordinary reality and half-truth to enlighten and lead others toward the same knowledge. In this sense, the knower or teacher, ideally, is one who serves others, not by force of his own personality or accomplishments alone, but through motivation by a higher purpose and truth than any mere mortal may lay claim to. The task of educating, in this sense, is divinely inspired. And for some throughout history, the teacher as prophet and seer has been a role that has a religious as well as a humanistic influence. At the same time, such a conception of educating can easily become an errant authoritarianism, even though it may masquerade as a truth of religious humanism.

Martin Buber, the existentialist thinker and rabbi, has been one of the most influential sources for humanistic thinking about education. Both of my selections are taken from his important book, *Between Man and Man.* In "Education," Buber uncovers education in the contexts of the *Thou,* Eros, and God. Starting with the dialectic or bipolar nature of creativity, Buber defines the *Thou* or Being of education as being made possible by the instincts of origination as well as communion. Furthermore, the completion or fulfillment of the originator instinct for creativity is found in the mutuality and sharing activity of communion with others. In this sense, the world, nature, and society—and not merely the self alone—educates and humanizes. In short, the focus for Buber is upon the experience of inclusion, which he distinguishes carefully from empathy, the latter experience failing to be the true extension of the great love that is found in the mother-child relationship. In feeling from outside, the teacher experiences the pupil in Present Being and not as he would rather want him or her to be. Friendship, in the teacher-student relationship, represents the transformation of the educative relationship into something greater, "community, turned to God."

In "The Education of Character," Buber defines character as the person as a whole, both in terms of actualities and possibilities. Furthermore he insists that it is only in the atmosphere of confidence that the teacher himself can be accepted as a person by the student. And "only in his whole being, in all his spontaneity can the educator truly affect the whole being of the pupil."

In agreement with Martin Heidegger and other theistic humanists, Buber states that modern man is blind to eternity.* Furthermore, the only way that the educator can help the pupil to overcome the contradictions of nature and society is through the unity of Being; or, in Buber's words: "The educator who helps to bring man back to his own unity will help to put him again face to face with God."

Donald Vandenberg's case study of the German Youth Movement at the turn of the century ends this section. It is a remarkable piece of writing, in touching so concretely upon so many existential themes. His concept of experiencing is very close to Buber's concept of inclusion; and since it speaks so well for itself, I will not comment upon it, except to say that it shows the strong imprint of Martin Heidegger's thinking. Also, it shows well how the "primordial way of living" found in the wanderer's quest is most utterly close to true Being. At the same time, Vandenberg's sensitivity to the connection between inner Being and the external world shines through strongly.

---

* I am aware that Sartre has described Heidegger as an atheist in "Existentialism Is a Humanism." However, Heidegger has protested the label "atheist" in "Letter on Humanism."

DISCUSSION QUESTIONS

1. In defining the philosophy of humanism, F. C. S. Schiller indicates that the academic attitude has been opposed to humanism. What, in your opinion, accounts for the opposition of humanism and academicism? Does academic activity necessarily imply a basis that is opposed to the scope of humanism? Or, does academicism breed a specialized, narrow, and merely intellectual bias because of its disciplined and departmentalized mentality? Also, is there or can there be a conflict between the logical and the psychological dimensions of education? Why?

2. Jean-Paul Sartre defines existential humanism as a philosophy based upon man's freedom. What threats are there, in society and in nature, to man's freedom? How does freedom express itself in the schools and colleges? If we are nothing but the choices we make, what does it mean to choose for another? Why is it important that persons involved in the educational process be free to choose for themselves? What are the limits to man's choosing for himself, or are we limitlessly free?

3. Do you agree with the implications of Plato's "Allegory of the Cave" that mankind is in half-darkness and blind to the truth of existence? Is there, in your opinion, a light or source of knowledge and truth that is more valuable than any other? Is there a world of becoming, or changing appearances, and a world of being, or permanent relationships, as Plato implies? What basis is there, intellectually and psychologically, for thinking that truth is in a higher realm, or in this merely a metaphorical way of thinking? What implications do Plato's assumptions about man, truth, and knowledge have for education?

4. Martin Buber's philosophy of education is heavily oriented towards theistic values. Do you think that entering into dialogue with the *other*, as pupil, is a way that the *Thou* or spiritual wholeness of existence can be experienced? Do you think that there is any danger in emphasizing the interpersonal dimension of learning to the extent that Buber does? Is the communal man the ideal that you hold for education? Do you think that there are ways other than those stated by Buber to reach the eternal values of education? If so, what are they?

5. Donald Vandenberg portrays the German Youth Movement as a protest against the lack of freedom and the authoritarian repression in the traditional schools. In their wandering the youths of the movement experienced not only a fundamental shift in their mode of being, toward the present as goallessness, but an awareness of the landscape itself as a part of their ground of being. How should schools and colleges be restructured to accomodate what Vanden-

berg calls the anthropological function of wandering? Are schools overstructured temporally and spatially, preventing students from wandering and experiencing primordially? Can schools become places where joy, play, and trust in present being is experienced? How?

FURTHER READING

Bergson, Henri. *Time and Free Will*. New York: Harper Torchbooks, 1960.

Binswanger, Ludwig. *Being-in-the-World*. New York: Harper Torchbooks, 1967.

Chardin, Teilhard de. *The Phenomenon of Man*. New York: Harper Torchbooks, 1959.

Dewey, John. *Art as Experience*. New York: Capricorn Books, 1958.

Farber, Marvin. *Phenomenology and Existence*. New York: Harper Torchbooks, 1967.

Gasset, Jose Ortega y. *What is Philosophy?* New York: W. W. Norton & Company Inc., 1964.

Heidegger, Martin. "Letter on Humanism." In *The Existentialist Tradition*, edited by Nino Langiulli. Garden City, New York: Anchor Books, 1971.

Heidegger, Martin. *An Introduction to Metaphysics*. Garden City, New York: Anchor Books, 1961.

Reps, Paul. *Zen Flesh, Zen Bones*. Garden City, New York: Anchor Books, 1957.

Tzu, Lao. *The Way of Life*. New York: Capricorn Books, 1962.

The Definition of Pragmatism and Humanism

F. C. S. SCHILLER

Humanism is really in itself the simplest of philosophic standpoints; it is merely the perception that the philosophic problems concerns human beings striving to comprehend a world of human experience by the resources of human minds. Not even Pragmatism could be simpler or nearer to an obvious truism of cognitive method. For if man may not presume his own nature in his reasonings about his experience, wherewith, pray, shall he reason? What prospect has he of comprehending a radically alien universe? And yet not even Pragmatism has been more bitterly assailed than the great principle that man is the measure of his experience, and so an ineradicable factor in any world he experiences. The Protagorean principle may sometimes seem paradoxical to the uninstructed, because they think it leaves out of account the "independence" of the "external" world. But this is mere misunderstanding. Humanism has no quarrel with the assumptions of common-sense realism; it does not deny what is popularly described as the "external" world. It has far too much respect for the pragmatic value of conceptions which *de facto* work far better than those of the metaphysics which despise and try to supersede them. It insists only that the "external world" of realism is still dependent on human experience, and perhaps ventures to add also that the data of human experience are not completely used up in the construction of a real external world. Moreover, its assailants are not realists, though, for the purpose of such attacks, they may masquerade as such.

The truth is rather that Humanism gives offence, not because it leaves out, but because it leaves in. It leaves in a great deal Intellectualism would like to leave out, a great deal it has no use for, which it would like to extirpate, or at least to keep out of its sight. But Humanism will not assent to the mutilations and expurgations of human nature which have become customary barbarisms in the initiation ceremonies of too many philosophic schools. It demands that man's integral nature shall be used as the whole premiss which philosophy must argue from wholeheartedly, that man's complete satisfaction shall be the conclusion philosophy must aim at, that philosophy shall not cut itself loose from the real problems of life by making initial abstractions which are false, and would not be admirable, even if they were true. Hence it insists on *leaving in* the whole rich luxuriance of individual minds, instead of compressing them all into a single type of "mind," feigned to be one and immutable; it leaves in also the psychological wealth of every human mind and the complexities of its interests, emotions, volitions, aspirations. By so doing it sacrifices, no doubt, much illusory simplicity in abstract formulas, but it appreciates and explains vast masses of what before had had to be slurred over as unintelligible fact.[1]

The dislike of Humanism, therefore, is psychological in origin. It arises from the nature of certain human minds who have become too enamoured of the artificial simplifications, or too accustomed to the self-inflicted mutilations, and the self-imposed torments, whereby they hope to merit absorption in absolute truth. These ascetics of the intellectual world must steadfastly oppose the free indulgence in all

---

[1] Contrast Mr. Joachim's *Nature of Truth* throughout, especially pp. 167–78.

human powers, the liberty of moving, or improving, of making, of manipulating, which Humanism vindicates for man, and substitutes for the old ideal of an inactive contemplation of a static truth. It is no wonder that the Simeons Stylitae of the old order, hoisted aloft each on the pillar of his metaphysical "system," resent the disturbance of their restful solitude, "alone with the Alone," by the hoots of intrusive motorcars; that the Saint Antonys of the deserts of Pure Thought are infuriated by their conversion into serviceable golf links; and that the Juggernaut Car of the Absolute gets fewer and fewer votaries to prostrate themselves beneath its wheels every time it is rolled out of the recesses of its sanctuary—for when man has grown conscious of his powers he will prefer even to chance an encounter with a useful machine to being run over by a useless "deity."

The active life of man is continuously being transformed by the progress of modern science, by the knowledge which is power. But not so the "knowledge" which is "contemplation," which postpones the test of action, and struggles to evade it. Unfortunately, it is hard to modernize the academic life, and it is this life which is the fountainhead of Intellectualism. Academic life naturally tends to produce a certain intellectualistic bias, and to select the natures which incline to it. Intellectualism, therefore, in some form will always be a congenial philosophy which is true to the academic life.

Genuine wholehearted Humanism, on the other hand, is a singularly difficult attitude to sustain in an academic atmosphere; for the tendencies of the whole mode of life are unceasingly against it. If Protagoras had been a university professor, he would hardly have discovered Humanism; he would more likely have constructed a Nephelococcygia of a system that laid claim to absolute, universal, and eternal truth, or spent his life in overthrowing the discrepant, but no less presumptuous, systems of his colleagues. Fortunately he lived before universities had been invented to regulate, and quench, the thirst for knowledge; he had to earn his living by the voluntary gratitude for instructions which could justify themselves only in his pupils' lives; and so he had to be human and practical, and to take the chill of pedantry off his discourses.

Just because Humanism, then, is true to the larger life of man, it must be in some measure false to the artificially secluded studies of a "seat of learning"; and its acceptance by an academic personage must always mean a triumph over the obvious temptation to idealize and adore the narrownesses of his actual life. However much it exalts the function of man in general, it may always be taken to hint a certain disparagement of the academic man. It needs a certain magnanimity, in short, in a professor to avow himself a humanist.

Thorough humanists, therefore, will always be somewhat rare in academic circles. There will always be many who will not be able to avoid convincing themselves of the truth of a method which works like the pragmatic one (and indeed in another twenty years pragmatic convictions will be practically universal), without being able to overcome the intellectualistic influences of their nature and their mode of life. Such persons will be psychologically incapacitated to advance in the path which leads from Pragmatism to Humanism.

Yet this advance is in a manner logical as well as psychological. For those whose nature predisposes them towards it will find it reasonable and satisfying, and when they have reached the humanist position and reflect upon the expansion of Pragmatism which it involves, there will seem to be a "logical" connexion. Pragmatism will seem a special application of Humanism to the theory of knowledge. But Humanism will seem more universal. It will seem to be possessed of a method which is applicable universally, to ethics, to aesthetics, to metaphysics, to theology, to every concern of man, as well as to the theory of knowledge.

Yet there will be no "logical" compulsion. Here, as always when we come to the important choices of life, we must be free to stop at the lower lever, if we are to be free to advance to the higher. We can stop at the epistemological level of Pragmatism (just as we can stop short of philosophy on the scientific plane, and of science on the plane of ordinary life), accepting Pragmatism indeed as the method and analysis of our cognitive procedure, but without seeking to generalize it, or to turn it into a metaphysic. Indeed, if our interest is not keen in life as a whole, we are very likely to do something of the kind.

Existentialism Is a Humanism

JEAN-PAUL SARTRE

Translated by Philip Mairet

My purpose here is to offer a defence of existentialism against several reproaches that have been laid against it.

First, it has been reproached as an invitation to people to dwell

Reprinted by permission of Methuen & Co. Ltd. and Les Edition Nagel from *Existentialism Is a Humanism* by Jean-Paul Sartre.

in quietism of despair. For if every way to a solution is barred, one would have to regard any action in this world as entirely ineffective, and one would arrive finally at a contemplative philosophy. Moreover, since contemplation is a luxury, this would be only another bourgeois philosophy. This is, especially, the reproach made by the Communists.

From another quarter we are reproached for having underlined all that is ignominious in the human situation, for depicting what is mean, sordid or base to the neglect of certain things that possess charm and beauty and belong to the brighter side of human nature: for example, according to the Catholic critic, Mlle. Mercier, we forget how an infant smiles. Both from this side and from the other we are also reproached for leaving out of account the solidarity of mankind and considering man in isolation. And this, say the Communists, is because we base our doctrine upon pure subjectivity—upon the Cartesian "I think": which is the moment in which solitary man attains to himself; a position from which it is impossible to regain solidarity with other men who exist outside of the self. The *ego* cannot reach them through the *cogito*.

From the Christian side, we are reproached as people who deny the reality and seriousness of human affairs. For since we ignore the commandments of God and all values prescribed as eternal, nothing remains but what is strictly voluntary. Everyone can do what he likes, and will be incapable, from such a point of view, of condemning either the point of view or the action of anyone else.

It is to these various reproaches that I shall endeavour to reply to-day; that is why I have entitled this brief exposition "Existentialism and Humanism." Many may be surprised at the mention of humanism in this connection, but we shall try to see in what sense we understand it. In any case, we can begin by saying that existentialism, in our sense of the word, is a doctrine that does render human life possible; a doctrine, also, which affirms that every truth and every action imply both an environment and a human subjectivity. The essential charge laid against us is, of course, that of overemphasis upon the evil side of human life. I have lately been told of a lady who, whenever she lets slip a vulgar expression in a moment of nervousness, excuses herself by exclaiming, "I believe I am becoming an existentialist." So it appears that ugliness is being identified with existentialism. That is why some people say we are "naturalistic," and if we are, it is strange to see how much we scandalise and horrify them, for no one seems to be much frightened or humiliated nowadays by what is properly called naturalism. Those who can quite well keep down a novel by Zola such as *La Terre* are sickened as soon as they read an existentialist novel. Those who appeal to the wisdom of the people—which is a sad wisdom—find ours sadder still. And yet, what could be more disillusioned than such sayings as "Charity begins at home" or "Promote a rogue and he'll sue you for damage, knock him down and he'll do you homage"? We all know how many common sayings can be quoted to this effect, and they all mean much the same—that you must not oppose the powers-that-be; that you must not fight against superior force; must not meddle in matters that are above your station. Or that any action not in accordance with some tradition is mere romanticism; or that any undertaking which has not the support of proven experience is foredoomed to frustration; and that since experience has shown men to be invariably inclined to evil, there must be firm rules to restrain them, otherwise we shall have anarchy. It is, however, the people who are forever mouthing these dismal proverbs and, whenever they are told of some more or less repulsive action, say "How like human nature!"—it is these very people, always harping upon realism, who complain that existentialism is too gloomy a view of things. Indeed their excessive protests make me suspect that what is annoying them is not so much our pessimism, but, much more likely, our optimism. For at bottom, what is alarming in the doctrine that I am about to try to explain to you is—is it not?—that it confronts man with a possibility of choice. To verify this, let us review the whole question upon the strictly philosophic level. What, then, is this that we call existentialism?

Most of those who are making use of this word would be highly confused if required to explain its meaning. For since it has become fashionable, people cheerfully declare that this musician or that painter is "existentialist." A columnist in *Clartés* signs himself "The Existentialist," and, indeed, the word is now so loosely applied to so many things that it no longer means anything at all. It would appear that, for the lack of any novel doctrine such as that of surrealism, all those who are eager to join in the latest scandal or movement now seize upon this philosophy in which, however, they can find nothing to their purpose. For in truth this is of all teachings the least scandalous and the most austere: it is intended strictly for technicians and philosophers. All the same, it can easily be defined.

The question is only complicated because there are two kinds of existentialists. There are, on the one hand, the Christians, amongst whom I shall name Jaspers and Gabriel Marcel, both professed Catholics; and on the other the existential atheists, amongst whom we must place Heidegger as well as the French existentialists and myself. What they have in common is simply the fact that they believe that *existence* comes before *essence*—or, if you will, that we must begin from the subjective. What exactly do we mean by that?

If one considers an article of manufacture—as, for example, a book or a paper-knife—one sees that it has been made by an artisan who had a conception of it; and he has paid attention, equally, to the conception of a paper-knife and to the preexistent technique of production which is a part of that conception and is, at bottom, a formula. Thus the paper-knife is at the same time an article producible in a certain manner and one which, on the other hand, serves a definite purpose, for one cannot suppose that a man would produce a paper-knife without knowing what it was for. Let us say, then, of the paper-knife that its essence—that is to say the sum of the formulae and the qualities which made its production and its definition possible—precedes its existence. The presence of such-and-such a paper-knife or book is thus determined before my eyes. Here, then, we are viewing the world from a technical standpoint, and we can say that production precedes existence.

When we think of God as the creator, we are thinking of him, most of the time, as a supernal artisan. Whatever doctrine we may be considering, whether it be a doctrine like that of Descartes, or of Leibnitz himself, we always imply that the will follows, more or less, from the understanding or at least accompanies it, so that when God creates he knows precisely what he is creating. Thus, the conception of man in the mind of God is comparable to that of the paper-knife in the mind of the artisan: God makes man according to a procedure and a conception, exactly as the artisan manufactures a paper-knife, following a definition and a formula. Thus each individual man is the realisation of a certain conception which dwells in the divine understanding. In the philosophic atheism of the eighteenth century, the notion of God is suppressed, but not, for all that, the idea that essence is prior to existence; something of that idea we still find everywhere, in Diderot, in Voltaire and even in Kant. Man possesses a human nature; that "human nature," which is the conception of human being, is found in every man; which means that each man is a particular example of an universal conception, the conception of Man. In Kant, this universality goes so far that the wild man of the woods, man in the state of nature and the bourgeois are all contained in the same definition and have the same fundamental qualities. Here again, the essence of man precedes that historic existence which we confront in experience.

Atheistic existentialism, of which I am a representative, declares with greater consistency that if God does not exist there is at least one being whose existence comes before its essence, a being which exists before it can be defined by any conception of it. That being is man or, as Heidegger has it, the human reality. What do we mean by saying that existence precedes essence? We mean that man first of all exists, encounters himself, surges up in the world—and defines himself afterwards. If man as the existentialist sees him is not definable, it is because to begin with he is nothing. He will not be anything until later, and then he will be what he makes of himself. Thus, there is no human nature, because there is no God to have a conception of it. Man simply is. Not that he is simply what he conceives himself to be but he is what he wills, and as he conceives himself after already existing—as he wills to be after that leap towards existence Man is nothing else but that which he makes of himself. That is the first principle of existentialism. And this is what people call its "subjectivity," using the word as a reproach against us. But what do we mean to say by this, but that man is of a greater dignity than a stone or a table? For we mean to say that man primarily exists—that man is, before all else, something which propels itself towards a future and is aware that it is doing so. Man is, indeed, a project which possesses a subjective life, instead of being a kind of moss, or a fungus or a cauliflower. Before that projection of the self nothing exists; not even in the heaven of intelligence: man will only attain existence when he is what he purposes to be. Not, however, what he may wish to be. For what we usually understand by wishing or willing is a conscious decision taken—much more often than not—after we have made ourselves what we are. I may wish to join a party, to write a book or to marry—but in such a case what is usually called my will is probably a manifestation of a prior and more spontaneous decision. If, however, it is true that existence is prior to essence, man is responsible for what he is. Thus, the first effect of existentialism is that it puts every man in possession of himself as he is, and places the entire responsibility for his existence squarely upon his own shoulders. And, when we say that man is responsible for himself, we do not mean that he is responsible only for his own individuality, but that he is responsible for all men. The word "subjectivism" is to be understood in two senses, and our adversaries play upon only one of them. Subjectivism means, on the one hand, the freedom of the individual subject and, on the other, that man cannot pass beyond human subjectivity. It is the latter which is the deeper meaning of existentialism. When we say that man chooses himself, we do mean that every one of us must choose himself; but by that we also mean that in choosing for himself he chooses for all men. For in effect, of all the actions a man may take in order to create himself as he wills to be, there is not one which is not creative, at the same time, of an image of man such as he believes he ought to be. To choose between this or that is at the same time to affirm the value of that which is chosen; for we are unable ever to choose the worse. What we choose is always the better; and nothing can be better for us unless it is better for all. If, moreover, existence precedes essence and we will to exist at the same time as we fashion our image, that image is valid for all and for the entire epoch in which we find ourselves. Our responsibility is thus much greater than we had supposed, for it concerns mankind as a whole. If I am a worker, for instance, I may choose to join a Christian rather than a Communist trade union. And if, by that membership, I choose to signify that resignation is, after all, the attitude that best becomes a man, that man's kingdom is not upon this earth, I do not commit myself alone to that view. Resignation is my will for everyone, and my action is, in consequence, a commitment on behalf of all mankind. Or if, to take a more personal case, I decide to marry and to have children, even though this decision proceeds simply from my situation, from my passion or my desire, I am thereby committing not only myself, but humanity as a whole, to the practice of monogamy. I am thus responsible for myself and for all men, and I am creating a certain image of man as I would have him to be. In fashioning myself I fashion man.

This may enable us to understand what is meant by such terms—perhaps a little grandiloquent—as anguish, abandonment and despair. As you will soon see, it is very simple. First, what do we mean by anguish? The existentialist frankly states that man is in anguish. His meaning is as follows—When a man commits himself to anything, fully realising that he is not only choosing what he will be, but is thereby at the same time a legislator deciding for the whole of mankind—in such a moment a man cannot escape from the sense of complete and profound responsibility. There are many, indeed, who show no such anxiety. But we affirm that they are merely disguising their anguish or are in flight from it. Certainly, many people think that in what they are doing they commit no one but themselves to anything: and if you ask them, "What would happen if everyone did so?" they shrug their shoulders and reply, "Everyone does not do so." But in truth, one ought always to ask oneself what would happen if everyone did as one is doing; nor can one escape from that disturbing thought except by a kind of self-deception. The man who lies in self-excuse, by saying "Everyone will not do it" must be ill at ease in his conscience, for the act of lying implies the universal value which it denies. By its very disguise his anguish reveals itself. This is the anguish that Kierkegaard called "the anguish of Abraham." You know the story: An angel commanded Abraham to sacrifice his son: and obedience was obligatory, if it really was an angel who had appeared and said, "Thou, Abraham, shalt sacrifice thy son." But anyone in such a case would wonder, first, whether it was indeed an angel and secondly, whether I am really Abraham. Where are the proofs? A certain mad woman who suffered from hallucinations said that people were telephoning to her, and giving her orders. The doctor asked, "But who is it that speaks to you?" She replied: "He says it is God." And what, indeed, could prove to her that it was God? If an angel appears to me, what is the proof that it is an angel; or, if I hear voices, who can prove that they proceed from heaven and not from hell, or from my own subconsciousness or some pathological condition? Who can prove that they are really addressed to me?

Who, then, can prove that I am the proper person to impose, by my own choice, my conception of man upon mankind? I shall never find any proof whatever; there will be no sign to convince me of it. If a voice speaks to me, it is still I myself who must decide whether the voice is or is not that of an angel. If I regard a certain course of action as good, it is only I who choose to say that it is good and not bad. There is nothing to show that I am Abraham: nevertheless I also am obliged at every instant to perform actions which are examples. Everything happens to every man as though the whole human race had its eyes fixed upon what he is doing and regulated its conduct accordingly. So every man ought to say, "Am I really a man who has the right to act in such a manner that humanity regulates itself by what I do." If a man does not say that, he is dissembling his anguish. Clearly, the anguish with which we are concerned here is not one that could lead to quietism or inaction. It is anguish pure and simple, of the kind well known to all those who have borne responsibilities. When, for instance, a military leader takes upon himself the responsibility for an attack and sends a number of men to their death, he chooses to do it and at bottom he alone chooses. No doubt he acts under a higher command, but its orders, which are more general, require interpretation by him and upon that interpretation depends the life of ten, fourteen or twenty men. In making the decision, he cannot but feel a certain anguish. All leaders know that anguish. It does not prevent their acting, on the contrary it is the very condition of their action, for the action presupposes that there is a plurality of possibilities, and in choosing one of these, they realise that it has value only because it is chosen. Now it is anguish of that kind which existentialism describes, and moreover, as we shall see, makes explicit through direct responsibility towards other men who are concerned. Far from being a screen which could separate us from action, it is a condition of action itself.

And when we speak of "abandonment"—a favorite word of Heidegger—we only mean to say that God does not exist, and that it is necessary to draw the consequences of his absence right to the end. The existentialist is strongly opposed to a certain type of secular moralism which seeks to suppress God at the least possible expense. Towards 1880, when the French professors endeavoured to formulate a secular morality, they said something like this:—God is a useless and costly hypothesis, so we will do without it. However, if we are to have morality, a society and a law-abiding world, it is essential that certain values should be taken seriously; they must have an *à priori* existence ascribed to them. It must be considered obligatory *à priori* to be honest, not to lie, not to beat one's wife, to bring up children and so forth; so we are going to do a little work on this subject; which will enable us to show that these values exist all the same, inscribed in an intelligible heaven although, of course, there is no God. In other words—and this is, I believe, the purport of all that we in France call radicalism—nothing will be changed if God does not exist; we shall re-discover the same norms of honesty, progress and humanity, and we shall have disposed of God as an out-of-date hypothesis which will die away quietly of itself. The existentialist, on the contrary, finds it extremely embarrassing that God does not exist, for there disappears with Him all possibility of finding values in an intelligible heaven. There can no longer be any good *à priori*, since there is no infinite and perfect consciousness to think it. It is nowhere written that "the good" exists, that one must be honest or must not lie, since we are now upon the plane where there are only men. Dostoievsky once wrote "If God did not exist, everything would be permitted"; and that, for existentialism, is the starting point. Everything is indeed permitted if God does not exist, and man is in consequence forlorn, for he cannot find anything to depend upon either within or outside himself. He discovers forthwith, that he is without excuse. For if indeed existence precedes essence, one will never be able to explain one's action by reference to a given and specific human nature; in other words, there is no determinism—man is free, man *is* freedom. Nor, on the other hand, if God does not exist, are we provided with any values or commands that could legitimise our behaviour. Thus we have neither behind us, nor before us in a luminous realm of values, any means of justification or excuse. We are left alone, without excuse. That is what I mean when I say that man is condemned to be free. Condemned, because he did not create himself, yet is nevertheless at liberty, and from the moment that he is thrown into this world he is responsible for everything he does. The existentialist does not believe in the power of passion. He will never regard a grand passion as a destructive torrent upon which a man is swept into certain actions as by fate, and which, therefore, is an excuse for them. He thinks that man is responsible for his passion. Neither will an existentialist think that a man can find help through some sign being vouchsafed upon earth for his orientation: for he thinks that the man himself interprets the sign as he chooses. He thinks that every man, without any support or help whatever, is condemned at every instant to invent man. As Ponge has written in a very fine article, "Man is the future of man." That is exactly true. Only, if one took this to mean that the future is laid up in Heaven, that God knows what it is, it would be false, for then it would no longer even be a future. If, however, it means that, whatever man may now appear to be, there is a future to be fashioned, a virgin future that awaits him—then it is a true saying. But in the present one is forsaken.

As an example by which you may the better understand this state of abandonment, I will refer to the case of a pupil of mine, who sought me out in the following circumstances. His father was quarrelling with his mother and was also inclined to be a "collaborator"; his elder brother had been killed in the German offensive of 1940 and this young man, with a sentiment somewhat primitive but generous, burned to avenge him. His mother was living alone with him, deeply afflicted by the semi-treason of his father and by the death of her eldest son, and her one consolation was in this young man. but he, at this moment, had the choice between going to England to join the Free French Forces or of staying near his mother and helping her to live. He fully realised that this woman lived only for him and that his disappearance—or perhaps his death—would plunge her into despair. He also realised that, concretely and in fact, every action he performed on his mother's behalf would be sure of effect in the sense of aiding her to live, where as anything he did in order to go and fight would be an ambiguous action which might vanish like water into sand and serve no purpose. For instance, to set out for England he would have to wait indefinitely in a Spanish camp on the way through Spain; or, on arriving in England or in Algiers he might be put into an office to fill up forms. Consequently, he found himself confronted by two very different modes of action; the one concrete, immediate, but directed towards only one individual; and the other an action addressed to an end infinitely greater, a national collectivity, but for that very reason ambiguous—and it might be frustrated on the way. At the same time, he was hesitating between two kinds of morality; on the one side the morality of sympathy, of personal devotion and, on the other side, a morality of wider scope but of more debatable validity. He had to choose between those two. What could help him to choose? Could the Christian doctrine? No. Christian doctrine says: Act with charity, love your neighbour, deny yourself for others, choose the way which is hardest, and so forth. But which is the harder road? To whom does one owe the more brotherly love, the patriot or the mother? Which is the more useful aim, the general one of fighting in and for the whole community, or the precise aim of helping one particular person to live? Who can give an

answer to that *à priori?* No one. Nor is it given in any ethical scrip-
ture. The Kantian ethic says, Never regard another as a means, but
always as an end. Very well; if I remain with my mother, I shall be
regarding her as the end and not as a means: but by the same token I
am in danger of treating as means those who are fighting on my
behalf; and the converse is also true, that if I go to the aid of the com-
batants I shall be treating them as the end at the risk of treating my
mother as a means.

If values are uncertain, if they are still too abstract to determine
the particular, concrete case under consideration, nothing remains
but to trust in our instincts. That is what this young man tried to do;
and when I saw him he said, "In the end, it is feeling that counts;
the direction in which it is really pushing me is the one I ought to
choose. If I feel that I love my mother enough to sacrifice everything
else for her—my will to be avenged, all my longings for action and
adventure—then I stay with her. If, on the contrary, I feel that my
love for her is not enough, I go." But how does one estimate the
strength of a feeling? The value of his feeling for his mother was determined precisely by the fact that he was standing by her. I may say
that I love a certain friend enough to sacrifice such or such a sum of
money for him, but I cannot prove that unless I have done it. I may
say, "I love my mother enough to remain with her," if actually I have
remained with her I can only estimate the strength of this affection if
I have performed an action by which it is defined and ratified. But if
I then appeal to this affection to justify my action, I find myself
drawn into a vicious circle.

Moreover, as Gide has very well said, a sentiment which is play-
acting and one which is vital are two things that are hardly distin-
guishable one from another. To decide that I love my mother by staying beside her, and to play a comedy the upshot of which is that I do
so—these are nearly the same thing. In other words, feeling is
formed by the deeds that one does; therefore I cannot consult it as a
guide to action. And that is to say that I can neither seek within
myself for an authentic impulse to action, nor can I expect, from
some ethic, formulae that will enable me to act. You may say that the
youth did, at least, go to a professor to ask for advice. But if you seek
counsel—from a priest, for example—you have selected that priest;
and at bottom you already knew, more or less, what he would advise.
In other words, to choose an adviser is nevertheless to commit oneself by that choice. If you are a Christian, you will say, Consult a
priest; but there are collaborationists, priests who are resisters and
priests who wait for the tide to turn: which will you choose? Had this
young man chosen a priest of the resistance, or one of the collabo-
ration, he would have decided beforehand the kind of advice he was

to receive. Similarly, in coming to me, he knew what advice I should give him, and I had but one reply to make. You are free, therefore choose—that is to say, invent. No rule of general morality can show you what you ought to do: no signs are vouchsafed in this world. The Catholics will reply, "Oh, but they are!" Very well; still, it is I myself, in every case, who have to interpret the signs. Whilst I was imprisoned, I made the acquaintance of a somewhat remarkable man, a Jesuit, who had become a member of that order in the following manner. In his life he had suffered a succession of rather severe setbacks. His father had died when he was a child, leaving him in poverty, and he had been awarded a free scholarship in a religious institution, where he had been made continually to feel that he was accepted for charity's sake, and, in consequence, he had been denied several of those distinctions and honours which gratify children. Later, about the age of eighteen, he came to grief in a sentimental affair; and finally, at twenty-two—this was a trifle in itself, but it was the last drop that overflowed his cup—he failed in his military examination. This young man, then, could regard himself as a total failure: it was a sign—but a sign of what? He might have taken refuge in bitterness or despair. But he took it—very cleverly for him—as a sign that he was not intended for secular successes, and that only the attainments of religion, those of sanctity and of faith, were accessible to him. He interpreted his record as a message from God, and became a member of the Order. Who can doubt but that this decision as to the meaning of the sign was his, and his alone? One could have drawn quite different conclusions from such a series of reverses—as, for example, that he had better become a carpenter or a revolutionary. For the decipherment of the sign, however, he bears the entire responsibility. That is what "abandonment" implies, that we ourselves decide our being. And with this abandonment goes anguish.

As for "despair," the meaning of this expression is extremely simple. It merely means that we limit ourselves to a reliance upon that which is within our wills, or within the sum of the probabilities which render our action feasible. Whenever one wills anything, there are always these elements of probability. If I am counting upon a visit from a friend, who may be coming by train or by tram, I presuppose that the train will arrive at the appointed time, or that the tram will not be derailed. I remain in the realm of possibilities; but one does not rely upon any possibilities beyond those that are strictly concerned in one's action. Beyond the point at which the possibilities under consideration cease to affect my action, I ought to disinterest myself. For there is no God and no prevenient design, which can adapt the world and all its possibilities to my will. When

Descartes said, "Conquer yourself rather than the world," what he meant was, at bottom, the same—that we should act without hope.

Marxists, to whom I have said this, have answered: "Your action is limited, obviously, by your death; but you can rely upon the help of others. That is, you can count both upon what the others are doing to help you elsewhere, as in China and in Russia, and upon what they will do later, after your death, to take up your action and carry it forward to its final accomplishment which will be the revolution. Moreover you must rely upon this; not to do so is immoral." To this I rejoin, first, that I shall always count upon my comrades-in-arms in the struggle, in so far as they are committed, as I am, to a definite, common cause; and in the unity of a party or a group which I can more or less control—that is, in which I am enrolled as a militant and whose movements at every moment are known to me. In that respect, to rely upon the unity and the will of the party is exactly like my reckoning that the train will run to time or that the tram will not be derailed. But I cannot count upon men whom I do not know, I cannot base my confidence upon human goodness or upon man's interest in the good of society, seeing that man is free and that there is no human nature which I can take as foundational. I do not know whither the Russian revolution will lead. I can admire it and take it as an example in so far as it is evident, to-day, that the proletariat plays a part in Russia which it has attained in no other nation. But I cannot affirm that this will necessarily lead to the triumph of the proletariat. I must confine myself to what I can see. Nor can I be sure that comrades-in-arms will take up my work after my death and carry it to the maximum perfection, seeing that those men are free agents and will freely decide, to-morrow, what man is then to be. To-morrow, after my death, some men may decide to establish Fascism, and the others may be so cowardly or so slack as to let them do so. If so, Fascism will then be the truth of man, and so much the worse for us. In reality, things will be such as men have decided they shall be. Does that mean that I should abandon myself to quietism? No. First I ought to commit myself and then act my commitment, according to the time-honoured formula that "one need not hope in order to undertake one's work." Nor does this mean that I should not belong to a party, but only that I should be without illusion and that I should do what I can. For instance, if I ask myself "Will the social ideal as such, ever become a reality?" I cannot tell, I only know that whatever may be in my power to make it so, I shall do; beyond that, I can count upon nothing.

Quietism is the attitude of people who say, "Let others do what I cannot do." The doctrine I am presenting before you is precisely the opposite of this, since it declares that there is no reality except in action. It goes further, indeed, and adds, "Man is nothing else but what he purposes, he exists only in so far as he realises himself, he is therefore nothing else but the sum of his actions, nothing else but what his life is." Hence we can well understand why some people are horrified by our teaching. For many have but one resource to sustain them in their misery, and that is to think, "Circumstances have been against me, I was worthy to be something much better than I have been. I admit I have never had a great love or a great friendship; but that is because I never met a man or a woman who were worthy of it; if I have not written any very good books, it is because I had not the leisure to do so; of, if I have had no children to whom I could devote myself it is because I did not find the man I could have lived with. So there remains within me a wide range of abilities, inclinations and potentialities, unused but perfectly viable, which endow me with a worthiness that could never be inferred from the mere history of my actions." But in reality and for the existentialist, there is no love apart from the deeds of love; no potentiality of love other than that which is manifested in loving; there is no genius other than that which is expressed in works of art. The genius of Proust is the totality of the works of Proust; the genius of Racine is the series of his tragedies, outside of which there is nothing. Why should we attribute to Racine the capacity to write yet another tragedy when that is precisely what he did not write? In life, a man commits himself, draws his own portrait and there is nothing but that portrait. No doubt this thought may seem comfortless to one who has not made a success of his life. On the other hand, it puts everyone in a position to understand that reality alone is reliable; that dreams, expectations and hopes serve to define a man only as deceptive dreams, abortive hopes, expectations unfulfilled; that is to say, they define him negatively, not positively. Nevertheless, when one says, "You are nothing else but what you live," it does not imply that an artist is to be judged solely by his works of art, for a thousand other things contribute no less to his definition as a man. What we mean to say is that a man is no other than a series of undertakings, that he is the sum, the organisation, the set of relations that constitute these undertakings.

In the light of all this, what people reproach us with is not, after all, our pessimism, but the sternness of our optimism. If people condemn our works of fiction, in which we describe characters that are base, weak, cowardly and sometimes even frankly evil, it is not only because those characters are base, weak, cowardly or evil. For suppose that, like Zola, we showed that the behaviour of these characters was caused by their heredity, or by the action of their environment upon them, or by determining factors, psychic or organic. People would be reassured, they would say, "You see, that is what we are like, no one can do anything about it." But the existentialist, when he portrays a coward, shows him as responsible for his coward-ice. He is not like that on account of a cowardly heart or lungs or cerebrum, he has not become like that through his physiological or-ganism; he is like that because he has made himself into a coward by his actions. There is no such thing as a cowardly temperament. There are nervous temperaments; there is what is called impover-ished blood, and there are also rich temperaments. But the man whose blood is poor is not a coward for all that, for what produces cowardice is the act of giving up or giving way; and a temperament is not an action. A coward is defined by the deed that he has done. What people feel obscurely, and with horror, is that the coward as we present him is guilty of being a coward. What people would prefer would be to be born either a coward or a hero. One of the charges most often laid against the *Chemins de la Liberté* is something like this—"But, after all these people being so base, how can you make them into heroes?" That objection is really rather comic, for it im-plies that people are born heroes: and that is, at bottom, what such people would like to think. If you are born cowards, you can be quite content, you can do nothing about it and you will be cowards all your lives whatever you do; and if you are born heroes you can again be quite content; you will be heroes all your lives, eating and drinking heroically. Whereas the existentialist says that the coward makes himself cowardly, the hero makes himself heroic; and that there is always a possibility for the coward to give up cowardice and for the hero to stop being a hero. What counts is the total commitment, and it is not by a particular case or particular action that you are commit-ted altogether.

We have now, I think, dealt with a certain number of the re-proaches against existentialism. You have seen that it cannot be regarded as a philosophy of quietism since it defines man by his ac-tion: nor as a pessimistic description of man, for no doctrine is more optimistic, the destiny of man is placed within himself. Nor is it an attempt to discourage man from action since it tells him that there is no hope except in his action, and that the one thing which permits him to have life is the deed. Upon this level therefore, what we are considering is an ethic of action and self-commitment. However, we are still reproached, upon these few data, for confining man within his individual subjectivity. There again people badly misunderstand us.

Our point of departure is, indeed, the subjectivity of the individ-ual, and that for strictly philosophic reasons. It is not because we are bourgeois, but because we seek to base our teaching upon the truth, and not upon a collection of fine theories, full of hope but lacking real foundations. And at the point of departure there cannot be any other truth than this, *I think, therefore I am,* which is the absolute truth of consciousness as it attains to itself. Every theory which begins with man, outside of this moment of self-attainment, is a theory which thereby suppresses the truth, for outside of the Cartesian *cogito,* all objects are no more than probable, and any doctrine of probabilities which is not attached to a truth will crumble into nothing. In order to define the probable one must possess the true. Before there can be any truth whatever, then, there must be an absolute truth, and there is such a truth which is simple, easily attained and within the reach of everybody; it consists in one's immediate sense of one's self.

In the second place, this theory alone is compatible with the dignity of man, it is the only one which does not make man into an object. All kinds of materialism lead one to treat every man including oneself as an object—that is, as a set of pre-determined reactions, in no way different from the patterns of qualities and phenomena which constitute a table, or a chair or a stone. Our aim is precisely to establish the human kingdom as a pattern of values in distinction from the material world. But the subjectivity which we thus postulate as the standard of truth is no narrowly individual subjectivism, for as we have demonstrated, it is not only one's own self that one discovers in the *cogito,* but those of others too. Contrary to the philosophy of Descartes, contrary to that of Kant, when we say "I think" we are attaining to ourselves in the presence of the other, and we are just as certain of the other as we are of ourselves. Thus the man who discovers himself directly in the *cogito* also discovers all the others, and discovers them as the condition of his own existence. He recognises that he cannot be anything (in the sense in which one says one is spiritual, or that one is wicked or jealous) unless others recognise him as such. The other is indispensable to my existence, and equally so to any knowledge I can have of myself. Under these conditions, the intimate discovery of myself is at the same time the revelation of the other as a freedom which confronts mine, and which cannot think or will without doing so either for or against me. Thus at once, we find ourselves in a world which is, let us say, that of "inter-subjectivity." It is in this world that man has to decide what he is and what others are.

Furthermore, although it is impossible to find in each and every man a universal essence that can be called human nature, there is nevertheless a human universality of *condition.* It is not by chance that the thinkers of to-day are so much more ready to speak of the

condition than of the nature of man. By his condition they understand, with more or less clarity, all the *limitations* which *à priori*
define man's fundamental situation in the universe. His historical situations are variable: man may be born a slave in a pagan society, or
may be a feudal baron, or a proletarian. But what never vary are the
necessities of being in the world, of having to labour and to die
there. These limitations are neither subjective nor objective, or
rather there is both a subjective and an objective aspect of them. Objective, because we meet with them everywhere and they are everywhere recognisable: and subjective because they are *lived* and are
nothing if man does not live them—if, that is to say, he does not
freely determine himself and his existence in relation to them. And,
diverse though man's purposes may be, at least none of them is
wholly foreign to me, since every human purpose presents itself as
an attempt either to surpass these limitations, or to widen them, or
else to deny or to accommodate oneself to them. Consequently every
purpose, however individual it may be, is of universal value. Every
purpose, even that of a Chinese, an Indian or a Negro, can be understood by a European. To say it can be understood, means that the
European of 1945 may be striving out of a certain situation towards
the same limitations in the same way, and that he may re-conceive in
himself the purpose of the Chinese, of the Indian or the African. In
every purpose there is universality, in this sense that every purpose
is comprehensible to every man. Not that this or that purpose defines
man for ever, but that it may be entertained again and again. There is
always some way of understanding an idiot, a child, a primitive man
or a foreigner if one has sufficient information. In this sense we may
say that there is a human universality, but it is not something given;
it is being perpetually made. I make this universality in choosing
myself; I also make it by understanding the purpose of any other
man, of whatever epoch. This absoluteness of the act of choice does
not alter the relativity of each epoch.

What is at the very heart and centre of existentialism, is the
absolute character of the free commitment, by which every man realises himself in realising a type of humanity—a commitment always
understandable, to no matter whom in no matter what epoch—and its
bearing upon the relativity of the cultural pattern which may result
from such absolute commitment. One must observe equally the relativity of Cartesianism and the absolute character of the Cartesian
commitment. In this sense you may say, if you like, that every one of
us makes the absolute by breathing, by eating, by sleeping or by behaving in any fashion whatsoever. There is no difference between
free being—being as self-committal, as existence choosing its essence—and absolute being. And there is no difference whatever be-

tween being as an absolute, temporarily localised—that is, localised in history—and universally intelligible being.

This does not completely refute the change of subjectivism. Indeed that objection appears in several other forms, of which the first is as follows. People say to us, "Then it does not matter what you do," and they say this in various ways. First they tax us with anarchy; then they say, "You cannot judge others, for there is no reason for preferring one purpose to another"; finally, they may say, "Everything being merely voluntary in this choice of yours, you give away with one hand what you pretend to gain with the other." These three are not very serious objections. As to the first, to say that it matters not what you choose is not correct. In one sense choice is possible, but what is not possible is not to chose. I can always choose, but I must know that if I do not choose, that is still a choice. This, although it may appear merely formal, is of great importance as a limit to fantasy and caprice. For, when I confront a real situation—for example, that I am a sexual being, able to have relations with a being of the other sex and able to have children—I am obliged to choose my attitude to it, and in every respect I bear the responsiblity of the choice which, in committing myself, also commits the whole of humanity. Even if my choice is determined by no à priori value whatever, it can have nothing to do with caprice: and if anyone thinks that this is only Gide's theory of the acte gratuit over again, he has failed to see the enormous difference between this theory and that of Gide. Gide does not know what a situation is, his "act" is one of pure caprice. In our view, on the contrary, man finds himself in an organised situation in which he is himself involved: his choice involves mankind in its entirety, and he cannot avoid choosing. Either he must remain single, or he must marry without having children, or he must marry and have children. In any case, and whichever he may choose, it is impossible for him, in respect of this situation, not to take complete responsibility. Doubtless he chooses without reference to any pre-established values, but it is unjust to tax him with caprice. Rather let us say that the moral choice is comparable to the construction of a work of art.

But here I must at once digress to make it quite clear that we are not propounding an aesthetic morality, for our adversaries are disingenuous enough to reproach us even with that. I mention the work of art only by way of comparison. That being understood, does anyone reproach an artist when he paints a picture for not following rules established à priori? Does one ever ask what is the picture that he ought to paint? As everyone knows, there is no pre-defined picture for him to make; the artist applies himself to the composition of a picture, and the picture that ought to be made is precisely that which he will have made. As everyone knows, there are no aesthetic values *à priori*, but there are values which will appear in due course in the coherence of the picture, in the relation between the will to create and the finished work. No one can tell what the painting of tomorrow will be like; one cannot judge a painting until it is done. What has that to do with morality? We are in the same creative situation. We never speak of a work of art as irresponsible; when we are discussing a canvas by Picasso, we understand very well that the composition became what it is at the time when he was painting it, and that his works are part and parcel of his entire life.

It is the same upon the plane of morality. There is this in common between art and morality, that in both we have to do with creation and invention. We cannot decide *à priori* what it is that should be done. I think it was made sufficiently clear to you in the case of that student who came to see me, that to whatever ethical system he might appeal, the Kantian or any other, he could find no sort of guidance whatever; he was obliged to invent the law for himself. Certainly we cannot say that this man, in choosing to remain with his mother—that is, in taking sentiment, personal devotion and concrete charity as his moral foundations—would be making an irresponsible choice, nor could we do so if he preferred the sacrifice of going away to England. Man makes himself; he is not found ready-made; he makes himself by the choice of his morality, and he cannot but choose a morality, such is the pressure of circumstances upon him. We define man only in relation to his commitments; it is therefore absurd to reproach us for irresponsibility in our choice.

In the second place, people say to us, "You are unable to judge others." This is true in one sense and false in another. It is true in this sense, that whenever a man chooses his purpose and his commitment in all clearness and in all sincereity, whatever that purpose may be it is impossible to prefer another for him. It is true in the sense that we do not believe in progress. Progress implies amelioration; but man is always the same, facing a situation which is always changing, and choice remains always a choice in the situation. The moral problem has not changed since the time when it was a choice between slavery and antislavery—from the time of the war of Secession, for example, until the present moment when one chooses between the M.R.P.* and the Communists.

We can judge, nevertheless, for, as I have said, one chooses in view of others, and in view of others one chooses himself. One can judge, first—and perhaps this is not a judgment of value, but it is a logical judgment—that in certain cases choice is founded upon an

error, and in others upon the truth. One can judge a man by saying
that he deceives himself. Since we have defined the situation of man
as one of free choice, without excuse and without help, any man who
takes refuge behind the excuse of his passions, or by inventing some
deterministic doctrine, is a self-deceiver. One may object: "But why
should he not choose to deceive himself?" I reply that it is not for me
to judge him morally, but I define his self-deception as an error.
Here one cannot avoid pronouncing a judgment of truth. The self-
deception is evidently a falsehood, because it is a dissimulation of
man's complete liberty of commitment. Upon this same level, I say
that it is also a self-deception if I choose to declare that certain values are incumbent upon me; I am in contradiction with myself if I
will these values and at the same time say that they impose themselves upon me. If anyone says to me, "And what if I wish to deceive
myself?" I answer, "There is no reason why you should not, but I
declare that you are doing so, and that the attitude of strict consistency alone is that of good faith. Furthermore, I can pronounce a
moral judgment. For I declare that freedom, in respect of concrete
circumstances, can have no other end and aim but itself; and when
once a man has seen that values depend upon himself, in that state of
forsakenness he can will only one thing, and that is freedom as the
foundation of all values. That does not mean that he wills it in the
abstract: it simply means that the actions of men of good faith have,
as their ultimate significance, the quest of freedom itself as such. A
man who belongs to some communist or revolutionary society wills
certain concrete ends, which imply the will to freedom, but that
freedom is willed in community. We will freedom for freedom's
sake, and in through particular circumstances. And in thus willing
freedom, we discover that it depends entirely upon the freedom of
others and that the freedom of others depends upon our own. Obviously, freedom as the definition of a man does not depend upon
others, but as soon as there is a commitment, I am obliged to will the
liberty of others at the same time as mine. I cannot make liberty my
aim unless I make that of others equally my aim. Consequently,
when I recognise, as entirely authentic, that man is a being whose
existence precedes his essence, and that he is a free being who cannot, in any circumstances, but will his freedom, at the same time I
realise that I cannot not will the freedom of others. Thus, in the
name of that will to freedom which is implied in freedom itself, I can
form judgments upon those who seek to hide from themselves the
wholly voluntary nature of their existence and its complete freedom.
Those who hide from this total freedom, in a guise of solemnity or
with deterministic excuses, I shall call cowards. Others, who try to
show that their existence is necessary, when it is merely an accident

of the appearance of the human race on earth,—I shall call scum. But neither cowards nor scum can be identified except upon the plane of strict authenticity. Thus, although the content of morality is variable, a certain form of this morality is universal. Kant declared that freedom is a will both to itself and to the freedom of others. Agreed: but he thinks that the formal and the universal suffice for the constitution of a morality. We think, on the contrary, that principles that are too abstract break down when we come to defining action. To take once again the case of that student; by what authoity, in the name of what golden rule of morality, do you think he could have decided, in perfect peace of mind, either to abandon his mother or to remain with her? There are no means of judging. The content is always concrete, and therefore unpredictable; it has always to be invented. The one thing that counts, is to know whether the invention is made in the name of freedom.

Let us, for example, examine the two following cases, and you will see how far they are similar in spite of their difference. Let us take *The Mill on the Floss*. We find here a certain young woman, Maggie Tulliver, who is an incarnation of the value of passion and is aware of it. She is in love with a young man, Stephen, who is engaged to another, an insignificant young woman. This Maggie Tulliver, instead of heedlessly seeking her own happiness, chooses in the name of human solidarity to sacrifice herself and to give up the man she loves. On the other hand, La Sanseverina in Stendhal's *Chartreuse de Parme*, believing that it is passion which endows man with his real value, would have declared that a grand passion justifies its sacrifices, and must be preferred to the banality of such conjugal love as would unite Stephen to the little goose he was engaged to marry. It is the latter that she would have chosen to sacrifice in realising her own happiness, and, as Stendhal shows, she would also sacrifice herself upon the plane of passion if life made that demand upon her. Here we are facing two clearly opposed moralities; but I claim that they are equivalent, seeing that in both cases the over-ruling aim is freedom. You can imagine two attitudes exactly similar in effect, in that one girl might prefer, in resignation, to give up her lover whilst the other preferred, in fulfilment of sexual desire, to ignore the prior engagement of the man she loved; and, externally, these two cases might appear the same as the two we have just cited, while being in fact entirely different. The attitude of La Sanseverina is much nearer to that of Maggie Tulliver than to one of careless greed. Thus, you see, the second objection is at once true and false. One can choose anything, but only if it is upon the plane of free commitment.

The third objection, stated by saying, "You take with one hand what you give with the other," means, at bottom, "your values are not serious, since you choose them yourselves." To that I can only say that I am very sorry that it should be so; but if I have excluded God the Father, there must be somebody to invent values, We have to take things as they are. And moreover, to say that we invent values means neither more nor less than this; that there is no sense in life *à priori.* Life is nothing until it is lived; but it is yours to make sense of, and the value of it is nothing else but the sense that you choose. Therefore, you can see that there is a possibility of creating a human community. I have been reproached for suggesting that existentialism is a form of humanism: people have said to me, "But you have written in your *Nausée* that the humanists are wrong, you have even ridiculed a certain type of humanism, why do you now go back upon that?" In reality, the word humanism has two very different meanings. One may understand by humanism a theory which upholds man as the end-in-itself and as the supreme value. Humanism in this sense appears, for instance, in Cocteau's story *Round the World in 80 Hours,* in which one of the characters declares, because he is flying over mountains in an aeroplane, "Man is magnificent!" This signifies that although I, personally, have not built aeroplanes I have the benefit of those particular inventions and that I personally, being a man, can consider myself responsible for, and honoured by, achievements that are peculiar to some men. It is to assume that we can ascribe value to man according to the most distinguished deeds of certain men. That kind of humanism is absurd, for only the dog or the horse would be in a position to pronounce a general judgment upon man and declare that he is magnificent, which they have never been such fools as to do—at least, not as far as I know. But neither is it admissible that a man should pronounce judgment upon Man. Existentialism dispenses with any judgment of this sort: an existentialist will never take man as the end, since man is still to be determined. And we have no right to believe that humanity is something to which we could set up a cult, after the manner of Auguste Comte. The cult of humanity ends in Comtian humanism, shut-in upon itself, and—this must be said—in Fascism. We do not want a humanism like that.

But there is another sense of the word, of which the fundamental meaning is this: Man is all the time outside of himself: it is in projecting and losing himself beyond himself that he makes man to exist; and, on the other hand, it is by pursuing transcendent aims that he himself is able to exist. Since man is thus self-surpassing, and can grasp objects only in relation to his self-surpassing, he is himself the heart and centre of his transcendence. There is no other universe except the human universe, the universe of human subjectivity. This relation of transcendence as constitutive of man (not in the sense that God is transcendent, but in the sense of self-surpassing) with subjectivity (in such a sense that man is not shut up in himself but forever present in a human universe)—it is this that we call existential humanism. This is humanism, because we remind man that there is no legislator but himself; that he himself, thus abandoned, must decide for himself; also because we show that it is not by turning back upon himself, but always by seeking, beyond himself, an aim which is one of liberation or of some particular realisation, that man can realise himself as truly human.

You can see from these few reflections that nothing could be more unjust than the objections people raise against us. Existentialism is nothing else but an attempt to draw the full conclusions from a consistently atheistic position. Its intention is not in the least that of plunging men into despair. And if by despair one means—as the Christians do—any attitude of unbelief, the despair of the existentialists is something different. Existentialism is not atheist in the sense that it would exhaust itself in demonstrations of the non-existence of God. It declares, rather, that even if God existed that would make no difference from its point of view. Not that we believe God does exist, but we think that the real problem is not that of his existence; what man needs is to find himself again and to understand that nothing can save him from himself, not even a valid proof of the existence of God. In this sense existentialism is optimistic, it is a doctrine of action, and it is only by self-deception, by confusing their own despair with ours that Christians can describe us as without hope.

Allegory of the Cave

PLATO

And now, I said, let me show in a figure how far our nature is enlightened or unenlightened:—Behold! human beings living in an underground den, which has a mouth open towards the light and reaching all along the den; here they have been from their childhood, and have their legs and necks chained so that they cannot move, and can only see before them, being prevented by the chains from turning

From *The Republic of Plato* trans. by Benjamin Jowett, 4th ed., 1953, pp. 253–259. By permission of The Clarendon Press, Oxford.

round their heads. Above and behind them a fire is blazing at a distance, and between the fire and the prisoners there is a raised way; and you will see, if you look, a low wall built along the way, like the screen which marionette players have in front of them, over which they show the puppets.

I see.

And do you see, I said, men passing along the wall carrying all sorts of vessels, and statues and figures of animals made of wood and stone and various materials, which appear over the wall? Some of them are talking, others silent.

You have shown me a strange image, and they are strange prisoners.

Like ourselves, I replied; and they see only their own shadows, or the shadows of one another, which the fire throws on the opposite wall of the cave?

True, he said; how could they see anything but the shadows if they were never allowed to move their heads?

And of the objects which are being carried in like manner they would only see the shadows?

Yes, he said.

And if they were able to converse with one another, would they not suppose that they were naming what was actually before them? [1]

Very true.

And suppose further that the prison had an echo which came from the other side, would they not be sure to fancy when one of the passers-by spoke that the voice which they heard came from the passing shadow?

No question, he replied.

To them, I said, the truth would be literally nothing but the shadows of the images.

That is certain.

And now look again, and see what will naturally follow if the prisoners are released and disabused of their error. At first, when any of them is liberated and compelled suddenly to stand up and turn his neck round and walk and look towards the light, he will suffer sharp pains; the glare will distress him, and he will be unable to see the realities of which in his former state he had seen the shadows; and then conceive some one saying to him, that what he saw before was an illusion, but that now, when he is approaching nearer to being and his eye is turned towards more real existence, he has a clearer vision,—what will be his reply? And you may further imagine that his instructor is pointing to the objects as they pass and requiring

[1] Reading παρόντα.

him to name them,—will he not be perplexed? Will he not fancy that the shadows which he formerly saw are truer than the objects which are now shown to him?

Far truer.

And if he is compelled to look straight at the light, will he not have a pain in his eyes which will make him turn away to take refuge in the objects of vision which he can see, and which he will conceive to be in reality clearer than the things which are now being shown to him?

True, he said.

And suppose once more, that he is reluctantly dragged up a steep and rugged ascent, and held fast until he is forced into the presence of the sun himself, is he not likely to be pained and irritated? When he approaches the light his eyes will be dazzled, and he will not be able to see anything at all of what are now called realities.

Not all in a moment, he said.

He will require to grow accustomed to the sight of the upper world. And first he will see the shadows best, next the reflections of men and other objects in the water, and then the objects themselves; then he will gaze upon the light of the moon and the stars and the spangled heaven; and he will see the sky and the stars by night better than the sun or the light of the sun by day?

Certainly.

Last of all he will be able to see the sun, and not mere reflections of him in the water, but he will see him in his own proper place, and not in another; and he will contemplate him as he is.

Certainly.

He will then proceed to argue that this is he who gives the season and the years, and is the guardian of all that is in the visible world, and in a certain way the cause of all things which he and his fellows have been accustomed to behold?

Clearly, he said, he would first see the sun and then reason about him.

And when he remembered his old habitation, and the wisdom of the den and his fellow-prisoners, do you not suppose that he would felicitate himself on the change, and pity them?

Certainly, he would.

And if they were in the habit of conferring honours among themselves on those who were quickest to observe the passing shadows and to remark which of them went before, and which followed after, and which were together; and who were therefore best able to draw conclusions as to the future, do you think that he would care for such honours and glories, or envy the possessors of them? Would he not say with Homer,

'Better to be the poor servant of a poor master,'

and to endure anything, rather than think as they do and live after their manner?

Yes, he said, I think that he would rather suffer anything than entertain these false notions and live in this miserable manner.

Imagine once more, I said, such an one coming suddenly out of the sun to be replaced in his old situation; would he not be certain to have his eyes full of darkness? To be sure, he said. And if there were a contest, and he had to compete in measuring the shadows with the prisoners who had never moved out of the den, while his sight was still weak, and before his eyes had become steady (and the time which would be needed to acquire this new habit of sight might be very considerable) would he not be ridiculous? Men would say of him that up he went and down he came without his eyes; and that it was better not even to think of ascending; and if any one tried to loose another and lead him up to the light, let them only catch the offender, and they would put him to death.

No question, he said.

This entire allegory, I said, you may now append, dear Glaucon, to the previous argument; the prisonhouse is the world of sight, the light of the fire is the sun, and you will not misapprehend me if you interpret the journey upwards to be the ascent of the soul into the intellectual world according to my poor belief, which, at your desire, I have expressed—whether rightly or wrongly God knows. But, whether true or false, my opinion is that in the world of knowledge the idea of good appears last of all, and is seen only with an effort; and, when seen, is also inferred to be the universal author of all things beautiful and right, parent of light and of the lord of light in this visible world, and the immediate source of reason and truth in the intellectual; and that this is the power upon which he who would act rationally either in public or private life must have his eye fixed.

I agree, he said, as far as I am able to understand you.

Moreover, I said, you must not wonder that those who attain to this beatific vision are unwilling to descend to human affairs; for their souls are ever hastening into the upper world where they desire to dwell; which desire of theirs is very natural, if our allegory may be trusted.

Yes, very natural.

And is there anything surprising in one who passes from divine contemplations to the evil state of man, misbehaving himself in a ridiculous manner; if, while his eyes are blinking and before he has become accustomed to the surrounding darkness, he is compelled to fight in courts of law, or in other places, about the images or the shadows of images of justice, and is endeavouring to meet the conceptions of those who have never yet seen absolute justice?

Anything but surprising, he replied.

Any one who has common sense will remember that the bewilderments of the eyes are of two kinds, and arise from two causes, either from coming out of the light or from going into the light, which is true of the mind's eye, quite as much as of the bodily eye; and he who remembers this when he sees any one whose vision is perplexed and weak, will not be too ready to laugh; he will first ask whether that soul of man has come out of the brighter life, and is unable to see because unaccustomed to the dark, or having turned from darkness to the day is dazzled by excess of light. And he will count the one happy in his condition and state of being, and he will pity the other; or, if he have a mind to laugh at the soul which comes from below into the light, there will be more reason in this than in the laugh which greets him who returns from above out of the light into the den.

That, he said, is a very just distinction.

But then, if I am right, certain professors of education must be wrong when they say that they can put a knowledge into the soul which was not there before, like sight into blind eyes.

They undoubtedly say this, he replied.

Whereas, our argument shows that the power and capacity of learning exists in the soul already; and that just as the eye was unable to turn from darkness to light without the whole body, so too the instrument of knowledge can only by the movement of the whole soul be turned from the world of becoming into that of being, and learn by degrees to endure the sight of being, and of the brightest and best of being, or in other words, of the good.

Education

MARTIN BUBER

"The development of the creative powers in the child" is the subject of this conference. As I come before you to introduce it I must not conceal from you for a single moment the fact that of the nine words

in which it is expressed only the last three raise no question
for me.

The child, not just the individual child, individual children, but
the child, is certainly a reality. That in this hour, while we make a
beginning with the "development of creative powers," across the
whole extent of this planet new human beings are born who are characterized already and yet have still to be characterized—this is a
myriad realities, but also one reality. In every hour the human race
begins. We forget this too easily in face of the massive fact of past
life, of so-called world-history, of the fact that each child is born with
a given disposition of "world-historical" origin, that is, inherited
from the riches of the whole human race, and that he is born into a
given situation of "world-historical" origin, that is, produced from
the riches of the world's events. This fact must not obscure the other
no less important fact that in spite of everything, in this as in every
hour, what has not been invades the structure of what is, with ten
thousand countenances, of which not one has been seen before, with
ten thousand souls still undeveloped but ready to develop—a creative event if ever there was one, newness rising up, primal potential
might. This potentiality, streaming unconquered, however much of it
is squandered, is the reality *child:* this phenomenon of uniqueness,
which is more than just begetting and birth, this grace of beginning
again and ever again.

What greater care could we cherish or discuss than that this
grace may not henceforth be squandered as before, that the might of
newness may be preserved for renewal? Future history is not inscribed already by the pen of a causal law on a roll which merely
awaits unrolling; its characters are stamped by the unforeseeable
decisions of future generations. The part to be played in this by everyone alive to-day, by every adolescent and child, is immeasurable,
and immeasurable is our part if we are educators. The deeds of the
generations now approaching can illumine the grey face of the
human world or plunge it in darkness. So, then, with education: if it
at last rises up and exists indeed, it will be able to strengthen the
light-spreading force in the hearts of the doers—how much it can do
this cannot be guessed, but only learned in action.

The child is a reality; education must become a reality. But what
does the "development of the creative powers" mean? Is *that* the reality of education? Must education become that in order to become a
reality? Obviously those who arranged this session and gave it its
theme think this is so. They obviously think that education has failed
in its task till now because it has aimed at something different from
this development of what is in the child, or has considered and promoted other powers in the child than the creative. And probably they

are amazed that I question this objective, since I myself talk of the treasure of eternal possibility and of the task of unearthing it. So I must make clear that this treasure cannot be properly designated by the notion of "creative powers," nor its unearthing by the notion of "development."

Creation originally means only the divine summons to the life hidden in non-being. When Johann Georg Hamann and his contemporaries carried over this term metaphorically to the human capacity to give form, they marked a supreme peak of mankind, the genius for forming, as that in which man's imaging of God is authenticated in action. The metaphor has since been broadened; there was a time (not long ago) when "creative" meant almost the same as "of literary ability"; in face of this lowest condition of the word it is a real promotion for it to be understood, as it is here, quite generally as something dwelling to some extent in all men, in all children of men, and needing only the right cultivation. Art is then only the province in which a faculty of production, which is common to all, reaches completion. Everyone is elementally endowed with the basic powers of the arts, with that of drawing, for instance, or of music; these powers have to be developed, and the education of the whole person is to be built up on them as on the natural activity of the self.

We must not miss the importance of the reference which is the starting-point of this conception. It concerns a significant but hitherto not properly heeded phenomenon, which is certainly not given its right name here. I mean the existence of an autonomous instinct, which cannot be derived from others, whose appropriate name seems to me to be the "originator instinct." Man, the child of man, wants to make things. He does not merely find pleasure in seeing a form arise from material that presented itself as formless. What the child desires is its own share in this becoming of things: it wants to be the subject of this event of production. Nor is the instinct I am speaking of to be confused with the so-called instinct to busyness or activity which for that matter does not seem to me to exist at all (the child wants to set up or destroy, handle or hit, and so on, but never "busy himself"). What is important is that by one's own intensively experienced action something arises that was not there before. A good expression of this instinct is the way children of intellectual passion produce speech, in reality not as something they have taken over but with the headlong powers of utter newness: sound after sound tumbles out of them, rushing from the vibrating throat past the trembling lips into the world's air, and the whole of the little vital body vibrates and trembles, too, shaken by a bursting shower of selfhood. Or watch a boy fashioning some crude unrecognizable in-

strument for himself. Is he not astonished, terrified, at his own movement like the mighty inventors of prehistoric times? But it is also to
be observed how even in the child's apparently "blind" lust for destruction his instinct of origination enters in and becomes dominant.
Sometimes he begins to tear something up, for example, a sheet of
paper, but soon he takes an interest in the form of the pieces, and it
is not long before he tries—still by tearing—to produce definite
forms.

It is important to recognize that the instinct of origination is autonomous and not derivatory. Modern psychologists are inclined to
derive the multiform human soul from a single primal element—the
"libido," the "will to power," and the like. But this is really only the
generalization of certain degenerate states in which a single instinct
not merely dominates but also spreads parasitically through the others. They begin with the cases (in our time of inner loss of community and oppression the innumerable cases) where such a hyper-
trophy breeds the appearance of exclusiveness, they abstract rules
from them, and apply them with the whole theoretical and practical
questionableness of such applications. In opposition to these doctrines and methods, which impoverish the soul, we must continually
point out that human inwardness is in origin a polyphony in which
no voice can be "reduced" to another, and in which the unity cannot
be grasped analytically, but only heard in the present harmony. One
of the leading voices is the instinct of origination.

This instinct is therefore bound to be significant for the work of
education as well. Here is an instinct which, no matter to what
power it is raised, never becomes greed, because it is not directed to
"having" but only to doing; which alone among the instincts can
grow only to passion, not to lust; which alone among the instincts
cannot lead its subject away to invade the realm of other lives. Here
is pure gesture which does not snatch the world to itself, but expresses itself to the world. Should not the person's growth into form,
so often dreamed of and lost, at last succeed from this starting-point?
For here this precious quality may be unfolded and worked out un-
impeded. Nor does the new experiment lack demonstration. The
finest demonstration I know, that I have just got to know, is this
Children's Choir led by the marvellous Bakule of Prague, with
which our Conference opened. How under his leadership crippled
creatures, seemingly condemned to lifelong idleness, have been released to a life of freely moving persons, rejoicing in their achievement, formable and forming, who know how to shape sights and
sounds in multiform patterns and also how to sing out their risen
souls wildly and gloriously; more, how a community of achievement,
proclaimed in glance and response, has been welded together out of

dull immured solitary creatures: all this seems to prove irrefutably not merely what fruitfulness but also what power, streaming through the whole constitution of man, the life of origination has.

But this very example, seen more deeply, shows us that the decisive influence is to be ascribed not to the release of an instinct but to the forces which meet the released instinct, namely, the educative forces. It depends on them, on their purity and fervour, their power of love and their discretion, into what connexions the freed element enters and what becomes of it.

There are two forms, indispensable for the building of true human life, to which the originative instinct, left to itself, does not lead and cannot lead: to sharing in an undertaking and to entering into mutuality.

An individual achievement and an undertaking are two very different matters. To make a thing is mortal man's pride; but to be conditioned in a common job, with the unconscious humility of being a part, of participation and partaking, is the true food of earthly immortality. As soon as a man enters effectively into an undertaking, where he discovers and practises a community of work with other men, he ceases to follow the originative instinct alone.

Action leading to an individual achievement is a "one-sided" event. There is a force within the person, which goes out, impresses itself on the material, and the achievement arises objectively: the movement is over, it has run in one direction from the heart's dream into the world, and its course is finished. No matter how directly, as being approached and claimed, as perceiving and receiving, the artist experiences his dealings with the idea which he faces and which awaits embodiment, so long as he is engaged in his work spirit goes out from him and does not enter him, he replies to the world but he does not meet it any more. Nor can he foster mutuality with his work: even in the legend Pygmalion is an ironical figure.

Yes; as an originator man is solitary. He stands wholly without bonds in the echoing hall of his deeds. Nor can it help him to leave his solitariness that his achievement is received enthusiastically by the many. He does not know if it is accepted, if his sacrifice is accepted by the anonymous receiver. Only if someone grasps his hand not as a "creator" but as a fellow-creature lost in the world, to be his comrade or friend or lover beyond the arts, does he have an awareness and a share of mutuality. An education based only on the training of the instinct of origination would prepare a new human solitariness which would be the most painful of all.

The child, in putting things together, learns much that he can learn in no other way. In making some thing he gets to know its possibility, its origin and structure and connexions, in a way he cannot learn by observation. But there is something else that is not learned in this way, and that is the viaticum of life. The being of the world as an object is learned from within, but not its being as a subject, its saying of *I* and *Thou*. What teaches us the saying of *Thou* is not the originative instinct but the instinct for communion.

This instinct is something greater than the believers in the "libido" realize: it is the longing for the world to become present to us as a person, which goes out to us as we to it, which chooses and recognizes us as we do it, which is confirmed in us as we in it. The child lying with half-closed eyes, waiting with tense soul for its mother to speak to it—the mystery of its will is not directed towards enjoying (or dominating) a person, or towards doing something of its own accord; but towards experiencing communion in face of the lonely night, which spreads beyond the window and threatens to invade.

But the release of powers should not be any more than a *presupposition* of education. In the end it is not the originative instinct alone which is meant by the "creative powers" that are to be "developed." These powers stand for human spontaneity. Real education is made possible—but is it also established?—by the realization that youthful spontaneity must not be suppressed but must be allowed to give what it can.

Let us take an example from the narrower sphere of the originative instinct—from the drawing-class. The teacher of the "compulsory" school of thought began with rules and current patterns. Now you knew what beauty was, and you had to copy it; and it was copied either in apathy or in despair. The teacher of the "free" school places on the table a twig of broom, say, in an earthenware jug, and makes the pupils draw it. Or he places it on the table, tells the pupils to look at it, removes it, and then makes them draw it. If the pupils are quite unsophisticated soon not a single drawing will look like another. Now the delicate, almost imperceptible and yet important influence begins—that of criticism and instruction. The children encounter a scale of values that, however unacademic it may be, is quite constant, a knowledge of good and evil that, however individualistic it may be, is quite unambiguous. The more unacademic this scale of values, and the more individualistic this knowledge, the more deeply do the children experience the encounter. In the former instance the preliminary declaration of what alone was right made for resignation or rebellion; but in the latter, where the pupil gains the realization only after he has ventured far out on the way to his achievement, his heart is drawn to reverence for the form, and educated.

This almost imperceptible, most delicate approach, the raising of a finger, perhaps, or a questioning glance, is the other half of what happens in education.

Modern educational theory, which is characterized by tendencies to freedom, misunderstands the meaning of this other half, just as the old theory, which was characterized by the habit of authority, misunderstood the meaning of the first half. The symbol of the funnel is in course of being exchanged for that of the pump. I am reminded of the two camps in the doctrine of evolution, current in the seventeenth and eighteenth centuries, the animalculists, who believed that the whole germ was present in the spermatozoon, and the ovists who believed it was wholly present in the ovum. The theory of the development of powers in the child recalls, in its most extreme expressions, Swammerdam's "unfolding" of the "preformed" organism. But the growth of the spirit is no more an unfolding than that of the body. The dispositions which would be discovered in the soul of a new-born child—if the soul could in fact be analysed—are nothing but capacities to receive and imagine the world. The world engenders the person in the individual. The world, that is the whole environment, nature, and society, "educates" the human being: it draws out his powers, and makes him grasp and genetrate its objections. What we term education, conscious and willed, means *a selection by man of the effective world:* it means to give decisive effective power to a selection of the world which is concentrated and manifested in the educator. The relation in education is lifted out of the purposelessly streaming education by all things, and is marked off as purpose. In this way, through the educator, the world for the first time becomes the true subject of its effect.

There was a time, there were times, where there neither was nor needed to be any specific calling of educator or teacher. There was a master, a philosopher or a coppersmith, whose journeymen and apprentices lived with him and learned, by being allowed to share in it, what he had to teach them of his handwork or brainwork. But they also learned, without either their or his being concerned with it, they learned, without noticing that they did, the mystery of personal life: they received the spirit. Such a thing must still happen to some extent, where spirit and person exist, but it is expelled to the sphere of spirituality, of personality, and has become exceptional, it happens only "on the heights." Education as a purpose is bound to be summoned. We can as little return to the state of affairs that existed before there were schools as to that which existed before, say, technical science. But we can and must enter into the completeness of its growth to reality, into the perfect humanization of its reality. Our way is composed of losses that secretly become gains. Education has lost the paradise of pure instinctiveness and now consciously serves at the plough for the bread of life. It has been transformed; only in this transformation has it become visible.

Yet the master remains the model for the teacher. For if the educator of our day has to act consciously he must nevertheless do it "as though he did not." That raising of the finger, that questioning glance, are his genuine doing. Through him the selection of the effective world reaches the pupil. He fails the recipient when he presents this selection to him with a gesture of interference. It must be concentrated in him; and doing out of concentration has the appearance of rest. Interference divides the soul in his care into an obedient part and a rebellious part. But a hidden influence proceeding from his integrity has an integrating force.

The world, I said, has its influence as nature and as society on the child. He is educated by the elements, by air and light and the life of plants and animals, and he is educated by relationships. The true educator represents both; but he must be to the child as one of the elements.

The release of powers can be only a presupposition of education, nothing more. Put more generally, it is the nature of freedom to provide the place, but not the foundation as well, on which true life is raised. That is true both of inner, "moral" freedom and of outer freedom (which consists in not being hindered or limited). As the higher freedom, the soul's freedom of decision, signifies perhaps our highest moments but not a fraction of our substance, so the lower freedom, the freedom of development, signifies our capacity for growth but by no means our growth itself. This latter freedom is charged with importance as the actuality from which the work of education begins, but as its fundamental task it becomes absurd.

There is a tendency to understand this freedom, which may be termed evolutionary freedom, as at the opposite pole from compulsion, from being under a compulsion. But at the opposite pole from compulsion there stands not freedom but communion. Compulsion is a negative reality; communion is the positive reality; freedom is a possibility, possibility regained. At the opposite pole of being compelled by destiny or nature or men there does not stand being free of destiny or nature or men but to commune and to covenant with them. To do this, it is true that one must first have become independent; but this independence is a foot-bridge, not a dwelling-place. Freedom is the vibrating needle, the fruitful zero. Compulsion in education means disunion, it means humiliation and rebelliousness. Communion in education is just communion, it means being opened up and drawn in. Freedom in education is the possibility of communion; it cannot be dispensed with and it cannot be made use of in itself; without it nothing succeeds, but neither does anything succeed by means of it: it is the run before the jump, the tuning of the violin, the confirmation of that primal and mighty potentiality which it cannot even begin to actualize.

Freedom—I love its flashing face: it flashes from the darkness and dies away, but it has made the heart invulnerable. I am devoted to it, I am always ready to join in the fight for it, for the appearance of the flash, which lasts no longer than the eye is able to endure it, for the vibrating of the needle that was held down too long and was stiff. I give my left hand to the rebel and my right to the heretic: forward! But I do not trust them. They know how to die, but that is not enough. I love freedom, but I do not believe in it. How could one believe in it after looking in its face? It is the flash of a significance comprising all meanings, of a possibility comprising all potentiality. For it we fight, again and again, from of old, victorious and in vain.

It is easy to understand that in a time when the deterioration of all traditional bonds has made their legitimacy questionable, the tendency to freedom is exalted, the springboard is treated as a goal and a functional good as substantial good. Moreover, it is idle sentimentality to lament at great length that freedom is made the subject of experiments. Perhaps it is fitting for this time which has no compass that people should throw out their lives like a plummet to discover our bearings and the course we should set. But truly *their* lives! Such an experiment, when it is carried out, is a neck-breaking venture which cannot be disputed. But when it is talked about and talked around, in intellectual discussions and confessions and in the mutual pros and cons of their life's "problems," it is an abomination of disintegration. Those who stake themselves, as individuals or as a community, may leap and crash out into the swaying void where senses and sense fail, or through it and beyond into some kind of existence. But they must not make freedom into a theorem or a programme. To become free of a bond is destiny; one carries that like a cross, not like a cockade. Let us realize the true meaning of being free of a bond: it means that a quite personal responsibility takes the place of one shared with many generations. Life lived in freedom is personal responsibility or it is a pathetic farce.

I have pointed out the power which alone can give a content to empty freedom and a direction to swaying and spinning freedom. I believe in it, I trust those devoted to it.

This fragile life between birth and death can nevertheless be a fulfilment—if it is a dialogue. In our life and experience we are addressed; by thought and speech and action, by producing and by influencing we are able to answer. For the most part we do not listen to the address, or we break into it with chatter. But if the word comes to us and the answer proceeds from us then human life exists, though brokenly, in the world. The kindling of the response in that "spark" of the soul, the blazing up of the response, which occurs time and again, to the unexpectedly approaching speech, we term responsibility. We practise responsibility for that realm of life allotted and entrusted to us for which we are able to respond, that is, for which we have a relation of deeds which may count—in all our inadequacy—as a proper response. The extent to which a man, in the strength of the reality of the spark, can keep a traditional bond, a law, a direction, is the extent to which he is permitted to lean his responsibility on something (more than this is not vouchsafed to us, responsibility is not taken off our shoulders). As we "become free" this leaning on something is more and more denied to us, and our responsibility must become personal and solitary.

From this point of view education and its transformation in the hour of the crumbling of bonds are to be understood.

It is usual to contrast the principle of the "new" education as "Eros" with that of the "old" education as the "will to power."

In fact the one is as little a principle of education as the other. A principle of education, in a sense still to be clarified, can only be a basic relation which is fulfilled in education. But Eros and the will to power are alike passions of the soul for whose real elaboration a place is prepared elsewhere. Education can supply for them only an incidental realm and moreover one which sets a limit to their elaboration; nor can this limit be infringed without the realm itself being destroyed. The one can as little as the other constitute the educational attitude.

The "old" educator, in so far as he was an educator, was not "the man with a will to power," but he was the bearer of assured values which were strong in tradition. If the educator represents the world to the pupil, the "old" educator represented particularly the historical world, the past. He was the ambassador of history to this intruder, the "child"; he carried to him, as the Pope in the legend did to the prince of the Huns, the magic of the spiritual forces of history; he instilled values into the child or he drew the child into the values. The man who reduces this encounter between the cosmos of history and its eternally new chaos, between Zeus and Dionysos, to the formula of the "antagonism between fathers and sons," has never beheld it in his spirit. Zeus the Father does not stand for a generation but for a world, for the olympic, the formed world; the world of history faces a particular generation, which is the world of nature renewed again and again, always without history.

This situation of the old type of education is, however, easily used, or misused, by the individual's will to power, for this will is inflated by the authority of history. The will to power becomes convulsive and passes into fury, when the authority begins to decay, that is, when the magical validity of tradition disappears. Then the moment comes near when the teacher no longer faces the pupil as an ambassador but only as an individual, as a static atom to the whirling atom. Then no matter how much he imagines he is acting from the fullness of the objective spirit, in the reality of his life he is thrown back on himself, cast on his own resources, and hence filled with longing. Eros appears. And Eros finds employment in the new situation of education as the will to power did in the old situation. But Eros is not a bearer or the ground or the principle any more than the will to power was. He only claims to be that, in order not to be recognized as longing, as the stranger given refuge. And many believe it.

Nietzsche did not succeed in glorifying the will to power as much as Plato glorified Eros. But in our concern for the creature in this great time of concern, for both alike we have not to consider the myths of the philosophers but the actuality of present life. In entire opposition to any glorification we have to see that Eros—that is, not "love," but Eros the male and magnigicent—whatever else may belong to him, necessarily includes this one thing, that he desires to enjoy men; and education, the peculiar essence bearing this name which is composed of no others, excludes precisely this desire. However, mightily an educator is possessed and inspired by Eros, if he obeys him in the course of his educating then he stifles the growth of his blessings. It must be one or the other: either he takes on himself the tragedy of the person, and offers an unblemished daily sacrifice, or the fire enters his work and consumes it.

Eros is choice, choice made from an inclination. This is precisely what education is not. The man who is loving in Eros chooses the beloved, the modern educator finds his pupil there before him. From this unerotic situation the *greatness* of the modern educator is to be seen—and most clearly when he is a teacher. He enters the school-room for the first time, he sees them crouching at the desks, indiscriminately flung together, the misshapen and the well-proportioned, animal faces, empty faces, and noble faces in indiscriminate confusion, like the presence of the created universe; the glance of the educator accepts and receives them all. He is assuredly no descendant of the Greek gods, who kidnapped those they loved. But he seems to me to be a representative of the true God. For if God "forms the light and creates darkness," man is able to love both—to love light in itself, and darkness towards the light.

If this educator should ever believe that for the sake of education he has to practise selection and arrangement, then he will be guided by another criterion than that of inclination, however legitimate this may be in its own sphere; he will be guided by the recognition of values which is in his glance as an educator. But even then his selection remains suspended, under constant correction by the special humility of the educator for whom the life and particular being of all his pupils is the decisive factor to which his "hierarchic" recognition is subordinated. For in the manifold variety of the children the variety of creation is placed before him.

In education, then, there is a lofty asceticism: an asceticism which rejoices in the world, for the sake of the responsibility for a realm of life which is entrusted to us for our influence but not our interference—either by the will to power or by Eros. The spirit's service of life can be truly carried out only in the system of a reliable counterpoint—regulated by the laws of the different forms of relation—of giving and withholding oneself, intimacy and distance, which of course must not be controlled by reflection but must arise from the living tact of the natural and spiritual man. Every form of relation in which the spirit's service of life is realized has its special objectivity, its structure of proportions and limits which in no way resists the fervour of personal comprehension and penetration, though it does resist any confusion with the person's own spheres. If this structure and its resistance are not respected then a dilettantism will prevail which claims to be aristocratic, though in reality it is unsteady and feverish: to provide it with the most sacred names and attitudes will not help it past its inevitable consequence of disintegration. Consider, for example, the relation of doctor and patient. It is essential that this should be a real human relation experienced with the spirit by the one who is addressed; but as soon as the helper is touched by the desire—in however subtle a form—to dominate or to enjoy his patient, or to treat the latter's wish to be dominated or enjoyed by him other than as a wrong condition needing to be cured, the danger of a falsification arises, beside which all quackery appears peripheral.

The objectively ascetic character of the sphere of education must not, however, be misunderstood as being so separated from the instinct to power and from Eros that no bridge can be flung from them to it. I have already pointed out how very significant Eros can be to the educator without corroding his work. What matters here is the threshold and the transformation which takes place on it. It is not the church alone which has a testing threshold on which a man is transformed or becomes a lie. But in order to be able to carry out this ever renewed transition from sphere to sphere he must have carried it out once in a decisive fashion and taken up in himself the essence of education. How does this happen? There is an elemental experience which shatters at least the assurance of the erotic as well as the ascetic man, but sometimes does more, forcing its way at white-heat into the heart of the instinct and remoulding it. A reversal of the single instinct takes place, which does not eliminate it but reverses its system of direction. Such a reversal can be effected by the elemental experience with which the real process of education begins and on which it is based. I call it experiencing the other side.

A man belabours another, who remains quite still. Then let us assume that the striker suddenly receives in his soul the blow which he strikes: the same blow; that he receives it as the other who remains still. For the space of a moment he experiences the situation from the other side. Reality imposes itself on him. What will he do? Either he will overwhelm the voice of the soul, or his impulse will be reversed.

A man caresses a woman, who lets herself be caressed. Then let us assume that he feels the contact from two sides—with the palm of his hand still, and also with the woman's skin. The twofold nature of the gesture, as one that takes place between two persons, thrills through the depth of enjoyment in his heart and stirs it. If he does not deafen his heart he will have—not to renounce the enjoyment but—to love.

I do not in the least mean that the man who has had such an experience would from then on have this two-sided sensation in every such meeting—that would perhaps destroy his instinct. But the one extreme experience makes the other person present to him for all time. A transfusion has taken place after which a mere elaboration of subjectivity is never again possible or tolerable to him.

Only an inclusive power is able to take the lead; only an inclusive Eros is love. Inclusiveness is the complete realization of the submissive person, the desired person, the "partner," not by the fancy but by the actuality of the being.

It would be wrong to identify what is meant here with the familiar but not very significant term "empathy." Empathy means, if anything, to glide with one's own feeling into the dynamic structure of an object, a pillar or a crystal or the branch of a tree, or even of an animal or a man, and as it were to trace it from within, understanding the formation and motoriality of the object with the perceptions of one's own muscles; it means to "transpose" oneself over there and in there. Thus it means the exclusion of one's own concreteness, the extinguishing of the actual situation of life, the absorption in pure æstheticism of the reality in which one participates. Inclusion is the opposite of this. It is the extension of one's own concreteness, the fulfilment of the actual situation of life, the complete presence of the reality in which one participates. Its elements are, first, a relation, of no matter what kind, between two persons, second, an event experienced by them in common, in which at least one of them actively participates, and, third, the fact that this one person, without forfeiting anything of the felt reality of his activity, at the same time lives through the common event from the standpoint of the other.

A relation between persons that is characterized in more or less degree by the element of inclusion may be termed a dialogical relation.

A dialogical relation will show itself also in genuine conversation, but it is not composed of this. Not only is the shared silence of two such persons a dialogue, but also their dialogical life continues, even when they are separated in space, as the continual potential presence of the one to the other, as an unexpressed intercourse. On the other hand, all conversation derives its genuineness only from the consciousness of the element of inclusion—even if this appears only abstractly as an "acknowledgement" of the actual being of the partner in the conversation; but this acknowledgement can be real and effective only when it springs from an experience of inclusion, of the other side.

The reversal of the will to power and of Eros means that relations characterized by these are made dialogical. For that very reason it means that the instinct enters into communion with the fellow-man and into responsibility for him as an allotted and entrusted realm of life.

The element of inclusion, with whose recognition this clarification begins, is the same as that which constitutes the relation in education.

The relation in education is one of pure dialogue.

I have referred to the child, lying with half-closed eyes waiting for his mother to speak to him. But many children do not need to wait, for they know that they are unceasingly addressed in a dialogue which never breaks off. In face of the lonely night which threatens to invade, they lie preserved and guarded, invulnerable, clad in the silver mail of trust.

Trust, trust in the world, because this human being exists—that is the most inward achievement of the relation in education. Because this human being exists, meaninglessness, however hard pressed you are by it, cannot be the real truth. Because this human being exists, in the darkness the light lies hidden, in fear salvation, and in the callousness of one's fellow-men the great Love.

Because this human being exists: therefore he must be really there, really facing the child, not merely there in spirit. He may not let himself be represented by a phantom: the death of the phantom would be a catastrophe for the child's pristine soul. He need possess none of the perfections which the child may dream he possesses; but he must be really there. In order to be and to remain truly present to the child he must have gathered the child's presence into his own store as one of the bearers of his communion with the world, one of the focuses of his responsibilities for the world. Of course he cannot be continually concerned with the child, either in thought or in deed, nor ought he to be. But if he has really gathered the child into his life then that subterranean dialogic, that steady potential presence of the one to the other is established and endures. Then there is reality *between* them, there is mutuality.

But this mutuality—that is what constitutes the peculiar nature of the relation in education—cannot be one of inclusion, although the true relation of the educator to the pupil is based on inclusion. No other relation draws its inner life like this one from the element of inclusion, but no other is in that regard like this, completely directed to one-sidedness, so that if it loses one-sidedness it loses essence.

We may distinguish three chief forms of the dialogical relation.

The first rests on an abstract but mutual experience of inclusion.

The clearest example of this is a disputation between two men, thoroughly different in nature and outlook and calling, where in an instant—as by the action of a messenger as anonymous as he is invisible—it happens that each is aware of the other's full legitimacy, wearing the insignia of necessity and of meaning. What an illumination! The truth, the strength of conviction, the "standpoint," or rather the circle of movement, of each of them, is in no way reduced by this. There is no "relativizing," but we may say that, in the sign of the limit, the essence of mortal recognition, fraught with primal destiny, is manifested to us. To recognize means for us creatures the fulfilment by each of us, in truth and responsibility, of his own relation to the Present Being, through our receiving all that is manifested of it and incorporating it into our own being, with all our force, faithfully, and open to the world and the spirit. In this way living truth arises and endures. We have become aware that it is with the other as with ourselves, and that what rules over us both is not a truth of recognition but the truth-of-existence and the existence-of-truth of the Present Being. In this way we have become able *to acknowledge*.

I have called this form abstract, not as though its basic experience lacked immediacy, but because it is related to man only as a spiritual person and is bound to leave out the full reality of his being and life. The other two forms proceed from the inclusion of this full reality.

Of these the first, the relation of education, is based on a concrete but one-sided experience of inclusion.

If education means to let a selection of the world affect a person through the medium of another person, then the one through whom this takes place, rather, who makes it take place through himself, is caught in a strange paradox. What is otherwise found only as grace, inlaid in the folds of life—the influencing of the lives of others with one's own life—becomes here a function and a law. But since the educator has to such an extent replaced the master, the danger has arisen that the new phenomenon, the will to educate, may degenerate into arbitrariness, and that the educator may carry out his selection and his influence from himself and his idea of the pupil, not from the pupil's own reality. One only needs to read, say, the accounts of Pestalozzi's teaching method to see how easily, even with the noblest teachers, arbitrary self-will is mixed up with will. This is almost always due to an interruption or a temporary flagging of the act of inclusion, which is not merely regulative for the realm of education, as for other realms, but is actually constitutive; so that the realm of education acquires its true and proper force from the constant return of this act and the constantly renewed connexion with it. The man whose calling is to influence the being of persons that can be determined, must experience this action of his (however much it may have assumed the form of non-action) ever anew from the other side. Without the action of his spirit being in any way weakened he must at the same time be over there, on the surface of that other spirit which is being acted upon—and not of some conceptual, contrived spirit, but all the time the wholly concrete spirit of this individual and unique being who is living and confronting him, and who stands with him in the common situation of "educating" and "being educated" (which is indeed one situation, only the other is at the other end of it). It is not enough for him to imagine the child's individuality, nor to experience him directly as a spiritual person and then to acknowledge him. Only when he catches himself "from over there," and feels how it affects one, how it affects this other human being, does he recognize the real limit, baptize his self-will in Reality and make it true will, and renew his paradoxical legitimacy. He is of all men the one for whom inclusion may and should change from an alarming and edifying event into an atmosphere.

But however intense the mutuality of giving and taking with which he is bound to his pupil, inclusion cannot be mutual in this case. He experiences the pupil's being educated, but the pupil cannot experience the educating of the educator. The educator stands at both ends of the common situation, the pupil only at one end. In the moment when the pupil is able to throw himself across and experience from over there, the educative relation would be burst asunder, or change into friendship.

We call friendship the third form of the dialogical relation, which is based on a concrete and mutual experience os inclusion. It is the true inclusion of one another by human souls.

The educator who practises the experience of the other side and stands firm in it, experiences two things together, first that he is limited by otherness, and second that he receives grace by being bound to the other. He feels from "over there" the acceptance and the rejection of what is approaching (that is, approaching from himself, the educator)—of course often only in a fugitive mood or an uncertain feeling; but this discloses the real need and absence of need in the soul. In the same way the foods a child likes and dislikes is a fact which does not, indeed, procure for the experienced person but certainly helps him to gain an insight into what substances the child's body needs. In learning from time to time what this human being needs and does not need at the moment, the educator is led to an ever deeper recognition of what the human being needs in order to grow. But he is also led to the recognition of what he, the "educator," is able and what he is unable to give of what is needed—and what he can give now, and what not yet. So the responsibility for this realm of life allotted and entrusted to him, the constant responsibility for this living soul, points him to that which seems impossible and yet is somehow granted to us—to self-education. But self-education, here as everywhere, cannot take place through one's being concerned with oneself but only through one's being concerned, knowing what it means, with the world. The forces of the world which the child needs for the building up of his substance must be chosen by the educator from the world and drawn into himself.

The education of men by men means the selection of the effective world by a person and in him. The educator gathers in the constructive forces of the world. He distinguishes, rejects, and confirms in himself, in his self which is filled with the world. The constructive forces are eternally the same: they are the world bound up in community, turned to God. The educator educates himself to be their vehicle.

Then is this the "principle" of education, its normal and fixed maxim?

No; it is only the *principium* of its reality, the beginning of its reality—wherever it begins.

There is not and never has been a norm and fixed maxim of education. What is called so was always only the norm of a culture, of a society, a church, an epoch, to which education too, like all stirring

and action of the spirit, was submissive, and which education translated into its language. In a formed age there is in truth no autonomy
of education, but only in an age which is losing form. Only in it, in
the disintegration of traditional bonds, in the spinning whirl of freedom, does personal responsibility arise which in the end can no
longer lean with its burden of decision on any church or society or
culture, but is lonely in face of Present Being.

In an age which is losing form the highly-praised "personalities", who know how to serve its fictitious forms and in their name
to dominate the age, count in the truth of what is happening no more
than those who lament the genuine forms of the past and are diligent
to restore them. The ones who count are those persons who—though
they may be of little renown—respond to and are responsible for the
continuation of living spirit, each in the active stillness of his sphere
of work.

The question which is always being brought forward—"To
where, to what, must we educate?"—misunderstands the situation.
Only times which know a figure of general validity—the Christian,
the gentleman, the citizen—know an answer to that question, not
necessarily in words, but by pointing with the finger to the figure
which rises clear in the air, out-topping all. The forming of this figure in all individuals, out of all materials, is the formation of a "culture". But when all figures are shattered, when no figure is able any
more to dominate and shape the present human material, what is
there left to form?

Nothing but the image of God.

That is the indefinable, only factual, direction of the responsible
modern educator. This cannot be a theoretical answer to the question
"To what?", but only, if at all, an answer carried out in deeds; an answer carried out by non-doing.

The educator is set now in the midst of the need which he experiences in inclusion, but only a bit deeper in it. He is set in the midst
of the service, only a bit higher up, which he invokes without words;
he is set in the *imitatio Dei absconditi sed non ignoti.*

When all "directions" fail there arises in the darkness over the
abyss the one true direction of man, towards the creative Spirit, towards the Spirit of God brooding on the face of the waters, towards
Him of whom we know not whence He comes and whither He goes.

That is man's true autonomy which no longer betrays, but responds.

Man, the creature, who forms and transforms the creation, cannot
create. But he, each man, can expose himself and others to the cre-

ative Spirit. And he can call upon the Creator to save and perfect His image.

The Education of Character

MARTIN BUBER

Education worthy of the name is essentially education of character. For the genuine educator does not merely consider individual functions of his pupil, as one intending to teach him only to know or be capable of certain definite things; but his concern is always the person as a whole, both in the actuality in which he lives before you now and in his possibilities, what he can become. But in this way, as a whole in reality and potentiality, a man can be conceived either as personality, that is, as a unique spiritual-physical form with all the forces dormant in it, or as character, that is, as the link between what this individual is and the sequence of his actions and attitudes. Between these two modes of conceiving the pupil in his wholeness there is a fundamental difference. Personality is something which in its growth remains essentially outside the influence of the educator; but to assist in the moulding of character is his greatest task. Personality is a completion, only character is a task. One may cultivate and enhance personality, but in education one can and one must aim at character.

However—as I would like to point out straightaway—it is advisable not to over-estimate what the educator can even at best to develop character. In this more than in any other branch of the science of teaching it is important to realize, at the very beginning of the discussion, the fundamental limits to conscious influence, even before asking what character is and how it is to be brought about.

If I have to teach algebra I can expect to succeed in giving my pupils an idea of quadratic equations with two unknown quantities. Even the slowest-witted child will understand it so well that he will amuse himself by solving equations at night when he cannot fall asleep. And even one with the most sluggish memory will not forget, in his old age, how to play with x and y. But if I am concerned with the education of character, everything becomes problematic. I try to explain to my pupils that envy is despicable, and at once I feel the secret resistance of those who are poorer than their comrades. I try to explain that it is wicked to bully the weak, and at once I see a suppressed smile on the lips of the strong. I try to explain that lying destroys life, and something frightful happens: the worst habitual liar of the class produces a brilliant essay on the destructive power of lying. I have made the fatal mistake of *giving instruction* in ethics, and what I said is accepted as current coin of knowledge; nothing of it is transformed into character-building substance.

But the difficulty lies still deeper. In all teaching of a subject I can announce my intention of teaching as openly as I please, and this does not interfere with the results. After all, pupils do want, for the most part, to learn something, even if not overmuch, so that a tacit agreement becomes possible. But as soon as my pupils notice that I want to educate their characters I am resisted precisely by those who show most signs of genuine independent character: they will not let themselves be educated, or rather, they do not like the idea that somebody wants to educate them. And those, too, who are seriously labouring over the question of good and evil rebel when one dictates to them, as though it were some long established truth, what is good and what is bad; and they rebel just because they have experienced over and over again how hard it is to find the right way. Does it follow that one should keep silent about one's intention of educating character, and act by ruse and subterfuge? No; I have just said that the difficulty lies deeper. It is not enough to see that education of character is not introduced into a lesson in class; neither may one conceal it in cleverly arranged intervals. Education cannot tolerate such politic action. Even if the pupil does not notice the hidden motive it will have its negative effect on the actions of the teacher himself by depriving him of the directness which is his strength. Only in his whole being, in all his spontaneity can the educator truly affect the whole being of his pupil. For educating characters you do not need a moral genius, but you do need a man who is wholly alive and able to communicate himself directly to his fellow beings. His aliveness streams out to them and affects them most strongly and purely when he has no thought of affecting them.

The Greek word character means *impression*. The special link between man's being and his appearance, the special connexion between the unity of what he is and the sequence of his actions and attitudes is impressed on his still plastic substance. Who does the impressing? Everything does: nature and the social context, the house and the street, language and custom, the world of history and the world of daily news in the form of rumour, of broadcast and newspaper, music and technical science, play and dream—

everything together. Many of these factors exert their influence by stimulating agreement, imitation, desire, effort; others by arousing questions, doubts, dislike, resistance. Character is formed by the interpenetration of all those multifarious, opposing influences. And yet, among this infinity of form-giving forces the educator is only one element among innumerable others, but distinct from them all by his *will* to take part in the stamping of character and by his *consciousness* that he represents in the eyes of the growing person a certain *selection* of what is, the selection of what is "right", of what *should* be. It is in this will and this consciousness that his vocation as an educator finds its fundamental expression. From this the genuine educator gains two things: first, humility, the feeling of being only one element amidst the fullness of life, only one single existence in the midst of all the tremendous inrush of reality on the pupil; but secondly, self-awareness, the feeling of being therein the only existence that *wants* to affect the whole person, and thus the feeling of responsibility for the selection of reality which he represents to the pupil. And a third thing emerges from all this the recognition that in this realm of the education of character, of wholeness, there is only *one* access to the pupil: his *confidence*. For the adolescent who is frightened and disappointed by an unreliable world, confidence means the liberating insight that there is human truth, the truth of human existence. When the pupil's confidence has been won, his resistance against being educated gives way to a singular happening: he accepts the educator as a person. He feels he may trust this man, that this man is not making a business out of him, but is taking part in his life, accepting him before desiring to influence him. And so he learns to *ask*.

The teacher who is for the first time approached by a boy with somewhat defiant bearing, but with trembling hands, visibly opened-up and fired by a daring hope, who asks him what is the right thing in a certain situation—for instance, whether in learning that a friend has betrayed a secret entrusted to him one should call him to account or be content with entrusting no more secrets to him—the teacher to whom this happens realizes that this is the moment to make the first conscious step towards education of character; he has to answer, to answer under a responsibility, to give an answer which will probably lead beyond the alternatives of the question by showing a third possibility which is the right one. To dictate what is good and evil in general is not his business. His business is to answer a concrete question, to answer what is right and wrong in a given situation. This, as I have said, can only happen in an atmosphere of confidence. Confidence, of course, is not won by the strenuous endeavour to win it, but by direct and ingenuous participation in the life of the people one is dealing with—in this case in the life of one's pupils—and by assuming the responsibility which arises from such participation. It is not the educational intention but it is the meeting which is educationally fruitful. A soul suffering from the contradictions of the world of human society, and of its own physical existence, approaches me with a question. By trying to answer it to the best of my knowledge and conscience I help it to become a character that actively overcomes the contradictions.

If this is the teacher's standpoint towards his pupil, taking part in his life and conscious of responsibility, then everything that passes between them can, without any deliberate or politic intention, open a way to the education of character: lessons and games, a conversation about quarrels in the class, or about the problems of a world-war. Only, the teacher must not forget the limits of education; even when he enjoys confidence he cannot always expect agreement. Confidence implies a break-through from reserve, the bursting of the bonds which imprison an unquiet heart. But it does not imply unconditional agreement. The teacher must never forget that conflicts too, if only they are decided in a healthy atmosphere, have an educational value. A conflict with a pupil is the supreme test for the educator. He must use his own insight wholeheartedly; he must not blunt the piercing impact of his knowledge, but he must at the same time have in readiness the healing ointment for the heart pierced by it. Not for a moment may he conduct a dialectical manœuvre instead of the real battle for truth. But if he is the victor he has to help the vanquished to endure defeat; and if he cannot conquer the self-willed soul that faces him (for victories over souls are not so easily won), then he has to find the word of love which alone can help to overcome so difficult a situation.

2

So far I have referred to those personal difficulties in the education of character which arise from the relation between educator and pupil, while for the moment treating character itself, the object of education, as a simple concept of fixed content. But it is by no means that. In order to penetrate to the real difficulties in the education of character we have to examine critically the concept of character itself.

Kerschensteiner in his well-known essay on *The Concept and Education of Character* distinguished between "character in the most general sense", by which he means "a man's attitude to his human surroundings, which is constant and is expressed in his actions", and real "ethical character", which he defines as "a special attitude, and one which in action gives the preference before all others to absolute values". If we begin by accepting this distinction unreservedly—and undeniably there is some truth in it—we are faced with such heavy odds in all education of character in our time that the very possibility of it seems doubtful.

The "absolute values" which Kerschensteiner refers to cannot, of course, be meant to have only subjective validity for the person concerned. Don Juan finds absolute and subjective value in seducing the greatest possible number of women, and the dictator sees it in the greatest possible accumulation of power. "Absolute validity" can only relate to universal values and norms, the existence of which the person concerned recognizes and acknowledges. But to deny the presence of universal values and norms of absolute validity—that is the conspicuous tendency of our age. This tendency, is not, as is sometimes supposed, directed merely against the sanctioning of the norms by religion, but against their universal character and absolute validity, against their claim to be of a higher order than man and to govern the whole of mankind. In our age values and norms are not permitted to be anything but expressions of the life of a group which translates its own needs into the language of objective claims, until at last the group itself, for example a nation, is raised to an absolute value—and moreover to the only value. Then this splitting up into groups so pervades the whole of life that it is no longer possible to re-establish a sphere of values common to mankind, and a commandment to mankind is no longer observed. As this tendency grows the basis for the development of what Kerschensteiner means by moral character steadily diminishes. How, under these circumstances, can the task of educating character be completed?

At the time of the Arab terror in Palestine, when there were single Jewish acts of reprisal, there must have been many discussions between teacher and pupils on the question: Can there be any suspension of the Ten Commandments, i.e. can murder become a good deed if committed in the interest of one's own group? One such discussion was once repeated to me. The teacher asked: "When the commandment tells you 'Thou shalt not bear false witness against thy neighbour', are we to interpret it with the condition, 'provided that it does not profit you'?" Thereupon one of the pupils said, "But it is not a question of my profit, but of the profit of my people." The teacher: "And how would you like it, then, if we put our condition this way: 'Provided that it does not profit your family'?" The pupil: "But family—that is still something more or less like myself; but the people—that is something quite different; there all question of *I* disappears." The teacher: "Then if you are thinking, 'we want victory', don't you feel at the same time, 'I want victory'?" The pupil: "But the people, that is something infinitely more than just the people of to-day. It includes all past and future generations." At this point the teacher felt the moment had come to leave the narrow compass of the present and to invoke historical destiny. He said: "Yes; all past generations. But what was it that made those past generations of the Exile live? What made them outlive and overcome all their trials? Wasn't it that the cry 'Thou shalt not' never faded from their hearts and ears?" The pupil grew very pale. He was silent for a while, but it was the silence of one whose words threatened to stifle him. Then he burst out: "And what have we achieved that way? This!" And he banged his fist on the newspaper before him, which contained the report on the British White Paper. And again he burst out with "Live? Outlive? Do you call that life? We want to live!"

I have already said that the test of the educator lies in conflict with his pupil. He has to face this conflict and, whatever turn it may take, he has to find the way through it into life, into a life, I must add, where confidence continues unshaken—more, is even mysteriously strengthened. But the example I have just given shows the extreme difficulty of this task, which seems at times to have reached an impassable frontier. This is no longer merely a conflict between two generations, but between a world which for several millennia has believed in a truth superior to man, and an age which does not believe in it any longer—will not or cannot believe in it any longer.

But if we now ask, "How in this situation can there be any education of character?", something negative is immediately obvious: it is senseless to want to prove by any kind of argument that nevertheless the denied absoluteness of norms exists. That would be to assume that the denial is the result of reflection, and is open to argument, that is, to material for renewed reflection. But the denial is due to the disposition of a dominant human type of our age. We are justified in regarding this disposition as a sickness of the human race. But we must not deceive ourselves by believing that the disease can be cured by formulæ which assert that nothing is really as the sick person imagines. It is an idle undertaking to call out, to a mankind that has grown blind to eternity: "Look! the eternal values!" To-day host upon host of men have everywhere sunk into the slavery of collectives, and each collective is the supreme authority for its own slaves; there is no longer, superior to the collectives, any universal sovereignty in idea, faith, or spirit: Against the values, decrees and decisions of the collective no appeal is possible. This is true, not only for the totalitarian countries, but also for the parties and party-like groups in the so-called democracies. Men who have so lost themselves to the collective Moloch cannot be rescued from it by any reference, however eloquent, to the absolute whose kingdom the Moloch has usurped. One has to begin by pointing to that sphere where man himself, in the hours of utter solitude, occasionally becomes aware of the disease through sudden pain: by pointing to the relation of the individual to his own self. In order to enter into a personal relation with the absolute, it is first necessary to be a person again, to rescue one's real personal self from the fiery jaws of collectivism which devours all selfhood. The desire to do this is latent in the pain the individual suffers through his distorted relation to his own self. Again and again he dulls the pain with a subtle poison and thus suppresses the desire as well. To keep the pain awake, to waken the desire—that is the first task of everyone who regrets the obscuring of eternity. It is also the first task of the genuine educator in our time.

The man for whom absolute values in a universal sense do not exist cannot be made to adopt "an attitude which in action gives the preference over all others to absolute values". But what one can inculcate in him is the desire to attain once more to a real attitude, and that is, the desire to become a person following the only way that leads to this goal to-day.

But with this the concept of character formulated by Kerschensteiner and deriving, as we know, from Kant is recognized to be useless for the specifically modern task of the education of character. Another concept has to be found if this task is to be more precisely defined.

We cannot conceal from ourselves that we stand to-day on the ruins of the edifice whose towers were raised by Kant. It is not given to us living to-day to sketch the plan for a new building. But we can perhaps begin by laying the first foundations without a plan, with only a dawning image before our mind's eye.

3

According to Kerschensteiner's final definition character is "fundamentally nothing but voluntary obedience to the maxims which have been moulded in the individual by experience, teaching, and self-reflection, whether they have been adopted and then completely assimilated or have originated in the consciousness through self-legislation". This voluntary obedience "is, however, only a form of self-control". At first, love or fear of other people must have produced in man "the *habit* of self-conquest". Then, gradually, "this outer obedience must be transformed into inner obedience".

The concept of habit was then enlarged, especially by John

Dewey in his book, *Human Nature and Conduct*. According to him character is "the interpenetration of habits". Without "the continued operation of all habits in every act" there would be no unified character, but only "a juxtaposition of disconnected reactions to separated situations".

With this concept of character as an organization of self-control by means of the accumulation of maxims, or as a system of interpenetrating habits, it is very easy to understand how powerless modern educational science is when faced by the sickness of man. But even apart from the social problems of the age, this concept can be no adequate basis for the construction of a genuine education of character. Not that the educator could dispense with employing useful maxims or furthering good habits. But in moments that come perhaps only seldom, a feeling of blessed achievement links him to the explorer, the inventor, the artist, a feeling of sharing in the revelation of what is hidden. In such moments he finds himself in a sphere very different from that of maxims and habits. Only on this, the highest plane of his activity, can he fix his real goal, the real concept of character which is his concern, even though he might not often reach it.

For the first time a young teacher enters a class independently, no longer sent by the training college to prove his efficiency. The class before him is like a mirror of mankind, so multiform, so full of contradictions, so inaccessible. He feels "These boys—I have not sought them out; I have been put here and have to accept them as they are—but not as they now are in this moment, no, as they *really* are, as they can become. But how can I find out what is in them and what can I do to make it take shape?" And the boys do not make things easy for him. They are noisy, they cause trouble, they stare at him with impudent curiosity. He is at once tempted to check this or that trouble-maker, to issue orders, to make compulsory the rules of decent behaviour, to say No, to say No to everything rising against him from beneath: he is at once tempted to start from beneath. And if one starts from beneath one perhaps never arrives above, but everything comes down. But then his eyes meet a face which strikes him. It is not a beautiful face nor particularly intelligent; but it is a real face, or rather, the chaos preceding the cosmos of a real face. On it he reads a question which is something different from the general curiosity: "Who are you? Do you know something that concerns me? Do you bring me something? What do you bring?"

In some such way he reads the question. And he, the young teacher, addresses this face. He says nothing very ponderous or important, he puts an ordinary introductory question: "What did you talk about last in geography? The Dead Sea? Well, what about the Dead Sea?" But there was obviously something not quite usual in the question, for the answer he gets is not the ordinary schoolboy answer; the boy begins to *tell a story*. Some months earlier he had stayed for a few hours on the shores of the Dead Sea and it is of this he tells. He adds: "And everything looked to me as if it had been created a day before the rest of creation." Quite unmistakably he had only in this moment made up his mind to talk about it. In the meantime his face has changed. It is no longer quite as chaotic as before. And the class has fallen silent. They all listen. The class, too, is no longer a chaos. Something has happened. The young teacher has started from above.

The educator's task can certainly not consist in educating great characters. He cannot select his pupils, but year by year the world, such as it is, is sent in the form of a school class to meet him on his life's way as his destiny; and in this destiny lies the very meaning of his life's work. He has to introduce discipline and order, he has to establish a law, and he can only strive and hope for the result that discipline and order will become more and more inward and autonomous, and that at last the law will be written in the heart of his pupils. But his real goal which, once he has well recognized it and well remembers it, will influence all his work, is the great character.

The great character can be conceived neither as a system of maxims nor as a system of habits. It is peculiar to him to act from the whole of his substance. That is, it is peculiar to him to react in accordance with the uniqueness of every situation which challenges him as an active person. Of course there are all sorts of similarities in different situations; one can construct types of situations, one can always find to what section the particular situation belongs, and draw what is appropriate from the hoard of established maxims and habits, apply the appropriate maxim, bring into operation the appropriate habit. But what is untypical in the particular situation remains unnoticed and unanswered. To me that seems the same as if, having ascertained the sex of a new-born child, one were immediately to establish its type as well, and put all the children of one type into a common cradle on which not the individual name but the name of the type was inscribed. In spite of all similarities every living situation has, like a new-born child, a new face, that has never been before and will never come again. It demands of you a reaction which cannot be prepared beforehand. It demands nothing of what is past. It demands presence, responsibility; it demands you. I call a great character one who by his actions and attitudes satisfies the claim of situations out of deep readiness to respond with his whole life, and in such a way that the sum of his actions and attitudes expresses at the same time the unity of his being in its willingness to accept responsibility. As his being is unity, the unity of accepted responsibility, his active life, too, coheres into unity. And one might perhaps say that for him there rises a unity out of the situations he has responded to in responsibility, the indefinable unity of a moral destiny.

All this does not mean that the great character is beyond the acceptance of norms. No responsible person remains a stranger to norms. But the command inherent in a genuine norm never becomes a maxim and the fulfilment of it never a habit. Any command that a great character takes to himself in the course of his development does not act in him as part of his consciousness or as material for building up his exercises, but remains latent in a basic layer of his substance until it reveals itself to him in a concrete way. What it has to tell him is revealed whenever a situation arises which demands of him a solution of which till then he had perhaps no idea. Even the most universal norm will at times be recognized only in a very special situation. I know of a man whose heart was struck by the lightning flash of "Thou shalt not steal" in the very moment when he was moved by a very different desire from that of stealing, and whose heart was so struck by it that he not only abandoned doing what he wanted to do, but with the whole force of his passion did the very opposite. Good and evil are not each other's opposites like right and left. The evil approaches us as a whirlwind, the good as a direction. There is a direction, a "yes", a command, hidden even in a prohibition, which is revealed to us in moments like those. In moments like these the command addresses us really in the second person, and the Thou in it is no one else but one's own self. Maxims command only the third person, the each and the none.

One can say that it is the unconditioned nature of the address which distinguishes the command from the maxim. In an age which has become deaf to unconditioned address we cannot overcome the dilemma of the education of character from that angle. But insight into the structure of great character can help us to overcome it.

Of course, it may be asked whether the educator should really start "from above", whether, in fixing his goal, the hope of finding a great character, who is bound to be the exception, should be his starting-point; for in his methods of educating character he will always have to take into consideration the others, the many. To this I reply that the educator would not have the right to do so if a method inapplicable to these others were to result. In fact, however, his very insight into the structure of a great character helps him to find the way by which alone (as I have indicated) he can begin to influence also the victims of the collective Moloch, pointing out to them the sphere in which they themselves suffer—namely, their relation to their own selves. From this sphere he must elicit the values which he can make credible and desirable to his pupils. That is what insight into the structure of a great character helps him to do.

A section of the young is beginning to feel today that, because of their absorption by the collective, something important and irreplaceable is lost to them—personal responsibility for life and the world. These young people, it is true, do not yet realize that their blind devotion to the collective, e.g. to a party, was not a genuine act of their personal life; they do not realize that it sprang, rather, from the fear of being left, in this age of confusion, to rely on themselves, on a self which no longer receives its direction from eternal values. Thus they do not yet realize that their devotion was fed on the unconscious desire to have responsibility removed from them by an authority in which they believe or want to believe. They do not yet realize that this devotion was an escape. I repeat, the young people I am speaking of do not yet realize this. But they are beginning to notice that he who no longer, with his whole being, decides what he does or does not, and assumes responsibility for it, becomes sterile in soul. And a sterile soul soon ceases to be a soul.

This is where the educator can begin and should begin. He can help the feeling that something is lacking to grow into the clarity of consciousness and into the force of desire. He can awaken in young people the courage to shoulder life again. He can bring before his pupils the image of a great character who denies no answer to life and the world, but accepts responsibility for everything essential that he meets. He can show his pupils this image without the fear that those among them who most of all need discipline and order will drift into a craving for aimless freedom: on the contrary, he can teach them in this way to recognize that discipline and order too are starting-points on the way towards self-responsibility. He can show that even the great character is not born perfect, that the unity of his being has first to mature before expressing itself in the sequence of his actions and attitudes. But unity itself, unity of the person, unity of the saved life, has to be emphasized again and again. The confusing contradictions cannot be remedied by the collectives, not one of which knows the taste of genuine unity and which if left to themselves would end up, like the scorpions imprisoned in a box, in the witty fable, by devouring one another. This mass of contradictions can be met and conquered only by the rebirth of personal unity, unity of being, unity of life, unity of action—unity of being, life and action together. This does not mean a static unity of the uniform, but the great dynamic unity of the multiform in which multiformity is formed into unity of character. Today the great characters are still "enemies of the people", they who love their society, yet wish not only to preserve it but to raise it to a higher level. To-morrow they will be the architects of a new unity of mankind. It is the longing for personal unity, from which must be born a unity of mankind, which the educator should lay hold of and strengthen in his pupils. Faith in this unity and the will to achieve it is not a "return" to individualism, but a step beyond all the dividedness of individualism and collectivism. A great and full relation between man and man can only exist between unified and responsible persons. That is why it is much more rarely found in the totalitarian collective than in any historically earlier form of society; much more rarely also in the authoritarian party than in any earlier form of free association. Genuine education of character is genuine education for community.

In a generation which has had this kind of upbringing the desire will also be kindled to behold again the eternal values, to hear again the language of the eternal norm. He who knows inner unity, the innermost life of which is mystery, learns to honour the mystery in all its forms. In an understandable reaction against the former domination of a false, fictitious mystery, the present generations are obsessed with the desire to rob life of all its mystery. The fictitious mystery will disappear, the genuine one will rise again. A generation which honours the mystery in all its forms will no longer be deserted by eternity. Its light seems darkened only because the eye suffers from a cataract; the receiver has been turned off, but the resounding ether has not ceased to vibrate. To-day, indeed, in the hour of upheaval, the eternal is sifted from the pseudo-eternal. That which flashed into the primal radiance and blurred the primal sound will be extinguished and silenced, for it has failed before the horror of the new confusion and the questioning soul has unmasked its futility. Nothing remains but what rises above the abyss of to-day's monstrous problems, as above every abyss of every time: the wing-beat of the spirit and the creative word. But he who can see and hear out of unity will also behold and discern again what can be beheld and discerned eternally. The educator who helps to bring man back to his own unity will help to put him again face to face with God.

The Return to the Origin of Being

DONALD VANDENBERG

In an attempt to gain perspective an existential interpretation of a very dead historical phenomenon will be repeated as a "case study." Empirical researchers sometimes use the case study method to exam-

Donald Vandenberg, Being and Education: An Essay in Existential Phenomenology, © 1971, pp. 78–82. Reprinted by permission of Prentice-Hall, Inc., Englewood Cliffs, New Jersey.

ine phenomena in their context in the real world. Clinical psychologists, e.g., employ it to generate understandings and generalizations of a certain kind of validity. Likewise is the "field study" beginning to be used to investigate problems of schooling from the viewpoint of the administrator. The following "case study" of the German Youth Movement at the beginning of the century illustrates in a paradigmatic way the authority-crisis that may occur in youth as it has been manifested at large scale in the United States in the lost generation after the First World War, then in the beat generation after the Second World War, then in the hippie-yippie generation during the Vietnam War, etc., etc. It also concerns related phenomena such as student unrest, disinterestedness in schooling, and the "drop-out" predicament, which are at bottom an alienation from schooling and what it stands for. The remoteness in time and place might assist in yielding balanced perspective on the significance of the being of youth for educating and the singificance of the being of education for youth; the reality of the occurrence might assist in the grounding of education with in the conditions of human being.

In the German Youth Movement the school boys in a college preparatory high school, a *gymnasium,* in Steglitz near Berlin, left their school and homes and tramped around Europe. They were soon followed by youth from elsewhere, until the abandonment of school and home became a general societal phenomenon. Why did they leave opportunities that, since they were the academic elite, might seem very enviable? *What* did they leave? To describe their situation from their point of view without interpreting it or judging it moralistically one has to use words that are moralistic, in the way the youth were moralistic, to convey their mooded understanding. Why did they themselves think they were leaving?

In their own minds the German youth fled the increasing drabness resulting from the industrialization of the city in protest against the mendacity and materialism of the age. They left to protest a tradition that seemed pretentious and lifeless and that interfered with their orientation to the future. The whole tradition and way of life "forced" upon them in school and at home seemed torpid, ungenuine, and uncreative. They fled what seemed to be a rigid life-order to seek genuineness, unobligatedness, and continuous becoming. By fleeing the overorganized "traditional" school at its best, they fled what seemed to be an overstructured milieu: neither the structured knowledge, daily assignments, nor school and community mores gave them room for their desires, interests, purposes, and goals. They fled a stifling atmosphere in order to breathe and consciously sought the precise opposite of what they fled. As they wandered around Europe, they had in mind to seek the new, far, and distant, but their actions revealed their true "goal," that of goallessness.

They had no goals in mind, for they went nowhere. They did not go to Paris or to Rome, but wandered through the Black Forest, through the pines. Their wandering, in other words, had no aim but itself, to move around the landscape aimlessly.

The wandering was the manifestation of a quest for a primordial way of living, a mode of being, that corresponded to the wanderer's own aimlessness. That it was an expression of the wanderer's simple having to be (for himself) can be seen through the shifts in the youth's temporal structure and concomitant shifts in the underlying moods or states-of-being. The temporal structure of the youth had become very bound in school. The organizing of their lives by the hours and days of schooling was not "natural," i.e., authentic, but was to great extent imposed upon their existence. The routine bound the youth's temporalizings into the anonymous pattern of schooling, "capturing" them so that the future was the next examination, etc., that impinged upon the individual, rather than promoting a free futurizing movement into which the youth might expand freely. The wandering freed the youth's temporal structure (and his temporalizings) from its bindings, from its being bound into public time with its objective past and future. The freeing of the present from its bonds to the earlier and the later made the experiencing of the present "timeless," and the disclosure of the world that occurred within that present became unique: as the present became loosened from the public time of schooling, it became worth while in its own right. The availability of the possibilities therein restored the youth to the childlike trust in the possibilities of the present. It restored his trust in present being. Each hour and each day became worth while in and for itself; each tomorrow became an inviting place to enter, acquiring an aura of holiness. In this progressive development of the sacredness of the present and the morrow, the world became open, bright, and promising. The *world* became an inviting place to enter because the disclosure of the world gradually came to occur within the wanderer's mood of high-spiritedness.

All disclosure of world occurs through mooded understanding, through an understanding that is enveloped in a "mood" or state-of-being. The state-of-being, moreover, is primary in determining how the world is disclosed to one; to be in a constricted mood reveals a limited and limiting world, whereas to be in an expansive mood reveals an expanding, open world. This simply means that all disclosure occurs to existing people, i.e., to human existence, and human being is such that it is always in some state-of-being that is felt by the individual: the taste and smell of one's being is always present as part of one's self-conscious being. Everything, including the disclosure of world, happens within a state-of-being. Even the colorless, disinterested "lack of mood" appropriate to theoretical or scientific understanding is precisely a mood. It is a mood approaching a satiation with being wherein the world disclosed is a dull place and being is almost a burden. As the youth wandered through the landscape, they underwent a gradual shifting of moods, or states-of-being, and with this shifting the mode of the disclosure of the world gradually shifted as well. This is most noticeable in the experiencing of time because the form of the temporal structure is the state-of-being: each mood has its own temporal structure; the temporal structure forced on the youth in home and school forced a state-of-being, or mood, of boredom upon them. As they wandered, the freeing from the public time of the schools was accompanied by a freeing from the state-of-being it induced. Therewith occurred, gradually, the child-like disclosure of world wherein the present possibilities became of great value.

The gradual shifting of the youth's state-of-being constitutes the anthropological significance of the wandering movement because of the accompanying changes in the general quality or valence of the world disclosed. The youth experienced extremely high spirits with the initial escape from schooling; this became a general elation as equanimity began to be restored. This became joy with the further restoral of equanimity, and this in turn gradually became the more primordial optimism of the child in his open communion with the world. The anthropological function of wandering was its return to the primary optimism of the child at play in a safe world. It was in the basal joy of wandering that was attained after the overly exuberant elation had subsided that the present moment became unbound from the "urgent future" and "dragging past" in an existential freeing from externally imposed learnings and goals. Then in the sheer joy of abandonment to the wandering itself the apprehensiveness of the past and future slid away and disappeared. Rather than tradition or external obligations covering over the present moment, the "instant" stretched itself out and became not a place to be passed over quickly but one in which to dwell. In this stretching out of the present moment in which the moment became livable, the past and future simply foundered.

Through wandering, the youth were freed to spatialize and temporalize from their own centers, i.e., for authentic existence. Then in the accompanying joy they could trust "nature," which became more open to them because of the trust, which increased the joy of wandering, which enabled the youth to became more and more open to the landscape as such. They became able to abandon themselves with confidence to the continuous movement of "nature," to drift along the stream of life therein. They identified with flowing brooks and streams, with the endless revolutions of days, months, and years, with mornings and springs, and these moments became expressed in song and lyric poetry. They identified, i.e., had a personal I-Thou relationship, an immediate at-oneness, with things encountered in nature analogous to the unification of the child with his toys. This relationship was extended to plants, animals, and natural phenomena, even to the ordinarily repelling aspects of "nature." Even violent storms, for example, raised the wanderer's spirits because their own kind of greatness was experienced: the being of the wanderer opened to encompass the spatiality of the storm, rather than retreating from it in the more customary oppressiveness experienced of storms. In this gradual union with the things of "nature," the youth came to dwell more and more in the landscape as such in the completely open communion with it that belongs to the earliest phase of childhood existence. They gradually became the landscape. The aimlessness of the wandering and the shifts of the states-of-being through which the world was disclosed made the disclosure of the landscape quite different from the world disclosed to a farmer, woodsman, sportsman, or scientist, because the provinces of meaning in which *their* disclosures occur cause them to look at and objectify the landscape and things therein. Instead of observing the landscape, the wanderers experienced it, for the landscape presented itself to them. It cannot present itself within the other provinces of meaning because their bracketing constitutes a distancing that landscape has difficulty breaking through. The shifts in their state-of-being, in other words, were initiated as much by the landscape they were experiencing as it was by their own wandering movement. In the state of primary optimism and open communion with "nature," the landscape presented itself and enabled the experiencing in depth.

The anthropological function of wandering was its return to nature, but if "nature" is given the interpretation of thinkers of the Romantic Movement, e.g., Rousseau, Wordsworth, or Emerson, it is interpreted sentimentally, youthfully, falsely. Rather than being a return to nature, the wandering of the youth movement represents a return to the origin, to the source. It was *a return to the ground of being*. Through the changes in the state-of-being, the wanderer's being opened to landscape and the landscape opened to the wanderer. The landscape, however, was not "nature"; it was being, simple being in itself. It was being qua being. Then what happened in the return to the origin when the wanderer's being opened to the landscape's being and the landscape's being opened to the wanderer's being was the movement whereby *being cleared a space for itself*. This worlding of the world, the truth of being, could not occur while the boys were in school because of the obstructiveness of the between-world of constructs that developed within the bracketing of the public time-structure of schooling and of the provinces of meaning of the academic disciplines studied therein. Although the anthropological function of the wandering was the return to an unconditional relation to being, its non-anthropocentric function was to allow being to clear a space for itself. What happened in the wandering was not merely a return to the ground of being, but a return of being. It occurred through joy because the matter of returning to the origin of one's being, the homecoming, is the originary joy.

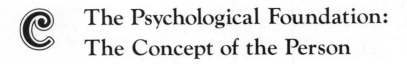

The Psychological Foundation:
The Concept of the Person

As a humanistic, existential, and phenomenological ideal, nothing transcends the significance of being a person. In fact, we can only begin to grasp the existential significance of humanity, if we sense ourselves, psychologically, as whole beings or persons in the here-and-now. The concept of the person has figured very largely in the development of most contemporary versions of humanistic education, and I consider it the main psychological foundation of humanistic education.

A concept is a scientific or cognitive means whereby thinking can proceed, as in formulating the solution to a problem. Thus the concept of the person provides the intellectual and philosophical framework within which humanistic and existential psychologists have begun to think holistically and ontologically about the individual. The "person" is by no means a static or frozen category that pertrifies thinking about the human being. The concept of the person connotes change as well as permanence, sameness as well as differences, the subjective as well as the objective, the inner as well as the outer, the mental as well as the bodily, the intellectual as well as the intuitive, the spiritual as well as the physical, the individual as well as the social being. In short, the concept of the person points toward the dialectical and holistic quality of existence. For this reason it provides a uniquely humanistic way of thinking about man and education.

Few have contributed as significantly to the psychological foundation of humanistic education as the late Abraham H. Maslow. Maslow approaches education as a psychologist who was deeply influenced by Taoist, phenomenological, and existential thinking. Taoism is an Eastern philosophy that believes the way of nature lies in a receptive attitude, rather than in the aggressive and intrusive attitude of Western science. Maslow believes the ideal method of teaching is based upon the Taoist need to "accept the person and help him to learn what kind of person he is already." In the context of phenomenology, or the philosophical and psychological study of consciousness, Maslow presents a view that he terms biological phenomenology, calling upon the individual to meditate and to listen to the deep inner impulses and animal instincts, that exist below roles, goals, and external conditioning. The influence of existential philosophy on Maslow is visible in his concern for the identity of the individual, particularly in the educational process.

Both of the selections from Maslow, "Education and Peak Experiences" and "Goals and Implications of Humanistic Education," show what a remarkable psychologist he was in thinking humanistically about education. His concepts of self-actualization, peak experiences, and the higher and lower needs of the self have made decisively important contributions to the rise of humanistic education. In the psychological realm of humanistic education Maslow's importance can hardly be overestimated.

A psychologist of perhaps no less stature is Carl R. Rogers, who was also influenced by existential and phenomenological thinking. His article, "The Goal: The Fully Functioning Person," delineates his concept of the "optimal end point of therapy, or . . . of education." Rogers approaches the subject of education from the viewpoint of client-centered therapy, which requires a person-to-person relationship rather than the role-playing of traditional therapy. In this context, Rogers presents the concept of empathic understanding, which entails, among other things, an openness to experience, living existentially moment by moment, and a trust in the organism. Rogers believes that man is not irrational but "exquisitely rational." Thus, the person's quest for discovery of the form of behavior that most closely satisfies his needs, such as affiliation and communication with others, is "appropriate to the survival and enhancement of a highly social animal." Rogers also thinks that the fully functioning person, admittedly a theoretical ideal, realizes that his organism is more wise than his conscious self may be.

Hence, the fully functioning person makes full use of his organism, sensing inwardly and outwardly through it and living completely in the existential here-and-now.

Frederick S. Perls is the founder of Gestalt therapy in America. Chapter 3 of his *Gestalt Therapy Verbatim* is included here to show his important concept of the here-and-now of human experiencing and also to introduce the reader to a psychological viewpoint that has influenced the thinking of classroom teachers at all levels of education. Essentially, Perls believes that nothing exists except the here-and-now of immediate, concrete, sensory experiencing, Most phenomena that pass for knowledge he calls "mind-fucking." This zone of consciousness constitutes the DMZ [demilitarized zone], or the space between self and world where only fantasy, illusion, and the three classes of verbiage ("chicken shit, bullshit, and elephantshit") exist. Despite Perls' unconventional rhetoric, his viewpoint shows the profound influences of phenomenology and existential philosophy, as well as behaviorism. His presence in America, particularly at the Esalen Institute, spurred the rise of Gestalt therapy at growth centers across the country, and his ideas and disciples have penetrated the classrooms of many schools and colleges. Perls' viewpoint is also important in understanding the human potential movement, because many of his ideas are similar to those of other leaders in the movement. His views are a most important contribution to a tough-minded approach to the psychological knowledge of the person.*

The selection entitled "Behavioral Humanism," by Carl E. Thoresen, assumes that a synthesis is possible between behavioral learning principles and the goals and values of humanistic psychology. Thoresen asserts that the humanistic goal of the good person is not incongruent with behaviorism, especially when the latter considers that the "here-and-now contemporary environment is a prime focus of concern. . . ." Thoresen's article is a serious, intellectual effort to combine the values of behaviorism and humanism, since he feels that so much vicious stereotyping and frivolous polemics have gone on between the two positions. His aim is to create productive dialogue between behaviorism and humanism, and he distinguishes carefully between the conflicting viewpoints of behaviorism in this effort.

Thoresen's article is important because Skinnerian behaviorism is so often described today as if it were the archenemy of anything humanistic in education. Thoresen offers solutions to the spurious antagonism of behaviorism and humanism, especially in his notion of the "intensive study of the individual." His views should contribute toward correcting psychological distortions of the self, especially when they rest upon artificial and intellectually self-deceptive constructions. I offer here a somewhat abridged version of the original article.

---

* Despite Perls' valuable contribution to the rise of the human potential movement and Gestaltism in America, I feel that his influence has also been harmful in contributing to the anti-intellectualism that is sometimes rife at growth centers. Recognizing that he was reacting against a heavy German intellectual background, it is understandable that Perls said some of the things that he did. However, I believe that for those who are seriously interested in actualizing and realizing the values of the person in the educational setting, a contemptuous, adolescent disregard of the mind or intellect will seriously weaken the effort.

Herbert A. Otto's "New Light on the Human Potential" is the last article in this section. Otto's central contention is that "in the area of human potentialities . . . it has become ever clearer that personality, to a much greater degree than previously suspected, functions in response to the environment." Otto, through his own leadership role in the human potential movement, is keenly aware of the extent to which "here-and-now inputs" affect the funtioning of personality. His view, shared by others, that the human person is only functioning at a fraction of his potential receives new confirmation daily. His article is valuable in offering an intimate and enthusiastic view of the burgeoning human potential movement (at the time of his writing). At the same time, Otto's sensitivity to the extent to which personal functioning is tied to society and the forces within it anticipates the sociological foundation of humanistic education.

Finally, in the context of the psychological foundations of humanistic education, I would urge the reader to consider the views of two thinkers, Robert Assagioli and Alexander Lowen. Considerations of space prevent me from including extracts from their writings, but their works are cited in Further Readings.

The Italian psychologist Roberto Assagioli presents a provocative view of the self, both in personalistic and spiritual contexts, that he calls psychosynthesis. According to Assagioli, "We are dominated by everything with which our self becomes identified. We can dominate and control everything from which we disidentify ourselves." Thus, Assagioli's method or guiding principle for training of the will and realization of the higher self, is called disidentification. Specifically, the principle of disidentification means the "disintegration of the harmful images and complexes" and the "control and utilization of the energies thus set free." Assagioli's psychology has new and profound implications for the task of humanizing education and actualizing the energies contained at the many levels of the personality. His claim that psychosynthesis is a "method of integral education," engaging the Spirit and Being of the cosmos through self-knowledge, has possibly deep meaning for realizing the higher needs of the person in education.

Alexander Lowen, one of the leaders in the field of bio-energetics, or the theory of health that the ego and mind of the person is grounded in the reality and experiences of the body, has made a provocative contribution to humanistic education. Basically, Lowen believes that a healthy ego is grounded in and needs identification with (1) the body or feeling and (2) the mind or knowledge. Educationally it is clear that no adequate form of teaching or learning can ignore either the experiences of the body or the knowledge made possible through the mind. Lowen claims that an ego that is not adequately grounded in reality becomes "bewitched." By this he means that the ego of the person becomes dissociated from both community (feelings with others) and causality (the natural laws of cause and effect). A full acceptance and appreciation of Lowen's viewpoint may be frustrated in education because of a "bias against the body still exists in high and low places." However, his views are well-worth considering by those interested in the implications of bio-energetics for education.

DISCUSSION QUESTIONS

1. Abraham H. Maslow's ultimate goal of self-actualization implies that the person transcend cultural conditioning and becomes a world citizen. How is it possible for a person to actually accomplish this? When, or under what conditions, can one transcend or go beyond anything? Also, in transcending or peak-experiencing Maslow says that there are at least two components: "an emotional one of ecstasy and an intellectual one of illumination." How can peak experience or experiences of self-actualization be promoted in the classroom? In what ways would the experience of self-actualization contribute to the humanization of education? What have been your own experiences of self-actualization?

2. Carl R. Rogers believes that more concepts and models are needed for the educated man. What criticisms do you have of his own model or concept of man? Do you believe, for example, that the "defensively organized man" cannot make an effective choice? What implications and consequences would "the power of naked choice" have in education? Do you believe that it is possible to experience absolute freedom through our choosing? Have you experienced this in education or elsewhere? If so, what was it like?

3. One of Frederick Perls' main assumptions about the person is that he is made whole by being in touch with reality. Does it appear that Perls depreciates the value of thinking by reducing it to the level of doing? Also, in view of how Perls feels about thinking, i.e., that it is fantasy-ridden and takes us out of the here-and-now, what problems does his viewpoint present to the educational establishment? How do you reconcile Perls view that "verbal communication is usually a lie. The real communication is beyond words" with the way most classrooms are structured? What is the main value of the concept of the here-and-now for the education of the person?

4. Do you think that Carl Thoresen overdraws the case for behavioral principles of learning being humanistic? From your knowledge of humanism, what appears to be true about humanism that is not true for behaviorism, and vice versa? Do you agree with Thoresen that the person should be used as a scientific tool in the under-

standing of man? What dangers are there in treating the person as a means rather than as an end, an object rather than a subject, as certain varieties of behaviorism advocate? To what extent is the school run on behavioristic rather than humanistic and existential principles? Do you believe in the potential value of a dialogue between humanists and behaviorists? Why?

5. Herbert Otto states that a "considerable number of studies indicate that much in our educational system—including conformity pressures exerted by teachers, emphasis upon memory development, and rote learning, plus the overcrowding of classrooms—militates against the development of creative capacities." Do you agree with his assessment of the educational system? What do you think can be done to actualize the hidden potential of the individual? Do you agree with Otto that we should focus more upon our strengths than our weaknesses to actualize our potentialites and to create a healthy culture? Do any of the areas of human potential, i.e., sensory training, parapsychology, hypnosis, group experience, and so on interest you? What are the implications of Otto's view of human potentiality for education? Would an active concern for the hidden potential of man realize the ideal of the whole person in education and society to a greater degree?

FURTHER READING

Assagioli, Roberto. *Psychosynthesis.* New York: The Viking Press, Inc., 1973.

Fromm, Erich. *Man for Himself.* New York: Fawcett Premier Book, 1967.

Laing, R. D. *The Divided Self.* Baltimore, Maryland: Penguin Books, 1966.

Lowen, Alexander. *The Betrayal of the Body.* New York: Collier Books, 1973.

Macmurray, John. *Persons in Relation.* London: Farber and Farber, 1961.

May, Rollo (ed.). *Existence.* New York: Simon and Schuster, Inc., 1967.

Moustakas, Clark. *Personal Growth.* Cambridge, Massachusetts: Howard A. Doyle Publishing Company, 1971.

Murphy, Gardner. *Human Potentialities.* New York: Basic Books, Inc., 1958.

Roger, Carl R. *On Becoming a Person.* Boston: Houghton Mifflin Company, 1961.

Ruitenbeek, Hendrik. *The New Group Therapies.* New York: Avon Books, 1972.

Tournier, Paul. *The Meaning of Persons.* New York: Perennial Library, 1973.

Education and Peak Experiences

ABRAHAM H. MASLOW

If one took a course or picked up a book on the psychology of learning, most of it, in my opinion, would be beside the point—that is, beside the "humanistic" point. Most of it would present learning as the
acquisition of associations of skills and capacities that are *external*
and not *intrinsic* to the human character, to the human personality,
to the person himself. Picking up coins or keys or possessions or
something of the sort is like picking up reinforcements and conditioned reflexes that are, in a certain, very profound sense, expen-
dable. It does not really matter if one has a conditioned reflex; if I
salivate to the sound of a buzzer and then this extinguishes, nothing
has happened to me; I have lost nothing of any consequence whatever. We might almost say that these extensive books on the psychology of learning are of no consequence, at least to the human center,
to the human soul, to the human essence.

Generated by this new humanistic philosophy is also a new conception of learning, of teaching, and of education. Stated simply,
such a concept holds that the function of education, the goal of education—the human goal, the humanistic goal, the goal so far as
human beings are concerned—is ultimately the "self-actualization"
of a person, the becoming fully human, the development of the fullest height that the human species can stand up to or that the particular individual can come to. In a less technical way, it is helping the
person to become the best that he is able to become.

Such a goal involves very serious shifts in what we would teach
in a course in the psychology of learning. It is not going to be a matter of associative learning. Associative learning in general is certainly
useful, extremely useful for learning things that are of no real consequence, or for learning means—techniques which are after all interchangeable. And many of the things we must learn are like that. If
one needs to memorize the vocabulary of some other language, he
would learn it by sheer rote memory. Here, the laws of association
can be a help. Or if one wants to learn all sorts of automatic habits in
driving, responding to a red signal light or something of the sort,
then conditioning is of consequence. It is important and useful,
especially in a technological society. But in terms of becoming a better person, in terms of self-development and self-fulfillment, or in

terms of "becoming fully human," the greatest learning experiences are very different.

In my life, such experiences have been far more important than classes, listening to lectures, memorizing the branches of the twelve cranial nerves and dissecting a human brain, or memorizing the insertions of the muscles, or the kinds of thing that one does in medical schools, in biology courses, or other such courses.

Far more important for me have been such experiences as having a child. Our first baby changed me as a psychologist. It made the behaviorism I had been so enthusiastic about look so foolish that I could not stomach it any more. It was impossible. Having a second baby, and learning how profoundly different people are even before birth, made it impossible for me to think in terms of the kind of learning psychology in which one can teach anybody anything. Or the John B. Watson [1] theory of "Give me two babies and I will make one into this and one into the other." It is as if he never had any children. We know only too well that a parent cannot make his children into anything. Children make themselves into something. The best we can do and frequently the most effect we can have is by serving as something to react against if the child presses too hard.

Another profound learning experience that I value far more highly than any particular course or any degree that I have ever had was my personal psychoanalysis: discovering my own identity, my own self. Another basic experience—far more important—was getting married. This was certainly far more important than my Ph.D. by way of instructiveness. If one thinks in terms of the developing of the kinds of wisdom, the kinds of understanding, the kinds of life skills that we would want, then he must think in terms of what I would like to call *intrinsic* education—*intrinsic* learning; that is, learning to be a human being in general, and second, learning to be *this* particular human being. I am now very busily occupied in trying to catch up with all the epiphenomena of this notion of intrinsic education. Certainly one thing I can tell you. Our conventional education looks mighty sick. Once you start thinking in this framework, that is, in terms of becoming a good human being, and if then you ask the question about the courses that you took in high school, "How did my trigonometry course help me to become a better human being?" an echo answers, "By gosh, it didn't!" In a certain sense, trigonometry was for me a waste of time. My early music education was also not very successful, because it taught a child who had a very profound feeling for music and a great love for the piano *not*

---

[1] John B. Watson, 1875–1958, was an American psychologist who originated behaviorism. He believed that behavior is shaped by physiological response to stimuli, and he rejected the concept of inner consciousness (Ed.).

to learn it. I had a piano teacher who taught me in effect that music is something to stay away from. And I had to relearn music as an adult, all by myself.

Observe that I have been talking about ends. This is a revolutionary repudiation of nineteenth-century science and of contemporary professional philosophy, which is essentially a technology and not a philosophy of ends. I have rejected thereby, as theories of human nature, positivism, behaviorism, and objectivism. I have rejected thereby the whole model of science and all its works that have been derived from the historical accident that science began with the study of nonpersonal, nonhuman things, which in fact had no ends. The development of physics, astronomy, mechanics, and chemistry was in fact impossible until they had become value-free, value-neutral, so that pure descriptiveness was possible. The great mistake that we are now learning about is that this model, which developed from the study of objects and of things, has been illegitimately used for the study of human beings. It is a terrible technique. It has not worked.

Most of the psychology on this positivitic model, on this objectivistic, associationistic, value-free, value-neutral model of science, as it piles up like a coral reef or like mountains and mountains of small facts about this and that, is certainly not false, but merely trivial. I would like to point out here that, in order not to sell my own science short, I think we do know a great deal about things that *do* matter to the human being, but I would maintain that what has mattered to the human being that we have learned has been learned mostly by non-physicalistic techniques, by the humanistic science techniques of which we have become more conscious.

In speaking of the world situation at the opening ceremonies of a recent Lincoln Center Festival, Archibald MacLeish said in part:

What is wrong is not the great discoveries of science—information is always better than ignorance, no matter what information or what ignorance. What is wrong is the belief behind the information, the belief that information will change the world. It won't. Information without human understanding is like an answer without its question—meaningless. And human understanding is only possible through the arts. It is the work of art that creates the human perspective in which information turns to truth. . . . .

In a certain sense I disagree with MacLeish, although I can understand why he said this. What he is talking about is information *short of this new revolution,* short of the humanistic psychologies, short of the conceptions of the sciences that not only repudiate the notion of being value-free and value-neutral, but actually assume as an obligation, as a duty, the necessity for discovery of values—the empirical discovery, demonstration, and verification of the values that are inherent in human nature itself. This work is now busily going on.

What Mr. MacLeish said was appropriate for the era from 1920 to 1930. It is appropriate today if one doesn't know about the new psychologies. "And human understanding is only possible through the arts." That *was* true. Fortunately, it is no longer true. It now is possible to gather *information* that can contribute to human understanding, that carries imbedded within it value hints, vectorial and directional information, information that goes someplace.

"It is the work of art that creates the human perspective in which information turns to truth." I deny that, and we had better argue about that. We must have some criteria for distinguishing good art from bad art. They do not yet exist in the realms of art criticism so far as I know. They are *beginning* to exist, and I would like to leave one hint, an empirical hint. A possibility is beginning to emerge that we would have some objective criteria for discriminating good art from bad art.

If your situation is like mine, you know that we are in a complete and total confusion of values in the arts. In music, just try to prove something about the virtues of John Cage as against Beethoven—or Elvis Presley. In painting and architecture similar confusion is present. We have no shared values anymore. I don't bother to read music criticism. It is useless to me. So is art criticism, which I have also given up reading. Book reviews I find useless frequently. There is a complete chaos and anarchy of standards. For instance, the *Saturday Review* recently carried a favorable review of one of Jean Genet's crummy books. Written by a professor of theology, it was total confusion. It was the approach that Evil now has become Good because there is some kind of paradox while playing with words: If evil becomes totally evil, then it somehow becomes good, and there were rhapsodies to the beauties of sodomy and drug addiction, which, for a poor psychologist who spends much of his time trying to rescue people from the anguish of these kinds of things, were incomprehensible. How can a grown man recommend this book as a chapter in ethics and a guide to the young?

If Archibald MacLeish says that works of art lead to the truth, Archibald MacLeish is thinking about particular works of art that Archibald MacLeish has picked out, but ones his son might not agree with. And *then*, MacLeish really has nothing much to say. There is no way of convincing anybody about this point. I think this could be some symbol of the way in which I feel that we are at a turning point. We are moving around the corner. Something new is happening. There are discernible differences—and these are not differences in taste or arbitrary values. These are empirical discoveries. They are new things that are being found out, and from these are generated all sorts of propositions about values and education.

One is the discovery that the human being *has higher needs*, that he has instinctlike needs, which are a part of his biological equipment—the need to be dignified, for instance, and to be respected, and the need to be free for self-development. The discovery of higher needs carries with it all sorts of revolutionary implications.

Secondly, the point I have already made about the social sciences: Many people are beginning to discover that the physicalistic, mechanistic model was a mistake and that it has led us . . . where? To atom bombs. To a beautiful technology of killing, as in the concentration camps. To Eichmann. An Eichmann cannot be refuted with a positivistic philosophy or science. He just cannot; and he never got it until the moment he died. He didn't know what was wrong. As far as he was concerned, nothing was wrong; he had done a good job. He *did* do a good job, if you forget about the ends and the values. I point out that professional science and professional philosophy are dedicated to the proposition of forgetting about the values, excluding them. This, therefore, must lead to Eichmanns, to atom bombs, and to who knows what!

I'm afraid that the tendency to separate good style or talent from content and ends can lead to this kind of danger.

The great discoveries Freud made, we can now add to. His one big mistake, which we are correcting now, is that he thought of the unconscious merely as undesirable evil. But unconsciousness carries in it also the roots of creativeness, of joy, of happiness, of goodness, of its own human ethics and values. We know that there is such a thing as a healthy unconscious as well as an unhealthy one. And the new psychologies are studying this at full tilt. The existential psychiatrists and psychotherapists are actually putting it into practice. New kinds of therapies are being practiced.

So we have a good conscious and a bad conscious—and a good unconscious and a bad unconscious. Furthermore, the good is real, in a non-Freudian sense. Freud was committed by his own positivism. Remember, Freud came out of a physicalistic, chemicalistic science. He was a neurologist. And a sworn oath that is in print called for a project to develop a psychology that could be entirely reduced to physical and chemical statements. This is what he dedicated himself to. He himself disproved his point, of course.

And about this higher nature that I claim we have discovered, the question is, how do we explain it? The Freudian explanation has been reductive. Explain it away. If I am a kind man, this is a reaction formation against my rage to kill. Somehow, here the killing is more basic than the kindness. And the kindness is a way of trying to cover up, repress, and defend myself against realizing the fact that I am truly a murderer. If I am generous, this is a reaction formation against stinginess. I am really stingy inside. This is a very peculiar thing. Somehow there is the begging of the question that is so obvious now. Why did he not say, for instance, that maybe killing people was a reaction formation against loving them? It is just as legitimate a conclusion and, as a matter of fact, more true for many people.

But to return to the principal idea, this exciting new development in science, this new moment in history. I have a very strong sense of being in the middle of a historical wave. One hundred and fifty years from now, what will the historians say about this age? What was really important? What was going? What was finished? My belief is that much of what makes the headlines is finished, and the "growing tip" of mankind is what is now growing and will flourish in a hundred or two hundred years, if we manage to endure. Historians will be talking about this movement as the sweep of history, that here, as Whitehead pointed out, when you get a new model, a new paradigm, a new way of perceiving, new definitions of the old words, words which now mean something else, suddenly, you have an illumination, an insight. You can see things in a different way.[2]

For instance, one of the consequences generated by what I have been talking about, is a flat denial, an *empirical* denial (not pious, or arbitrary, or *a priori*, or wishful) of the Freudian contention of a necessary, intrinsic, built-in opposition between the needs of the individual and the needs of society and civilization. It just is not so. We now know something about how to set up the conditions in which the needs of the individual become synergic with, not opposed to, the needs of society, and in which they both work to the same ends. This is an empirical statement, I claim.

Another empirical statement is about the peak experiences. We have made studies of peak experiences by asking groups of people and individuals such questions as, What was the most ecstatic moment of your life? Or as one investigator asked, Have you experienced transcendent ecstasy? One might think that in a general population, such questions might get only blank stares, but there were many answers. Apparently, the transcendent ecstasies had all been kept private, because there is no way of speaking about them in public. They are sort of embarrassing, shameful, not "scientific"—which, for many people, is the ultimate sin.

In our investigations of peak experiences, we found many, many

---

[2] Maslow is referring to the experience of a fundamental intuition that triggers the creative process in a person. Alfred North Whitehead is merely one among many persons who have attested to its actualizing or peak-like knowledge (Ed.).

triggers, many kinds of experiences that would set them off. Apparently most people, or almost all people, have peak experiences, or ecstasies. The question might be asked in terms of the single most joyous, happiest, most blissful moment of your whole life. You might ask questions of the kind I asked. How did you feel different about yourself at that time? How did the world look different? What did you feel like? What were your impulses? How did you change if you did? I want to report that the two easiest ways of getting peak experiences (in terms of simple statistics in empirical reports) are through music and through sex. I will push aside sex education, as such discussions are premature—although I am certain that one day we will not giggle over it, but will take it quite seriously and teach children that like music, like love, like insight, like a beautiful meadow, like a cute baby, or whatever, that there are many paths to heaven, and sex is one of them, and music is one of them. These happen to be the easiest ones, the most widespread, and the ones that are easiest to understand.

For our purposes in identifying and studying peak experiences, we can say it is justified to make a list of kinds of triggers. The list gets so long that it becomes necessary to make generalizations. It looks as if any experience of real excellence, of real perfection, of any moving toward the perfect justice or toward perfect values tends to produce a peak experience. Not always. But this is the generalization I would make for the many kinds of things that we have concentrated on. Remember, I am talking here as a scientist. This doesn't sound like scientific talk, but this is a new kind of science. A dissertation will soon be published which will show that out of this humanistic science has come, I would say, one of the real childbearing improvements since Adam and Eve. It is a dissertation on peak experiences in natural childbirth. And this can be a potent source of peak experiences. We know just how to encourage peak experiences; we know the best way for women to have children in such a fashion that the childbearing mother is apt to have a great and mystical experience, a religious experience if you wish—an illumination, a revelation, an insight. That is what they call it, by the way, in the interviews—to simply become a different kind of person because, in a fair number of peak experiences, there ensues what I have called "the cognition of being."

We must make a new vocabulary for all these untilled, these unworked problems. This "cognition of being" means really the cognition that Plato and Socrates were talking about; almost, you could say, a technology of happiness, or pure excellence, pure truth, pure goodness, and so on. Well, why *not* a technology of joy, of happiness? I must add that this is the only known technique for inducing peak experiences in fathers. It had occurred to us, as my wife and I had first gotten to these surveys in college students, that many triggers were discovered. One of them was that while women talked about peak experiences from having children, men didn't. Now we have a way to teach men also to have peak experiences from childbirth. This means, in a certain condensed sense, being changed, seeing things differently, living in a different world, having different cognitions, in a certain sense some move toward living happily ever after. Now these are data, various paths to mystical experiences. I think that I had better pass them by as they are so numerous.

So far, I have found that these peak experiences are reported from what we might call "classical music." I have not found a peak experience from John Cage or from an Andy Warhol movie, from abstract-expressionistic kind of painting, or the like. I just haven't. The peak experience that has reported the great joy, the ecstasy, the visions of another world, or another level of living, has come from classical music—the great classics. Also I must report that this melts over, fuses over, into dancing or rhythm. So far as this realm of research is concerned, there really isn't much difference between them; they melt into each other. I may add, even, that when I was talking about music as a path to peak experiences, I included dancing. For me they have already melted together. The rhythmic experience, even the very simple rhythmic experience—the good dancing of a rumba, or the kinds of things that the kids can do with drums: I don't know whether you want to call that music, dancing, rhythm, athletics, or something else. The love for the body, awareness of the body, and a reverence of the body—these are clearly good paths to peak experiences. These in turn are good paths (not guaranteed, but statistically likely to be good paths; to the "cognition of being," to the perceiving of the Platonic essences, the intrinsic values, the ultimate values of being, which in turn is a therapeutic-like help toward both the curing-of-sicknesses kind of therapy and also the growth toward self-actualization, the growth toward full humanness.

In other words, peak experiences often have consequences. They can have very, very important consequences: Music and art in a certain sense can do the same; there is a certain overlap. They can do the same there as psychotherapy, if one keeps his goals right, and if one knows just what he is about, and if one is conscious of what he is going toward. We can certainly talk, on the one hand, of the breaking up of symptoms, like the breaking up of clichés, of anxieties, or the like; or on the other hand, we can talk about the development of spontaneity, and of courage, and of Olympian or Godlike humor and suchness, sensory awareness, body awareness, and the like.

Far from least, it happens that music and rhythm and dancing

are excellent ways of moving toward the discovering of identity. We
are built in such a fashion that this kind of trigger, this kind of stimulation, tends to do all kinds of things to our autonomic nervous systems, endocrine glands, to our feelings, and to our emotions. It just
does. We just do not know enough about physiology to understand
why it does. But it does, and these are unmistakable experiences. It
is a little like pain, which is also an unmistakable experience. In experientially empty people, which includes a tragically large proportion of the population, people who do not know what is goin on inside themselves and who live by clocks, schedules, rules, laws, hints
from the neighbors—other-directed people—this is a way of discovering what the self is like. There are signals from inside, there are
voices that yell out, "By gosh this is good, don't ever doubt it!" This
is a path, one of the ways that we try to teach self-actualization and
the discovery of self. The discovery of identity comes via the impulse voices, via the ability to listen to your own guts, and to their reactions and to what is going on inside of you. This is also an experimental kind of education that, if we had the time to talk about it,
would lead us into another parallel educational establishment, another *kind* of school.

Mathematics can be just as beautiful, just as peak-producing as
music; of course, there are mathematics teachers who have devoted
themselves to preventing this. I had no glimpse of mathematics as a
study in aesthetics until I was thirty years old, until I read some
books on the subject. So can history, or anthropology (in the sense of
learning another culture), social anthropology, or paleontology, or
the study of science. Here again I want to talk data. If one works
with great creators, great scientists, the creative scientists, *that* is the
way they talk. The picture of the scientist must change, and is giving
way to an understanding of the creative scientist, and the creative
scientist lives by peak experiences. He lives for the moments of
glory when a problem solves itself, when suddenly through a micro-
scope he sees things in a very different way, the moments of revelation, of illumination, insight, understanding, ecstasy. These are vital
for him. Scientists are very, very shy and embarrassed about this.
They refuse to talk about this in public. It takes a very, very delicate
kind of a midwifery to get these things out, but I have gotten them
out. They are there, and if one can manage to convince a creative scientist that he is not going to be laughed at for these things, then he
will blushingly admit the fact of having a high emotional experience
from, for example, the moment in which the crucial correlation turns
out right. They just don't talk about it, and as for the usual textbook
on how you do science, it is total nonsense.

My point here is that it is possible; that if we are conscious enough of what we are doing, that is, if we are philosophical enough in the insightful sense too, we may be able to use those experiences that most easily produce ecstasies, that most easily produce revelations, experiences, illumination, bliss, and rapture experiences. We may be able to use them as a model by which to re-evaluate history teaching or any other kind of teaching.

Finally, the impression that I want to try to work out—and I would certainly suggest that this is a problem for everyone involved in arts education—is that effective education in music, education in art, education in dancing and rhythm, is intrinsically far closer than the usual "core curriculum" to intrinsic education of the kind that I am talking about, of learning one's identity as an essential part of education. If education doesn't do that, it is useless. Education is learning to grow, learning what to grow toward, learning what is good and bad, learning what is desirable and undesirable, learning what to choose and what not to choose. In this realm of intrinsic learning, intrinsic teaching, and intrinsic education, I think that the arts, and especially the ones that I have mentioned, are so close to our psychological and biological core, so close to this identity, this biological identity, that rather than think of these courses as a sort of whipped cream or luxury, they must become basic experiences in education. I mean that this kind of education can be a glimpse into the infinite, into ultimate values. This intrinsic education may very well have art education, music education, and dancing education as its core. (I think dancing is the one I would choose first for children. It is the easiest for the two-, three-, or four-year-old children—just plain rhythm.) Such experiences could very well serve as the model, the means by which perhaps we could rescue the rest of the school curriculum from the value-free, value-neutral, goal-less meaninglessness into which it has fallen.

Goals and Implications of Humanistic Education

ABRAHAM H. MASLOW

Just before he died, Aldous Huxley was on the brink of an enormous breakthrough, on the verge of creating a great synthesis between science, religion, and art. Many of his ideas are illustrated in his last novel, *Island*. Although *Island* is not very signficant as a work of art, it is very exciting as an essay on what man is capable of becoming. The most revolutionary ideas in it are those pertaining to education, for the educational system in Huxley's Utopia is aimed at radically different goals than the educational system of our own society.

If we look at education in our own society, we see two sharply different factors. First of all, there is the overwhelming majority of teachers, principals, curriculum planners, school superintendents, who are devoted to passing on the knowledge that children need in order to live in our industrialized society. They are not especially imaginative or creative, nor do they often question *why* they are teaching the things they teach. Their chief concern is with efficiency, that is, with implanting the greatest number of facts into the greatest possible number of children, with a minimum of time, expense, and effort. On the other hand, there is the minority of humanistically oriented educators who have as their goal the creation of better human beings, or in psychological terms, self-actualization and self-transcendence.

Classroom learning often has as its unspoken goal the reward of pleasing the teacher. Children in the usual classroom learn very quickly that creativity is punished, while repeating a memorized response is rewarded, and concentrate on what the teacher wants them to say, rather than understanding the problem. Since classroom learning focuses on behavior rather than on thought, the child learns exactly how to behave while keeping his thoughts his own.

Thought, in fact, is often inimical to extrinsic learning. The effects of propaganda, indoctrination, and operant conditioning all disappear with insight. Take advertising, for example. The simplest medicine for it is the truth. You may worry about subliminal advertising and motivational research, but all you need are the data which prove that a particular brand of toothpaste stinks, and you'll be impervious to all the advertising in the world. As another example of destructive effect of truth upon extrinsic learning, a psychology class played a joke on their professor by secretly conditioning him while he was delivering a lecture on conditioning. The professor, without realizing it, began nodding more and more, and by the end of the lecture he was nodding continually. As soon as the class told the professor what he was doing, however, he stopped nodding, and of course after that no amount of smiling on the part of the class could make him nod again. Truth made the learning disappear. Extending this point, we ought to ask ourselves how much classroom learning is actually supported by ignorance, would be destroyed by insight.

Students, of course, have been steeped in attitudes of extrinsic learning and respond to grades and examiniations as the chimps responded to the poker chips. In one of the best universities in the country a boy sat on the campus reading a book, and a friend passing by asked him why he was reading that particular book as it hadn't been assigned. The only reason for reading a book could be the extrinsic rewards that it would bring. In the poker-chip milieu of the university, the question was logical.

The difference between the intrinsic and the extrinsic aspects of a college education is illustrated by the following story about Upton Sinclair. When Sinclair was a young man, he found that he was unable to raise the tuition money needed to attend college. Upon careful reading of the college catalogue, however, he found that if a student failed a course, he received no credit for the course, but was obliged to take another course in its place. The college did not charge the student for the second course, reasoning that he had already paid once for his credit. Sinclair took advantage of this policy and got a free education by deliberately failing all his courses.

The phrase "earning a degree" summarizes the evils of extrinsically oriented education. The student automatically gets his degree after investing a certain number of hours at the university, referred to as credits. All the knowledge taught in the university has its "cash value" in credits, with little or no distinction made between various subjects taught at the university. A semester of basketball coaching, for example, earns the student as many credits as a semester in French philology. Since only the final degree is considered to have any real value, leaving college before the completion of one's senior year is considered to be a waste of time by the society and a minor tragedy by parents. You have all heard of the mother bemoaning her daughter's foolishness in leaving school to get married during her senior year since the girl's education had been "wasted." The learning value of spending three years at the university has been completely forgotten.

In the ideal college, there would be no credits, no degrees, and no required courses. A person would learn what he wanted to learn. A friend and I attempted to put this ideal into action by starting a series of seminars at Brandeis called "Freshman Seminars—Introduction to the Intellectual Life." We announced that the course would have no required reading or writing and give no credits, and that whatever was discussed would be of the student's own choosing. We also stated who we were—a professor of psychology and a practicing psychiatrist, expecting that the description of the seminar and of our own interests would indicate to the student who should come and who should not. The students who came to this seminar came of their own volition and were at least partially responsible for its successes and failures. The exact opposite holds true for the classical schoolroom—it is compulsory, people have been forced into it one way or another.

In the ideal college, intrinsic education would be available to anyone who wanted it—since anyone can improve and learn. The student body might include creative, intelligent children as well as adults; morons as well as geniuses (for even morons can learn emotionally and spiritually). The college would be ubiquitous—that is, not restricted to particular buildings at particular times, and the teachers would be any human beings who had something that they wanted to share with others. The college would be lifelong, for learning can take place all through life. Even dying can be a philosophically illuminating, highly educative experience.

The ideal college would be a kind of educational retreat in which you could try to find yourself; find out what you like and want; what you are and are not good at. People would take various subjects, attend various seminars, not quite sure of where they were going, but moving toward the discovery of vocation, and *once they found it,* they could then make good use of technological education. The chief goals of the ideal college, in other words, would be the *discovery of identity,* and with it, the *discovery of vocation.*

What do we mean by the discovery of identity? We mean finding out what your real desires and characteristics are, and being able to live in a way that expresses them. You learn to be authentic, to be honest in the sense of allowing your behavior and your speech to be the true and spontaneous expression of your inner feelings. Most of us have learned to avoid authenticity. You may be in the middle of a fight, and your guts are writhing with anger, but if the phone rings, you pick it up and sweetly say hello. Authenticity is the reduction of phoniness toward the zero point.

There are many techniques for teaching authenticity. The T group is an effort to make you aware of who you really are, of how you really react to other people, by giving you a chance to be honest, to tell what is really going on inside of you instead of presenting façades or giving polite evasions.

People whom we describe as healthy, strong, and definite seem to be able to hear their inner-feeling-voices more clearly than most people. They know what they want, and they know equally clearly what they don't want. Their inner preferences tell them that one color doesn't go with another, and that they don't want wool clothing because it makes them itch, or that they dislike superficial sexual relations. Other people, in contrast, seem to be empty, out of touch with their own inner signals. They eat, defecate, and go to sleep by the clock's cues, rather than by the cues of their own bodies. They use external criteria for everything from choosing their food ("it's good for you") and clothing ("it's in style") to questions of values and ethics ("my daddy told me to").

We do a very good job of confusing our young children about their own inner voices. A child may say, "I don't want any milk," and his mother replies, "Why, you know you want some milk." Or he may say, "I don't like spinach," and she tells him, "We love spinach." An important part of self-knowledge is being able to hear clearly these signals from the inside, and the mother is not helping her child when she confuses their clarity for him. It would be just as easy for her to say, "I know you don't like spinach, but you have to eat it anyway for such-and-such reasons."

Aesthetic people seem to have clearer impulse voices than most people about matters of colors, relationships of appearances, suitability of patterns, etc. People with high IQs seem to have similarly strong impulse voices about perceiving truth seeing that this relationship is true and that one is not, in the same way that aesthetically gifted people seem to be able to see that this tie goes well with this jacket but not that one. Presently a lot of research is being done on the relationshp between creativity and high IQ in children. Creative children seem to be those who have strong impulse voices that tell them what is right and what is wrong. Noncreative high IQ children seem to have lost their impulse voices and become domesticated, so that they look to the parent or the teacher for guidance or inspiration.

Healthy people seem to have clear impulse voices about matters of ethics and values, as well. Self-actualizing people have to a large extent transcended the values of their culture. They are not so much merely Americans as they are world citizens, members of the human species first and foremost. They are able to regard their own society objectively, liking some aspects of it, disliking others. If an ultimate goal of education is self-actualization, then education ought to help people transcend the conditioning imposed upon them by their own culture and become world citizens. Here the technical question of how to enable people to overcome their enculturation arises. How do you awaken the sense of brotherhood to all mankind in a young child that is going to enable him to hate war as an adult and do all that he can to avoid it? The churches and Sunday schools have carefully avoided this task, and instead teach the children colorful Bible tales.

Another goal which our schools and teachers should be pursuing is the discovery of vocation, of one's fate and destiny. Part of learning who you are, part of being able to hear your inner voices, is discovering what it is that you want to do with your life. Finding one's identity is almost synonymous with finding one's career, revealing the altar on which one will sacrifice oneself. Finding one's lifework is a little like finding one's mate. One custom is for young people to "play the field," to have a lot of contacts with people, a love affair or two, and perhaps a serious trial marriage before getting married. In this way they discover what they like and don't like in members of the opposite sex. As they become more and more conscious of their own needs and desires, those people who know themselves well enough eventually just find and recognize one another. Sometimes very similar things happen when you find your career, your lifework. It feels right and suddenly you find that twenty-four hours aren't a long-enough time span for the day, and you begin bemoaning the shortness of human life. In our schools, however, many vocational counselors have no sense of the possible goals of human existence, or even of what is necessary for basic happiness. All this type of counselor considers is the need of the society for aeronautical engineers or dentists. No one ever mentions that if you are unhappy with your work, you have lost one of the most important means of self-fulfillment.

Summarizing what we have said, the schools should be helping the children to look within themselves, and from this self-knowledge derive a set of values. Yet values are not taught in our schools today. This may be a holdover from the religious wars in which the church and the state were made separate and the rulers decided that the discussion of values would be the church's concern, whereas the secular schools would concern themselves with other problems. Perhaps it is fortunate that our schools, with their grievous lack of a real philosophy and of suitably trained teachers, do *not* teach values, just as it is fortunate they have not taught sex education for the same reasons.

Among the many educational consequences generated by the humanistic philosophy of education is a different conception of the self. This is a very complex conception, difficult to describe briefly, because it talks for the first time in centuries of an *essence*, of an *intrinsic* nature, of specieshood, of a kind of animal nature. This is in sharp contrast with the European existentialist, most especially with Sartre, for whom man is *entirely* his own project, *entirely* and merely a product of his own arbitrary, unaided will. For Sartre and all those whom he has influenced, one's self becomes an arbitrary choice, a willing by fiat to be something or do something without any guidelines about which is better, which is worse, what's good and what's bad. In essentially denying the existence of biology, Sartre has given up altogether any absolute or at least any species-wide conception of values. This comes very close to making a life-philosophy of the obsessive-compulsive neurosis in which one finds what I have called "experiental emptiness," the absence of impulse voices from within.

The American humanistic psychologists and existential psychiatrists are mostly closer to the psychodynamicists than they are to Sartre. Their clinical experiences have led them to conceive of the human being as having an essence, a biological nature, membership in a species. It is very easy to interpret the "uncovering" therapies as helping the person to *discover* his Identity, his Real Self, in a word, his own subjective biology, which he can *then* proceed to actualize, to "make himself," to "choose."

The trouble is that the human species is the only species which finds it hard to be a species. For a cat there seems to be no problem about being a cat. It's easy; cats seem to have no complexes or ambivalences or conflicts, and show no signs of yearning to be dogs instead. Their instincts are very clear. But *we* have no such unequivocal animal instincts. Our biological essence, our instinct remnants, are weak and subtle, and they are hard to get at. Learnings of the extrinsic sort *are more powerful than our deepest impulses.* These deepest impulses in the human species, at the points where the instincts have been lost almost entirely, where they are extremely weak, extremely subtle and delicate, where you have to dig to find them, *this* is where I speak of introspective biology, of biological phenomenology, implying that one of the necessary methods in the search for identity, the search for self, the search for spontaneity and for naturalness is a matter of closing your eyes, cutting down the noise, turning off the thoughts, putting away all busyness, just relaxing in a kind of Taoistic and receptive fashion (in much the same way that you do on the psychoanalyst's couch). The technique here is to just wait to see what happens, what comes to mind. This is what Freud called free association, free-floating attention rather than task orientation, and if you are successful in this effort and learn how to do it, you can forget about the outside world and its noises and begin to hear these small, delicate impulse voices from within, the hints from your animal nature, not only from your common species-nature, but also from your own uniqueness.

There's a very interesting paradox here, however. On the one hand I've talked about uncovering or discovering your idiosyncrasy, the way in which you are different from everybody else in the whole world. Then on the other hand I've spoken about discovering your specieshood, your humanness. As Carl Rogers has phrased it: "How does it happen that the deeper we go into ourselves as particular and unique, seeking for our own individual identity, the more we find the whole human species?" Doesn't that remind you of Ralph Waldo Emerson and the New England Transcendentalists? Discovering your specieshood, at a deep enough level, merges with discovering your selfhood. Becoming (learning how to be) fully human means *both* enterprises carried on simultaneously. You are learning (subjectively experiencing) what you peculiarly are, how you are you, what your potentialities are, what your style is, what your pace is, what your tastes are, what your values are, what direction your body is going, where your personal biology is taking you, i.e., how you are *different* from others. And at the same time it means learning what it means to be a human animal like other human animals, i.e., how you are *similar* to others.

One of the goals of education should be to teach that life is precious. If there were no joy in life, it would not be worth living. Unfortunately many people never experience joy, those all-too-few moments of total life-affirmation which we call peak experiences. Fromm spoke about the life-wishers who often experienced joy, and the death-wishers who never seemed to experience moments of joy and whose hold on life was very weak. The latter group would take all sorts of idiotic chances with their lives, as though they were hoping that an accident would save them from the trouble of committing suicide. Under adverse conditions, such as in concentration camps, those to whom every moment of life was precious struggled to keep alive, while the others let themselves die without resistance. We are beginning to find out through such agencies as Synanon that drug addicts, who are killing a part of themselves, will give up drugs easily if you offer them instead some meaning to their lives. Psychologists have described alcoholics as being fundamentally depressed, basically bored with life. They describe their existence as an endless flat plain with no ups or downs. Colin Wilson, in his book, *Introduction to the New Existentialism,* pointed out that life has to have meaning, has to be filled with moments of high intensity that validate life and make it worthwhile. Otherwise the desire to die makes sense, for who would want to endure endless pain or endless boredom?

We know that children are capable of peak experiences and that they happen frequently during childhood. We also know that the present school system is an extremely effective instrument for crushing peak experiences and forbidding their possibility. The natural child-respecting teacher who is not frightened by the sight of children enjoying themselves is a rare sight in classrooms. Of course, with the traditional model of thirty-five children in one classroom and a curriculum of subject matter which has to be gotten through in a given period of time, the teacher is forced to pay more attention to orderliness and lack of noise than she is making learning a joyful experience. But then our official philosophies of education and teachers' colleges seem to have as an implicit assumption that it is dangerous for a child to have a good time. Even the difficult tasks of learning to read and subtract and multiply, which are necessary in an industrialized society, can be enhanced and made joyful.

What can the schools do to counteract the death wish in kindergarten, to strengthen the wish for life in the first grade? Perhaps the most important thing they can do is to give the child a sense of accomplishment. Children get a great deal of satisfaction in helping someone younger or weaker than themselves accomplish something. The child's creativity can be encouraged by avoiding regimentation. Since the children imitate the attitudes of the teacher, the teacher can be encouraged to become a joyful and self-actualizing person. The parents convey their own distorted patterns of behavior to the child, but if the teacher's are healthier and stronger, the children will imitate these instead.

In the first place, unlike the current model of teacher as lecturer, conditioner, reinforcer, and boss, the Taoist helper is receptive rather than intrusive. I was told once that in the world of boxers, a youngster who feels himself to be good and who wants to be a boxer will go to a gym, look up one of the managers, and say, "I'd like to be a pro, and I'd like to be in your stable. I'd like you to manage me." In this world, what is then done characteristically is to try him out. The good manager will select one of his professionals and say, "Take him on in the ring. Stretch him. Strain him. Let's see what he can do. Just let him show his very best. Draw him out." If it turns out that the boxer has promise, if he's a "natural," then what the good manager does is to take that boy and train him to be, if this is Joe Dokes, a *better Joe Dokes*. That is, he takes his style as given and builds upon that. He does not start all over again, and say, "Forget all you've learned, and do it this new way," which is like saying, "Forget what kind of body you have," or "Forget what you are good for." He takes him and builds upon his *own* talents and builds him up into the very best Joe Dokes-type boxer that he possibly can.

It is my strong impression that this is the way in which much of the world of education could function. If we want to be helpers, counselors, teachers, guiders, or psychotherapists, what we must do is to accept the person and help him learn what kind of person he is already. What is his style, what are his aptitudes, what is he good for, not good for, what can we build upon, what are his good raw materials, his good potentialities? We would be nonthreatening and would supply an atmosphere of acceptance of the child's nature which reduces fear, anxiety, and defense to the minimum possible. Above all, we would care for the child, that is, enjoy him and his growth and self-actualization. So far this sounds much like the Rogerian therapist, his "unconditional positive regard," his congruence, his openness and his caring. And indeed there is evidence by now that this "brings the child out," permits him to express and to act, to experiment, and even to make mistakes; to let himself be seen. Suitable feedback at this point, as in T-groups or basic encounter groups, or nondirective counseling, then leads the child to discover what and who he is. We must learn to treasure the "jags" of the child in school, his fascination, absorptions, his persistent wide-eyed wonderings, his Dionysian enthusiasms. At the very least, we can value his more diluted raptures, his "interests," and hobbies, etc. They can lead to much. Especially can they lead to hard work, persistent, absorbed, fruitful, educative.

And conversely I think it is possible to think of the peak experience, the experience of awe, mystery, wonder, or of perfect completion, as the goal and reward of learning as well, its end as well as its beginning. If this is true for the *great* historians, mathematicians, scientists, musicians, philosophers, and all the rest, why should we not try to maximize these studies as sources of peak experiences for the child as well?

I must say that whatever little knowledge and experience I have to support these suggestions comes from intelligent and creative children rather than from retarded or underprivileged or sick ones. However, I must also say that my experience with such unpromising adults in Synanon, in T-groups, in Theory-Y industry, in Esalen-type educative centers, in Grof-type work with psychedelic chemicals, not to mention Laing-type work with psychotics, and other such experiences, has taught me never to write *anybody* off in advance.

Another important goal of intrinsic education is to see that the child's basic psychological needs are satisfied. A child cannot reach self-actualization until his needs for security, belongingness, dignity, love, respect, and esteem are all satisfied. In psychological terms, the child is free from anxiety because he feels himself to be love-worthy, and knows that he belongs in the world, that someone respects and wants him. Most of the drug addicts who come to Synanon have had a life devoid of almost all need-gratification. Synanon creates an atmosphere in which they are treated as if they were four-year-olds, and then slowly lets them grow up in an atmosphere which will allow their fundamental needs to be satisfied one by one.

Another goal of education is to refreshen consciousness so that we are continually aware of the beauty and wonder of life. Too often in this culture we become desensitized so that we never really see things we look at or hear the things we listen to. Laura Huxley had a little cube of magnifying glasses into which you could insert a tiny flower and look at the flower while it was illuminated from lights at the sides of the cubes. After a while the watcher would become lost in the experience of total attention, and from that would arise the psychedelic experience, which is seeing the absolute concreteness of a thing and the wonder of its existence. A very good trick for refreshening the quality of daily experience is imagining that you are going to die—or that the other person you are with is going to die. If you are actually threatened by death, you perceive in a different way with closer attention than you do ordinarily. If you know that a particular person is going to die, you see him more intensely, more personally, without the casual categorizing that marks so much of our experience. You must fight stereotyping, never allowing yourself to get used to anything. Ultimately the best way of teaching, whether the subject is mathematics, history, or philosophy, is to make the students aware of the beauties involved. We need to teach our children unitive perception, the Zen experience of being able to see the temporal and the eternal simultaneously, the sacred and the profane in the same object.

We must once again learn to control our impulses. The days in which Freud treated overinhibited people are now long past, and today we are confronted with the opposite problem—that of expressing every impulse immediately. It is possible to teach people that controls are not necessarily repressive. Self-actualized people have a system of Apollonian controls in which the control and the gratification work together to make the gratification more pleasurable. They know, for example, that eating is more fun if you sit down at a well-set table with well-cooked food even though it takes more control to prepare the table and the food. Something similar is true for sex.

One of the tasks of real education is to transcend pseudoproblems and to grapple with the serious existential problems of life. All neurotic problems are pseudoproblems. The problems of evil and suffering, however, are real and must be faced by everybody sooner or later. Is it possible to reach a peak experience through suffering? We have found that the peak experience contains two components—an emotional one of ecstasy and an intellectual one of illumination. Both need not be present simultaneously. For example, the sexual orgasm can be extremely satisfying emotionally but not illuminate the person in any way. In confrontation with pain and death, a nonecstatic illumination can occur, as pointed out in Marghanita Laski's book, *Ecstasy*. We now have a fairly extensive literature on the psychology of death in which it is evident that some people do experience illumination and gain philosophical insight as they approach death. Huxley, in his book, *Island*, illustrates how a person can die with reconciliation and acceptance rather than being dragged out of life in an undignified way.

Another aspect of intrinsic education is learning how to be a good chooser. You can teach yourself to choose. Place yourself before two glasses of sherry, a cheap one and an expensive one, and see which one you like the best. Try seeing if you can tell the difference between two brands of cigarettes with your eyes closed. If you can't tell the difference, there is none. I found myself that I can tell the difference between good and cheap sherry, so I now buy expensive sherry. On the other hand, I can't tell the difference between good gin and cheap gin, so I buy the cheapest gin I can. If I can't tell the difference, why bother?

What do we really mean by self-actualization? What are the psychological characteristics that we are hoping to produce in our ideal educational system? The self-actualized person is in a state of good psychological health; his basic needs are satisfied so what is it that motivates him to become such a busy and capable person? For one thing, all self-actualized people have a cause they believe in, a vocation they are devoted to. When they say, "my work," they mean their mission in life. If you ask a self-actualized lawyer why he entered the field of law, what compensates for all the routine and trivia, he will eventually say something like, "Well, I just get mad when I see somebody taking advantage of somebody else. It isn't fair." Fairness to him is an ultimate value; he can't tell you *why* he values fairness any more than an artist can tell you why he values beauty. Self-actualizing people, in other words, seem to do what they do for the sake of ultimate, final values, which is for the sake of principles which seem *intrinsically worthwhile*. They protect and love these values, and if the values are threatened, they will be aroused to indignation, action, and often self-sacrifice. These values are not abstract to the self-actualizing person; they are as much a part of them as their bones and arteries. Self-actualizing people are motivated by the eternal verities, the B-Values, by pure truth and beauty in perfection. They go beyond polarities and try to see the underlying oneness; they try to integrate everything and make it more comprehensive.

The next question is, are these values instinctoid, inherent in the organism, just as the need for love or vitamin D are inherent in the organism? If you eliminate all vitamin D from your diet, you will become sick. We can call love a need for the same reason. If you take away all love from your children, it can kill them. Hospital staffs have learned that unloved babies die early from colds. Do we need truth in the same way? I find that if I am deprived of truth, I come down with a peculiar kind of sickness—I become paranoid, mistrusting everybody and trying to look behind everything, searching for hidden meanings to every event. This sort of chronic mistrustfulness is certainly a psychological disease. So I would say that being deprived of truth results in a pathology—a metapathology. A metapathology is the illness which results in being deprived of a B-Value.

The deprivation of beauty can cause illness. People who are aesthetically very sensitive become depressed and uncomfortable in ugly surroundings. It probably affects their menstruation, gives them headaches, etc.

I performed a series of experiments on beautiful and ugly surroundings to prove this point. When subjects saw pictures of faces to be judged in an ugly room, they viewed the people as being psychotic, paranoid, or dangerous, indicating that faces and presumably human beings look bad in ugly surroundings. How much the ugliness affects you depends on your sensitivity and the ease with which you can turn your attention away from the obnoxious stimuli. To carry the point further, living in an unpleasant environment with nasty people is a pathological force. If you choose beautiful and decent people to spend your time with, you will find that you feel better and more uplifted.

Justice is another B-Value, and history has given us plenty of examples of what happens to people when they are deprived of it over a long period of time. In Haiti, for example, people learn distrust of everything, cynicism about all other human beings, believing that underneath everything there must be rot and corruption.

The metapathological state of uselessness is of great interest to me. I have met many youngsters who fulfill all the criteria of self-actualization; their basic needs are gratified, they are using their capacities well and show no obvious psychological symptoms.

Yet they are disrupted and disturbed. They mistrust all the B-Values, all the values that people over thirty espouse, and regard such words as truth, goodness, and love as empty clichés. They have even lost faith in their ability to make a better world, and so all they can do is protest in a meaningless and destructive way. If you don't have a value-life, you may not be neurotic, but you suffer from a cognitive and spiritual sickness, for to a certain extent your relationship with reality is distorted and disturbed.

If B-Values are as necessary as vitamins and love, and if their absence can make you sick, then what people have talked about for thousands of years as the religious or platonic or rational life seems to be a very basic part of human nature. Man is a hierarchy of needs, with the biological needs at the base of the hierarchy and the spiritual needs at the top. Unlike the biological needs, however, the B-Values are not hierarchical in and of themselves. One is as important as the next, and each one can be defined in terms of all the others. Truth, for example, must be complete, aesthetic, comprehensive, and strangely enough, it must be funny in an Olympian godlike sense. Beauty must be true, good, comprehensive, etc. Now if the B-Values are all definable in terms of each other, we know from factor-analysis that some general factor underlies them all—a G-factor, to use the statistical term. The B-Values are not separate piles of sticks, but rather the different facets of one jewel. Both the scientist who is devoted to truth and the lawyer who is devoted to justice are devoted to the same thing. Each has found out that the aspect of the general value which suits him best is the one he is using in his life's work.

An interesting aspect of the B-Values is that they transcend many of the traditional dichotomies, such as selfishness and unselfishness, flesh and spirit, religious and secular. If you are doing the work that you love and are devoted to the value that you hold highest, you are being as selfish as possible, and yet are also being unselfish and altruistic. If you have introjected truth as a value so that it is as much a part of you as your blood, then if a lie is told anywhere in the world, it hurts you to find out about it. The boundaries of yourself in that sense now extend far beyond your personal sphere of interests to include the entire world. If an injustice is being committed against a person in Bulgaria or China, it is also being committed against you. Though you may never meet the person involved, you can feel his betrayal as your own.

Take the dichotomy of "religious" and "secular." The form of religion that was offered to me as a child seemed so ludicrous that I abandoned all interest in religion and experienced no desire to "find God." Yet my religious friends, at least those who had gotten beyond the peasants' view of God as having a skin and beard, talk about God the way I talk about B-Values. The questions that theologians consider of prime importance nowadays are questions such as the meaning of the universe, and whether or not the universe has a direction. The search for perfection, the discovery of adherence to values is the essence of the religious tradition. And many religious groups are beginning to declare openly that the external trappings of religion, such as not eating meat on Friday, are unimportant, even detrimental, because they confuse people as to what religion really is, and are beginning once again to commit themselves in practice as well as in theory to the B-Values.

People who enjoy and are committed to the B-Values also enjoy their basic need-gratifications more because they make them sacred. To lovers who view each other in terms of the B-Values as well as in terms of need fulfillment, sexual intercourse becomes a sacred ritual. To live the spiritual life, you don't have to sit on top of a pillar for ten years. Being able to live in the B-Values somehow makes the body and all its appetites holy.

If we were to accept as a major educational goal the awakening and fulfillment of the B-Values, which is simply another aspect of self-actualization, we would have a great flowering of a new kind of civilization. People would be stronger, healthier, and would take their own lives into their hands to a greater extent. With increased personal responsibility for one's personal life, and with a rational set of values to guide one's choosing, people would begin to actively change the society in which they lived. The movement toward psychological health is also the movement toward spiritual peace and social harmony.

The Goal: The Fully Functioning Person

CARL R. ROGERS

What are we striving for? Why is it that we desire the "best" (however we define that term) in family life, in the school, in the university, in the community? It is, I believe, because we hope to develop the "best" of human beings. But rarely do we give explicit thought to the exact meaning of this goal. What sort of human being do we wish to grow?

A number of years ago, writing as a psychotherapist, I tried to state my personal answer to this question. I make no apology for the fact that this chapter is cast in the framework of therapy. To my mind the "best" of education would produce a person very similar to the one produced by the "best" of therapy. Indeed it may be of help to teachers and educators to think of this issue in a setting outside the school. It may make it easier for them to see, in sharper focus, those points where they agree with the picture I paint, and those points where they disagree.

I suspect that each one of us, from time to time, speculates on the general characteristics of the optimal person. If education were as completely successful as we could wish it to be in promoting personal growth and development, what sort of person would emerge? Or, speaking from the field in which I have had the most experience, suppose psychotherapy were completed in optimal fashion, what sort of person would have developed? What is the hypothetical endpoint, the ultimate, of psychological growth and development? I wish to discuss this question from the point of view of therapy, but I believe the tentative answers which I formulate would be equally applicable to education, or to the family, or to any other situation

From *The Freedom to Learn* by Carl R. Rogers, pp. 279–297. Copyright © *Psychotherapy: Theory, Research and Practice*, 1963, 1, No. 1, 17–26. First two paragraphs credited to Charles E. Merrill Publishing Company. Permission granted by *Psychotherapy: Theory, Research and Practice*, Charles E. Merrill Publishing Company, and Carl R. Rogers.

which has as its aim the constructive development of persons. I am really raising the issue, what is the goal? What is the optimal person?

I have often asked myself this question and have felt an increasing dissatisfaction with the kind of answers which are current. They seem too slippery, too relativistic, to have much value in a developing science of personality. They often contain too, I believe, a concealed bias which makes them unsatisfactory. I think of the commonly held notion that the person who has completed therapy or is fully mature will be adjusted to society. But what society? Any society, no matter what its characteristics? I cannot accept this. I think of the concept, implicit in much psychological writing, that successful therapy means that a person will have moved from a diagnostic category considered pathological to one considered normal. But the evidence is accumulating that there is so little agreement on diagnostic categories as to make them practically meaningless as scientific concepts. And even if a person becomes "normal," is that a suitable outcome of therapy? Furthermore, the experience of recent years has made me wonder whether the term psychopathology may not be simply a convenient basket for all those aspects of personality which diagnosticians as a group are most afraid of in themselves. For these and other reasons, change in diagnosis is not a description of therapeutic outcome which is satisfying to me. If I turn to another type of concept, I find that the person whose psychological growth is optimal is said to have achieved a positive mental health. But who defines mental health? I suspect that the Menninger Clinic and the Center for Studies of the Person would define it rather differently. I am sure that the Soviet state would have still another definition.

Pushed about by questions such as these, I find myself speculating about the characteristics of the person who comes out of therapy, if therapy is maximally successful. I should like to share with you some of these tentative personal speculations. What I wish to do is to formulate a theoretical concept of the optimal end-point of therapy, or, indeed, of education. I would hope that I could state it in terms which would be free from some of the criticisms I have mentioned, terms which might eventually be given operational definition and objective test.

The Background from Which the Problem Is Approached

I shall have to make it clear at the outset that I am speaking from a background of client-centered therapy. Quite possibly all successful psychotherapy has a similar personality outcome, but I am less sure of that than formerly, and hence wish to narrow my field of consideration. So I shall assume that this hypothetical person whom I describe has had an intensive and extensive experience in client-centered therapy, and that the therapy has been as completely successful as is theoretically possible. This would mean that the therapist has been able to enter into an intensely personal and subjective relationship with this client—relating not as a scientist to an object of study, not as a physician expecting to diagnose and cure, but as a person to a person. It would mean that the therapist feels this client to be a person of unconditional self-worth; of value no matter what his condition, his behavior, or his feelings. It means that the therapist is able to let himself go in understanding this client; that no inner barriers keep him from sensing what it feels like to be the client at each moment of the relationship; and that he can convey something of his empathic understanding to the client. It means that the therapist has been comfortable in entering this relationship fully, without knowing cognitively where it will lead, satisfied with providing a climate which will free the client to become himself.

For the client, this optimal therapy has meant an exploration of increasingly strange and unknown and dangerous feelings in himself; the exploration proving possible only because he is gradually realizing that he is accepted unconditionally. Thus he becomes acquainted with elements of his experience which have in the past been denied to awareness as too threatening, too damaging to the structure of the self. He finds himself experiencing these feelings fully, completely, in the relationship, so that for the moment he is *his fear, or his anger, or his tenderness, or his strength. And as he lives these widely varied feelings, in all their degrees of intensity, he discovers that he has experienced himself,* that he *is* all these feelings. He finds his behavior changing in constructive fashion in accordance with his newly experienced self. He approaches the realization that he no longer needs to fear what experience may hold, but can welcome it freely as a part of his changing and developing self.

This is a thumbnail sketch of what client-centered therapy might be at its optimum. I give it here simply as an introduction to my main concern: What personality characteristics would develop in the client as a result of this kind of experience?

The Characteristics of the Person After Therapy

What then is the end-point of optimal psychotherapy, of maximal psychological growth? I shall try to answer this question for myself, basing my thinking upon the knowledge we have gained from clinical experience and research, but pushing this to the limit in order better to see the kind of person who would emerge if therapy were most effective. As I have puzzled over the answer, the description seems to me quite unitary, but for clarity of presentation I shall break it down into three facets.

1. THIS PERSON WOULD BE OPEN TO HIS EXPERIENCE. This is a phrase which has come to have increasingly definite meaning for me. It is the polar opposite of defensiveness. Defensiveness we have described in the past as being the organism's response to experiences which are perceived or anticipated as incongruent with the structure of the self. In order to maintain the self-structure, such experiences are given a distorted symbolization in awareness, which reduces the incongruity. Thus the individual defends himself against any threat of alteration in the concept of self.

In the person who is open to his experience, however, every stimulus, whether originating within the organism or in the environment, would be freely relayed through the nervous system without being distorted by a defensive mechanism. There would be no need of the mechanism of "subception" whereby the organism is forewarned of any experience threatening to the self. On the contrary, whether the stimulus was the impact of a configuration of form, color, or sound in the environment on the sensory nerves, or a memory trace from the past, or a visceral sensation of fear or pleasure or disgust, the person would be "living it," would have it completely available to awareness.

Perhaps I can give this concept a more vivid meaning if I illustrate it from a recorded interview. A young professional man reports in the 48th interview the way in which he has become more open to some of his bodily sensations, as well as other feelings.

Client: "It doesn't seem to me that it would be possible for anybody to relate all the changes that I feel. But I certainly have felt recently that I have more respect for, more objectivity toward my physical makeup. I mean I don't expect too much of myself. This is how it works out: It feels to me that in the past I used to fight a certain tiredness that I felt after supper. Well now I feel pretty sure that I really am *tired*—that I am not making myself tired—that I am just physiologically lower. It seemed that I was just constantly criticizing my tiredness."

Therapist: "So you can let yourself *be* tired, instead of feeling along with it a kind of criticism of it."

Client: "Yes, that I *shouldn't* be tired or something. And it seems in a way to be pretty profound that I can just not fight this tiredness, and along with it goes a real feeling of *I've* got to slow down, too, so that being tired isn't such an awful thing. I think I can also kind of pick up a thread here of why I should be that way in the way my father is and the way he looks at some of these things. For instance, say that I was sick, and I would report this, and it would seem that overtly he would want to do something about it but he would also communicate, 'Oh, my gosh, more trouble.' You know, something like that."

Therapist: "As though there were something quite annoying, really, about being physically ill."

Client: "Yeah, I am sure that my father has the same disrespect for his own physiology that I have had. Now last summer I twisted my back, I wrenched it, I heard it snap and everything. There was real pain there all the time at first, real sharp. And I had the doctor look at it and he said it wasn't serious, it should heal by itself as long as I didn't bend too much. Well this was months ago—and I have been noticing recently that—hell, this is a real pain and it's still there—and it's not my fault, I mean it's—"

Therapist: "It doesn't prove something bad about you—"

Client: "No—and one of the reasons I seem to get more tired than I should maybe is because of this constant strain and so on. I have already made an appointment with one of the doctors at the hospital that he would look at it and take an X-ray or something. In a way I guess you could say that I am just more accurately sensitive—or objectively sensitive to this kind of thing. I can say with certainty that this has also spread to what I eat and how much I eat. And this is really a profound change, as I say. And of course my relationship with my wife and the two children is—well you just wouldn't recognize it if you could see me inside—as you have—I mean—there just doesn't seem to be anything more wonderful than really and genuinely—really *feeling* love for your own child and at the same time *receiving* it. I don't know how to put this. We have such an increased respect—both of us—for Judy and we've noticed just—as we participated in this—we have noticed such a tremendous change in her—it seems to be a pretty deep kind of thing."

Therapist: "It seems to me you are saying that you can listen more accurately to yourself. If your body says it's tired, you listen to it and believe it, instead of criticizing it; if it's in pain you can listen to that; if the feeling is really loving your wife or child, you can *feel* that, and it seems to show up in the differences in them too."

Here, in a relatively minor but symbolically important excerpt, can be seen much of what I have been trying to say about openness to experience. Formerly he could not freely feel pain or illness, because being ill meant being unacceptable. Neither could he feel tenderness and love for his child, because such feelings meant being weak, and he had to maintain his façade of being strong. But now he can be genuinely open to the experience of his organism—he can be tired when he is tired, he can feel pain when his organism is in pain, he can freely experience the love he feels for his daughter, and he can also feel and express annoyance toward her, as he went on to say in the next portion of the interview. He can fully live the experiences of his total organism, rather than shutting them out of awareness.

I have used this concept of availability to awareness to try to make clear what I mean by openness to experience. This might be misunderstood. I do not mean that this individual would be self-consciously aware of all that was going on within himself, like the centipede who became aware of all of his legs. On the contrary, he would be free to live a feeling subjectively, as well as be aware of it. He might experience love, or pain, or fear, living in this attitude subjectively. Or he might abstract himself from this subjectivity and realize in awareness, "I am in pain," "I am afraid," "I do love." The crucial point is that there would be no barriers, no inhibitions, which would prevent the full experiencing of whatever was organismically present, and availability to awareness is a good measure of this absence of barriers.

2. THIS PERSON WOULD LIVE IN AN EXISTENTIAL FASHION.   I believe it would be evident that for the person who was fully open to his experience, completely without defensiveness, each moment would be new. The complex configuration of inner and outer stimuli which exists in this moment has never existed before in just this fashion. Consequently our hypothetical person would realize that "What I will be in the next moment, and what I will do, grows out of that moment, and cannot be predicted in advance either by me or by others." Not infrequently we find clients expressing this sort of feeling. Thus one, at the end of therapy, says in rather puzzled fashion, "I haven't finished the job of integrating and reorganizing myself, but that's only confusing, not discouraging, now that I realize this is a continuing process. . . . It is exciting, sometimes upsetting, but deeply encouraging to feel yourself in action and apparently knowing where you are going even though you don't always consciously know where that is."

One way of expressing the fluidity which would be present in such existential living is to say that the self and personality would emerge *from* experience, rather than experience being translated or twisted to fit a preconceived self-structure. It means that one becomes a participant in and an observer of the ongoing process of organismic experience, rather than being in control of it. In Chapter 6, I have tried to describe how this type of living seems to me.

This whole train of experiencing, and the meaning that I have thus far discovered in it, seem to have launched me on a process which is both fascinating and at times a little frightening. It seems to mean letting my experience carry me on, in a direction which appears to be forward, toward goals that I can but dimly define, as I try to understand at least the current meaning of that experience. The sensation is that of floating with a complex stream of experience, with the fascinating possibility of trying to comprehend its everchanging complexity.

Such living in the moment, then, means an absence of rigidity, of tight organization, of the imposition of structure on experience. It means instead a maximum of adaptability, a discovery of structure *in* experience, a flowing, changing organization of self and personality.

The personality and the self would be continually in flux, the only stable elements being the physiological capacities and limitations of the organism, the continuing or recurrent organismic needs for survival, enhancement, food, affection, sex, and the like. The most stable personality traits would be openness to experience, and the flexible resolution of the existing needs in the existing environment.

3. THIS PERSON WOULD FIND HIS ORGANISM A TRUSTWORTHY MEANS OF ARRIVING AT THE MOST SATISFYING BEHAVIOR IN EACH EXISTENTIAL SITUATION. He would do what "felt right" in this immediate moment and he would find this in general to be a competent and trustworthy guide to his behavior.

If this seems strange, let me explain the reasoning behind it. Since he would be open to his experience he would have access to all of the available data in the situation, on which to base his behavior; the social demands, his own complex and possibly conflicting needs; his memories of similar situations, his perception of the uniqueness of this situation, etc., etc. The dynamic aspects of each situation would be very complex indeed. But he could permit his total organism, his consciousness participating, to consider each stimulus, need, and demand, its relative intensity and importance, and out of this complex weighing and balancing, discover that course of action which would come closest to satisfying all his needs in the situation. An analogy which might come close to a description would be to compare this person to a giant electronic computing machine. Since he is open to his experience, all of the data from his sense impressions, from his memory, from previous learning, from his visceral and internal states, is fed into the machine. The machine takes all of these multitudinous pulls and forces which were fed in as data, and quickly computes the course of action which would be the most economical avenue of need satisfaction in this existential situation. This is the behavior of our hypothetical person.

The defects which in most of us make this process untrustworthy are the inclusion of non-existential material, or the absence of data. It is when memories and previous learnings are fed into the computation as if they were *this* reality, and not memories and learnings, that erroneous behavioral answers arise. Or when certain threatening experiences are inhibited from awareness, and hence are withheld from the computation or fed into it in distorted form, this too produces error. But our hypothetical person would find his organism thoroughly trustworthy, because all the available data would be used, and it would be present in accurate rather than distorted form. Hence his behavior would come as close as possible to satisfying all his needs—for enhancement, for affiliation with others, and the like.

In this weighing, balancing, and computation, his organism would not by any means be infallible. It would always give the best possible answer for the available data, but sometimes data would be missing. Because of the element of openness to experience however, any errors, any following of behavior which was not satisfying would be quickly corrected. The computations, as it were, would always be in process of being corrected, because they would be continually checked in behavior.

Perhaps you will not like my analogy of an electronic computing machine. Let me put it in more human terms. The client I previously quoted found himself expressing annoyance to his daugher when he "felt like it," as well as affection. Yet he found himself doing it in a way which not only released tension in himself, but which freed this small girl to voice her annoyances. He describes the differences between communicating his angry annoyance or imposing it on her. He continues, "Because it just doesn't feel like I'm imposing my feelings on her, and it seems to me I must show it on my face. Maybe she sees it as 'Yes, daddy is angry, but I don't have to cower.' Because she never does *cower*. This in itself is a topic for a novel, it just feels that good." In this instance, being open to his experience, he selects, with astonishing intuitive skill, a subtly guided course of behavior which meets his need for the release of his angry tension, but also satisfies his need to be a good father, and his need to find satisfaction in his daughter's healthy development. Yet he achieves all this by simply doing the thing that feels right to him.

On quite another level, it seems to be this same kind of complex organismic selection that determines the behavior of the creative person. He finds himself moving in a certain direction long before he can give any completely conscious and rational basis for it. During this period, whether he is moving toward a new type of artistic expression, a new literary style, a new theory in the field of science, a new approach in his classroom, he is simply trusting his total organismic reaction. He feels an assurance that he is on his way, even though he could not describe the end point of that journey. This is the type of behavior which is, I believe, also characteristic of the person who has gained greatly from therapy, or of the person whose educational experience has enabled him to learn how to learn.

The Fully Functioning Person

I should like to pull together these three threads into one more unified descriptive strand. It appears that the person who emerges from a theoretically optimal experience of personal growth, whether through client-centered therapy or some other experience of learning and development, is then a fully functioning person. He is able to live fully in and with each and all of his feelings and reactions. He is making use of all his organic equipment to sense, as accurately as possible, the existential situation within and without. He is using all of the data his nervous system can thus supply, using it in awareness, but recognizing that his total organism may be, and often is, wiser than his awareness. He is able to permit his total organism to function in all its complexity in selecting, from the multitude of possibilities, that behavior which in this moment of time will be most generally and genuinely satisfying. He is able to trust his organism in this functioning, not because it is infallible, but because he can be fully open to the consequences of each of his actions and correct them if they prove to be less than satisfying.

He is able to experience all of his feelings, and is afraid of none of his feelings; he is his own sifter of evidence, but is open to evidence from all sources; he is completely engaged in the process of being and becoming himself, and thus discovers that he is soundly and realistically social; he lives completely in this moment, but learns that this is the soundest living for all time. He is a fully functioning organism, and because of the awareness of himself which flows freely in and through his experiences, he is a fully functioning person.

Some Implications of This Description

This, then, is my tentative definition of the hypothetical endpoint of therapy, my description of the ultimate picture which our actual clients approach but never fully reach, the picture of the person who is continually learning how to learn. I have come to like this description, both because I believe it is rooted in and is true of my clinical and educational experience, and also because I believe it has significant clinical, scientific, and philosophical implications. I should like to present some of these ramifications and implications as I see them.

A. Appropriate to Clinical Experience

In the first place it appears to contain a basis for the phenomena of clinical experience in successful therapy. We have noted the fact that the client develops a locus of evaluation within himself; this is consistent with the concept of the trustworthiness of the organism. We have commented on the client's satisfaction at being and becoming himself, a satisfaction associated with functioning fully. We find that clients tolerate a much wider range and variety of feelings, including feelings which were formerly anxiety-producing; and that these feelings are usefully integrated into their more flexibly organized personalities. In short, the concepts I have stated appear to be sufficiently broad to contain the positive outcomes of therapy as we know it.

B. Leads Toward Operational Hypotheses

While the formulation as given is admittedly speculative, it leads, I believe, in the direction of hypotheses which may be stated in rigorous and operational terms. Such hypotheses would be culture-free or universal, I trust, rather than being different for each culture.

It is obvious that the concepts given are not easily tested or measured, but with our growing research sophistication in this area, their measurability is not an unreasonable hope.

C. Explains a Paradox of Personal Growth

We have found, in some of our research studies in psychotherapy, some perplexing differences in the analyses of before-and-after personality tests, by different outside experts. In clients whose personal gain in therapy is amply supported by other evidence, we have found contradictions among the experts in the interpretation of their personality tests. Briefly, psychologists who are oriented strictly toward personality *diagnosis*, who are comparing the individual with general norms, tend to be concerned over what they see as a lack of personality defenses, or a degree of disorganization, at the conclusion of therapy. They may be concerned that the person is "falling apart." The psychologist who is therapeutically oriented tends to see the same evidence as indicative of fluidity, openness to experience, an existential rather than a rigid personality organization.

To me it seems possible that the "looseness," the openness, of the person who is undergoing marked personal growth may be seen, in terms of population norms, as deviating from those norms, as "not normal." But these same qualities may indicate that all personal growth is marked by a certain degree of disorganization followed by reorganization. The pain of new understandings, of acceptance of new facets of oneself, the feeling of uncertainty, vacillation, and even turmoil within oneself, are all an integral part of the pleasure and satisfaction of being more of oneself, more fully oneself, more fully functioning. This to me is a meaningful explanation of what would otherwise be a puzzling paradox.

D. Creativity As an Outcome

One of the elements which pleases me in the theoretical formulation I have given is that this is a creative person. This person at the hypothetical end-point of therapy could well be one of Maslow's "self-actualizing people." With his sensitive openness to the world, his trust of his own ability to form new relationships with his environment, he would be the type of person from whom creative products and creative living emerge. He would not necessarily be "adjusted" to his culture, and he would almost certainly not be a conformist. But at any time and in any culture he would live constructively, in as much harmony with his culture as a balanced satisfaction of needs demanded. In some cultural situations he might in some ways be very unhappy, but he would continue to be himself, and to behave in such a way as to provide the maximum possible satisfaction of his deepest needs.

Such a person would, I believe, be recognized by the student of evolution as the type most likely to adapt and survive under changing environmental conditions. He would be able creatively to make sound adjustments to new as well as old conditions. He would be a fit vanguard of human evolution.

E. Builds on Trustworthiness of Human Nature.

It will have been evident that one implication of the view I have been presenting is that the basic nature of the human being, when functioning freely, is constructive and trustworthy. For me this is an inescapable conclusion from more than thirty years of experience in psychotherapy. When we are able to free the individual from defensiveness, so that he is open to the wide range of his own needs, as well as the wide range of environmental and social demands, his reactions may be trusted to be positive, forward-moving, constructive.

We do not need to ask who will socialize him, for one of his own deepest needs is for affiliation with and communication with others. When he is fully himself, he cannot help but be realistically socialized. We do not need to ask who will control his aggressive impulses, for when he is open to all of his impulses, his need to be liked by others and his tendency to give affection are as strong as his impulses to strike out or to seize for himself. He will be aggressive in situations in which aggression is realistically appropriate, but there will be no runaway need for aggression. His total behavior, in these and other areas, when he is open to all his experience, is balanced and realistic, behavior which is appropriate to the survival and enhancement of a highly social animal.

I have little sympathy with the rather prevalent concept that man is basically irrational, and thus his impulses, if not controlled, would lead to destruction of others and self. Man's behavior is exquisitely rational, moving with subtle and ordered complexity toward the goals his organism is endeavoring to achieve. The tragedy for most of us is that our defenses keep us from being aware of this rationality, so that consciously we are moving in one direction, while organismically we are moving in another. But in our hypothetical person there would be no such barriers, and he would be a participant in the rationality of his organism. The only control of impulses which would exist or which would prove necessary, is the natural and internal balancing of one need against another, and the discovery of behaviors which follow the avenue most closely approximating the satisfaction of all needs. The experience of extreme satisfaction of one need (for aggression, or sex, etc.) in such a way as to do violence to the satisfaction of other needs (for companionship, tender relationship, etc.)—an experience very common in the defensively organized person—would simply be unknown in our hypothetical individual. He would participate in the vastly complex self-regulatory activities of his organism—the psychological as well as physiological thermostatic controls—in such a fashion as to live harmoniously, with himself and with others.

F. Behavior Dependable But Not Predictable

There are certain implications of this view of the optimum human being which have to do with predictability, which I find fascinating to contemplate. It should be clear from the theoretical picture I have sketched that the particular configuration of inner and outer stimuli in which the person lives at this moment has never existed in precisely this fashion before; and also that his behavior is a realistic reaction to an accurate apprehension of all this internalized evidence. It should therefore be clear that this person will seem to himself to be dependable but not specifically predictable. If he is entering a new situation with an authority figure, for example, he cannot predict what his behavior will be. It is contingent upon the behavior of this authority figure, and his own immediate internal reactions, desires, etc., etc. He can feel confident that he will behave appropriately, but he has no knowledge in advance of what he will do. I find this point of view often expressed by clients, and I believe it is profoundly important.

But what I have been saying about the client himself, would be equally true of the scientist studying his behavior. The scientist would find this person's behavior lawful, and would find it possible to postdict it, but could not forecast or predict the specific behavior of this individual. The reasons are these. If the behavior of our hypothetical person is determined by the accurate sensing of all of the complex evidence which exists in this moment of time, and by that evidence only, then the data necessary for prediction is clear. It would be necessary to have instruments available to measure every one of the multitudinous stimuli of the input, and a mechanical computer of great size to calculate the most economical vector of reaction. While this computation is going on, our hypothetical person has already made this complex summation and appraisal within his own organism and has acted. Science, if it can eventually collect all this data with sufficient accuracy, should theoretically be able to analyze it and come to the same conclusion and thus postdict his behavior. It is doubtful that it could ever collect and analyze the data instantaneously, and this would be necessary if it were to predict the behavior before it occurred.

It may clarify this if I point out that it is the maladjusted person whose behavior can be specifically predicted, and some loss of predictability should be evident in every increase in openness to experience and existential living. In the maladjusted person, behavior is predictable precisely because it is rigidly patterned. If such a person has learned a pattern of hostile reaction to authority, and if this "badness of authority" is a part of his conception of himself-in-relation-to-authority, and if because of this he denies or distorts any experience which should supply contradictory evidence, *then* his behavior is specifically predictable. It can be said with assurance that when he enters a new situation with an authority figure, he will be hostile to him. But the more that therapy, or any growth-promoting relationship, increases the openness to experience of this individual, the less predictable his behavior will be. This receives some crude confirmation from the Michigan study (Kelly & Fiske, 1951) attempting to predict success in clinical psychology. The predictions for the men who were in therapy during the period of investigation were definitely less accurate than for the group as a whole.

What I am saying here has a bearing on the common statement that the long range purpose of psychology as a science is "the prediction and control of human behavior" a phrase which for me has had disturbing philosophical implications. I am suggesting that as the individual approaches this optimum of complete functioning his behavior, though always lawful and determined, becomes more difficult to predict; and though always dependable and appropriate, more difficult to control. This would mean that the science of psychology, at its highest levels, would perhaps be more of a science of understanding than a science of prediction, an analysis of the lawfulness of that which has occurred, rather than primarily a control of what is about to occur.

In general this line of thought is confirmed by our clients, who feel confident that what they will do in a situation will be appropriate and comprehensible and sound, but who cannot predict in advance how they will behave. It is also confirmed by our experience as therapists, where we form a relationship in which we can be sure the person will discover himself, become himself, learn to function more freely, but where we cannot forecast the specific content of the next statement, of the next phase of therapy, or of the behavioral solution the client will find to a given problem. The general direction is dependable, and we can rest assured it will be appropriate; but its specific content is unpredictable.

G. Relates Freedom and Determinism

I should like to give one final philosophical implication which has meaning for me. For some time I have been perplexed over the living paradox which exists in psychotherapy between freedom and determinism, as I have indicated in the preceding chapter. I would like to add one more thought on that topic. In the therapeutic relationship some of the most compelling subjective experiences are those in which the client feels within himself the power of naked choice. He is *free*—to become himself or to hide behind a façade; to move forward or to retrogress; to behave in ways which are destructive of self and others, or in ways which are enhancing; quite literally free to live or die, in both the physiological and psychological meaning of those terms. Yet as we enter this field of psychotherapy with objective research methods, we are, like any other scientist, committed to a complete determinism. From this point of view every thought, feeling, and action of the client is determined by what precedes it. The dilemma I am trying to describe is no different than that found in other fields—it is simply brought to sharper focus. I tried to bring this out in a paper written some time ago contrasting these two views. In the field of psychotherapy,

Here is the maximizing of all that is subjective, inward, personal; here a relationship is lived, not examined, and a person, not an object, emerges, a person who feels, chooses, believes, acts, not as an automaton, but as a person. And here too is the ultimate in science—the objective exploration of the most subjective aspects of life; the reduction to hypotheses, and eventually to theorems, of all that has been regarded as most personal, most completely inward, most thoroughly a private world (Rogers, 1955).

In terms of the definition I have given of the fully functioning person, the relationship between freedom and determinism can, I believe, be seen in a fresh perspective. We could say that in the optimum of therapy the person rightfully experiences the most complete and absolute freedom. He wills or chooses to follow the course of action which is the most economical vector in relation to all the internal and external stimuli, because it is that behavior which will be most deeply satisfying. But this is the same course of action which from another vantage point may be said to be determined by all the factors in the existential situation. Let us contrast this with the picture of the person who is defensively organized. He wills or chooses to follow a given course of action, but finds that he *cannot* behave in the fashion that he chooses. He is determined by the factors in the existential situation, but these factors include his defensiveness, his denial or distortion of some of the relevant data. Hence it is certain that his behavior will be less than fully satisfying. His behavior is determined, but he is not free to make an effective choice. The fully functioning person, on the other hand, not only experiences, but utilizes, the most absolute freedom when he spontaneously, freely, and voluntarily chooses and wills that which is absolutely determined.

I am quite aware that this is not a new idea to the philosopher, but it has been refreshing to come upon it from a totally unexpected angle, in analyzing a concept in personality theory. For me it provides the rationale for the subjective reality of absolute freedom of choice, which is so profoundly important in therapy, and at the same time the rationale for the complete determinism which is the very foundation stone of science. With this framework I can enter subjectively the experience of naked choice which the client is experiencing; I can also as a scientist, study his behavior as being absolutely determined.

Conclusion

Here then is my theoretical model of the person who emerges from therapy or from the best of education, the individual who has experienced optimal psychological growth—a person functioning freely in all the fullness of his organismic potentialities; a person who is dependable in being realistic, self-enhancing, socialized, and appropriate in his behavior; a creative person, whose specific form-ings of behavior are not easily predictable; a person who is everchanging, ever developing, always discovering himself and the newness in himself in each succeeding moment of time.

Let me stress, however, that what I have described is a person who does not exist. He is the theoretical goal, the end-point of per-sonal growth. We see persons moving *in this direction* from the best of experiences in education, from the best of experiences in therapy, from the best of family and group relationships. But what we observe is the imperfect person moving *toward* this goal. What I have de-scribed is my version of the goal in its "pure" form.

I have written this chapter partly to clarify my own ideas. What sort of persons tend to come from my classes, from my groups, from my therapy? But much more important, I have written it to try to force educators to think much more deeply about their *own* goals. The assumption has been prevalent for so long that we all know what constitutes an "educated man," that the fact that this comfortable definition is now *completely irrelevant* to modern society is almost never faced. So this chapter constitutes a challenge to educators at all levels. If my concept of the fully functioning person is abhorrent to you as the goal of education, then give *your* definition of the person who should emerge from modern day education, and publish it for all to see. We need many such definitions so that there can be a re-ally significant *modern* dialogue as to what constitutes our optimum, our ideal citizen of *today*. I hope this chapter makes a small con-tribution toward the dialogue.

References

Kelley, E. L., & Fiske, Donald W. *The Prediction of Performance in Clinical Psychology*. Ann Arbor: University of Michigan Press, 1951.
Rogers, C. R. Persons or Science: A Philosophical Question. *American Psy-chologist*, 1955, *10*, 267–278.

Gestalt Therapy Verbatim

FREDERICK S. PERLS

Now let me tell you of a dilemma which is not easy to understand. It's like a *koan*—those Zen questions which seem to be insoluble. The *koan* is: *Nothing exists except the here and now.* The *now* is the present, is the phenomenon, is what you are aware of, is that moment in which you carry your so-called memories and your so-called anticipations with you. Whether you remember or anticipate, you do it *now.* The past is no more. The future is not yet. When I say, "I was," that's not now, that's the past. When I say, "I want to," that's the future, it's not yet. Nothing can possibly exist except the now. Some people then make a program out of this. They make a demand, "You *should* live in the here and now." And I say it's *not possible* to live in the here and now, and yet, nothing exists except the here and now.

How do we resolve this dilemma? What is buried in the word *now?* How come it takes years and years to understand a simple word like the word *now?* If I play a phonograph record, the sound of the record appears when the record and the needle touch each other, where they make contact. There is no sound of the before, there is no sound of the afterwards. If I stop the phonograph record, then the needle is still in contact with the record, but there is no music, because there is the *absolute* now. If you would blot out the past, or the anticipation of themes three minutes from now, you could not understand listening to that record you are now playing. But if you blot out the now, nothing will come through. So again, whether we remember or whether we anticipate, we do it *here and now.*

Maybe if I say the *now* is not the scale but the point of spspense, it's a zero point, it is a nothingness, and that is the *now.* The very moment I feel that I experience something and I talk about it, I pay attention to it, that moment is already gone. So what's the use of talking about the *now?* It has many uses, very many uses.

Let's talk first about the past. *Now,* I am pulling memories out of my drawer and possibly believe that these memories are identical with my history. That's never true, because a memory is an abstraction. Right now, you experience something. You experience me, you experience your thoughts, you experience your posture perhaps, but you can't experience *everything.* You always abstract the relevant gestalt from the total context. Now if you take these abstractions and file them away, then you call them memories. If these memories are unpleasant, especially if they are unpleasant to our self-esteem, we change them. As Nietsche said: "Memory and Pride were fighting. Memory said, 'It was like this' and Pride said, 'It couldn't have been like this'—and Memory gives in." You all know how much you are lying. You all know how much you are deceiving yourselves, how many of your memories are exaggerations and projections, how many of your memories are patched up and distorted.

The past is past. And yet—in the now, in our being, we carry much of the past with us. But we carry much of the past with us only as far as we have unfinished situations. What happened in the past is either assimilated and has become a part of us, or we carry around an unfinished situation, an incomplete gestalt. Let me give you as an example, the most famous of the unfinished situations is the fact that we have not forgiven our parents. As you know, parents are never right. They are either too large or too small, too smart or too dumb. If they are stern, they should be soft, and so on. But when do you find parents who are all right? You can always blame the parents if you want to play the blaming game, and make the parents responsible for all your problems. Until you are willing to let go of your parents, you continue to conceive of yourself as a child. But to get closure and let go of the parents and say, "I am a big girl, now," is a different story. This is part of therapy—to let go of parents, and especially to forgive one's parents, which is the hardest thing for most people to do.

The great error of psychoanalysis is in assuming that the memory is reality. All the so-called *traumata*, which are supposed to be the root of the neurosis, are an invention of the patient to save his self-esteem. None of these traumata has ever been proved to exist. I haven't seen a single case of infantile trauma that wasn't a falsification. They are all lies to be hung onto in order to justify one's unwillingness to grow. To mature means to take responsibility for your life, to be on your own. Psychoanalysis fosters the infantile state by considering that the past is responsible for the illness. The patient isn't responsible—no, the trauma is responsible, or the Oedipus complex is responsible, and so on. I suggest that you read a beautiful little pocketbook called *I Never Promised You a Rose Garden,* by Hannah Green. There you see a typical example, how that girl invented this childhood trauma, to have her *raison d'etre,* her basis to fight the world, her justification for her craziness, her illness. We have got such an idea about the importance of this invented memory, where the whole illness is supposed to be based on this memory. No wonder that all the wild goose chase of the psychoanalyst to find out *why* I am now like this can never come to an end, can never prove a real opening up of the person himself.

Freud devoted his whole life to prove to himself and to others that sex is not bad, and he had to prove this scientifically. In his time, the scientific approach was that of causality, that the trouble was *caused* by something in the past, like a billiard cue pushing a billiard ball, and the cue then is the cause of the rolling of the ball. In the meantime, our scientific attitude has changed. We don't look to the world any more in terms of cause and effect: We look upon the world as a continuous ongoing process. We are back to Heraclitus, to the pre-Socratic idea that everything is in a flux. We never step into the same river twice. In other words, we have made—in science, but unfortunately not yet in psychiatry—the transition from linear causality to thinking of process, from the *why* to the *how*.

If you ask *how*, you look at the structure, you see what's going on now, a deeper understanding of the process. The *how* is all we need to understand how we or the world functions. The *how* gives us perspective, orientation. The *how* shows that one of the basic laws, the identity of structure and function, is valid. If we change the structure, the function changes. If we change the function, the structure changes.

I know you want to ask *why*, like every child, like every immature pe son asks *why*, to get rationalization or explanation. But the *why* at best leads to clever explanation, but never to an understanding. *Why* and *because* are dirty words in Gestalt Therapy. They lead only to rationalization, and belong to the second class of vergiage production. I distinguish three classes of verbiage production: chickenshit—this is "good morning," "how are you," and so on; bullshit—this is "because," rationalization, excuses; and elephant-shit—this is when you talk about philosophy, existential Gestalt Therapy, etc.—what I am doing now. The *why* gives only unending inquiries into the cause of the cause of the cause of the cause of the cause of the cause. And as Freud has already observed, every event is *over*-determined, has *many* causes; all kinds of things come together in order to create the specific moment that is the *now*. Many factors come together to create this specific unique person which is *I*. Nobody can at any given moment be different from what he is at this moment, including all the wishes and prayers that he should be different. We are what we are.

These are the two legs upon which Gestalt Therapy walks: *now* and *how*. The essence of the theory of Gestalt Therapy is in the understanding of these two words. *Now* covers all that exists. The past is no more, the future is not yet. *Now* includes the balance of being here, is experiencing, involvement, phenomenon, awareness. *How* covers everything that is structure, behavior, all that is actually going on—the ongoing process. All the rest is irrelevant—computing, apprehending, and so on.

Everything is grounded in *awareness*. *Awareness* is the only basis of knowledge, communication, and so on. In communication, you have to understand that you want to make the other person *aware of something:* aware of yourself, aware of what's to be noticed in the other person, etc. And in order to communicate, we have to make sure that we are *senders,* which means that the message which we send can be understood; and also to make sure that we are *receivers*—that we are willing to listen to the message from the other person. It is very rare that people can talk *and* listen. Very few people can listen without talking. Most people can talk without listening. And if you're busy talking you have no time to listen. The integration of talking and listening is a really rare thing. Most people don't listen and give an honest response, but just put the other person off with a question. Instead of listening and answering, immediately comes a counter-attack, a question or something that diverts, deflects, dodges. We are going to talk a lot about blocks in sending messages, in giving yourself, in making others aware of yourself, and in the same way, of being willing to be open to the other person—to be receivers. Without communication, there cannot be contact. There will be only isolation and boredom.

So I would like to reinforce what I just said, and I would like you to pair up, and to talk to each other for five minutes about your actual present awareness of yourself now and your awareness of the other. Always underline the *how—how* do you behave *now, how* do you sit, *how* do you talk, all the details of what goes on *now. How* does he sit, *how* does he look. . .

So how about the future? We don't know anything about the future. If we all had crystal balls, even then we wouldn't experience the future. We would experience a *vision* of the future. And all this is taking place here and now. We imagine, we anticipate the future because we don't want to have a future. So the most important existential saying is, we don't want to have a future, we are afraid of the future. We fill in the gap where there should be a future with insurance policies, status quo, sameness, *anything* so as not to experience the possibility of openness towards the future.

We also cannot stand the nothingness, the openness, of the past. We are not willing to have the idea of eternity—"It has always been"—so we have to fill it in with the story of creation. Time has started somehow. People ask, "When did time begin?" The same applies to the future. It seems incredible that we could live without goals, without worrying about the future, that we could be open and ready for what might come. No; we have to make sure that we have no future, that the status quo should remain, even be a little bit better. But we mustn't take risks, we mustn't be open to the future. Something could happen that would be new and exciting, and contributing to our growth. It's too dangerous to take the growth risk. We would rather walk this earth as half-corpses than live dangerously, and realize that this living dangerously is much safer than this insurance-life of safety and not taking risks, which most of us decide to do.

What is this funny thing, risk-taking? Has anybody a definition for risk-taking? What's involved in risk-taking?

A: Getting hurt.

B: Taking a dare.

C: Going too far.

D: A hazardous attempt.

E: Inviting danger.

Now you notice you all see the catastrophic expectation, the negative side. You don't see the possible gain. If there was only the negative side, you just would avoid it, wouldn't you? Risk-taking is a suspense between catastrophic and anastrophic expectations. You have to see *both* sides of the picture. You might gain, and you might lose.

One of the most important moments in my life was after I had escaped Germany and there was a position as a training analyst available in South Africa, and Ernest Jones wanted to know who wanted to go. There were four of us: three wanted guarantees. I said I take a risk. All the other three were caught by the Nazis. I took a risk and I'm still alive.

An absolutely healthy person is completely in touch with himself and with reality. The crazy person, the psychotic, is more or less completely *out* of touch with both, but mostly with *either* himself *or* the world. We are in between being psychotic and being healthy, and this is based upon the fact that we have *two* levels of existence. One is reality, the actual, realistic level, that we are in touch with whatever goes on now, in touch with our feelings, in touch with our senses. Reality is awareness of ongoing experience, actual touching, seeing, moving, doing. The other level we don't have a good word for, so I choose the Indian word *maya*. *Maya* means something like illusion, or fantasy, or philosophically speaking, the *as if* of Vaihinger. *Maya* is a kind of dream, a kind of trance. Very often this fantasy, this *maya*, is called the mind, but if you look a bit closer, what you call "mind" is fantasy. It's the rehearsal stage. Freud once said: *"Denken ist prober arbeit"*—thinking is rehearsing, trying out. Unfortunately, Freud never followed up this discovery because it would be inconsistent with his genetic approach. If he had accepted this statement of his, "Thinking is rehearsing," he would have realized how our fantasy activity is turned toward the future, because we rehearse for the future.

We live on two levels—the public level which is our *doing*, which is observable, verifiable; and the private stage, the thinking stage, the rehearsing stage, on which we prepare for the future roles we want to play. Thinking is a private stage, where you try out. You talk to some person unknown, you talk to yourself, you prepare for an important event, you talk to the beloved before your appointment or disappointment, whatever you expect it to be. For instance, if I were to ask, "Who wants to come up here to work?" you probably would quickly start to rehearse. "What shall I do there?" and so on. And of course probably you will get stage fright, because you leave the secure reality of the now and jump into the future. Psychiatry makes a big fuss out of the symptom *anxiety*, and we live in an age of anxiety, but anxiety is nothing but the tension from the *now* to the *then*. There are few people who can stand this tension, so they have to fill the gap with rehearsing, planning, "making sure," making sure that they don't have a future. They try to hold onto the sameness, and this of course will prevent any possibility of growth or spontaneity.

Q [1]: Of course the past sets up anxiety too, doesn't it?

F: No. The past sets up—or let's say is still present with un-finished situations, regrets and things like this. If you feel anxiety about what you have done, it's not anxiety about what you have done, but anxiety about what will be the punishment to come in the future.

Freud once said the person who is free from anxiety and guilt is healthy. I spoke about anxiety already. I didn't speak about guilt. Now, in the Freudian system, the guilt is very complicated. In Ge-stalt Therapy, the guilt thing is much simpler. We see guilt as pro-jected *resentment*. Whenever you feel guilty, find out what you re-sent, and the guilt will vanish and you will try to make the other person feel guilty.

Anything unexpressed which wants to be expressed can make you feel uncomfortable. And one of the most common unexpressed experiences is the resentment. This is the unfinished situation *par excellence*. If you are resentful, you're stuck; you neither can move forward and have it out, express your anger, change the world so that you'll get satisfaction, nor can you let go and forget whatever dis-turbs you. Resentment is the psychological equivalent of the hanging-on bite—the tight jaw. The hanging-on bite can neither let go, nor bite through and chew up—whichever is required. In resent-ment you can neither let go and forget, and let this incident or per-son recede in the background, nor can you actively tackle it. The expression of resentment is one of the most important ways to help

---

[1] "Q" stands for a questioner; "F" for Fritz Perls (Ed.)

you to make your life a little bit more easy. Now I want you all to do the following collective experiment:

I want each one of you to do this. First you evoke a person like father or husband, call the person by name—whoever it is—and just say briefly, "Clara, I resent—" Try to get the person to hear you, as if there was really communication and you felt this. So try to speak to the person, and establish in these communications that this person should listen to you. Just become aware of how difficult it is to mobilize your fantasy. Express your resentment—kind of present it right into his or her face. Try to realize at the same time that you don't dare, really, to express your anger, nor would you be generous enough to let go, to be forgiving. Okeh, go ahead. . .

There is another great advantage to using resentment in therapy, in growth. Behind every resentment there are demands. So now I want all of you to talk directly to the same person as before, and express the demands behind the resentments. The demand is the only real form of communication. Get your demands into the open. Do this also as self-expression: formulate your demands in the form of an imperative, a command. I guess you know enough of English grammar to know what an imperative is. The imperative is like "Shut up!" "Go to hell!" "Do this!" . . .

Now go back to the resentments you expressed toward the person. Remember *exactly* what you resented. Scratch out the word *resent* and say *appreciate*. Appreciate what you resented before. Then go on to tell this person what else you appreciate in them. Again try to get the feeling that you actually communicate with them . . .

You see, if there were no appreciations, you wouldn't be stuck with this person and you could just forget him. There is always the other side. For instance, my appreciation of Hitler: If Hitler had not come to power, I probably would have been dead by now as a good psychoanalyst who lives on eight patients for the rest of his life.

If you have any difficulties in communication with somebody, look for your resentments. Resentments are among the worst possible unfinished situations—unfinished gestalts. If you resent, you can neither let go nor have it out. Resentment is an emotion of central importance. The resentment is the most important expression of an impasse—of being stuck. If you feel resentment, be able to express your resentment. A resentment unexpressed often is experienced as, or changes into, feelings of guilt. Whenever you feel guilty, find out what you are resenting and express it and make your demands explicit. This alone will help a lot.

Awareness covers, so to speak, three layers or three zones: awareness of the *self,* awareness of the *world,* and awareness of what's between—the intermediate zone of fantasy that prevents a person from being in touch with either himself or the world. This is Freud's great discovery—that there is something between you and the world. There are so many processes going on in one's fantasies. A complex is what he calls it, or a prejudice. If you have prejudices, then your relationship to the world is very much disturbed and destroyed. If you want to approach a person with a prejudice, you can't get to the person. You always will contact only the prejudice, the fixed idea. So Freud's idea that the intermediate zone, the DMZ, this no-man's land between you and the world should be eliminated, emptied out, brainwashed or whatever you want to call it, was perfectly right. The only trouble is that Freud stayed in that zone and analyzed this intermediate thing. He didn't consider the self-awareness or world-awareness; he didn't consider what we can do to be in touch again.

This loss of contact with our authentic self, and loss of contact with the world, is due to this intermediate zone, the big area of *maya* that we carry with us. That is, there is a big area of fantasy activity that takes up so much of our excitement, of our energy, of our life force, that there is very little energy left to be in touch with reality. Now, if we want to make a person whole, we have first to understand what is merely fantasy and irrationality, and we have to discover where one is in touch, and with what. And very often if we work, and we empty out this middle zone of fantasy, this *maya,* then there is the experience of *satori,* of waking up. Suddenly the world is *there.* You wake up from a trance like you wake up from a dream. You're all there again. And the aim in therapy, the growth aim, is to lose more and more of your "mind" and come more to your *senses.* To be more and more in touch, to be in touch with yourself and in touch with the world, instead of only in touch with the fantasies, prejudices, apprehensions, and so on.

If a person confuses *maya* and reality, if he takes fantasy for reality, then he is neurotic or even psychotic. I give you an extreme case of psychosis, the schizophrenic who imagines the doctor is after him, so he decides to beat him to the punch and shoot the doctor, without checking up on reality. On the other hand, there is another possibility. Instead of being divided between *maya* and reality, we can integrate these two, and if *maya* and reality are integrated, we call it art. Great art is real, and great art is at the same time an illusion.

Fantasy can be creative, but it's creative only if you have the fantasy, whatever it is, in the *now.* In the *now,* you use what is available, and you are bound to be creative. Just watch children in their play. What's available is usable and then something happens, something comes out of the being in touch with what is *here* and *now.*

There is only one way to bring about this state of healthy spontaneity, to save the genuineness of the human being. Or, to talk in trite
religious terms, there is only one way to regain our soul, or in American terms, to revive the American corpse and bring him back to life.
The paradox is that in order to get this spontaneity, we need, like in
Zen, an utmost discipline. The discipline is simply to understand the
words *now* and *how,* and to bracket off and put aside anything that is
not contained in the words *now* and *how.*

Now what's the technique we are using in Gestalt Therapy? The
technique is to establish a *continuum of awareness.* This continuum
of awareness is required so that the organism can work on the
healthy gestalt principle: that the most important unfinished situation will always emerge and can be dealt with. If we prevent ourselves from achieving this gestalt formation, we function badly and
we carry hundreds and thousands of unfinished situations with us,
that always demand completion.

This continuum of awareness seems to be very simple, just to be
aware from second to second what's going on. Unless we are asleep,
we are always aware of something. However, as soon as this awareness becomes unpleasant, most people will interrupt it. Then suddenly they start intellectualizing, bullshitting, the flight into the past,
the flight into expectations, good intentions, or schizophrenically
using free associations, jumping like a grasshopper from experience
to experience, and none of these experiences are ever *experienced,*
but just a kind of a flash, which leaves all the available material unas-
similated and unused.

Now how do we proceed in Gestalt Therapy? What is nowadays
quite fashionable was very much pooh-poohed when I started this
idea of *everything is awareness.* The purely verbal approach, the
Freudian approach in which I was brought up, barks up the wrong
tree. Freud's idea was that by a certain procedure called free-association, you can liberate the disowned part of the personality and put it
at the disposal of the person and then the person will develop what
he called a strong ego. What Freud called association, I call *dis*socia-
tion, schizophrenic dissociation to avoid the experience. It's a computer game, an interpretation-computer game, which is exactly an
avoidance of the experience of what *is.* You can talk 'til doomsday,
you can chase your childhood memories to doomsday, but nothing
will change. You can associate—or dissociate—a hundred things to
one event, but you can only experience one reality.

So, in contrast to Freud who placed the greatest emphasis on
resistances, I have placed the greatest emphasis on *phobic attitude,
avoidance, flight from.* Maybe some of you know that Freud's illness
was that he suffered from an immense number of phobias, and as he

had this illness, of course he had to avoid coping with avoidance. His phobic attitude was tremendous. He couldn't look at a patient—couldn't face having an encounter with the patient—so he had him lie on a couch, and Freud's symptom became the trademark of psychoanalysis. He couldn't go into the open to be photographed, and so on. But usually, if you come to think of it, most of us would rather avoid unpleasant situations and we mobilize all the armor, masks, and so on, a procedure which is usually known as the "repression." So, I try to find out from the patient what he *avoids*.

The enemy of development is this pain phobia—the unwillingness to do a tiny bit of suffering. You see, pain is a signal of nature. The painful leg, the painful feeling, cries out, "Pay attention to me—if you don't pay attention, things will get worse." The broken leg cries, "Don't walk so much. Keep still." We use this fact in Gestalt Therapy by understanding that the awareness continuum is being interrupted—that you become phobic—as soon as you begin to feel something unpleasant. When you begin to feel uncomfortable, you take away your attention.

So the therapeutic agent, the means of development, is to integrate *attention* and *awareness*. Often psychology doesn't differentiate between awareness and attention. Attention is a deliberate way of listening to the emerging foreground figure, which in this case is something unpleasant. So what I do as therapist is to work as a catalyst both ways: provide situations in which a person can experience this being stuck—the unpleasantness—and I frustrate his avoidances still further, until he is willing to mobilize his own resources.

Authenticity, maturity, responsibility for one's actions and life, response-ability, and living in the now, having the creativeness of the now available, is all one and the same thing. Only in the now, are you in touch with what's going on. If the now becomes painful, most people are ready to throw the now overboard and avoid the painful situation. Most people can't even suffer themselves. So in therapy the person might simply become phobic and run away or he might play games which will lead our effort *ad absurdum*—like making a fool out of the situation or playing the bear-trapper game. You probably know the bear-trappers. The bear-trappers suck you in and give you the come-on, and when you're sucked in, down comes the hatchet and you stand there with a bloody nose, head, or whatever. And if you are fool enough to ram your head against the wall until you begin to bleed and be exasperated, then the bear-trapper enjoys himself and enjoys the control he has over you, to render you inadequate, impotent, and he enjoys his victorious self which does a lot for his feeble self-esteem. Or you have the Mona Lisa smiler. They smile and smile, and all the time think, "You're such a fool." And nothing penetrates. Or you have the drive-us-crazy, whose only interest in life is to drive themselves or their spouse or their environment crazy and then fish in troubled waters.

But with these exceptions, anyone who has a little bit of goodwill will benefit from the Gestalt approach because the simplicity of the Gestalt approach is that we pay attention to the obvious, to the utmost surface. We don't delve into a region which we don't know anything about, into the so-called "unconscious." I don't believe in repressions. The whole theory of repression is a fallacy. We can't repress a need. We have only repressed certain expressions of these needs. We have blocked one side, and then the self-expression comes out somewhere else, in our movements, in our posture, and most of all in our voice. A good therapist doesn't listen to the content of the bullshit the patient produces, but to the sound, to the music, to the hesitations. Verbal communication is usually a lie. The real communication is beyond words. There is a *very* good book available, *The Voice of Neurosis,* by Paul Moses, a psychologist from San Francisco who died recently. He could give you a diagnosis from the voice that is better than the Rorschach test.

So don't listen to the words, just listen to what the voice tells you, what the movements tell you, what the posture tells you, what the image tells you. If you have ears, then you know all about the other person. You don't have to listen to *what* the person says: listen to the sounds. *Per sona*—"through sound." The sounds tell you everything. Everything a person wants to express is all there—not in words. What we say is mostly either lies or bullshit. But the voice is there, the gesture, the posture, the facial expression, the psychosomatic language. It's all there if you learn to more or less let the content of the sentences play the second violin only. And if you don't make the mistake of mixing up sentences and reality, and if you use your eyes and ears, then you see that everyone expresses himself in one way or another. If you have eyes and ears, the world is open. Nobody can have any secrets because the neurotic only fools himself, nobody else—except for awhile, maybe, if he is a good actor.

In most psychiatry, the sound of the voice is not noticed, only the verbal contact is abstracted from the total personality. Movements like—you see how much this young man here expresses in his leaning forward—the total personality as it expresses itself with movements, with posture, with sound, with pictures—there is so much invaluable material here, that we don't have to do anything else except get to the obvious, to the outermost surface, and feed this back, so as to bring this into the patient's awareness. *Feedback* was

Carl Rogers' introduction into psychiatry. Again, he only mostly feeds back the sentences, but there is so much more to be fed back— something you might not be aware of, and here the attention and awareness of the therapist might be useful. So we have it rather easy compared with the psychoanalysts, because we see the whole being of a person right in front of us, and this is because Gestalt Therapy uses eyes and ears and the therapist stays absolutely in the now. He avoids interpretation, verbiage production, and all other types of mind-fucking. But mind-fucking is mind-fucking. It is also a symptom which might cover something else. But what is there is there. Gestalt Therapy is being in touch with the obvious.

Behavioral Humanism [1]

CARL E. THORESEN

Educators and behavioral scientists can act to help individuals experience life in more positive ways. There are many possible ways to take such actions. One offers considerable promise: the synthesizing of social learning-behavioral principles and techniques with the goals and concerns of humanistic psychology. This synthesis is termed behavioral humanism. We can benefit from the work of behaviorists and humanists if we act to reduce the confusion and ambiguity about contemporary behaviorism and humanism and if we develop and use new scientific methods tailored to the study of human phenomena. In this chapter an effort is made to reduce some of the misunderstanding about contemporary humanism and behaviorism. The intensive experimental study of individuals ($N = 1$ design) is discussed as an "intimate" research design well suited to the study of humanistic concerns. A behavioral approach to self-control is briefly presented as one way of helping the individual gain power for self-direction. A translation of humanistic concepts into human action (response) terms is suggested.

From the 72nd Yearbook, Part I (1973), the National Society for the Study of Education. Reprinted by permission.

[1] The work described herein was conducted at the Stanford Center for Research and Development in Teaching, which is supported in part as a Research and Development Center under Contract No. OEC-6-10-078 with the United States Office of Education, Department of Health, Education, and Welfare. The opinions expressed in this publication do not necessarily reflect the position or policy of the Office of Education, and no official endorsement by the Office of Education should be inferred.

On Humanism

A variety of humanisms have existed since the time of Hellenic civilization. Today there are classical, ethical, scientific, religious, Christian, and rational humanists. Many individuals are essentially humanists, although they do not label themselves as such. Those who identify with humanistic psychology can be seen as representing a blending of psychology as a discipline with ethical forms of humanism (118).

Humanism was and is primarily a philosophical and literary movement. It emerged in the early Renaissance as a reaction against the revealed truth of the Church and the dominance of Aristotelian thinking (1). The early humanists argued that man, through his own intellect, had the power (and the responsibility) to determine his own destiny. It was the Renaissance humanists who made the definitive break that opened the way for the rise of Western science. Interestingly, many contemporary humanists now oppose the scientific world view initiated by earlier humanists.

Kurtz (53) suggests that two basic principles characterize humanism: a rejection of any supernatural world view as established fact and a rejection of any metaphysical divinity as the source of human values. Some people may believe in supernatural powers but, since there is no known empirical means to prove or refute these views, the existence of such powers is a matter not of fact but of personal belief. For the humanist, man must be responsible for himself, especially in deciding what is good, desirable, and worthwhile. Man is the maker of values and man's actions represent, in effect, his values.

Not all humanists, however, accept two other basic principles offered by Kurtz (53): that ethical principles and value judgments should be open to empirical, rational scrutiny and that the methods of science can be applied in solving man's problems. The humanist is generally concerned with what people do in this life—with human actions in life's present circumstances. Many humanists further believe that the use of reason and methods of science provides the best single means of solving human problems and improving the quality of human life. For example, Eysenck (30:25) states that "the use of reason in human affairs applied in the service of compassion" reflects a basic spirit of many humanists.

Definitions of what constitutes humanism are as diverse as the individuals offering the definitions. Interestingly, many contemporary "behaviorists," i.e., behavior therapists, behavioral counselors, and operant psychologists or social learning psychologists consider themselves humanists (see 21, 43, 48, 58, 64, 97, 103, 110, 111). Several reasons explain why behavior-oriented professionals see themselves this way. First of all, they focus on what the individual person *does* in the present life and not on who he *is* in terms of vague social labels or obscure descriptions. Secondly, they emphasize human problems as primarily learning situations where the person is seen as capable of changing. Thirdly, they examine how environments can be altered to reduce and prevent human problems, and, finally, they use scientific procedures to improve techniques for helping individuals.

Differences or distinctions between contemporary behaviorists and humanists do exist. For example, many contemporary humanists have rejected methods of science as a means of problem-solving, whereas behaviorists are strongly committed to the need for rigorous empirical inquiry. As many differences exist, however, within heterogeneous groupings called behaviorist or humanist as between such groupings. The issue is not behaviorism versus humanism; that is a pseudoissue that has been promoted by crude caricatures of these positions. Instead, the issue is how best to utilize the concepts and methodologies of both behavioral and humanistic psychology. An examination of the literature of humanistic psychology should help us clarify the concerns of humanists.

Humanistic Psychology and Education

Many people have written about the concerns of humanistic psychology and education (e.g., see 2, 13, 15, 28, 31, 41, 45, 46, 57, 70, 71, 72, 80, 85, 89, 117). Humanistic psychology and education have been influenced by a host of Eastern and Western schools of philosophy, psychology, and religious thought. Abraham Maslow, Carl Rogers, Rollo May, and Viktor Frankl have in particular extended this influence. The tolerance for diversity and pluralism that characterizes humanistic psychology brings about a confluence of theoretical orientations such as neopsychoanalytic, phenomenological, gestalt, existential, and Rogerian. As a result, the field at present lacks a coherent, integrated, theoretical rationale. This theoretical looseness, though cherished by some, has discouraged empirical research. Buhler (15), in presenting the basic theoretical concepts of humanistic psychology, has distinguished it from the philosophy of humanism in that different concepts, methods, and goals are involved. For Buhler, humanistic psychology must use scientific methods to discover ways of helping the person "experience his existence as real." The humanistic psychologist is seen as more action-oriented than the traditional literary humanist who is seen as one engaged in philosophical disputes and antireligious quarrels.

Jourard (46) has emphasized transcendent behaviors, where the individual learns by committing himself fully in thinking, perceiving, and achieving, by going beyond the typical, by acting divergently, by taking risks, and by using fantasy. Transcendent behavior is made possible by an openness to experience, the ability to focus selectively, skill in using symbols and metaphors, and self-confidence. For Landsman (57) the key unit of behavior is "positive experiencing." He suggests that efforts should be directed toward the "experimental creation of positive experiences." Maslow (69, 70) sees the major task of humanistic psychology as collaborating with the behavioral sciences in the study of how to create physical and social environments that will nurture self-actualization. In discussing humanistic education, Brown (13) has stressed the need for a confluence of the cognitive and the affective aspects of learning. With this integration the curriculum could provide planned educational experiences for all kinds of human learning.

Maslow (70:732) offered what can be viewed as the basic theme of humanistic psychology and education: "The first and overarching Big Problem is to make the Good Person." This concept of creating the good person permeates the writings of humanistic psychology. The task of psychology is to develop methods to help the individual person act in more positive, meaningful ways with himself and with others. An examination of the literature of humanistic psychologists and educators reveals the following concerns:

1. The person as the unit of focus rather than the average performance of large groups and populations
2. The search for unity in human experience; the recognition that the person must exist in harmony with himself and nature
3. Awareness and awakening; attempts to increase the conscious range of the person's behavior, especially in his own internal behavior, such as thoughts, images, and physiological responses
4. The need for compassionate persons, individuals who can communicate personally and intimately with others in a variety of ways and who can also help others experience life more positively
5. Self-determination and responsibility; the ability to identify alternatives, clarify values, make decisions, and accept the responsibility for one's actions
6. Diversity and pluralism; a reverence for the idiosyncratic and the unique in individuals
7. The need for new research techniques and methodologies tailored to the intensive study of the individual person—techniques that avoid the detachment and impersonality of traditional physical science methods
8. The need for educational experiences that engage the individual in a comprehensive sense, involving social, emotional, and sensual actions as well as the so-called academic or cognitive

The focus of action-oriented humanists is on what the individual person does internally and externally. These concerns highlight the *interdependence* of action in stressing the need for unity and harmony in experience. The self-actualizing person is someone who knows what is happening, someone who is aware of a variety of responses taking place both within himself and with others in the external environment. Further, such a person is seen as one who has the skills to "make things happen."

Contemporary Behaviorism

The term *behaviorist* represents a variety of theoretical positions and technical practices. There is diversity and disagreement among those who consider themselves to be behaviorists (22, 88). While all aspects of what constitutes behaviorism cannot be discussed here, a brief discussion may clarify the situation enough to eliminate some stereotypes.

Clearly, the behaviorism lamented by its critics (50, 51, 71) is a dated and inaccurate representation. Behaviorism is not, for example, the simple (minded) application of reinforcement schedules to persons as if they were no different than rats or pigeons. Nor is all behaviorism a physicalistic, empty (headed) black-box psychology. Behaviorism or behavior therapy does not deny thoughts and complex emotions nor does it treat individuals as "simple mechanical entities" (86). At present there is no one type of behaviorism. Behaviorists today range from experimental psychologists who meticulously study specific animal responses in highly controlled laboratories to counselors and therapists who work with the immediate complex problems of individuals. Contemporary behaviorism is, in fact, a rich conglomeration of principles, assumptions, and techniques.

Perhaps what characterizes all behaviorists is their use of experimental methods, their reliance on empirical data based on careful observation, their concern for objectivity and replication of results, their focus on the environment and what the organism is doing currently, and their rejection of inner causes or entities as the sole or most important determinant of human action. To the behaviorist, the "here and now" contemporary environment is a prime focus of concern because much of what a person does is a function of environmental events.

Popular conceptions of behaviorism often fail to acknowledge differences between behaviorists. Some *conventional* behaviorists have emphasized internal processes such as drive reduction or habit strength to explain behavior (23, 44). Others have suggested curiosity and exploratory drives that are elicited by external stimuli (8, 40) while still others have conceptualized internal sensory feedback processes to explain behavior (79). In addition, conventional behaviorism has emphasized operational definitions and the direct observation of physical responses. Some conventional behaviorists are also dualistic in the Cartesian mind-body sense. To them the events of the mind are not to be understood in the same fashion as physical behavior, i.e., sensory motor (88). Conventional behaviorists have also relied heavily on extensive deductive theories and have typically employed experimental group designs in their research (e.g., 44).

In contrast, the *radical* behaviorist rejected this mind-body dualism, the reliance on operational definitions and mentalistic explanations such as drive states and drive reduction (101).[2] Private events, that is, what goes on within the person, are viewed as influenced by the same learning principles as is external behavior. The radical behaviorist also rejects elaborate experimental group designs and reliance on inferential statistics of the conventionalists based on the average performance of groups of subjects. Instead, he considers that the individual organism serves as the focus of research and that observations are to be made continuously before, during, and after planned interventions with an emphasis on careful description.

Besides conventional and radical behaviorists there are social learning or cognitive behaviorists (e.g., 6), who emphasize internal processes such as thoughts and imagery in explaining how learning occurs. At the present, the term *behaviorist* may therefore refer to conventional, radical, or cognitive-oriented behaviorism.

Watson and Skinner

The early behaviorism of Watson (115) sought to reduce all human action to physical terms and to explain it in those terms. Figuratively, the early S-R advocates believed that if the phenomenon could not be reduced to units that comfortably fitted in their scientific test tube, then the phenomenon was metaphysical and meaningless. Watson denied the existence of consciousness and awareness, rejected introspection (self-report) as a valid scientific method, and saw all of man's actions as determined by forces outside the person. The spirit of Watson's viewpoint is represented in a recent article (61) in which it is argued that much of what is called behavior ther-

[2] A distinction is sometimes made between the early radical behaviorism of John Watson and B. F. Skinner's contemporary radical behaviorism (Day, 22; Terrace, 107). Both are labeled radical in rejecting mentalistic inner explanations such as drives. However, Watson's highly physicalistic S-R rationale, coupled with a dualistic perspective, differs markedly from Skinner's operant theory (99).

apy today is not behavioristic since these therapies, e.g., the systematic desensitization of Wolpe (122), use covert processes, rely on self-reports from clients, and are not restricted to behavior directly observable by others. For the early Watsonian behaviorist and some conventional behaviorists today, the focus is on physically based operational definitions and direct physical assessment. If the phenomenon in question cannot be measured directly with some type of physical device—ruler, scale, calipers, polygraph—then the phenomenon is beyond scientific interest. Except for physiological responses such as heart rate, which can be measured directly and independent of the individual, covert events are deemed beyond controlled inquiry.

The radical behaviorism of Skinner differs from the conventional S-R framework in several ways. Skinner rejected the positivistic operationalism and the limited physicalistic rationale of the earlier behaviorists and functionalists (101). He argued that in an adequate science of behavior nothing that determines conduct can be overlooked, no matter how difficult of access it may be. Skinner acknowledged the role of private events in explaining behavior and the person's internal environment. He observed, "It would be a mistake to refuse to consider them (private events) as data just because a second observer cannot feel or see them . . ." (99:242). He remained skeptical, however, concerning how central a role internal responses play in determining what the individual does. Covert responses such as thoughts or internal sentences are not autonomous but, rather, owe their existence to a public history of learning.

Skinner also rejected the animistic and mentalistic explanations of behavior, such as ego, positive growth force, drive reduction or sensory drive mechanism, as explanatory fictions created to explain what is not yet understood. Skinner contended that the individual behaves internally and these covert responses are explainable by the same principles as are observable external responses (100, 102). Since the individual may be the only person with access to a private event such as a self-verbalization, self-reports of private events are justified. Skinner (97, 100, 102) has consistently acknowledged the difficulties in dealing scientifically with internal phenomena. While his own work has avoided inquiry into the area, his theoretical rationale clearly recognizes the import of the individual's internal behavior.

Skinner's basic unit of analysis, the three-term contingency, is very significant for its relevance in understanding the causes of individual action. Human behavior (internal or external) is influenced by preceding events (stimulus control) and by events that follow certain actions (outcome control). These antecedent and consequent events may be internal, within the person, as well as external to the person.

To understand why the individual does certain things, one must carefully observe the conditions and circumstances surrounding his actions.[3]

The most recent development in contemporary behaviorism can be called the social behavior or social learning approach (6, 78). This type of behaviorism does not conceptualize behavior in Skinner's operant response terms (e.g., the three-term contingency). Further, it does not utilize the traits, motives, and drive explanations of conventional behaviorists (23, 29), nor does it reject the relevance of internal processes and events. Indeed, to social learning behaviorists the often-cited empty "black box" is considered quite full.

In the social behavior view, individual actions are seen as regulated by three basic processes: stimulus control, internal symbolic control, and outcome control (6). A major focus of the social behavior theory is on the person's covert symbolic responses. Mediation, what goes on with the person, is viewed as important data, as is the "meaning" or significance of a particular situation to the person. Bandura (6) has emphasized the importance of vicarious or observational learning which takes place by means of symbolic processes within the individual. Observational learning is not explained in an external stimulus cue and reinforcement paradigm. Rather, observational learning is presented as a dynamic sequence of complex processes involving attentional, retentional, reproductive, and motivational factors.

In the social learning perspective a distinction is made between acquisition of behavior (learning) and its performance. Internal symbolic and sensory process play the major part in learning new behavior while the external contingencies of reinforcement (outcomes) determine if the behavior is then performed. Reinforcement is seen as primarily of informational and incentive value. The individual can learn without overtly performing and without any direct reinforcement. Social behaviorists view the individual person as a dynamically changing organism rather than as a passive receptacle of enduring responses. The internal and external actions of each person are primarily influenced by the specific "here and now" experiences.

Social behaviorism and Skinner's radical behaviorism are highly similar in stressing current environmental situations as prime deter-

[3] Interestingly, the "radical" position of Skinner is shared considerably by the radical phenomenology of Sartre and Merleau-Ponty (74) who reject what they consider the introspective, dualistic, idealistic views of American phenomenologists such as Rogers and May. These radical phenomenologists stress the primacy of observing and describing human behavior. Mentalistic causes and notions of inner man are rejected. Instead, human behavior is to be understood by examining the interaction between the person and his environment. See Kvale and Grenners (54).

minants of human action. While Skinner's theoretical work has clearly recognized private events and the individual's internal environment, the research and practice of radical behaviorists has generally avoided this area. Social behaviorists, however, have pursued the more complex area of symbolic behavior, seeking to understand how covert events as responses interact with external responses to regulate what the person does.

Behaviorism today is far more than the psychology of Watson with its physicalistic concerns or the drive reduction-oriented animal experiments of the conventionalists. *Behaviorism* as a term denotes an emphasis on the comprehensive and systematic study of the individual, which uses empirical methods to examine how current environments may be influencing the individual's action. What goes on within the individual—covert responses—represents important data.

Some basic characteristics of contemporary radical behaviorism and social learning approaches are as follows:

1. A monistic view of the individual and a rejection of a dualistic mind-body theory
2. A belief that public or observable events are functionally similar to private or covert events and that both kinds of events are influenced by the same learning processes and principles
3. A rejection of inner "mentalistic" explanations of behavior
4. A belief that behavior is determined primarily by the immediate environment, including the person's internal environment
5. A use of scientific methods that stress careful, systematic observation and control of behavior, including self-observation and self-control
6. A rejection of using trait-state labels (e.g. introvert) to describe the person, based on the belief that the individual is best described and understood by examining what he does in particular situations

Intensive Study of the Individual

Traditional research designs and techniques have been grossly inadequate for the scientific study of the individual person. Prevailing research methodologies have been criticized for their irrelevance in understanding the actions of individuals (19, 69, 105, 109, 123). Controlled psychological research has relied almost exclusively on a particular type of research design that requires the use of large groups of subjects and the concomitant need for elaborate statistical procedures. This type of design has been often exalted as the only true and legitimate strategy for scientific inquiry (19).

A cursory review of research textbooks used in psychology testifies to the dominance of comparative group designs. These extensive designs with their focus on the mean performance of groups of individuals have yielded limited information about the whats and whys of individual performance. A major reason for this has to do with the underlying assumptions of extensive designs, such as the concept of "intrinsic" variability of individuals within groups and the role of the central limit theorem (94). In effect, most psychological research has sought generalizations that apply to the performance of populations. Such generalizations have required the need for random sampling from populations—an assumption almost always violated by psychological researchers (27)—and the use of statistical techniques to handle troublesome individual variability. Such variability is sometimes referred to as error or nuisance variance or unexplained individual fluctuations. Extensive designs using group comparisons represent a powerful strategy to verify hypotheses about hypothetical populations. However, such designs are concerned with only one facet of the cycle of scientific inquiry, which includes discovery, description, observation, induction, deduction, and verification (55, 84). Scientific inquiry requires a variety of designs and techniques; there is no one best method.

Fortunately, an alternative design, one with a long and honorable history in science (25), is available. The intensive empirical study of the single case, $N = 1$, is an experimental design ideally suited for the kind of "intimate" inquiry required for the concerns of humanists. The intensive design avoids many of the problems of large-group studies deriving from the use of statistical techniques to control for individual variation rather than precise experimental control, from random sampling from hypothetical populations, from the failure to pinpoint specific cause-and-effect relationships for individual behavior, and from not providing continuous data on changes of every subject throughout all phases of the investigation. The intensive design, sometimes referred to as the experimental study of the individual, is based on different assumptions than the group designs. Further, it seeks to answer different questions, such as how specific conditions influence certain individual actions over time. The concern is not with what Kurt Lewin (59) once called "on the average thinking," but with understanding how each individual is influenced by specific interventions.

Comprehensive discussions of the intensive experimental study of individual behavior are available (14, 19, 94, 108, 120). These discussions provide detailed information on different types of intensive designs such as multiple time series, the base-line treatment reversals, and multiple base-line procedures. The discussion here is (a) to introduce the relevance of intensive designs for examining the kind of overt and covert human behavior of concern to humanists, (b) to suggest that criticism of behavioral or scientific research has been misdirected because of stereotyped conceptions, and (c) to summarize the merits of intensive designs in studying individual behavior.

Maslow (69), one of the founders of humanistic psychology, deplored the rigid conventionalism of psychological researchers. He believed it was possible and desirable to develop new methods and designs for studying the individual scientifically. Allport (3) long ago urged that idiographic rather than nomothetic strategies should be used if we are to understand individuals. Allport developed a variety of what he called morphogenic methods, such as personal letters, questionnaires, structured interviews, and biographies, along with self-anchoring rating scales, to study the structure of each individual. Similarly, Lewin (59) argued that the individual should be studied in relation to his current environment, which he described as "concrete whole situations." Lewin criticized the Aristotelian logic underlying extensive designs and classical statistics, which required the individual to be viewed as a random or capricious event. Instead, Lewin believed that the actions of each individual were lawful and understandable through scientific investigation if appropriate designs were developed. Skinner (98), somewhat in the tradition of the early $N = 1$ experimental psychologists of the late nineteenth century (e.g., Ebbinghaus), challenged the orthodoxy of statistical group research methodologies. Skinner argued that the prevalent use of inferential statistical operations kept investigators away from working directly with data, an argument also raised by others (5, 104). To Skinner, functional or causal relationships could best be discovered and confirmed by exercising tight experimental control of the situation. Elaborate group statistics were too often used as an excuse for failing to use experimental control.

Skinner's early work with animal subjects was based on a continuous observing and recording of data over long periods of time. Various interventions were tried and the results directly observed. On the basis of these observations, interventions were often altered. In this way the investigator learned from the data; his actions were determined by what the individual subject was observed to do. It is the potential for this rich interplay between the researcher and the individual subject that makes the intensive design a powerful research strategy—a design similar to the Taoist approach to inquiry advanced by Maslow (69).

Some critics of behavioral psychology have used the "subjective" revolution in physics with its concepts of indeterminacy, complementarity, and uncertainty as a basis of rejecting the methods of scientific psychology (71). Since the performance of individual atoms and electrons can neither be predicted nor controlled, man, it is argued, is also beyond prediction and control. Man is seen as just as complex as an atom or an electron. Therefore, behavioral psychology with its deterministic rationale of classical science derived from Newton and Hume is viewed as inappropriate for the study of man.

The problem of this kind of analogous thinking is that it assumes that *all* human action functions in the same way as subatomic particles. All human activity, from the movement of blood cells to verbal responses, cannot be explained by any single rationale. Physics did not reject classical determinism totally in the twentieth century but, instead, expanded its rationales to fit various phenomena. The question is what types of human behavior are best understood by what explanatory rationales. The determinism versus indeterminism argument is a pseudoissue that fails to capture the complexities involved. We do not know enough at present about how different types of human behavior are influenced. Undoubtedly the rigid, mechanistic determinism of classical Western science with its notions of absolute prediction is invalid for much of the human activity of concern to humanists. Clearly there is a need for a variety of causal models and research strategies (9). Our task is to find out which human actions are best explained by what principles and which kinds of research designs are most appropriate to facilitate such inquiry.

Given the limited status of our understanding about individual human behavior, the intensive experimental study of individuals seems very promising. Every design of course has its limitations. Bandura (6:243–44) presents shortcomings of intensive designs, such as the problem of not being able to return to the base line after treatment and the confounding of sequential treatment effects. However, much is to be learned from focusing carefully on the individual through controlled observation and description. An intensive approach to research promises to create inquiry that is more personal and intimate in dealing with the individual. If we are to learn, the individual person cannot be treated as an inanimate object to be manipulated, but must be viewed as a dynamic, active organism. The individual has much to teach us. When it comes to understanding man, perhaps the person himself can be one of the best scientific tools in existence.

The intensive experimental study of the individual offers the following advantages:

1. The unit of focus is the specific actions of the individual subjects rather than average performance of groups.
2. The frequency, magnitude and/or variability of the individual's actions can be examined continuously during and between each phase of the investigation.
3. The individual subject serves as his own control in that the magnitude

and duration of change is compared to his own base line of actions. In this way, past experience and individual differences are fully controlled.

4. Experimental control of variables is greatly facilitated, thereby reducing the need for statistical control through complex inferential statistics.

5. The effects of treatment administered simultaneously or sequentially on one or more individual behaviors can be examined over time for a particular individual.

6. Causal or functional relationships are established by replication (reproducibility) of specific results for the same individual and across individuals. In this way, evidence of generalization is systematically gathered without recourse to the often untenable assumption of random sampling.

7. The clinician as researcher can determine the extent of specific changes in individual actions continuously before, during, and after treatment; changes in treatment can be made and evaluated promptly.

8. Scientific inquiry into both external and internal behavior is possible.

Freedom and Self-Control

A growing area of behavioral research concerns self-control. What are the internal and external controlling responses that influence internal and external actions? Behavioral researchers are particularly interested in developing techniques to teach individuals how to manage their own actions. Some humanistic writers (10, 72) have criticized behaviorists for their failure to consider freedom and self-direction. Believing that the person is and should be free to decide what he shall do in a given situation, that human action is not predetermined and is not predictable, they see the behaviorist as someone who would deprive man of this freedom to determine his own actions. They equate the prediction and control of human behavior by others with the demise of freedom and dignity. But they view the individual's ability to predict and control his *own* actions as freedom.

The problem with this view of the individual's freedom is that past and present experiences with other persons do subtly influence what an individual may decide to do in the present. Common sense would suggest that the person can decide to do something completely independent of anything else. And a venerable literary tradition supports the view that self-direction operates entirely within the person. The person who thus charts his own course and makes his own choices is a free and dignified individual (56).

Freedom and dignity, however, are measured in individual actions. The free person has the power to take certain actions. The power, and therefore the freedom, depends on awareness, that is, the conscious processing of all kinds of information. Recall the premium placed on awareness by humanistic psychologists. Awareness is crucial, since information (stimuli, to use a technical term) influences the individual's behavior. The person who has information and who can control it is free. Terrace (107) argues that awareness is actually a learned behavior. The person learns to distinguish certain internal responses which he then labels "angry," "happy," "upset," and so forth. Awareness therefore consists of discriminating items of information or stimuli and describing them in some way. How a person "labels" information about his own behavior has been studied recently in attribution research (91). Inaccurate labeling and faulty stimulus discrimination by a person may be one type of maladaptive behavior pattern. The person, unable to explain adequately to himself the high arousal he is experiencing, concludes he is irrational and mentally disturbed (124).

In many ways the difference between individual freedom and control by others lies in "who is manipulating what stimuli" (62:214) or who is using and controlling information that influences human action. Awareness is the basis of freedom and self-control because it provides the individual with the information he needs to change his own sources of stimulation, both internal and external. Freedom versus determinism is therefore a pseudoissue. The freedom to act depends on the person's being aware of, or knowing, what kinds of information (stimuli) influence his own behavior. This awareness must include internal or covert stimuli as well as external data for both internal and external behavior.

Staats (103) has suggested that the very young child learns self-control by observing others. The young child talks aloud to himself at first, then gradually replaces these overt verbalizations with covert talk or self-verbalization in the form of self-instructions. After the first few years of life, the person engages in a great deal of covert speech (63, 113). However, his awareness of this internal behavior quickly diminishes. Thus, over time it *seems* to the person as if what he does is spontaneous and totally determined from within. Once behavior such as covert speech is learned from environmental experiences, however, that behavior can determine, in part, what the person will do. In this way it may be said that the person causes his own current and future behavior through what he has learned in the past. The person therefore acquires covert responses such as self-verbalization from others in his verbal community. The availability of these learned covert responses to the person determines whether that person is "free to act."

A series of experiments by Meichenbaum (75) and his colleagues illustrates how persons can be taught through social learning techniques "to talk to themselves differently" as a way of gaining greater freedom and self-control. In one study, children who had difficulty attending to a task were first provided concrete examples (social models) of others instructing themselves by speaking aloud. The children then practiced self-verbalizations with fewer external cues until they could direct their own actions without external support. In another study, adults labeled as schizophrenics were taught how to use covert self-instructions along with how to become aware of certain information that usually preceded their "crazy behavior." This training in using covert responses helped these individuals to gain greater self-control.

Viktor Frankl's modern classic, *Man's Search for Meaning* (34), exemplifies how the verbal community in most Western cultures teaches the person to conceptualize self-control as a vague inner force. Throughout Frankl's moving description of life in a concentration camp, he describes circumstances in which he used self-verbalization or vivid imagery. For long periods of time Frankl managed his inner environment by carrying on covert conversations with his wife or with friends, coupled with "mental pictures" of persons and situations. In this way aversive external stimuli—the sight of dead bodies, the verbal abuse by guards, and physiological cues such as hunger—were controlled. Frankl did not conceptualize his covert actions as influencing other behaviors, however. Instead, he explained them in terms of inner life and freedom. Frankl survived, he states, not because he was able to use a variety of effective covert responses in an extremely aversive external environment, but because he possessed an inner strength, a sense of meaning, and dignity. It might also be said that he survived because he had learned to use vivid images and to carry on covert dialogues with himself.

Techniques for self-control have had a long, though somewhat obscure, history. Varieties of Yoga and Zen procedures for self-managing thoughts and physiological responses have existed for over two thousand years. There is evidence that certain individuals have achieved astonishing levels of self-control. Green (37), for example, has reported laboratory studies with a yoga master who radically altered his heart rate, body temperature, and brain wave patterns repeatedly on demand. The yogi was engaging in a complex pattern of covert behavior that altered these responses. The unanswered questions are, What were these controlling behaviors? How did they function to effect such changes?

Research by behavior-oriented investigators has been expanding recently into physiological feedback (biofeedback) training, cognitive focusing, and the instrumental (operant) conditioning of glandular and visceral responses (26, 38, 77, 83, 116). DuPraw (26), for example, utilizing the work of Schultz and Luthe (93) in autogenic training, demonstrated that some individuals could significantly reduce their heart rate by using self-instructions (covert verbalizations) and selected imagery responses. Miller (77) and his colleagues have provided data in a series of animal studies which show that a great variety of internal physiological responses can be "voluntarily" controlled by the organism if reinforcing stimuli are provided. The well-publicized biofeedback studies (e.g., 20) involving EEG alpha waves have suggested that the person can learn to alter his "state of consciousness" if information or awareness of his current performance is provided.[4]

Humanistic Behaviors

Earlier a summary of humanistic concerns was presented. These concerns were stated in rather abstract terms. It seems possible, however, to reconceptualize or translate these important ideas directly into statements of human action. Such a translation will encourage empirical research that examines how the frequency and magnitude of these human actions can be changed. In addition, it is reasonable to consider these humanistic concepts in terms of internal (covert) and external (overt) behavior (60). Because the human organism is a complex system which responds within and without *simultaneously*, the use of an internal-external classification is arbitrary. Such a classification may be helpful at this point, however, in facilitating understanding and in fostering controlled research.

Some humanists may argue that translating these concerns into human response terms is oversimplistic and reductionistic and that it is merely another thinly disguised effort at resurrecting the same old behaviorist mentality of only dealing with simple, readily observed behavior (72). Admittedly, the approach is simple and may fail to capture *all* aspects of the phenomena involved. However, proceeding from the simple to the more complex has been one of the most successful strategies of modern science (69). In an area where relatively little empirical data are available, moving from the simple to the complex on the basis of empirically derived data is crucial. The major question concerns the development of methods to help persons act in more humanistic ways. If a translation is indeed too simple, then the methods will not work. The answer is to be found empirically, not in logical argument.

INTERNAL RESPONSE. An examination of the humanistic literature suggests a variety of statements that can be translated into response

[4] Pages 402–411, on "Behavioral Self-Control" have been deleted from the original article (editor).

terms. First let us consider internal actions. The following is a sample of internal response categories in which the importance of the increase/decrease factor is evident. The humanistic phrases are in parentheses.

1. Increase the frequency, variety, and accuracy of internal self-observation responses (self-knowledge; *knows* what is going on within; is really aware of self).
2. Increase the frequency of perceptually accurate responses (can see things for what they really are; knows what others are experiencing).
3. Increase the frequency and variety of low-probability responses (has new and unusual thoughts, physical sensations, images).
4. Decrease the frequency of stress and tension responses within the body (experiences tranquility; calmness in everyday life).
5. Increase the frequency of highly consistent psychophysiological responses (experiences sense of unity within; the body is in agreement with the head).
6. Increase the frequency and variety of imagery responses (engages in rich fantasy; has a well-developed imagination).
7. Increase the frequency of using psychophysiological responses in specific situations as criteria (trusts his own experiences; reads himself and uses personal reactions to decide).
8. Decrease the frequency and variety of self-critical, negative responses (accepts oneself as worthy; experiences oneself as positive; thinks positively about self and others).

Let us explore a few of these translations. The first item on self-observation of internal responses (thoughts, images, and physiological responses) is one example of translating humanistic statements into response terms. One way of conceptualizing self-observation is the systematic recording of a particular internal response such as positive self-thoughts. Here the individual makes discriminations about whether certain covert verbalizations constitute positive self-thoughts. The individual can record these positive self-thoughts by tallying each occurrence on a card or using a wrist counter. At the end of a particular time period, such as a day, the person notes the total frequency of positive self-thoughts. This represents one way that self-knowledge of internal events can be examined.

Item 4, concerning stress and tension responses, might be dealt with by teaching the person how to use deep muscle relaxation techniques, or how to stop stressful thoughts when they occur. Once instructed, the person may experience more tranquility and calmness in his everyday life.

Self-critical, negative responses constitute a major factor in self-esteem and self-acceptance (39). Thus, helping a person reduce the frequency and variety of self-critical thoughts represents one way of encouraging self-esteem. The individual, of course, should also be engaging in external actions that encourage positive thoughts about himself. Since some persons manifest high frequencies of negative self-thoughts that lack any external basis, reducing these negative internal responses may be prerequisite to promoting more positive responses about oneself.

EXTERNAL RESPONSES. Here are a few tentative translations of other humanistic phrases into external response categories. Examples of external response categories are as follows:

1. Increase the frequency, variety, and accuracy of external observation responses, both of the self and of others (knows what is happening with others around him; knows what is happening with himself).
2. Increase the frequency and variety of positive verbal responses (can self-disclose; can be assertive when necessary; can empathize with others).
3. Increase the frequency and variety of positive nonverbal responses (can relate to others in many ways; seems to really care and be concerned).
4. Increase the frequency of using environmental stimulus cues by altering physical environments (makes things happen for himself and for others).
5. Decrease the frequency and variety of socially aversive, negative verbal and nonverbal responses (positive, accepting person; deals with disagreement and disapproval in constructive ways).
6. Increase the frequency and variety of positive verbal and nonverbal responses to animate and inanimate natural situations (good relationships with nature; feels close to nature).

Positive verbal responses (item 2) is obviously a very broad response category. The notion of what constitutes a positive verbal response is relative to the consequences of such behavior in particular situations. However, specific verbal responses such as self-disclosing behavior can be defined, and planned learning situations can be used to increase such behaviors (107). Similarly, aversive talk and gestures (item 5) can be specified and then altered through structured learning situations. One way of "making things happen" (item 4) is by changing certain features of the physical environment. For example, the person can rearrange room furnishings to prompt certain behaviors and to discourage others.

Since the concerns of humanists have to do with what the individual does, a translation of these concerns into more specific action or response terms will help in promoting humanistic behavior. Well-controlled empirical studies of how individuals change will reveal if the suggested translation into terms of specific actions has missed the humanistic mark.

In Summary

Contemporary environments, in their complexities and subtle manipulations, have reduced the individual person's power to manage his own life (76). Modern humanists and contemporary behaviorists are both concerned with helping the person experience life more positively. The translation of humanistic concerns into human response terms represents one way of encouraging meaningful scientific inquiry. Literary, nonempirical, and antiscientific orientations cannot provide the data needed to develop techniques for giving power to the individual. Polemics and stereotyping by humanists have accomplished little, except to retard scientific progress. Furthermore, the myopic perspective of conventional behaviorists and other scientists preoccupied with "hard" data have also impeded research.

We need a synthesizing perspective that draws from a variety of sources and avoids invidious dichotomies—humanist versus behaviorist. The beginnings of one such perspective has been suggested. Humanistic psychologists and educators share much with contemporary behaviorists. All are concerned with increasing our understanding of overt and covert processes that influence the actions of individuals. The intensive, empirical study of the individual offers a methodology highly relevant to the intimate study of the individual. One way of conceptualizing self-control that stresses the continuity of behavior has been suggested. Self-controlling actions are possible through self-observation as well as through individual and environmental planning. Some promising self-control techniques are already available.

Misunderstanding and misinformation among behavioral scientists, educators, and humanistic scholars has prevented much needed scientific inquiry. Well-controlled empirical research can provide valuable data. With such data we can learn how to help the individual engage in self-actualizing behavior.

REFERENCES

1. Abbagnano, N. *The Encyclopedia of Philosophy,* vol. 4. New York: Macmillan Co. and the Free Press, 1967.
2. Allport, G. W. *Pattern and Growth in Personality.* New York: Holt, Rinehart & Winston, 1963.
3. Allport, G. W. *Personality: A Psychological Interpretation.* New York: Holt, Rinehart & Winston, 1937.
4. Ashem, B., and Donner, L. "Covert Sensitization with Alcoholics: A

Controlled Replication." *Behaviour Research and Therapy* 6 (1968): 7–12.

5. Bakan, D. *On Method: Toward a Reconstruction of Psychological Investigation.* San Francisco: Jossey-Bass, 1967.

6. Bandura, A. *Principles of Behavior Modification.* New York: Holt, Rinehart & Winston, 1969.

7. Barber, T.; Di Cara, L. V.; Kamiya, J.; Miller, N. E.; Shapiro, D.; and Stoyva, J.; eds. *Biofeedback and Self-Control.* Chicago: Aldine Publishing Co., 1971.

8. Berlyne, D. E. *Conflict, Arousal, and Curiosity.* New York: McGraw-Hill Book Co., 1960.

9. Blackburn, J. R. "Sensuous-Intellectual Complementarity in Science." *Science* 172 (1971): 1003–7.

10. Blanshard, B. "The Limits of Naturalism." *Mind Science and History,* vol. 2 of Contemporary Philosophic Thought: The International Philosophy Year Conferences at Brockport. Albany: State University of New York Press, 1970.

11. Bolstad, O. D., and Johnson, S. M. "Self-Regulation in the Modification of Disruptive Classroom Behavior." Unpublished manuscript, University of Oregon, 1971.

12. Broden, M.; Hall, R. V.; and Mitts, B. "The Effect of Self-Recording on the Classroom Behavior of Two Eighth-Grade Students." *Journal of Applied Behavior Analysis* 4 (1971): 191–99.

13. Brown, G. *Human Teaching for Human Learning.* New York: Viking Press, 1970.

14. Browning, R. M.; and Stover, D. D. *Behavior Modification in Child Treatment.* Chicago: Aldine-Atherton, 1971.

15. Buhler, C. "Basic Theoretical Concepts of Humanistic Psychology." *American Psychologist* 26 (1971): 378–86.

16. Cautela, J. R. "Behavior Therapy and Self-Control." In *Behavior Therapy Appraisal and Status,* edited by C. Franks, pp. 323–40. New York: McGraw-Hill Book Co., 1969.

17. ———. "Covert Conditioning." *The Psychology of Private Events: Perspectives on Covert Response Systems,* edited by A. Jacobs and L. Sachs, pp. 112–30. New York: Academic Press, 1971.

18. ———. "Covert Sensitization." *Psychological Record* 20 (1967): 459–68.

19. Chassan, J. B. *Research Design in Clinical Psychology and Psychiatry.* New Appleton-Century-Crofts, Appleton-Centry-Crofts, 1967.

20. Collier, B. L. "Brain Power—the Case for Bio-Feedback Training." *Saturday Review,* April 10, 1971, 10–13ff.

21. Day, W. F. "Humanistic Psychology and Contemporary Humanism." *Humanist* 31 (1971): 13–16.

22. ———. "Radical Behaviorism in Reconciliation with Phenomenology." *Journal of the Experimental Analysis of Behavior* 12 (1969): 315–28.

23. Dollard, J., and Miller, N. E. *Personality and Psychotherapy: An Analysis in Terms of Learning, Thinking, and Culture.* New York: McGraw-Hill Book Co., 1950.

24. Dubos, R. *So Human an Animal*. New York: Charles Scribner's Sons, 1968.

25. Dukes, W. F. "N = 1." *Psychological Bulletin* 64 (1965): 74–79.

26. DuPraw, V. "Self-Management of Internal Responses: Heart Rate Control." Doctoral dissertation. Stanford University, 1972.

27. Edgington, E. S. "Statistical Inference and Nonrandom Samples." *Psychological Bulletin* 66 (1966): 485–87.

28. Edwards, I. *A Humanistic View*. Sydney: Angus & Robertson, 1969.

29. Eysenck, H. J. *Behaviour Therapy and the Neuroses*. London: Pergammon Press, 1960.

30. ———. "Behavior Therapy as a Scientific Discipline." *Journal of Consulting and Clinical Psychology* 36 (1971): 314–19.

31. Fairfield, R. P., ed. *Humanistic Frontiers in American Education*. Englewood Cliffs, N.J.: Prentice-Hall, 1971.

32. Ferster, C. B. "Classification of Behavioral Pathology." In *Research in Behavior Modification*, edited by L. Krasner and L. Ullmann, pp. 6–26. New York: Holt, Rinehart & Winston, 1965.

33. Ferster, C. B.; Nurnberger, J. I.; and Levitt, E. B. "The Control of Eating." *Journal of Mathematics* 1 (1962): 87–109.

34. Frankl, V. E. *Man's Search for Meaning: An Introduction to Logotherapy*. New York: Washington Square Press, 1959.

35. Goldfried, M. R. "Systematic Desensitization As Training in Self-Control." *Journal of Consulting and Clinical Psychology* 37 (1971): 228–34.

36. Goldiamond, I. "Self-Control Procedures in Personal Behavior Problems," *Psychological Reports* 17 (1965): 851–68.

37. Green, E. "Varieties of Healing Experiences." Invited address, De Anza College, October 30, 1971.

38. Green, E.; Green, A.; and Walters, E. "Self-Regulation of Internal States," *Progress of Cybernics: Proceedings of the International Congress of Cybernetics, London, 1969*, edited by J. Rose, et al. London, 1970.

38a. Hannum, J. W. "The Modification of Evaluative Self-Thoughts and Their Effects on Overt Behavior." Doctoral dissertation, Stanford University, 1972.

39. Harris, M. B. "Self-directed Program for Weight Control: A Pilot Study." *Journal of Abnormal Psychology* 74 (1969): 263–70.

40. Harlow, H. F. "Motivation as a Factor in the Acquisition of New Responses." In *Current Theory and Research in Motivation: A Symposium*, pp. 24–49. Lincoln: University of Nebraska Press, 1953.

41. Heath, R. S. *The Reasonable Adventurer*. Pittsburgh: University of Pittsburgh Press, 1969.

42. Homme, L. E. "Perspective in Psychology: XXIV. Control of Coverants, the Operants of the Mind." *Psychological Record* 15 (1965): 501–11.

43. Hosford, R. E., and Zimmer, J. "Humanism through Behaviorism." *Counseling and Values* 16 (1972): 1–7.

44. Hull, C. L. *Principles of Behavior*. New York: Appleton-Century-Crofts, 1943.

45. Huxley, A. "Education on the Non-Verbal Level." In *Contemporary Educational Psychology*, edited by R. M. Jones, pp. 44–60. New York: Harper Torchbooks, 1966.
46. Jourard, S. M. *Disclosing Man to Himself.* Princeton, N.J.: D. Van Nostrand Co., 1968.
47. Kanfer, F. H. "The Maintenance of Behavior by Self-generated Stimuli and Reinforcement." In *The Psychology of Private Events*, edited by A. Jacobs and L. Sachs, pp. 39–59. New York: Academic Press, 1971.
48. Kanfer, F. H., and Phillips, J. S. *Learning Foundations of Behavior Therapy.* New York: John Wiley & Sons, 1970.
49. Kelly, G. *The Psychology of Personal Constructs*, vol. 1. New York: W. W. Norton & Co., 1955.
50. Koch, S. "Psychology and Emerging Conceptions of Knowledge as Unitary." In *Behaviorism and Phenomenology: Contrasting Bases for Modern Psychology*, edited by T. W. Wann. Chicago: University of Chicago Press, 1964.
51. Koestler, A. *The Ghost in the Machine.* New York: Macmillan Co., 1967.
52. Krasner, L. "Behavior Therapy." In *Annual Review of Psychology* 22 (1971): 483–532.
53. Kurtz, P. "What Is Humanism?" In *Moral Problems in Contemporary Society*, edited by P. Kurtz. New York: Prentice-Hall, 1969.
54. Kvale, S., and Grenness, C. E. "Skinner and Sartre: Towards a Radical Phenomenology of Behavior?" *Review of Existential Psychology and Psychiatry* 7 (1967): 128–48.
55. Lackenmeyer, C. W. "Experimentation—A Misunderstood Methodology in Psychological and Social-Psychological Research." *American Psychologist* 25 (1970): 617–24.
56. Lamont, C. *Freedom of Choice Affirmed.* New York: Horizon Press, 1967.
57. Landsman, T. "Positive Experience and the Beautiful Person." Presidential address, Southeastern Psychological Association, April 5, 1968.
58. Lazarus, A. *Behavior Therapy and Beyond.* New York: McGraw-Hill Book Co., 1971.
59. Lewin, K. *A Dynamic Theory of Personality—Selected Papers.* New York: McGraw-Hill Book Co., 1935.
60. Lichtenstein, P. E. "A Behavioral Approach to 'Phenomenological Data'." *Psychological Record* 21 (1971): 1–16.
61. Locke, E. A. "Is 'Behavior Therapy' Behavioristic? (An Analysis of Wolpe's Psychotherapeutic Methods)." *Psychological Bulletin* 76 (1971): 318–27.
62. London, P. *Behavior Control*, New York: Harper & Row, 1969.
63. Luria, A. R. *The Role of Speech in the Regulation of Normal and Abnormal Behavior.* New York: Liveright, 1961.
64. MacCorquodale, K. "Behaviorism Is a Humanism." *Hummanist* 31 (April-May 1971): 12–13.
65. Mahoney, M. J. "Research Issues in Self-Management." *Behavior Therapy* 3 (1972): 45–63.

66. ———. "The Self-Management of Covert Behaviors: A Case Study." *Behavior Therapy* 2 (1971): 575–78.
67. ———. "Toward an Experimental Analysis of Coverant Control." *Behavior Therapy* 1 (1970): 510–21.
68. Marston, A., and McFall, R. M. "Comparison of Behavior Modification Approaches to Smoking Reduction." *Journal of Consulting and Clinical Psychology* 36 (1971): 153–62.
69. Maslow, A. H. *The Psychology of Science.* New York: Harper & Row, 1966.
70. ———. "Towards a Humanistic Biology." *American Psychologist* 24 (1965): 724–35.
71. Matsen, F. *The Broken Image.* New York: George Braziller, 1964.
72. Matsen, F. W. "Counterrebuttal." *Humanist* 31 (April–May 1971): 18–19.
73. McFall, R. "Effects of Self-Monitoring on Normal Smoking Behavior." *Journal of Consulting and Clinical Psychology* 35 (1970): 135–42.
74. Merleau-Ponty, M. *The Structure of Behaviour.* London: Metheun, 1965.
75. Meichenbaum, D. H. "Cognitive Factors in Behavior Modification: Modifying What Clients to Themselves." Paper presented at annual meeting of Association for Advancement of Behavior Therapy, Washington, D.C., September, 1970.
76. Michael, D. N. *The Unprepared Society: Planning for a Precarious Future.* New York: Basic Books, 1968.
77. Miller, N. E. "Learning of Visceral and Glandular Responses." *Science* 163 (1969): 434–53.
78. Mischel, W. *Introduction to Personality.* New York: Holt, Rinehart & Winston, 1971.
79. Mowrer, O. H. *Learning Theory and Behavior.* New York: John Wiley & Sons, 1960.
80. Murphy, G. "Psychology in the Year 2000." *American Psychologist* 24 (1969): 523–30.
81. Nelson, C. M., and McReynolds, W. T. "Self-Recording and Control of Behavior: A Reply to Simkins." *Behavior Therapy* 2 (1971): 594–97.
82. Nolan, J. D. "Self-Control Procedures in the Modification of Smoking Behavior." *Journal of Consulting and Clinical Psychology* 32 (1968): 92–93.
83. Nowlis, D., and Kamiya, J. "The Control of Electroencephalographic Alpha Rhythms through Auditory Feedback and the Associated Mental Activity." *Psychophysiology,* in press.
84. Paul, G. L. "Behavior Modification Research: Design and Tactics." In *Behavior Therapy: Appraisal and Status,* edited by C. Frank, pp. 29–62. New York: McGraw-Hill Book Co., 1969.
85. Platt, J. R. *The Step to Man.* New York: John Wiley & Sons, 1966.
86. Portes, A. "On the Emergence of Behavior Therapy in Modern Society." *Journal of Consulting and Clinical Psychology* 36 (1971): 303–16.
87. Premack, D. "Reinforcement Theory." In *Nebraska Symposium on Mo-*

tivation: 1965, edited by D. Levine, pp. 123–80. Lincoln: University of Nebraska Press, 1965.

88. Rachlin, H. *Introduction to Modern Behaviorism*. San Francisco: Freeman, 1970.

89. Rogers, C. *Freedom to Learn*. Columbus, Ohio: Charles Merrill Books, 1969.

90. ――――. "The Person of Tomorrow." Commencement address, Sonoma State College, June, 1968.

91. Ross, L.; Rodin, J.; and Zimbardo, P. "Toward an Attribution Therapy: The Reduction of Fear through Induced Cognitive Misattribution." *Journal of Personality and Social Psychology* 12 (1960): 279–88.

92. Rutner, I. T., and Bugle, C. "An Experimental Procedure for the Modification of Psychotic Behavior." *Journal of Consulting and Clinical Psychology* 33 (1969): 651–53.

93. Schultz, H. H., and Luthe, W. *Autogenic Methods*, vol. 1. New York: Grune & Stratton, 1969.

94. Sidman, M. *The Tactics of Scientific Research: Evaluating Experimental Data in Psychology*. New York: Basic Books, 1960.

95. Simkins, L. "The Reliability of Self-recorded Behavior." *Behavior Therapy* 2 (1971): 83–87.

96. Skinner, B. F. "Behaviorism at Fifty." *Science* 140 (1963): 951–58.

97. ――――. *Beyond Freedom and Dignity*. New York: A. Knopf, 1971.

98. ――――. "A Case History in Scientific Method." In *Psychology: A Study of a Science*, vol. 2, edited by S. Koch. New York: McGraw-Hill Book Co., 1959.

99. ――――. *The Contingencies of Reinforcement*. New York: Appleton-Century-Crofts, 1969.

100. ――――. "Discussion of Behaviorism at Fifty." In *Behaviorism and Phenomenology*, edited by T. W. Wann. Chicago: University of Chicago Press, 1964.

101. ――――. "The Operational Analysis of Psychological Terms." *Psychological Review* 52 (1945): 270–73.

102. ――――. *Science and Human Behavior*. New York: Macmillan Co., 1953.

103. Staats, A. W. *Child Learning, Intelligence and Personality*. New York: Harper & Row, 1971.

104. Stevens, S. S. "Measurement, Statistics, and the Schemapriric View." *Science* 171 (1972): 849–56.

105. Strupp, H. H., and Bergin, A. W. "Some Empirical and Conceptual Bases for Coordinated Research in Psychotherapy: A Critical Review of Issues, Trends, and Evidence." *International Journal of Psychiatry* 72 (1969): 1–90.

106. Stuart, R. B. "Behavioral Control of Overeating." *Behaviour Research and Therapy* 5 (1967): 357–65.

106a. Stuhr, D. E. "The Effects of Social Model Characteristics in Eliciting Personal Feeling Questions." Doctoral dissertation, Stanford University, 1972.

107. Terrace, H. S. "Awareness As Viewed by Conventional and Radical

Behaviorism." Paper presented at annual meeting of American Psychological Association, Washington, D.C., September, 1971.

108. Thoresen, C. E. "The Intensive Design: An Intimate Approach to Counseling Research." Paper presented at the American Educational Research Association, Chicago, 1972.

109. ———. "Relevance and Research in Counseling." *Review of Educational Research* 39 (1969): 264–82.

110. Thoresen, S. E., and Mahoney, M. J. *Behavioral Self-Control.* New York: Holt, Rinehart & Winston, forthcoming.

111. Ullmann, L. P., and Krasner, L. *A Psychological Approach to Abnormal Behavior.* Englewood Cliffs, N.J.: Prentice-Hall, 1969.

112. Upper, D., and Meredith, L. "A Stimulus Control Approach to the Modification of Smoking Behavior." *Proceedings of the 78th Annual Convention,* American Psychological Association, 1970.

113. Vygotsky, L. S. *Thought and Language.* New York: John Wiley & Sons, 1962.

114. Wagner, M. K., and Bragg, R. A. "Comparing Behavior Modification Approaches to Habit Decrement—Smoking." *Journal of Consulting and Clinical Psychology* 34 (1970): 258–63.

115. Watson, J. B. *Psychology from the Standpoint of a Behaviorist.* Philadelphia: J. B. Lippincott Co., 1924.

116. Wegner, M. A.; Bagchi, B. U.; and Anand, G. "Voluntary Heart and Pulse Control by Yoga Methods." *International Journal of Parapsychology* 5 (1963): 25–40.

117. Weinstein, G., and Fanbini, M., eds. *Toward Humanistic Education: A Curriculum of Affect.* New York: Frederick A. Praeger, 1970.

118. Wilson, E. H. "Humanism's Many Dimensions." *Humanist* 30 (1970): 35–36.

119. Wisocki, P. "Treatment of Obsessive-Compulsive Behavior by Covert Sensitization and Covert Reinforcement: A Case Report." *Journal of Behaviour Therapy and Experimental Psychiatry* 1 (1970): 223–39.

120. Wolf, M., and Risley, T. "Reinforcement: Applied Research." In *The Nature of Reinforcement,* edited by R. Glaser, pp. 310–25. New York: Academic Press, 1971.

121. Wolman, B. B. "Does Psychology Need Its Own Philosophy of Science?" *American Psychologist* 26 (1971): 877–86.

122. Wolpe, J. *Psychotherapy by Reciprocal Exhibition.* Stanford: Stanford University Press, 1958.

123. Yates, A. *Behavior Therapy.* New York: John Wiley & Sons, 1970.

124. Zimbardo, P.; Maslach, C.; and Marshall, G. "Unexplained Arousal." In *Current Trends in Hypnosis Research,* edited by E. Fromm and R. Shor, forthcoming.

New Light on the Human Potential

HERBERT A. OTTO

William James once estimated that the healthy human being is functioning at less than 10 per cent of his capacity. It took more than half a century before this idea found acceptance among a small proportion of behavioral scientists. In 1954, the highly respected and widely known psychologist Gardner Murphy published his pioneering volume *Human Potentialities*. The early Sixties saw the beginnings of the human potentialities research project at the University of Utah and the organization of Esalen Institute in California, the first of a series of "Growth Centers" that were later to be referred to as the Human Potentialities Movement.

Today, many well-known scientists such as Abraham Maslow, Margaret Mead, Gardner Murphy, O. Spurgeon English, and Carl Rogers subscribe to the hypothesis that man is using a very small fraction of his capacities. Margaret Mead quotes a 6 per cent figure, and my own estimate is 5 per cent or less. Commitment to the hypothesis is not restricted to the United States. Scientists in the U.S.S.R. and other countries are also at work. Surprisingly, the so-called human potentialities hypothesis is still largely unknown.

What are the dimensions of the human potential? The knowledge we do have about man is minimal and has not as yet been brought together with the human potentialities hypothesis as an organizing force and synthesizing element. Of course, we know more about man today than we did fifty years ago, but this is like the very small part of the iceberg we see above the water. Man essentially remains a mystery. From the depths of this mystery there are numerous indicators of the human potential.

Certain indicators of man's potential are revealed to us in childhood. They become "lost" or submerged as we succumb to the imprinting of the cultural mold in the "growing up" process. Do you remember when you were a child and it rained after a dry spell and there was a very particular, intensive earthy smell in the air? Do you remember how people smelled when they hugged you? Do you recall the brilliant colors of leaves, flowers, grass, and even brick surfaces and lighted signs that you experienced as a child? Furthermore, do you recall that when father and mother stepped into the room you *knew* how they felt about themselves, about life, and about you—at that moment?

Today we know that man's sense of smell, one of the most powerful and primitive senses, is highly developed. In the average man this capacity has been suppressed except for very occasional use. Some scientists claim that man's sense of smell is almost as keen as a hunting dog's. Some connoisseurs of wines, for example, can tell by the bouquet not only the type of grape and locality where they were grown but even the vintage year and vineyard. Perfume mixers can often detect fantastically minute amounts in mixed essences; finally there are considerable data on odor discrimination from the laboratory. It is also clear that, since the air has become an overcrowded garbage dump for industrial wastes and the internal combustion engine, it is easier to turn off our sense of smell than to keep it functioning. The capacity to experience the environment more fully through our olfactory organs remains a potential.

It is possible to regain these capacities through training. In a similar manner, sensory and other capacities, including visual, kinesthetic, and tactile abilities, have become stunted and dulled. We perceive less clearly, and as a result we feel less—we use our dulled senses to close ourselves off from both our physical and interpersonal environments. Today we also dull our perceptions of how other people feel and we consistently shut off awareness of our own feelings. For many who put their senses to sleep it is a sleep that lasts unto death. Again, through sensory and other training the doors of perception can be cleansed (to use Blake's words) and our capacities reawakened. Anthropological research abounds with reports of primitive tribes that have developed exceptional sensory and perceptive abilities as a result of training. Utilization of these capacities by modern man for life-enrichment purposes awaits the future.

Neurological research has shed new light on man's potential. Work at the UCLA Brain Research Institute points to enormous abilities latent in everyone by suggesting an incredible hypothesis: The ultimate creative capacity of the human brain may be, for all practical purposes, infinite. To use the computer analogy, man is a vast storehouse of data, but we have not learned how to program ourselves to utilize these data for problem-solving purposes. Recall of experiential data is extremely spotty and selective for most adults. My own research has convinced me that the recall of experiences can be vastly improved by use of certain simple training techniques, provided sufficient motivation is present.

Under emergency conditions, man is capable of prodigious feats of physical strength. For example, a middle-aged California woman with various ailments lifted a car just enough to let her son roll out from under it after it had collapsed on him. According to newspaper reports the car weighed in excess of 2,000 pounds. There are numerous similar accounts indicating that every person has vast physical reserve capacities that can be tapped. Similarly, the extraordinary feats of athletes and acrobats—involving the conscious and specialized development of certain parts of the human organism as a result of consistent application and a high degree of motivation—point to the fantastic plasticity and capabilities of the human being.

Until World War II, the field of hypnosis was not regarded as respectable by many scientists and was associated with stage performances and charlatanism. Since that time hypnosis has attained a measure of scientific respectability. Medical and therapeutic applications of hypnosis include the use of this technique in surgery and anesthesiology (hypnoanesthesia for major and minor surgery), gynecology (infertility, frigidity, menopausal conditions), pediatrics (enuresis, tics, asthma in children, etc.), and in dentistry. Scores of texts on medical and dental hypnosis are available. Dr. William S. Kroger, one of the specialists in the field and author of the well-known text *Clinical and Experimental Hypnosis,* writes that hypnotherapy is "directed to the patient's needs and is a methodology to tap the 'forgotten assets' of the *hidden potentials* of behavior and response that so often lead to new learnings and understanding." (My italics.) As far as we know now, the possibilities opened by hypnosis for the potential functioning of the human organism are not brought about by the hypnotist. Changes are induced by the subject, utilizing his belief-structure, with the hypnotist operating as an "enabler," making it possible for the subject to tap some of his unrealized potential.

The whole area of parapsychology that deals with extrasensory perception (ESP), "mental telepathy," and other paranormal phenomena, and that owes much of its development to the work of Dr. J. B. Rhine and others is still regarded by much of the scientific establishment with the same measure of suspicion accorded hypnosis in the pre-World War II days. It is of interest that a number of laboratories in the U.S.S.R. are devoted to the study of telepathy as a physical phenomenon, with research conducted under the heading "cerebral radiocommunication" and "bioelectronics." The work is supported by the Soviet government. The reluctance to accept findings from this field of research is perhaps best summarized by an observation of Carl C. Jung's in 1958:

[Some] people deny the findings of parapsychology outright, either for philosophical reasons or from intellectual laziness. This can hardly be considered a scientifically responsible attitude, even though it is a popular way out of quite extraordinary intellectual difficulty.

Although the intensive study of creativity had its beginnings in fairly recent times, much of value has been discovered about man's creative potential. There is evidence that every person has creative abilities that can be developed. A considerable number of studies indicate that much in our educational system—including conformity pressures exerted by teachers, emphasis on memory development, and role learning, plus the overcrowding of classrooms—militates against the development of creative capacities. Research has established that children between the ages of two and three can learn to read, tape record a story, and type it as it is played back. Hundreds of children between the ages of four and six have been taught by the Japanese pedagogue Suzuki to play violin concertos. Japanese research with infants and small children also suggests the value of early "maximum input" (music, color, verbal, tactile stimuli) in the personality development of infants. My own observations tend to confirm this. We have consistently underestimated the child's capacity to learn and his ability to realize his potential while *enjoying* both the play elements and the discipline involved in this process.

In contrast to the Japanese work, much recent Russian research appears to be concentrated in the area of mentation, with special emphasis on extending and enlarging man's mental processes and his capacity for learning. As early as 1964 the following appeared in *Soviet Life Today*, a U.S.S.R. English language magazine:

The latest findings in anthropology, psychology, logic, and physiology show that the potential of the human mind is very great indeed. "As soon as modern science gave us some understanding of the structure and work of the human brain, we were struck with its enormous reserve capacity," writes Yefremov (Ivan Yefremov, eminent Soviet scholar and writer). "Man, under average conditions of work and life, uses only a small part of his thinking equipment. . . . If we were able to force our brain to work at only half its capacity, we could, without any difficulty whatever, learn forty languages, memorize the large Soviet Encyclopedia from cover to cover, and complete the required courses of dozens of colleges."

The statement is hardly an exaggeration. It is the generally accepted theoretical view of man's mental potentialities.

How can we tap this gigantic potential? It is a big and very complex problem with many ramifications.

Another signpost of man's potential is what I have come to call the "Grandma Moses effect." This artist's experience indicates that artistic talents can be discovered and brought to full flowering in the latter part of the life cycle. In every retirement community there can be found similar examples of residents who did not use latent artistic abilities or other talents until after retirement. In many instances the presence of a talent is suspected or known but allowed to remain fallow for the best part of a lifetime.

Reasons why well-functioning mature adults do not use specific abilities are complex. Studies conducted at the University of Utah as a part of the Human Potentialities Research Project revealed that unconscious blocks are often present. In a number of instances a person with definite evidence that he has a specific talent (let's say he won a state-wide contest in sculpture while in high school) may not wish to realize this talent at a later time because he fears this would introduce a change in life-style. Sometimes fear of the passion of creation is another roadblock in self-actualization. On the basis of work at Utah it became clear that persons who live close to their capacity, who continue to activate their potential, have a pronounced sense of well-being and considerable energy and see themselves as leading purposeful and creative lives.

Most people are unaware of their strengths and potentialities. If a person with some college background is handed a form and asked to write out his personality strengths, he will list, on an average, five or six strengths. Asked to do the same thing for his weaknesses, the list will be two to three times as long. There are a number of reasons for this low self-assessment. Many participants in my classes and marathon group weekends have pointed out that "listing your strengths feels like bragging about yourself. It's something that just isn't done." Paradoxically, in a group, people feel more comfortable about sharing problem areas and hang-ups than they do about personality resources and latent abilities. This is traceable to the fact that we are members of a pathology-oriented culture. Psychological and psychiatric jargon dealing with emotional dysfunction and mental illness has become the parlance of the man in the street. In addition, from early childhood in our educational system we learn largely by our mistakes—by having them pointed out to us repeatedly. All this results in early "negative conditioning" and influences our attitude and perception of ourselves and other people. An attitudinal climate has become established which is continually fed and reinforced.

As a part of this negative conditioning there is the heavy emphasis by communications media on violence in television programs and motion pictures. The current American news format of radio, television, and newspapers—the widely prevalent idea of what constitutes news—results from a narrow, brutalizing concept thirty or forty years behind the times and is inimical to the development of human potential.

The news media give much time and prominent space to violence and consistently underplay "good" news. This gives the consumer the impression that important things that happen are various types of destructive activities. Consistent and repeated emphasis on bad news not only creates anxiety and tension but instills the belief that there is little except violence, disasters, accidents, and mayhem abroad in the world. As a consequence, the consumer of such news gradually experiences a shift in his outlook about the world leading to the formation of feelings of alienation and separation. The world is increasingly perceived as a threat, as the viewer becomes anxious that violence and mayhem may be perpetrated on him from somewhere out of the strange and unpredictable environment in which he lives. There slowly grows a conviction that it is safer to withdraw from such a world, to isolate himself from its struggles, and to let others make the decisions and become involved.

As a result of the steady diet of violence in the media, an even more fundamental and insidious erosion in man's self-system takes place. The erosion affects what I call the "trust factor." If we have been given a certain amount of affection, love, and understanding in our formative years, we are able to place a certain amount of trust in our fellow man. Trust is one of the most important elements in today's society although we tend to minimize its importance. *We basically trust people.* For example, we place an enormous amount of trust in our fellow man when driving on a freeway or in an express lane. We trust those with whom we are associated to fulfill their obligations and responsibilities. The element of trust is the basic rule in human relations. When we distrust people, they usually sense our attitude and reciprocate in kind.

The consistent emphasis in the news on criminal violence, burglarizing, and assault makes slow but pervasive inroads into our reservoir of trust. As we hear and read much about the acts of violence and injury men perpetrate upon one another, year after year, with so little emphasis placed on the loving, caring, and humanitarian acts of man, we begin to trust our fellow man less, and we thereby diminish ourselves. It is my conclusion the media's excessive emphasis on violence, like the drop of water on the stone, erodes and wears away the trust factor in man. By undermining the trust factor in man, media contribute to man's estrangement from man and prevent the full flourishing and deeper development of a sense of community and communion with all men.

Our self-concept, how we feel about ourselves and our fellow man and the world, is determined to a considerable extent by the inputs from the physical and interpersonal environment to which we are exposed. In the physical environment, there are the irritants in the air, i.e., air pollution plus the ugliness and noise of megapolis. Our interpersonal environment is characterized by estrangement and distance from others (and self), and by the artificiality and superficiality of our social encounters and the resultant violation of authenticity. Existing in a setting that provides as consistent inputs multiple irritants, ugliness and violence, and lack of close and meaningful relationships, man is in danger of becoming increasingly irritated, ugly, and violent.

As work in the area of human potentialities progressed, it has become ever clearer that personality, to a much greater degree than previously suspected, functions in response to the environment. This is additional confirmation of what field theorists and proponents of the holistic approach to the study of man have long suspected.

Perhaps the most important task facing us today is the regeneration of our environment and institutional structures such as school, government, church, etc. With increasing sophistication has come the recognition that institutions are not sacrosanct and that they have but one purpose and function—to serve as a framework for the actualization of human potential. It is possible to evaluate both the institution and the contribution of the institution by asking this question: "To what extent does the function of the institution foster the realization of human potential?"

Experimental groups consistently have found that the more a person's environment can be involved in the process of realizing potential, the greater the gains. It is understandable why scientists concerned with the study of personality have been reluctant to consider the importance of here-and-now inputs in relation to personality functioning. To do so would open a Pandora's box of possibilities and complex forces that until fairly recently were considered to be the exclusive domain of the social scientist. Many scientists and professionals, particularly psychotherapists, feel they have acquired a certain familiarity with the topography of "intra-psychic forces" and are reluctant to admit the reality of additional complex factors in the functioning of the personality.

It is significant that an increasing number of psychologists, psychiatrists, and social workers now realize that over and beyond keeping up with developments in their respective fields, the best way to acquire additional professional competence is through group experiences designed for personal growth and that focus on the unfolding of individual possibilities. From this group of aware professionals and others came much of the initial support and interest in Esalen Institute and similar "Growth Centers" later referred to as the Human Potentialities Movement.

Esalen Institute in Big Sur, California, was organized in 1962 by Michael Murphy and his partner, Dick Price. Under their imaginative management the institute experienced a phenomenal growth, established a branch in San Francisco, and is now famous for its seminars and weekend experiences offered by pioneering professionals. Since 1962 more than 100,000 persons have enrolled for one of these activities.

The past three years have seen a rapid mushrooming of Growth Centers. There are more than fifty such organizations ranging from Esalen and Kairos Institutes in California to Oasis in Chicago and Aureon Institute in New York. The experiences offered at these Growth Centers are based on several hypotheses: 1) that the average healthy person functions at a fraction of his capacity; 2) that man's most exciting life-long adventure is actualizing his potential; 3) that the group environment is one of the best settings in which to achieve growth; and 4) that personality growth can be achieved by anyone willing to invest himself in this process.

Human potentialities is rapidly emerging as a discrete field of scientific inquiry. Exploring the human potential can become the meeting ground for a wide range of disciplines, offering a dynamic synthesis for seemingly divergent areas of research. It is possible that the field of human potentialities offers an answer to the long search for a synthesizing and organizing principle which will unify the sciences. The explosive growth of the Human Potentialities Movement is indicative of a growing public interest. Although there exist a considerable number of methods—all designed to tap human potential—work on assessment or evaluation of these methods has in most instances not progressed beyond field testing and informal feedback of results. The need for research in the area of human potentialities has never been more pressing. The National Center for the Exploration of Human Potential in La Jolla, California, has recently been organized for this purpose. A nonprofit organization, the center will act as a clearing house of information for current and past approaches that have been successful in fostering personal growth. One of the main purposes of the center will be to conduct and coordinate basic and applied research concerning the expansion of human potential.

Among the many fascinating questions posed by researchers are some of the following: What is the relationship of body-rhythms, biorhythms, and the expansion of sensory awareness to the uncovering of human potential? What are the applications of methods and approaches from other cultures such as yoga techniques, Sufi methods, types of meditation, etc.? What is the role of ecstasy and play vis-á-vis the realizing of human possibilities? The exploration of these and similar questions can help us create a society truly devoted to the full development of human capacities—particularly the capacities for love, joy, creativity, spiritual experiencing. This is the challenge and promise of our lifetime.

The Sociological Foundation: The Reality of the World

The concept of culture, or the historical and social existence of man, is very important for the understanding and appreciation of the sociological foundation of humanistic education. For the purpose of this analysis we will focus upon the existential and humanistic term *world,* to denote the meaning and experiences conventionally communicated by the concept of culture. Basically, the term *world,* as used here, denotes the dialectical state of man's being, which is existentially, i.e., temporally and spatially, constituted. The concept points to the human dialectic of *self* and *other,* which involves the problems and possibilities of intersubjectivity.

Historically the dehumanization of man by man has been well-documented. On the sociological level of existence the freedom, and by implication the consciousness, of the individual has important consequences not only for sociology as a science, but for the real, day-to-day world that we actually live in. The existential and phenomenological view of the world holds that the basic freedom and self-consciousness of man prevents the possibility that "society," the "system," the "state," or "they" can ever totally annihilate the identity of the individual against his or her will. Thus in every case of a "takeover" of the world by "others," the individual in a sense chooses freely to give up his or her personal sense of being for "others."

Existential and phenomenological sociology is concerned, among other things, with the existence of the individual in the world in terms of the subjectivity/objectivity of human consciousness. Basically, because of the dialectical nature of consciousness and existence, the so-called real world of external, objective reality also lies within, subjectively. And, on experiential and epistemological levels, the actual encounter with and meaning of the world lies within the freedom and self-being of the person.

Otherwise, the existential and phenomenological nature of the world may be viewed on at least three levels of being. (1) The concept of *Eigenwelt* defines the individual's relationship to the world entirely in terms of the inner world of the self. In this view the world exists only in an inward or immanent way, limiting yet, paradoxically, making possible the experiential relationship of the individual to the surrounding world. (2) The *Mitwelt* is that relationship toward the world that is constituted by the existence of others, namely other human beings. It describes the "between-ness" of man in his human relatedness, the interpersonal dimension of existence. (3) the concept of *Umwelt,* or the surrounding world, of which the individual is part, accounts for man's experience and knowledge of the world as being "out there" rather than "in here." This concept of the world is focused or centered outside the inner being of the individual, although it is inextricably linked to the subjective freedom of consciousness, experientially and epistemologically.* The concepts of *Eigenwelt, Miltwelt,* and *Umwelt,* as "in here," "between," and "out there," could serve to clarify the nature of the world of education.

Heretofore we have left the concept of education largely undefined. In terms of our existential, phenomenological view of the *world, education* refers to the experimental and epistemological inclusiveness of being an individual in the context of immediate, social reality. Further, the term *social* refers to the dynamic, cultural totality of events, relationships, and other phenomena that can be found in existence. This includes webs of personal relationships, institutions, belief systems, customs, economic and political changes, role- expectations, physical and intellectual resources, and so on—the totality of given externals.

No education that is humanistic can be adequately grounded in terms of knowledge and experience if it is not cognizant of and actively oriented toward the social surroundings of the learner. It must take into account the real nature and state of the world—both the immediate and more distant world—so that the student may be prepared to live in it. No school administration, teacher-student relationship, or curriculum exists in a vacuum, separated from the outside realities of the world of political, economic, and social change. For this very reason, humanistic education, if it is to be holistic and oriented toward the growth and development of the person, must not and cannot ignore the cultural world of man.

The first selection dealing with the reality of the world for humanistic

* The "link" between the world, as out-there, and the freedom of consciousness, as in-here, occurs through the dialectical structure of consciousness as in-here and out-there, simultaneously.

education is from the exciting book *The Greening of America,* by Charles A. Reich. "The Lost Self" is an incisively provocative chapter that describes how the meritocracy, or the system of rewards and punishments of the Corporate State, shapes not only the "whole structure of education" but the development of the human person. In the meritocratic world, education serves the state and its impersonal ends by teaching the individual that it is better to play a role, with a substitute self, rather than be authentic and real. In such a system of education and the social world that it reflects, merit implies no humanistic or ethical judgment, because it is an impersonal system that sets the standards and guidelines for behavior rather than the individual himself. The evils of such a social system are legion: people in identity crises, uptight, obedient, demeaned in their work, unfree, phony, suspicious and mistrustful, driven by false needs and values, and unable to experience themselves as full, human beings. In such a world can there be any doubt about the need for a truly humanistic education?

In "Human Prospects," Lewis Mumford, the famous observer of modern culture, outlines his ideal for the One World man and the educational model of *paideia* that accompanies it. Basically, Mumford believes that the human person is the highest value of human existence and that the One World order, or the educational system that makes such an order possible, cannot ignore the philosophy of the person. Mumford links the goal of a One World culture with the consciousness that man has gone through four stages of development: the archaic, civilized, axial, and mechanical. He pleads for a Nietzschean "transvaluation of values" in order to build a new man who takes cognizance of the four stages of human history as well as the significance of goal-seeking and future time. Yet, in order to really start toward the new man who sees and experiences all, we must realize that contemporary man lives in a half-world of externalism. Therefore, we must reorient ourselves inwardly to stir the quality of life, integrating the inner with the outer, the higher with the lower, in a dialectic that the educational ideal of *paideia* easily encompasses. The Greek ideal of *paideia* integrates love with power, life with work, self with world, the private with the public, leisure with learning, making possible the prospect of man's continuous and infinite growth into the future.

Irving H. Buchen's "Humanism and Futurism: Enemies or Allies?" is the last article in this section. As a futurist, Buchen argues against the traditional, humanistic notion of individuality and asserts that the "individual man is stirred by interdependence, autonomy and self-reliance." Man is through and through a social being, mostly because of the kind of world he lives in; and education, to be truly humanistic, should be oriented toward the collectivized individual. Furthermore, education should be focused upon the image of multiple selves rather than one self for the growth of the person. Rightly or wrongly, Buchen castigates the humanities for bewailing the dehumanization of technology and the physical sciences, when the humanities themselves have trained specialists and fragmented knowers, while positing the goal of the whole man.

In the context of the sociological realities of the world, I would like to draw the reader's attention to the educational viewpoints of Hannah Arendt and Paulo Freire, although space prevents me from including extracts from their works. In "The Crisis in Education," Hannah Arendt trenchantly describes the "New Order of the world" that was made possible in America particularly through its educational system. The "crisis" lies in the extent to which education has been used for political ends, i.e., in establishing of belief in utopia and in the Americanization of immigrant children. The essence or core concept of education, Arendt asserts, is in the fact of "natality" or "that human beings are born into the world." And although natality implies a responsibility and an obligation to teach and to prepare children for the world, adults have given up responsibility for the world. Furthermore, although the child exists in a double relationship toward the world and life, "life qua life does not matter" in the public world. Nonetheless the first function of education is to teach world-mindedness, according to Arendt, and not the art of living.

Arendt raises some controversial points in asserting that education in America has given authority over to the child group rather than to the adult—by promoting the role of the nonauthoritarian teacher who can teach anything and by substituting doing for knowing and playing for working in the learning process. A serious question is raised about the possibility not only of humanistic education but of any education in America, if Arendt is right.

Paulo Freire, a Brazilian by birth, goes beyond Arendt in advancing a revolutionary method for educational reform, his aim being liberation of the oppressed and dehumanized people of the Third World. In his book *Pedagogy of the Oppressed,* Freire uses the term *prescription* to denote the imposition of one man's choice upon another, in which man is forced to give up the freedom of his world in order to conform to the wishes of the oppressor. Following Hegel and Karl Marx, Freire notes the interrelationship between the oppressor and the oppressed classes of the world. However, his revolutionary educational methods for social and political reform transcend the passive dialectic of armchair philosophizing. *Praxis,* to Freire, denotes reflective action upon the world in order to transform it, and dialogue the process and act by which the oppressed are prepared intellectually to take liberating action against their oppressors. On the subject of a method to transform and humanize the world Freire is uncompromising: liberators must not use the same dehumanizing methods in the interests of the oppressed as have been used by the oppressor class.

Consequently "propaganda, management, and manipulation" are out, and the method of dialogue is in. Finally, asserting that "a real humanist trusts people," Freire proposes the method of consciousness or intentionality, or the method by which people are treated as subjects rather than objects and action and thought becomes "co-intentional" and cooperative, to achieve revolutionary ends through education.

In conclusion it must be said that the ideals, values, and goals of humanism, in the context of the sociology of education, present a highly problematic view of the world. Perhaps the solution to the differences uncovered through the debates of humanistic sociology may only be sought through the values and beliefs that we hold to be true, philosophically, psychologically, and theologically. Anyway, I hope that the reader will find more explicit realization of the ideas and values outlined in this part of the book in Part II.

DISCUSSION QUESTIONS

1. One of the main reasons why the mass of people are suffering from the loss of self, according to Charles A. Reich, is because they have been schooled to play a role rather than to become and experience their real selves. Do you believe that Reich makes a good case for what has been lost experientially through Consciousness II of the meritocracy? Do you think that it is possible to avoid playing a role in the meritocracy that Reich describes? Or, is it possible to play a role authentically or in a way that is true to your real self? To what extent do you feel that you have lost your self? And what, in your own opinion, can the schools do to correct the abuses of the meritocracy?

2. Lewis Mumford holds that the One World culture requires a new man, one made possible through the educational ideal of *paideia*. Do you think that work can become "an educative force" for everyone, or is this ideal unrealistic in a world that is oriented toward machines rather than people? What do you think Mumford means when he says that "leisure makes possible the school?" Do you feel that the world is suffering from externalism and needs to concentrate upon the development of the inner man? Why? Also, do you believe that love is the "symbol and agent of . . . organic wholeness," as Mumford does? How can the experience and value of love become an integral part of the world? Mumford implies that humanistic education can not exist without a philosophy that integrates all experience. Do you agree?

3. Irving H. Buchen thinks that the traditional, romantic concept

of the individual as independent and self-reliant is antithetical to the humanistic concept of the whole man. Do you believe that the "individual isolated from the surrounding social environment is not and cannot be whole?" In addition, do you think we are suffereing from "over-individualization" and need to focus upon the "collectivized individual" in teaching and learning? What psychological basis is there for thinking that we have many selves rather than one, as Buchen contends? Is futurism an ally of humanism? Finally, can there be any wholeness of being for the individual without a future? And if not, what implications does this have for realizing the ideal of the person in education?

FURTHER READING

Arendt, Hannah. "The Crisis in Education" in *Between Past and Future*. New York: The Viking Press, Inc., 1968.

Berger, Peter L. *Invitation to Sociology: A Humanistic Perspective*. Garden City, New York: Anchor Books, 1963.

Broudy, Harry S. *The Real World of the Public Schools*. New York: Harcourt Brace Jovanovich, Inc., 1972.

Dewey, John. *Freedom and Culture*. New York: Capricorn Books. 1963.

Freire, Paulo. *Pedagogy of the Oppressed*. New York: Herder and Herder, 1972.

Henry, Jules. *Culture Against Man*. New York: Vintage Books, 1963.

Illich, Ivan. *DeSchooling Society*. New York: Harrow Books, 1972.

Reimer, Everett. *School Is Dead: Alternatives in Education*. Garden City, New York: Anchor Books., 1972.

Roszak, Theodore. *Where the Wasteland Ends*. Garden City, New York: Anchor Books, 1973.

Silberman, Charles E. *Crisis In the Classroom*. New York: Vintage Books, 1970.

The Lost Self

CHARLES A. REICH

What kind of life does man live under the domination of the Corporate State? It is the life that was foreseen in *The Cabinet of Dr. Caligari*, *Metropolis*, and *M*, a robot life, in which man is deprived of his own being, and he becomes instead a mere role, occupation, or function. The self within him is killed, and he walks through the remainder of his days mindless and lifeless, the inmate and instrument of a machine world.

The process by which man is deprived of his self begins with his institutionalized training in public school for a place in the machinery of the State. The object of the training is not merely to teach him how to perform some specific function, it is to make him become that function; to see and judge himself and others in terms of functions, and to abandon any aspect of self, thinking, questioning, feeling, loving, that has no utility for either production or consumption in the Corporate State. The training for the role of consumer is just as important as the training for a job, and at least equally significant for loss of self.

Job training in school consists of learning goal-behavior and an accompanying discipline and repression of unrelated instincts and interests. Goal-behavior is simply the substitution of outside ends for inner objectives. In the classroom, the goals set for the child include memorizing and being able to repeat certain information and opinions, completing papers and tests according to prescribed standards, and conforming to certain rules of deportment. The more senseless the goals the better, for that child is best prepared who will pursue any goal that is set with equal effort.

Consumer training in school consists of preventing the formation of individual consciousness, taste, aesthetic standards, self-knowledge, and the ability to create one's own satisfactions. Solitude, separateness, undirected time, and silence, which are necessary for consciousness, are not permitted. Groups are encouraged to set values, inhibiting the growth of self-knowledge. Since activity and initiative are the key to finding one's own standards and satisfactions, the child is taught passivity, so that it must depend for satisfactions on what is provided by the society. Thus the child is taught to depend on the fun of cheering for the basketball team, rather than spending the same two hours searching for some individual interest.

While learning to be a producer and a consumer, the child is also trained in how to go about making a substitute-self, one that will get the maximum approval and rewards from the State, a self that will get along better than the real self, the self that might-have-been. The child learns to play a role, to dress, talk, behave, and enjoy things in a certain way, and at the same time to judge others by their success in playing roles. The child also learns to base relationships with others on criteria fixed by the State; other booys and girls can be rated on a fixed objective scale. Further, the child learns that life as defined by the State is not an experience-in-common but an individual position on a scale of relative positions, so that individuals must compete for places in life; "life" consists of a position-achieved, and not in living-as-process. Accordingly, the student is trained to submerge his personality in a series of organizations, teams, groups, and classroom situations; he is compelled to accept the judgment of his peers on many issues, and to believe that "social acceptability" should be a major personal goal.

School is intensely concerned with training students to stop thinking and start obeying. Any course that starts with a textbook and a teacher and ends with an examination runs this danger unless great pains are taken to show students that they are supposed to think for themselves; in most school and college classes, on the other hand, thinking for oneself is actually penalized, and the student learns the value of repeating what he is told. Public school is "obedience school"; the student is taught to accept authority without question, to respect authority simply because of its position, to obey not merely in the area of school regulations but in the area of facts and ideas as well. He is told to accept hierarchical authority—that principals, deans, "adults" have the right to make decisions concerning him without consulting him or being responsible to him in any way. Everything that happens is decided by someone other than the student—the curriculum (some of which may even be dictated by state law), and all other school activities; what apparent freedom the students have, such as publishing their own newspaper, is like the "freedom" of a prison newspaper; it can be suspended at any time. Democracy, while praised in theory, is rejected in practice by the school. The student is trained away from democracy; instead, he is most elaborately trained in joining a hierarchy. Every organization he belongs to has a hierarchy similar to that which he will encounter in the outside world. From the school paper to the camera club there is a president, secretary-treasurer, and underlings. In a structure such as the school newspaper, almost all of the subtleties of the corporate executive suite are reporduced and practiced. In short, democracy and independence are among the greatest sins in public school.

From the outside, reading textbooks, writing papers and essays, doing homework, engaging in classroom recitations and discussions, may have all the appearance of work that is good for the mind. But a closer look (and this is true of college as well as high school) shows how little thinking is really going on. This is child labor, an ordeal that both keeps the child off the streets and trains him in the carrying out of prescribed tasks. A history examination reveals it all: it asks for names, dates, and conclusions found in the textbook or outside reading. The real questions on the test are: "Did you do the job that you were told to do?" "Do you remember what you were told?" "Have you learned to carry out a job carefully and accurately?" "Did you have the self-discipline to do this job despite all the temptations and other activities that offered themselves?" "Can you sit longer and concentrate harder than the others in the class?" The youngster who gets A's is well on his way to being suitable material for the Corporate State.

One of the great purposes of the school is to indoctrinate the inmates. Vast powers are set to work on remolding their thinking. Indoctrination is not the same as teaching. The purpose of teaching is to help the student to think for himself. The purpose of indoctrination is to compel him to accept someone else's ideas, someone else's version of the facts. It is indoctrination whenever the student can get a bad mark for disagreeing. Indoctrination may take many forms. There may be a blatant course entitled "Democracy versus Communism." Even if there is not, the usual courses in American studies, history, and civics will present a strongly biased point of view. As we have just begun to learn, the bias may not only be political, it often is racial as well. The school tries to force-feed a whole set of values and attitudes: about advertising, business, competition, success, and the American way of life. And this is carried on amid a pervasive atmosphere of dishonesty and hypocrisy. No one will admit that America might be a bad country, that the textbooks might be boring and stupid, that much of what the school does may not be in the best interests of students, that there could be other ways of doing what routine requires.

The productive side of the American State is organized as a meritocracy, a hierarchy of jobs or roles for which the individual is trained and fitted. His training, abilities, character, opinions, and loyalties, that is, the whole of his public, exterior self, must be shaped to this end. Most people who describe the American scene would prefer to emphasize the "voluntary" nature of the process; the individual *chooses* to seek and qualify for a position. But from the point of view of the process as a whole the "choice" to join organized society in some capacity does not really exist, and all of the arrangements we will describe, educational, legal, and otherwise, are designed to make it imperative for an individual to fit himself into the hierarchy. No measures, including use of the penal laws, are neglected in prodding lagging "volunteers." The meritocracy process produces two major consequences. First, it creates a working force for the machinery of the State. Second, for all but those at the top, it creates a condition of "inferiority" in which the individual is looked down upon by society and looks down upon himself because he is "not as good" as someone more successful. It is the meritocracy that makes the worker, white or black, into a "nigger" who despises himself.

A key to insight is to understand what is meant by "merit." The standards of "merit" are set by each organization or profession and its needs. The man best qualified flies the airplane, or seves as a doctor or automobile repairman. We would not want to fly in a jet piloted by the least qualified man. But we must recognize some further aspects of this. The word "merit" is used in a purely functional sense. It means only functional usefulness, it implies no ethical or humanistic judgment whatever, and to a considerable extent its standards are an "accident" of technology. At one stage of technology a big man may be valued, at another stage, a small man or a man with a rapid heartbeat, etc. These matters to a large degree lie outside the control of the individual, who is fortunate or unfortunate as the circumstances dictate.

In school, the meritocracy shapes the whole structure of education. The object is not simply to train each child for a function in the State, but to begin the process of arranging everyone in a hierarchy of statuses, a process which will be completed many years later. Accordingly, school is full of devices for measuring and comparing children. Tests—academic, psychological, physical, and social— dominate the curriculum. The tracking system, in many public high schools, separates students into "ability groups" for their training. The end of the high school training process comes with the State's decision: who goes to a good college, who goes to a bad college, who goes to the white-collar occupations, who is destined for the factory or the filling station. Except for those born to wealth or hopeless poverty, this classification is the most important thing that happens to a person in our society; it determines almost everything else about the kind of life he will have. It determines a man's entire standing in the community; the amount of honor, gain, and respect he receives; indeed, his entire value as a human being. It also determines his relationships to others, friendships, how he lives, his interests except for an ever-narrowing private area which in many cases vanishes into nothingness by middle age. "Merit" also constitutes the way in which a man forms a knowledge of himself; it becomes the key to his identity, self-respect, and self-knowledge. He learns to say "I *am* . . . a lawyer / auto worker," etc.

The opposite side of "merit" is doing one of society's undesirable jobs—that of a blue- or white-collar worker. For these jobs, the most important requirement is not any affirmative form of training, although that is of course necessary, but a negative form of training— training in giving up those sides of human nature that are incompatible with the job. No person with a strongly developed aesthetic sense, a love of nature, a passion for music, a desire for reflection, or a strongly marked independence could possibly be happy or contented in a factory or white-collar job. Hence these characteristics must be snuffed out in school. Taste must be lowered and vulgar-ized, internal reflection must be minimized, feeling for beauty cut off. All of these processes are begun in school, and then carried into later life in the case of those who are destined for the lower half of the nation's productive force.

What the school determines to accomplish it does so in a constant and total atmosphere of violence. We do not mean physical violence; we mean violence in the sense of any assault upon, or violation of, the personality. An examination or test is a form of violence. Compulsory gym, to one embarrassed or afraid, is a form of violence. The requirement that a student must get a pass to walk in the hallways is violence. Compelled attendance in the classroom, compulsory studying in study hall, is violence. We do not suggest that all violence is an evil, or that all of it could be avoided, but the amount of violence in a high school is staggering. There are more subtle kinds; humiliation, insults, embarrassments, and above all, judgments. A judgment, unasked for, is an act of violence; if one met a man at a party, and the man said, "I'd pronounce you approximately a B-minus individual," one would recognize how violent the act of grading or judging really is. It ceases to be violence only when it is made affirmative by affection and concern, emotions that rarely exist in a high school system.

The authority exercised by the school is in the purest sense lawless, in that the school authorities have virtually unlimited discretion. They make and change the rules, they provide whatever procedure there is for deciding if the rules have been violated, they determine punishments (backed, if necessary, by the law). There is no rule of law by which the student can assert any rights whatever. As in any total institution, all of the many different powers of the school can be brought to bear on an individual, so that he can be flunked and also removed from an athletic team if both are needed to ensure compliance. And the school's power extends out into the indefinite future. For the school can make possible, or thwart, the prospects of a job or a college education. Given black marks in high school, a student may find himself crippled for life, unable to get into a good college, unable to pursue a desired career in consequence. It is as if a prison had the authority to permanently maim or cripple prisoners for disobeying the rules; the school's jurisdiction lasts only three or four years, but its sentences can last a lifetime.

While the school's authority is lawless, school is nevertheless an experience made compulsory by the full power of the law, including criminal penalties. (The option to go to private school does exist for families that can afford it, but this is not the students' own option, and it is obviously available only to a few.) School has no prison bars, or locked doors like an insane asylum, but the student is no more free to leave it than a prisoner is free to leave the penitentiary.

Thus at the core of the high school experience is something more terrible than authority, indoctrination, or violence—it is an all-out assault upon the newly emerging adolescent self. The self needs, above all, privacy, liberty, and a degree of sovereignty to develop. It needs to try things, to search, to explore, to test, to err. It needs solitude—solitude to bring sense to its experiences and thereby to create a future. It needs, not enforced relationships with others, rigidly categorized into groups, teams, and organizations, but an opportunity to try different forms of relationships—to try them, to withdraw, to re-create. The school is a brutal machine for destruction of the self, controlling it, heckling it, hassling it into a thousand busy tasks, a thousand noisy groups, never giving it a moment to establish a knowledge within.

After a person has been classified by the meritocracy he is fitted into the personal prison that each individual carries with him in the form of a role. Roles are nothing new to the world—peasant, knight, and bishop had roles in the Middle Ages; medicine men and warriors have roles in a primitive tribe. But roles have changed somewhat; they are ever more highly specialized, and they grow constantly more pervasive, cutting deeper into every side of an individual. The basic process which is going on during all the years of schooling is learning to become the kind of person society wants, instead of the kind of person one is, or would like to be. At an elementary level, this is seen in the student's attempting to become "academic" when his real interests are mechanical, sensual, or just plain undeveloped. At a higher and more tragic level, one can observe the violent alienation of law students from their prior selves. Finding themselves in law school for many possible reasons, they discover that they are expected to become "argumentative" personalities who listen to what someone else is saying only for the purpose of disagreeing, "analytic" rather than receptive people, who dominate information rather than respond to it; and intensely competitive and self-assertive as well. Since many of them are not this sort of personality before they start law school, they react initially with anger and despair, and later with resignation as their self-alienation becomes complete. In a very real sense, they "become stupider" during law school, as the range of their imagination is limited, their ability to respond with sensitivity and to receive impressions is reduced, and the scope of their reading and thinking is progressively narrowed.

Training toward alienation, from elementary school onward, reaches its climax when the student is forced to make his choice, first

of a college major, then of a career. Surrounding these moments is a
gradually built-up picture of man as a creature who has one single
"right" vocation in life, the vocation for which he is "best fitted,"
and for which he can be aptitude tested and trained. The choice is
surrounded by great anxiety and doubt, particularly because the student may find that his own nature fails to conform to the expected
norm. He may find that he is seriously interested in music, surfing,
and astronomy, that no career can encompass these interests, and
that consequently he is faced with having to give up a part of himself. Often he has an "identity crisis" at this point, and it would only
seem fair to say that the crisis is really not of his making at all, but
one forced upon him by society's demand that he give up a portion of
the identity which he has already formed. This sort of "choice" can
only be a sad and desperate moment. For a young person is not only
asked to give up a large portion of the "identity" he already has in
favor of something unknown and perhaps far less satisfying; he must
also give up all the as yet undiscovered possibilities within him, and
thus commit a part of himself to death before it can be born and tried
out. When a college student decides on medicine, he puts out of his
mind the chance that he might learn about literature and discover a
special affinity there; he will never give that potential in him a
chance, but for a long time he will wonder about it.

In discussing Consciousness II, we dealt with role-playing in
the context of false consciousness—the modern young couple whose
activities and tastes are formed outside themselves, so that they ski
or collect antiques because of values they accept from their roles.
But role-playing can also be viewed as a set of limitations on each individual—our concern here. The role-prison drastically restricts such
fundamental aspects of personality as relationships with others, personal expression, modes of thought, and goals and aspirations. Indeed, it does so with such total effectiveness that we are usually not
at all aware of the prison we are in.

The deepest form of role-constraint is the fact that the individual's own "true" self, if still alive, must watch helplessly while the
role-self lives, enjoys, and relates to others. A young lawyer, out on a
date, gets praised for his sophistication, competence, the important
cases he is working on, the important people he knows, his quick
and analytical professional mind. His role-self accepts the praise, but
his true self withers from lack of recognition, from lack of notice,
from lack of appreciation and companionship, and as the young lawyer accepts the praise he feels hollow and lonely.

If the professional is imprisoned by his role, the policeman,
nurse, salesman, secretary, and factory worker are even more enclosed by the relationships, thoughts, and goals prescribed by their

occupations. On the job, most of what happens is sterile, impersonal, empty of experience. An airline ticket salesman, a stewardess, a pilot, a baggage handler, a telephone reservations girl, a plane mechanic, an air controller, are all expected to be mechanical people, thinking their own thoughts and expressing their own feelings as little as possible, putting in an entire working day that is dictated by the functional requirements of their jobs.

For both the professional and the nonprofessional, regulation does not stop with the job itself. Job requirements merge into requirements of the society as a whole. These broader and vaguer restraints are difficult to perceive, we are so accustomed to them. We are often aware of some of the particulars of this direct supervision, such as laws against the use of drugs, but as in most matters where the Corporate State is concerned we do not see the whole design. We think that the state has intervened to prevent certain excesses: murder, theft, drug addiction. But the pattern is not a series of negatives or prohibitions imposed on otherwise unregulated private lives for the good of the community. Instead, the state has undertaken to define, within rather strict limits, the life-style of its citizens with respect to sex life, culture and consciousness, and political thought and activity.

The prescribed way of life can be summarized quite easily. Sex life shall consist of a monogamous marriage; extramarital sex, premarital sex, sex exchanged between two couples, communal sex, homosexuality, and polymorphous sexual expression are all rejected. Cultural life shall include anything produced and prescribed by the machine, but it may not include even minor deviations such as long hair, marijuana, nude swimming, vagrancy. Political life shall be limited to loyalty to the Corporate State, enforced by loyalty oaths, internal security laws, and restrictions on speech and expression; for example, life is made distinctly unpleasant for the man who wishes to contend publicly that "our form of government" is wrong. All of this repression is upheld under the legal doctrine, mentioned earlier, that "the national interest" prevails over any "individual interest." And it is all enforced by an elaborate system of official surveillance, including wiretapping, eavesdropping, invasions of privacy by police searches, police photography of demonstrators, congressional investigations, and all of the other methods with which we have become familiar.

The full force of these restrictions can only be appreciated when they are seen not merely as a pattern, but as a seamless web in which each restraint augments all of the others. The individual feels pressure from the meritocracy, from the rules concerning him, from the organization he works for, from the draft and public welfare, from regulatory laws. Anything he does is likely to be the subject of notice by some official agency. Significantly, the law makes little distinction between the criminal and non-criminal areas; a "narcotics addict," for example, might be subject to "involuntary civil commitment" rather than "criminal punishment." In other words, the law is not particularly concerned with distinguishing between whether an individual has breached some rule or whether he is in need of affirmative correction; criminal and civil laws are simply different means to produce the desired result. And there is cooperation among the different agencies of pressure; thus, from time to time one notes in the newspaper that some political dissenter, not easily reached by any specific law, has been attacked by permitting some portion of the character information on file concerning him to be "leaked" to his enemies; for example, New Orleans District Attorney Garrison, who persisted in questioning the official version of President Kennedy's assassination, was suddenly made the subject of newspaper stories based on a highly "confidential" army psychiatrist's file concerning him. Or a college professor in upstate New York fighting the marijuana laws is faced with loss of his house due to cancellation of his fire insurance by "private" insurance companies. Or a hippie group living in a small town is driven out by zealous enforcement of zoning laws. This pervasive official power over individuals gives that special gray, oppressive feeling of totalitarian countries that appears in Kafka's *The Trial;* one may have obeyed all known laws, but still the authorities are watching.

One of the ways we can perceive this surveillance most clearly is in the use of the criterion of "character" when individuals are selected for college, graduate school, employment, and promotion. "Character" means the indidual's personality, habits, friends, activities, politics, opinions, associations, and disciplinary and police record. All of these are thought by an increasing number of organizations to be an appropriate subject for investigation in order to reach a decision on an individual's "merit." In many cases these matters are thought to have an importance equal to the individual's "ability" and "achievement." Surveillance of character has become pervasive in our society. Most colleges and graduate schools and large private employers investigate applicants' character, and the federal government has elaborate procedures and many thousands of people occupied full time with character investigations. Where the government is concerned, the chief emphasis is upon making sure of political loyalty. Most agencies that determine qualifications for the various professions and occupations, such as the committees governing admission to the bar, licensing authorities for physicians, taxi drivers, boxers, television station owners, real estate brokers, liquor dealers, and wilderness guides consider character an important element in determining their actions.

What does "good" character mean to all of these official investigators? First, that the individual has never violated, or been accused of violating, any laws, regulations, or rules of any private organization. Second, that the individual is not rebellious against the Corporate State, or against the specific objectives of organizations or against duly constituted authority, public or private, or against the conventions of life. Third, that he is a "team" man who goes along with the group, does not think or act with undue independence, and acts in ways that are approved by others. Fourth, that he is not emotionally unreliable or undesirable. Fifth, that he has commended himself to his superiors at various stages of his life and in the various institutions through which he has passed.

To ascertain "character," organizations make use of police and other official records, questioning of the applicant himself, and statements by school authorities, former employers, friends, and enemies. These sources of information are carefully and permanently kept secret from the applicant, who has no opportunity to refute anything reported concerning him. No adequate effort is made to ascertain the truth or reliability of statements made about an individual. A college teacher, for example, may fill out dozens of forms each year without having anyone check the basis for his opinions. Persons asked to supply information are not limited to reasonably objective facts, but invited to answer such questions as "cooperation with others," "ethical standards," "appropriateness of dress," "language and conduct," "ability to react constructively to criticisms, suggestions, advice," "emotional stability." Although few teachers, school authorities, or former employers know individuals in their school or organization very well, they are told to answer the quetions on the basis of whatever opinions or information they have.

The information and opinions concerning an individual's character are filed away and continue to be available down through the years. Nothing in the file is ever changed or disclosed to the individual, so that his character-on-file takes on an independent existence that may have an ever more remote relationship to the real individual, assuming that it ever did resemble him. The rule of most organizations is, when in doubt, don't take a chance. Thus, a file that suggests an individual may be a "risk" constitutes a permanent disability to him. The consequences to the individual of this stress upon character are profound. Beginning with childhood, he learns that he must trim his sails, be prudent, please those in authority, avoid experimentation and trouble, and try to force his individuality into the rigid mold of "good character" prescribed by the State. The State, not content with dictating his working life, has thus intruded deeply into his private life and private personality.

The personality that emerges from all of this processing is, in the language of the new generation, "uptight." Uptight means rigid, tense, afraid, narrowly limited. But the concept of uptightness, as developed by the new generation, carries a far deeper critique of the American personality. In part, uptightness might be defined as how much of society a person carries around within himself. The uptight person is concerned with goals, with competence, with coping, with managing the past and the future. He is a person with a coating or crust over him, so that he can tolerate impersonal relations, inauthenticity, loneliness, hassling, bad vibrations. He is preoccupied with the nonsensual aspects of existence, so that he has little capacity to receive or give out sensual vibrations. He is a person who can successfully handle the frustrations, difficulties, traumas, and demands of the Corporate State, and by that very fact is diminished in his humanity, tense, angry, and tight as he confronts the world. Anyone who can function efficiently in an airport or large hotel is uptight, because he has to be.

One place this tension can be felt with the greatest immediacy is in a "nice" "clean" suburb, preferably upper middle class, such as can be found outside any city in America. Here the casual walker *feels* the managerial world. He is watched with suspicion, whether on Main Street or on a residential street. Police cars cruise by slowly, inspecting him carefully; five minutes later the police are back, passing the stroller with an even slower, more deliberate scrutiny. Housewives look out from their windows, as if spying an unexpected patch of dirt in an otherwise spick-and-span house. Storekeepers and other "solid citizens" follow him with their eyes down the center of town. Is this small-town America, with its typically suspicious provincialism? No, this is Darien, Bethesda, or Paoli, and its residents are sophisticated people, men who work in the big city, women who went to college. Is the walker just a bit paranoid? He would answer that he feels no such paranoia in a city, or in the real country, or in a lower-class suburb, or in a high-class suburb that is also a college town. It is the business-managerial suburb that can tolerate nothing strange, different, unknown; it is here one feels the intensity of the demand that every individual be regulated and controlled in "the national interest."

To the description we have given so far, we must add the impoverishment of the individual in his relationship to the public community. In the first place, the individual finds himself with no meaningful work to do—his job is increasingly frustrating, artificial, and purposeless. In the second place, he finds himself powerless to take action that would have any meaningful impact on society, and on the social evils which are increasingly apparent. Thus, he is not only deprived of "private" experience, he is deprived of a man's role in society. Appearances cannot remove the fact of his impotency, or give him a sense of manhood in the public realm.

In the years following World War II the evils afflicting America were visible to all, and reflected in much of the art of the time. American painting showed the desolation of urban life, and the movies were even more vivid in their depiction of alienation, violence, and claustrophobia. Such films as *A Place in the Sun* or Sam Fuller's *Pickup on South Street* showed that the dehumanization of life and environment was seen and felt by many people. This being the case, it was demeaning that no one was able to act. At the very end of *Casablanca*, a film made when America had just entered World War II, Humphrey Bogart is a man who can still change fate by taking action. Perhaps *Casablanca* was that last moment when most Americans believed that.

The individual was placed in the position of seeing much that was wrong in his society but remaining personally aloof. He could not be passionate; he could not be moral. He might have private feelings but publicly, and especially in his work, he went along with the system. Writing in 1967, Arthur Miller called the present age the Age of Abdication (*The New York Times*, December 23, 1967); it is equally an age without a public life. Sadly, many of those who took no public stand undoubtedly felt deeply concerned, but there was no communication between like-minded people, no solidarity which would have made effective action possible. To take a public stand meant being picked off, one by one, without even the satisfaction of having done any good. To perceive evil was to feel utterly alone.

For the individual of the Fifties and Sixties, deprived of his political and public manhood, denied work of which he could be proud, the Corporate State provided substitute images of the heroic life: the cowboy, the gangster, the detective, the virile romantic hero. Rare indeed was the popular entertainment which attempted to show that an individual could be proud of his job or, except in war, proud of his contribution to society. He must watch the deterioration of his community as a spectator in the bleachers, a nonparticipant in the great events of his times.

The product of the system we have described is the "new man" of the technological age, a man suitable for operating machines and working within organizations. He is a man who permits himself to be dominated by technique, by propaganda, by training, by advertising, by the state, all to the end that he shall be as perfectly suited as possible for playing his part. He is an artificially streamlined man, from whom irrationality, unpredictability, and complexity have been removed as far as possible. He is oversimplified in the service of reason; he tries to control himself by reason, and the result is not man but a smoothed-down man.

In John Barth's novel *End of the Road* we meet a young couple who attempt to "understand" each other perfectly, in verbal terms, disallowing all mysteries and contradictions. They want to be able to see right through each other, without any obstacles such as arbitrary or irrational fictions. What they achieve is a reductive and shallow view of each other. They banish uniqueness, expose everything that is hidden, assault every last corner of privacy, and end up as people without depth. Like overly functional architecture, they deny man's artistic need to elaborate his surroundings by carving them with designs that suggest the unknowable. Striving to know the past and the future perfectly, they have all but eliminated the richness of present experience. Adaptation to the machine not only precludes complexity, it prohibits personal growth. The individual can, of course, grow in the direction of increasing his specialty. But any other growth has a definite disutility. A person who continued to grow after he had chosen his occupation might want to change jobs or occupations in middle life; he might want to change wives; he might demand that other people relate to him in new ways; he might question his place in the hierarchy, and question his dedication to his present goals. Even if he is in one of the learned professions, he cannot grow, he becomes ever narrower. His human self is covered over by his alienated existence.

Consider a social event among professional people—a dinner, cocktail party, garden party, or just a lunch among friends. Everything that takes place occurs within incredibly narrow limits. The events are almost completely structured around conversation. No one pays any sensual attention to the food, the mind-altering experience of the drink, or to the weather, or to the nonverbal side of personality; the people do not listen to music together, or lie on the grass and look at the sky together, or share food, or sit silently and exchange vibrations. They do not talk about philosophy or subjective experience. They do not strive for genuine relationships, but keep their conversation at the level of sociability, one-upmanship, and banter, all of which leave the individual himself uncommitted, and not vulnerable. Above all, there is no exchange of brotherhood and love. Why not? There is no law against any of these possibilities, no employer forbids them, no file threatens to expose them. Professional people are so deeply in their roles that they simply cannot imagine any of these other possibilities; they may look sophisticated and free, but they are painfully stereotyped and constricted; to get them to stretch out on the floor and listen to music is to ask the impossible; for even if they wanted to, they could not bring themselves to do it freely.

Nor is this constraint limited to personal relationships and expression; if one overheard the conversation it would be clear that the modes of thought and purposes of a professional group are as limited as if thought-control had been imposed. They are dedicated to a certain pattern of "rational" thought, they limit their view of the world to their own specialty, and in fact they appear impervious to new ideas altogether, merely continuing to think in established channels for the rest of their lives, never allowing their minds to be startled into new realms after reaching maturity. If told there was a new philosophy or religion coming into prominence, few would be willing even to hear what it was about. Similarly, they allow their goals to continue to be guided by the tests, rewards, statuses, and honors which their world provides, never questioning these as valid goals. In short, what seems to be the freest class in American society turns out to be locked into a cage from which even the desire for real freedom seems to have fled; the party is a dull affair.

The end result of this personal and public imporverishment is a hollow man. Look again at our middle-class, professional people's party. Their goals—status, promotion, institutional approval, and a correct image for the outside world—are hollow in terms of personal satisfaction and meaning. They work under terrible stress, which prevents them from finding more genuine meaning and is likely to drive them to ulcers, heart attacks, or the psychiatrist's couch. In Marx's sense, they are alienated from their determinate selves, alienated from their work, and alienated from their needs. A few of them even go to plastic surgeons to change their faces, but many have done something plastic to their inner selves. Many have several different and separate selves, different roles which are not integrated and prevent anyone from confronting the individual as a whole. They have surrounded themselves by things, and rendered themselves passive in the process; it is as if they have given up the power to change and grow and create, and things have acquired this power instead; things change and dance, and the individual sits motionless, besotted, and empty. For he who can neither act to fulfill his own genuine needs, nor act to help his society in its dire need, has no genuine existence. The existentialists believe that man exists when he acts; Orestes, in Sartre's play The Flies, does not exist until he assumes responsibility for his country and himself. And so the party we have been watching is a party to which no real selves are invited to come, a social event for alienated selves. "I'd like you to meet Dr. Smith's alienated self," the host politely says to the alienated self of another of his guests. Nobody minds, so long as no real selves have been invited.

But the real tragedy of the lost self in America is not that of the professional middle class, who have had all the advantages, but the tragedy of the white-collar and blue-collar worker, who never had any chance. The meritocracy has placed them low on its scale, convincing them that they have little value as people. The productive state has demanded output from them all their lives, draining them of life, creativity, vitality, and never giving them a chance to be renewed. Competition has made them fearful and suspicious of their fellow men, believing that every other man is not a brother but a threatening rival with a knife at the throat of his adversaries. Imprisoned in masks, they endure an unutterable loneliness. Their lives are stories of disappointed hopes, hopes disintegrating into the bitterness and envy that is ever present in even the most casual conversation of the worker. If they had an individual excellence or greatness, in some area, it has been passed over by society; they are Joan Baez or Bob Dylan, working in a bank or a filling station until their minds and bodies have forgotten the poetry that once was in them. They are driven by outside authority, not merely that of the state and their employer, but by the nameless authority that says "it must be done this way," the authority of what Heidegger called "the they." Caring nothing about their work, nothing about what happens to them, they face a prospect stretching all the way to retirement, another form of death. But death is with them already, in their sullen boredom, their unchanging routines, their minds closed to new ideas and new feelings, their bodies slumped in front of television to watch the ball game on Sunday.

If anyone doubts these words, let him look at the faces of America. Stand at a commuter train station and see the blank, hollow, bitter faces. Sit in a government cafeteria and see the faces set in rigidity, in unawareness, in timid compliance, or bureaucratic obstinacy; the career women with all their beauty fled, the men with all their manhood drained. We do not look at faces very often in America, even less than we look at ruined rivers and devastated hills.

What have we all lost? What aspects of the human experience are either missing altogether from our lives or present only in feeble imitation of their real quality? Let us take our list off the yellow pad where it was jotted down one fine morning in early summer.

Adventure, Travel   The Yukon, the Hebrides, a blizzard, fog on the Grand Banks, the lost cities of Crete, climbing a mountain on rock and ice in elemental cold and wind.

Sex   Experiences with many different people, in different times, circumstances, and localities, in moments of happiness, sorrow, need, and comfortable familiarity, in youth and in age.

Nature   The experience of living in harmony with nature, on a farm, or by the sea, or near a lake or meadow, knowing, using, and returning the elements; Thoreau at Walden.

Physical Activity   Chopping wood, carrying a boat, running, walking, climbing, experiencing heat and cold, swimming, building a house, paddling a canoe.

Clothes   Clothes to express various moods, and to express the body, its strength, its shape, its sensuality, its harmony with the rest of nature. Clothes for fun, for work, for dignity.

Morality   Having a moral stand with respect to something happening to oneself, to others, or to society; maintaining that stand, and giving it expression.

Bravery
Worship
Magic and Mystery
Awe, Wonder, Reverence
Fear, Dread, Awareness of Death
Spontaneity
Romance
Dance
Play
Ceremony and Ritual
Performing for Others

Creativity   In more primitive cultures, creativity and art are part of everyday life, and each person has an opportunity to exercise his creative side.

Imagination
Mind-expanding Drugs
Music as a Part of Daily Life

Multimedia Experiences   Music, light, smell, dance, all together.

Alterations of Time   Staying up all night, getting up before dawn, sleeping all day, working three days straight, or being wholly oblivious to measured time.

Seasons   Observing the four changes of season by stopping other activities for a while and going to some place where the change is fully visible.

Growth, Learning, Change   Constantly learning new things, experiencing changes of feelings and personality, continually growing in experience and consciousness.

Harmony   Enough time and reflection to assemble various experiences and changes into a harmony within the individual, relating them to each other and to earlier experiences.

Inner Life   Introspection, reflection.

Responding to Own Needs   Staying in bed when the need is felt, drinking a milk shake on a hot afternoon, or stopping everything to watch a rainstorm.

Own Special Excellence   Having enough independence to disregard other people's standards of excellence, discover one's own special excellence, and then pursue it.

Wholeness Being completely present with another person, or completely given to some experience, rather than being partially withheld as most roles demand.

Sensuality Being sensually aware of all the stimuli at a given moment; smell, temperature, breeze, noises, the tempo of one's own body.

New Feelings Experiencing feelings or emotions qualitatively different from those previously known.

Expanded Consciousness Experiencing previously unknown kinds of awareness, new values, new understanding.

New Environments Experiencing a new total environment long enough to make adjustments to it and understand its terms (such as six months in the tropics).

Creating an Environment Taking whatever elements are given, natural, human, and social, and making a unique pattern out of them as one's own creation.

Conflict, Disorder
Suffering, Pain
Challenge
Transcendence
Myth Making and Telling
Literature, Art, Theatre, Films
Bare Feet
Aesthetic Enjoyment of Food
New Ways of Thinking
Nonrational Thoughts
New Ideas
Ability to Listen to Others
People: Perceiving Them Non-verbally
People: Seeing the Uniqueness of Each One
People: Creativity in Relationships
People: Exchanging Experiences
People: Exchanging Feelings
People: Being Vulnerable with Them
People: Friendship
Affection
Community
Solidarity
Brotherhood
Freedom.

In Ken Kesey's remarkable book *One Flew Over the Cuckoo's Nest,* the rowdy, full-blooded hero finds himself, although perfectly sane, confined to a mental hospital ward under the jurisdiction of "The Big Nurse." The Nurse is determined to "cure" McMurphy, the hero, of his refusal to accept the system of the hospital, and his

efforts to get other patients to reassert their independence and sense
of life. Slowly, the claustrophobic, suffocating net is drawn closer
around McMurphy, his struggles are taken as evidence that he is insane, and "for his own good" he is subjected to mind-damaging
shock treatments. When he still resists conforming to the total supervision and madness of the hospital, the Big Nurse has him lobotomized, leaving him a blank and helpless vegetable. Kesey's book is
about the American working man, deprived of his virility, his manhood, and his intellect by the system we have described. It is no
wonder that the book has created an extraordinary impression upon
today's young people. High school, the office, and the factory prepare a bleak fate for our youth. Indeed, the saddest thing of all in
America is probably the fate of most of its teen-agers. For at sixteen
or seventeen, no matter how oppressive the Corporate State, there is
still a moment when life is within their grasp. There are a few years
when they pulse to music, know beaches and the sea, value what is
raunchy, wear clothes that express their bodies, flare against authority, seek new experience, know how to play, laugh, and feel, and
cherish one another. But it is a short, short road from Teensville to
Squarestown; soon their senses have been dulled, their strength put
under restraint, their minds lobotomized; bodies still young, cut off
from selves, walk the windowless, endless corridors of the Corporate
State.

Human Prospects

LEWIS MUMFORD

The development of a world culture concerns mankind at large and
each individual human being. Every community and society, every
association and organization, has a part to play in this transformation;
and no domain of life will be unaffected by it. This effort grows naturally out of the crisis of our time: the need to redress the dangerous
overdevelopment of technical organization and physical energies by
social and moral agencies equally far-reaching and even more com-
manding. In that sense, the rise of world culture comes as a measure
to secure human survival. But the process would lose no small part of

its meaning were it not also an effort to bring forth a more complete kind of man than history has yet disclosed. That we need leadership and participation by unified personalities is clear; but the human transformation would remain desirable and valid, even if the need were not so imperative.

The kind of person called for by the present situation is one capable of breaking through the boundaries of culture and history, which have so far limited human growth. A person not indelibly marked by the tattooings of his tribe or restricted by the taboos of his totem: not sewed up for life in the stiff clothes of his caste and calling or encased in vocational armor he cannot remove even when it endangers his life. A person not kept by his religious dietary restrictions from sharing spiritual food that other men have found nourishing; and finally, not prevented by his ideological spectacles from ever getting more than a glimpse of the world as it shows itself to men with other ideological spectacles, or as it discloses itself to those who may, with increasing frequency, be able without glasses to achieve normal vision.

The immediate object of world culture is to break through the premature closures, the corrosive conflicts, and the cyclical frustrations of history. This breakthrough would enable modern man to take advantage of the peculiar circumstances today that favor a universalism that earlier periods could only dream about. But the ultimate purpose of One World culture is to widen the human prospect and open up new domains—on earth, not in interstellar space—for human development. If the chief result of a world civilization were only to provide each individual with a television set, a motor car, a social security card, and a one-way ticket on a spaceship, one might as well turn the planet over at once to post-historic man.

The resources for this human transformation have been available for only little more than a century; and many of the technical instruments and corporate agencies have still to be shaped. But for the first time in history, man now begins to know his planet as a whole and to respond to all the peoples who inhabit it: that is, he begins to see his own multiple image in a common mirror, or rather, in a moving picture that traverses backward and forward the dimension of time. Since the exploration of the earth was undertaken by Western man before he was spiritually prepared for it, the peoples and regions that were drawn together by trade, colonization, and conquest lost many of the most precious attributes of their cultures and their personalities. The New World expansion barbarized the conquerors instead of civilizing the conquered. By the same token, Western man impoverished his own future development, too, for the heritage he mangled and often extirpated was also his own, as a member of the human race. In his land hunger, in his greed for gold and silver, for coal and iron and oil, Western man overlooked far greater riches.

Though our dawning sense of interdependence and unity comes too belatedly to repair all the damage that has been done, we see that even the residue of past cultures still holds more values than any single nation has yet created or expressed. By his very consciousness of history, modern man may free himself at last from unconscious compulsions, derived from situations he has outlived, which continue to push him off the highway of development into rubbish-filled blind alleys. Yet if he achieves a fresh understanding of the potentialities he has buried through his own failure to know himself, he may repair his shattered confidence in his future and throw open new vistas.

The survey of human existence as a whole that has gone on systematically only for the last four centuries has not alone naturalized man by bringing him within the cycle of cosmic, geological, and biological processes: it has likewise humanized nature and made it more closely than ever before an integral part of human consciousness. Man's own creative works, whether they are a temple, an atomic pile, or a mathematical theorem, are themselves expressions of nature and witnesses of potentialities that were latent in the atom and in the formative process that built up, in rhythmic series, the stable elements.

Whatever the ultimate realities, that which man knows of nature is conditioned by his self, and it changes from moment to moment and age to age as his experience matures and his capacity for symbolic interpretation grows. His feelings are as much a part of this reality as his thoughts, for his very concept of an "objective," neutral world without feelings and values was itself the product of a particular moment in his own self-development and is no longer as important as it once seemed. Yet whatever man knows of himself is conditioned by nature: so that the more exact, the more self-detached, becomes his perception of natural processes, the more fully does he free himself from the delusions of arbitrary subjectivity. Brahman and Atman are indeed one, once they are conceived in dynamic interaction: the self-creating world and the world-creating self.

This exploration of nature has naturally opened up man's inner history, too. Within the individual soul man finds in symbolic form a whole universe that seems to contain the scattered debris of past cultures and the germinal nodes of future ones. Here, within himself, he finds primitive urges and civilized constraints, tribal fixations and axial liberations, animal lethargies and angelic flights. Through the agency of culture, if not through any more direct impress upon the psyche, all of man's past selves remain disconcertingly alive. Just as man's interpretation of the so-called physical world has now become multidimensional, spanning the whole distance from interstellar to intra-atomic space, and including an exact knowledge of phenomena, like ultraviolet rays, which are outside his sensory experience, so with the inner world of man: it ranges from the depths of the unconscious to the highest levels of conscious ideation, disciplined feeling, and purposeful action.

Our view of the self now includes earlier interpretations that New World science, in its confident externalism, had discarded. Augustine's picture of the mind is closer to Freud's than is John Locke's, and St. Paul's description of human nature seems far more adequate than Jeremy Bentham's. Heaven and hell, as the ultimate destinations of creativity or disintegration, are necessary cardinal points in any description of the human soul. It is not through scientific description, but through sympathy and empathy, through parallel acts of re-creation, that one explores this world, even after it has been opened up to other men in the symbols and forms of art.

Now the persistence of old biological or historic residues, whether active or inert, does not mean, as many still falsely suppose, that they have a preappointed or fated outcome. If certain aspects of man's nature are relatively fixed, since they are structured in his organs, they function like the warp in the loom: not merely is there considerable play in the fixed threads themselves, but the shuttle that weaves the fabric lies in man's hands, and by his conscious efforts, introducing new colors and figures, he modifies even the overall design. Every culture attaches different estimates to man's nature and history; and in its creative moments, it adds new values that enlarge the human personality and give it new destinations. Though man's release from nature's conditions or his own past selves can never be complete, the effort to achieve it is what gives individuality to every historic form: this indeed is what keeps even the most repetitive movements of history from being entirely meaningless. The making of the future is an essential part of man's self-revelation.

The problem for man today is to use his widened consciousness of natural processes and of his own historic nature to promote his own further growth. Such knowledge must now be turned to fuller uses, in the projection of a fresh plan of life and a new image of the self, which shall be capable of rising above man's present limitations and disabilities. This effort, as we have seen, is an old one; for even before man achieved any degree of self-consciousness, he was actively engaged in self-fabrication. If "Be yourself" is nature's first injunction to man, "Transform yourself" was her second—even as "Transcend yourself" seems, at least up to now, to be her final imperative. What will distinguish the present effort to create world culture, if once it takes form, is the richness and variety of the resources that are now open, and the multitude of people now sufficiently released from the struggle for existence to play a part in this new drama.

2

The readiness to face existence in all its dimensions, cosmic and human, is the first requirement for human development today. This readiness is itself a new fact, for even scientists, whose curiosity seems boundless, for long recoiled in fear against any exploration of the subjective self that penetrated beyond the threshold of isolated stimuli, abstracted sensations, and measured responses.

Not without a certain irony, the scientific rationalism of Dr. Sigmund Freud, with its fine surgical indifference to the seemingly morbid, brought to light the areas of the personality that positivism and rationalism had dismissed as "unreal"—the wish and the dream, the sense of guilt and original sin, the elaboration of fantasy into art; and by carrying his inquiry further, into the normal and healthy manifestations of these inner states, Dr. Carl Jung disclosed the integrating functions of the symbol, and thus opened a passage from self-enclosed subjectivity to those common aesthetic expressions and practical constructions that can be shared, in a spirit of love, with other people.

This opening up of every part of the psyche coincides, it would seem, with the new relationship that has begun to develop between cultures. This is symbolized by an appreciative awareness, hardly a generation old, of the aesthetic values of African or Polynesian or Aztec or Andean art, following an equally radical change in Western man's attitude toward the great arts of Egypt, Mesopotamia, Persia, India and China, once considered too far below the absolute standard of Greek art to merit study, still less appreciation. That change might, of course, lead to an abortive cultural relativism, innocent of any principle of development, were it not attached to the emergent purposes of world culture. The partial and fragmentary selves that man historically achieved sacrificed completeness for the sake of temporary order; and in the most partial and fragmentary form of all, that now sought by post-historic man, the order would be almost absolute, because so much that was essentially human would be left out of it.

From this negative universalism the acceptance of man's whole self, disclosed only in the fullness of history, helps to rescue us; for organic wholeness itself is impossible unless the creative and integrating processes remain uppermost. Religion and art, if not science, remind us of the constant reappearance of angelic saviors and redeemers: Promethean heroes who bring fire and light, defying the tortures of the envious gods: mother images of succor and loving devotion. We have learned nothing from historic experience if we have not learned that man lives by more than his applied intelligence alone.

Out of the depths of life itself come the superego, the conscience, the idealized image and the imagined ideal, the voice of reason and the promptings of divinity: all as integral to man's present nature as breathing or digestion. For it is not just the animal past that lives on in man's unconscious: the emergent future that has not yet taken form is likewise present: all that promises to release man from fixations and regressions and to open up untested modes of being and becoming, of transfiguration and transformation. Though no small part of human history has been preoccupied with the exploration of this inner world, even to the detriment of man's control over the external world, it has yet to enlist man's fullest capabilities. And as with the discovery of the New World there is an even more difficult stage that follows the surveying and mapping of the unknown area: that is, its settlement and cultivation.

3

With respect to man's inner development, we have seen it go roughly through four main stages: each of these has left a mark on both his ideas and his institutions.

In the primitive stage, the stage of magic and myth, he was innocent of self-consciousness, because his self, as an entity apart from the group, was still nonexistent; and he therefore lacked the capacity for independent action and invention which became feasible only after a certain separation had taken place. Subjectively, every part of human experience held together, expressible in meaningful images and symbols; but the price of this unity was insulation from any possibly contradictory reality. Primitive man, as we piece him together from the myths and relics that remain, was relatively whole; but in transcending his animal state he had left the real world, since he no longer recognized otherness: what he saw and felt and reacted to were his own projections, his own externalized feelings and urges, into which all outward events were somehow converted.

Civilization placed external curbs on this subjectivity; it exacted external obedience to powers other than his own, to gods and kings if not to actual conditions of nature; and it provided all human activities with a mechanical basis of order. The metes and bounds so provided secured man, in some degree, against subjective dissolution. To the extent that civilization made man recognize his own limitations, and released him from purely wishful fantasy, it enlarged the human grip on reality. But in recognizing as absolute claims outside the self, civilized man ceased to live in a unified world: the fragmentary man, with his split and contradictory selves, came into existence: the innocent paranoia of primitive man gave place to the schizoid state seemingly chronic to civilization in every phase.

With the development of axial religious consciousness a new self came into existence. In a determined effort to achieve wholeness, the inner man split himself off from the outer world and its imprisoning institutions. So real became the vision of a single unifying God, omniscient and omnipotent, that the outer world seemed, in comparison, trivial and unimportant. Meaning and value were attached to the inner, the disembodied, the subjective; and such aspects of nature as were manifestly part of another system were the expression of God's will and mind, not man's. This innerness was even more audacious in its revelations than that of primitive man; and it restored man's sense of his own self-importance, after civilization had reduced him to a mere fraction, virtually a nonentity, paralyzed by power and authority external to him.

But if axial religion escaped the fragmentation of the civilized order, it did so only by creating a dualism between "this world" and the "other world." This disturbed both inner tranquillity and practical effectiveness. Every external display of human order and power or even intelligence involved a betrayal of the inner man, or at least was a threat to his existence. That inveterate, underlying dualism of the axial self was challenged by another conception, first formulated in Ionia in the sixth century B.C., which shifted meaningful experience from the inner world to the outer world. This philosophy denied, in effect, the importance of the soul as an independent entity, with its conscious values and ideal goals, and gave weight only to the external manifestations of "earth, air, fire, and water," devoid of purpose or goal, and detached from any self-consciousness except that exhibited by rational intelligence. The self was thus reduced to the knower, and reality was reduced to that which could be known.

Unfortunately this view, which came to maturity in the seventeenth century, was only a dualism in reverse: it achieved unity by suppressing or ignoring every subjective expression except its own kind of thought. The conscious inner world that was thus brought into existence was ostentatiously antiseptic, like the operating theater in a hospital: within this special room, with its refined mechanical facilities, the mind learned to operate with a deftness and precision that only the rarest spirits had mastered before. But outside in the corridors there was dirt and disorder and disease: the rejected parts of the psyche were in a worse state under this new dispensation than the rejected parts of the physical world had been under the axial self.

At all these stages in the development of the self, only a small part of man's potentialities were consciously represented in image or idea. Fortunately, the repressed or neglected aspects, even in primitive society, were not effectively excluded from living experience. However well fortified the inner world, some of the outer world is constantly breaking through, making demands that must be met, offering suggestions that, even if unheeded, produce a certain effect. So, too, however heavy the crust formed by external nature, by human institutions and habits, the pressure from the inner world would produce cracks and fissures, and even from time to time explosively erupt. By no attention to magic formulae, by no probing of the unconscious, can one shape a tool. Similarly, by no feat of mechanical organization can one write a poem. In other words, by the very act of living men have always in some degree escaped the imperfections of their knowledge and belief. Just as life itself, in its constantly unfolding creativity, is far richer than any conception we are able to form of it, so with the human self. Man not merely builds but lives better than he knows.

At the same time, it should be plain that a great measure of man's potential energy and vitality and creativity has been dissipated, because he has not been fully oriented to every aspect of reality, outward and inward. His various historic selves have served as fine meshes that rejected far more than they admitted. We can hardly yet picture the transformation that would be wrought if every part of man's experience were hospitably received; and if every part of the inner world were as accesible and as subject to conscious direction as the outer world. So far we have lived mainly in partial worlds; and they have allowed only a small share of our energies to be directly employed. Neither the loose subjective wholeness achieved by primitive man nor, at the other extreme, the accurate, piecemeal objectivity now sought by science could do justice to every dimension of human experience. If the first was limited by its caprices, which recognized no external order or causality, the latter is equally limited by its compulsions, which recognize no inner flow of purpose and make no account of free creativity or potential divinity. Living in half-worlds, it is hardly strange that we have produced only half-men, of creatures even more distorted than these homunculi, "inverted cripples," magnified ears, eyes, bellies, or brains, whose other parts have shrunk away.

Perhaps an even better figure for the state of man, as disclosed by history, would be that of a series of experimental plants, each fed with some of the elements necessary for full growth, but none yet supplied with all of them: here an excess of nitrogen has favored a leggy growth of stem, there the absence of water has withered the whole plant; and, to make the figure even more accurate, in addition to these natural defects, the horticulturist himself has often clipped and pruned the growing plant or pinched its buds. What the experiment shows, if we may at last draw a lesson, is that man requires a sounder diet, including minute trace elements, than any self-enclosed historic culture has supplied him. He needs both a fuller exposure to sunlight above ground and a richer soil in the unconscious.

The ideal of wholeness itself is what has been lacking in the culture of man: his specialties and particularities have gotten the better of him. But from occasional periods, like the Renascence, when the ideal of the whole man has commanded the foremost representatives of the age, we have a hint of the immense energizing that may take place when every aspect of life is open to cultivation, when the instinctual life is no longer cut off from rational development, and when order and reason are not impoverished by torpid emotions or listless routines or limited purposes.

But even in unpropitious periods, individual figures, who had reached some degree of maturity in every department of life, may have appeared from time to time, only to be rejected by the society they transcended. At more than one moment in history, indeed, the effort to achieve wholeness, balance, universality, brought a measure of fulfillment. Greek culture, from the sixth century to the fourth, was remarkably peopled by such whole men: Solon, Socrates, Sophocles, were outstanding examples, but not rare ones: indeed, the proportion of highly developed persons in relation to the total population seems to have been greater than at possibly any other place and time.

These examples of wholeness may account for the attraction that Greek culture has exercised on the best minds of the West. To a degree that few other cultures could claim, the Greek self seems to stand for the truly and fully human. The development of any individual might show flaws: witness Socrates' serious failure to connect man in the city with man in nature. But in the main, no part of life was closed to them, and no part of the self claimed such exclusive respect that it crippled other capacities or closed other avenues of experience. Sophocles' readiness to do his duty as citizen, in service as a general, did not incapacitate him as a tragic playwright: for in both roles he was first of all a man. The ultimate mysteries and irrationalities of existence—symbolized by Chance, Fate, the Furies, Eros—entered their consciousness without upsetting their composure or undermining the real values they had won.

Yet even at its fullest development, this Hellenic self, so finely poised, so admirably complete within its own cultural boundaries, its own favored habitat, lacked universality. Their best representatives did not realize that the unity and balance they sought needed the help of other cultures and other types of personality: that in fact the barbarian they despised had had experiences and had produced values that might, for example, have kept one of their most creative minds, Plato, from conceiving such static and stultifying utopias as those he pictured in the *Republic* and the *Laws*. From the Jews, the Greeks needed to learn about the meaningfulness of time, change, and history; from the Persians, the fact that tension and struggle are essential to human growth, so that a polity that sought only a vegetative perfection, free from dialectic oppositions of good and evil, would be founded on illusion.

The example of the Greeks shows that the ideal possibilities of our own day have historic roots: their failures show that it is only by accepting the realities of a contemporary world society, instead of seeking a more limited province for a more limited self, that we can find a new foundation for our own further development. The self we seek, one that will have a heightened consciousness of its own still-unused resources, has still to be created. To the shaping of that self we must give no small part of the energies that we have so far recklessly squandered on our misdirected and muddled "conquest of nature." Only by a concentration on our inner world, sufficient to counterbalance our present externalism, can we hope in time to achieve the balance and wholeness which will permit a steady flow of energies back and forth between inner and outer. In the fullness of time, a unified self will bring a world culture into existence, and that world culture will in turn sustain and bring to a higher pitch of development this new self.

4

Every transformation of man, except that perhaps which produced neolithic culture, has rested on a new metaphysical and ideological base; or rather, upon deeper stirrings and intuitions whose rationalized expressions takes the form of a new picture of the cosmos and the nature of man. Even neolithic man may have been no exception; for who can say what images of fertility, what intuitions of the relation of seed and soil, phallus and womb, may not have been the prelude to that order? Our hope of creating one world within and without, accessible in all its reaches to all men, prompting a life more copious, vehement, and bold than any that has appeared before, rests upon a corresponding ideological change. To achieve unity between men, we must cultivate unity within ourselves; to enact that unity, we must have a vision of it before our eyes.

We have need, therefore, for a rational framework that will itself have the varied attributes of life: it must be capable of reconciling persistence with change, unity with variety, the internal with the external, the causal with the teleological, process with purpose. Many attempts to formulate such a philosophy during the last two centuries have been handicapped by the traditional tendency of philosophy itself to create a single watertight system, too confidently complete to admit repair or enlargement by other minds. We see this plainly in the early efforts at synthesis made by Hegel, Comte, Marx, Spencer, each of which, in excluding every rival system, undermined its own pretence to unity. Even the sciences themselves, which can modify their foundations and make additions to the superstructure without undermining the sound parts already built, have no place for any kind of experience except that which can be ratified by their methods, which exclude nonintellectual modes of creativity.

Certainly it would be presumptuous to attempt to rectify these errors by creating still another system; but it would be even more stultifying to follow the path taken by most contemporary philosophers and abandon the search for synthesis and unity as beyond human power. To effect a new transformation of man, we must be informed by a philosophy capable of uniting every aspect of human experience, and directing human development through every phase. Whilst the personless and purposeless *Weltbild* of seventeenth-century physics is already partly discredited in the sciences where it originated, the great corpus of scientific knowledge was largely formed under its influence. Most of our positive knowledge has passed through a filter devised to eliminate those aspects of experience that reveal autonomous and purposeful activities, not characteristic of purely physical systems.

Even in the human sciences the same limitation holds. The reductive technique of conventional science, interpreting the complex in terms of the simple, the higher in terms of the lower, the whole in terms of the part, is useless for revealing movement in the opposite direction. It has no method for working forward toward the future, following the path of integration and development and emergence: so it fails to understand those organic processes in which the end or goal plays a part in determining the earlier sequence of events, even though the end, as imagined or projected, is itself subject in the very act of realization to further changes in its own structure. In the case of organic or human development the reductive technique conceals the one characteristic that, above all others, signifies development as opposed to random change: namely, the continued forward movement toward a goal, or, at a lower stage, toward the completion of an organic sequence, like the life cycle of a species. With man, this movement toward a consciously projected ideal goal, though constantly modified by external conditions, has its origin in unconscious urges and dreams; and with the growth of knowledge and experience it takes in a much larger world than any visible environment suggests.

If ordered knowledge is to be at the service of man's further transformation, the sciences themselves will have to overcome the naïve bias against teleology they have inherited from the seventeenth century. At that time advanced thinkers like Galileo, Descartes, and even Spinoza found themselves constrained, in the pursuit of truth, to shake off the dogmatic finalism of axial thought. Theological dogma, which presumed to know the mind of God and the ultimate destination of man, on the basis of "revelation," had discredited itself by its very presumption. Though no finite mind can claim insight into the over-all processes of evolution and history, though, as Spinoza rightly said, "Nature has no fixed end in view," that is not to say that proximate ends and tentative goals are not visible and definable.

Doubtless the route that both nature and man have taken was not rigidly laid out at the beginning: indeed at every stage of the voyage we are greeted, as Columbus was, by unexpected landfalls and strange ports. But this does not say that the entire journey has been aimless and will never get one anywhere. A bottle thrown into the ocean may be carried, by the accidents of the tides and ocean currents, to a distant shore: but the great voyages of discovery were not conducted on the same terms, nor would they have succeeded without a purpose, a direction, and a goal. On the contrary, the end in view selectively controls and orders the sequence that brings about its accomplishment; and the better that end is interpreted, the more direct the voyage is likely to be. Organic activities create their own occasions, instead of being entirely at the mercy of nature's offerings.

Fortunately, biological knowledge has laid a fresh foundation for the teleological principle, Man has long known that the flow of life is directional and irreversible: corpses do not turn into embryos. Likewise, for a good part of an organism's existence, living processes oppose the tendency of energy to run downhill and disperse. The reversal of the natural trajectory of life is unbuilding and disintegration. We know, too, that certain attributes of organic existence have over long periods gained; that there was far more mind in existence at the point when man emerged than there had been a hundred million years before. Since man started on his career, there has not been merely an increase in the quantity of mind, but also in its qualitative attributes: in man's sensitiveness, his feeling, his capacity for love, and in his ability to encompass with the aid of symbols a larger and fuller sense of the whole. In man, the blind forces that stirred through matter and organic life have now achieved, as never before, a consciousness that reaches ever further back into origins and ever further forward into possible choices and possible destinies. Despite many setbacks and diversions, mind has matured, and love, which first sprang out of the needs of reproduction and nurture, has widened its domain. No theory of human development is adequate that does not include this widening of the province of love; it is this, rather than intelligence and the division of labor (which man shares with rats and termites), that marks man's full emergence into the human estate. In the act of maturation man has made existence more lovable by multiplying the objects and the ways of love.

As intuitions and scattered fragments of knowledge, all these facts and possibilities have been known to man at other times. But the growth of systematic thought has worked them into a unified body of knowledge. From Darwin to Freud, from Humboldt to Geddes, from Schliemann to Petrie and Evans, from Vico to Toynbee and Teilhard de Chardin, the disciplines that describe organic and human development have replaced guess and myth with accurate observation and a more comprehensive insight: though much of our existing knowledge needs the correction and amplification that only a more unified experience will be able to give it.

If life, in its fullness and wholeness, is to furnish our criterion for all development, then our philosophy must respect the main attributes of life, balance and growth, freedom and choice, persistence and variation, adaptation and insurgence, above all, the tendency to self-actualization and self-transcendence. In the interest of wholeness, we must counterbalance inhibition with expression, etherealization with materialization, extroversion with introversion, automatism with renewed creativity. For the new person, as for William James, "the real and the ideal are dynamically continuous." And only in the act of living can that dynamic interplay be maintained.

This new orientation does not merely declare the primacy of life: even more decisively, it challenges the one-sided reductive and analytic technique by placing the highest term in conscious existence, the human person, in a position of responsibility for interpreting and directing the course of life, in so far as that now lies increasingly within his hands. Instead of devaluating the person by reducing him to his animal lusts and drives, or to his even lower physico-chemical components, it attaches a fresh value to all natural events by bringing them within the purview of the person.

5

This polarization of thought around the concept of the person, as the highest emergent of known life, has been going on in many different minds during the past generation; but in a different sense than that of the axial religions. One means here, not the particular illumined person, the singular incarnation of axial religion, but the generic person, the last term in the development of the physical universe, the organic world, and the human community. As such, the person is endowed with the energies and vitalities of each earlier emergence. But he transcends his creaturely limitations by his capacity to interpret natural events, to conserve forms and values, to plan and project new goals and new destinies, to hold together in consciousness a meaningful world and to transform by action ever wider reaches of life, in accordance with that meaning.

The philosophy of the person includes every aspect of experience: the reality of love no less than the reality of power, the reality of the unique and the individualized no less than the reality of the repeated and the standardized. In the person both immanence and transcendence, necessity and freedom, are facts of experience. When we begin with the person we penetrate life at every level, not merely the past and the known, but the potential and the conceivable: that which still lies beyond our knowing. This is the polarizing idea that will presently radiate into every department of thought, quickening the perception of interrelations and integrations, and giving a new value to truths that would otherwise remain inert.

A world built up conceptually from the atom might remain forever in fragments and unfinished sequences: in such a world, if uncorrected by a theory of organic development, even the phenomena of life might seem disjointed and accidental, without direction, without ultimate value. Whereas a world penetrated downward from the person begins with the face of integration, with values and goals already embodied and incarnated. From that beginning one may interpret otherwise dispersed and aimless events in the light of the goal toward which they have moved and achieved conscious existence. Such a world assumes no pre-established harmony and no fixed destination. What it reveals is a multitude of organic patterns, which, in relation to further human designs, become cumulatively significant. The increase of creativity becomes accordingly man's measure of his success in life.

As man has gone on with his own development, he has become more conscious both of the general process of organic transformation and of the important role he himself has come to play. The concept of the person, associated with creativity and divinity, was originally confined to a single individual, the supreme ruler of the land, identified and worshipped as a god. Now it has become the essential mark of human development, in which all men share. Instead of man in person bowing himself out of the picture, as he did when he followed the old canons of the physical sciences, he now takes a central position on the stage, knowing that the performance itself, in the theater of consciousness at least, cannot go on without him. Without man's intervention it would be a meaningless dumb show.

Man begins as an actor, detached from his animal colleagues, already something of a star performer, but uncertain of what part he shall learn. In time, he becomes a scene painter, modifying the natural background and finding his own part modified by it, too: and he is driven to be a stagehand, likewise, shifting the "properties" to make his entrances and exits more manageable. Only after much practice in all these roles, as scene painter, stagehand, costumer, make-up artist, actor, does man discover that his main function is to write and direct the drama. In composing the play itself man uses, in Shakespearean fashion, many of the old plots left by nature, but he gives them a new turn of the imagination and works the events up to a climax that nature, without his aid, might not have blundered upon for countless million years.

In its early stages, this intensification of creativity is represented, not in man's actual acts, but in the attributes of his gods, to whom he at first fearfully attributed the omniscience and omnipotence he secretly coveted for himself. Only late in man's development did he find it necessary to project, in his conception of divinity, an attribute that would offset the grave threat to life hidden in this all-knowingness and all-powerfulness: a divine all-lovingness.

Love, like mind itself, has been slowly gathering momentum through the organic world: by reason of its late introduction into the drama conceived and enacted by man, it has absorbed only a small share of man's working and learning activities. But in the development of the person love is actually the central element of integration: love as erotic desire and procreativeness, love as passion and asthetic delight, lingering over images of beauty and shaping them anew, love as fellow feeling and neighborly helpfulness, bestowing its gifts on those who need them, love as parental solicitude and sacrifice, finally, love with its miraculous capacity for overvaluing its own object, thereby glorifying it and transfiguring it, releasing for life something that only the lover at first can see. Without a positive concentration upon love in all its phases, we can hardly hope to rescue the earth and all the creatures that inhabit it from the insensate forces of hate, violence, and destruction that now threaten it. And without a philosophy of the person, who dares to talk of love?

What is ideally desirable, at this stage of man's development, does not exist in any past form of man, either biological or social: not cerebral man, muscular man, or visceral man: not the pure Hindu, the pure Mohammedan, the pure Christian, nor yet the pure Marxist or the pure Mechanist: not Old World man or New World man. The unity we seek must do justice to all these fragments, and lovingly include them in a self that shall be capable of transcending them. Any doctrine of wholeness that does not begin with love itself as the symbol and agent of this organic wholeness can hardly hope to produce either a unified self or a united world; for it is not in the detached intellect alone that this transformation must be effected.

6

This radical transvaluation of values is a necessary prelude to the next phase of man's development. Up to the present the chief activity of mankind has been confined to its biological ambit—to keep alive and reproduce itself. The quantity of time and attention that man could give to art and play, to ritual and religion, to philosophy and science, in short, to the central drama of existence, was only a modicum of that which he was forced to devote to the preparatory economic processes. What was achieved in meaning and value was almost surreptitiously filched from the so-called serious business of life. But almost within the memory of living men, a radical change in the human condition has come about. This change rivals that brought in by neolithic culture, and far outstrips that produced by earlier forms of mechanical organization, for it brings with it the promise or release from compulsory labor and every form of external slavery. Thanks mainly to advances in science, almost unlimited energies are now at man's disposal; and in most of the servile modes of work, the automatic machine is capable of performing functions that heretofore were performed only at an immense sacrifice of human life.

Because the current activities of our society continued to flow into obsolete molds, this change at first produced only industrial crises and dislocations; and even now, only a small part of its bene-

fits is available. But already, in advanced industrial countries, the
number of hours in the working week has been almost halved, and
the proportion of people in the professions and in the services not
devoted to agriculture or industrial production has risen steadily. As
this change proceeds, a fact unknown outside the most primitive cultures comes once again into existence: no longer the domination of
life by work, but the possible integration of work into a more abun-
dant and significant life.

This relief from the demand that life shall be grimly subordinated to work holds out two great promises. The first of these is that
work itself, at least that which remains outside the province of the
automatic machine, may itself become an educative process, evoking
intelligence and feeling, giving back even to mechanical functions
the freedom the old cratsman used to exercise. This kind of creativity
is largely lacking in the meretricious art of the market place, but has
long been prophetically visible in art, such as the sculptures of
Naum Gabo or the architecture of Frank Lloyd Wright. At this point,
Le Play's great dictum, that the most important product that comes
out of the mine is the miner, will apply to every occupation. Even
more, we may now favor certain types of products and certain systems of production, and reject others, with reference to the effect that
the work has upon the human personality: we shall weigh its influence upon love, fellowship, family life, citizenship, not merely upon
mechanical efficiency.

The other great benefit of the transformation of the industrial
process is the fact that its outcome need not be a plethora of material
goods and gadgets, nor yet of instruments of warfare and genocide.
Once we revamp the institutions of the market, and distribute goods
mainly on the basis of need, rather than in proportion to toil or sacrifice or privileged status, our gains will be gains in leisure. In fact,
without leisure, our expansion in industrial production would be almost meaningless; for we need a plenitude of time if we are to select
and assimilate all the genuine goods that modern man now commands. *Schola* means leisure; and leisure makes possible the school.
The promise of a life economy is to provide schooling for the fullest
kind of human growth—not for the further expansion of the machine.

This does not mean simply that more of our lives will be devoted to education: it means rather that education will constitute the
principal business of life. This change promises to be so profound
that one must emphasize it by bestowing on it a new name, to indicate that the processes of infusing value and meaning into every
phase of life will not stop with the formal school.

The words education, self-development, character formation,
conversion all bear upon the process; but they carry with them the

limited references of their original use. That of education is still tied
to the bookish training that used to begin with the mastery of the
ABC's and even now lasts no longer, formally, than the attainment of
the highest professional degree. The concept of self-development
carries with it, if not a hint of humanistic priggishness or romantic
willfulness, the general axial belief that the welfare of the self can be
secured in separation from that of society, or at least that its cultivation has no public concerns: thus the personal is falsely identified
with the private.

As for character formation, it recalls the stern protestant discipline, with its daily assessment of weaknesses, its aesthetically
repressive regimen; and that flavor of narrowness and negation remains, though in classic British education it mingled with a strong
humanist influence that promoted manly athletic exercises and
nourished physical beauty. Finally, conversion, the axial term for the
birth of the second self, might be considered the most decisive of educational influences: yet in its formative stages it indicates only a
change of attitude and direction and does not provide the social context. One needs a term to indicate not alone these traditional aspects
of education, but something that world culture itself will add to the
process.

The word for this larger conception of education is the Greek
term *paideia,* which Werner Jaeger reintroduced in his brilliant and
exhaustive study of Greek education. *Paideia* is education looked
upon as a lifelong transformation of the human personality, in which
every aspect of life plays a part. Unlike education in the traditional
sense, *paideia* does not limit itself to the conscious learning processes, or to inducting the young into the social heritage of the community. *Paideia* is rather the task of giving form to the act of living itself: treating every occasion of life as a means of self-fabrication, and
as part of a larger process of converting facts into values, processes
into purposes, hopes and plans into consummations and realizations.
Paideia is not merely a learning: it is a making and a shaping; and
man himself is the work of art that *paideia* seeks to form.

We are too easily tempted today, by habits that belong to past
moments of civilization, into thinking of the kind of unity that might
be achieved by a formal assembly of specialists, by an organization of
"interdisciplinary activities," by an intellectual synthesis based upon
some logical scheme for uniting the sciences. But *paideia* demands
far more than that kind of formal synthesis: the unity it seeks must be
sought in experience, and it demands a readiness to interchange
roles, even at a sacrifice of expertness, for the sake of the greater gain
to learning and life. The lesson of *paideia* is fundamentally the
prime lesson of democracy: growth and self-transformation cannot be

delegated. What is more, the achievement of the human whole—and the achievement of the wholly human—take precedence over every specialized activity, over every narrower purpose. Though this new person will still doubtless cherish and develop the skills associated with specialized vocations, he will tend to be multi-occupational as a citizen, nourishing other interests and pursuing other activities, in harmony with a larger plan of life. To exercise all the capacities of a man will become more important than to learn the identifying badge of a vocation or an office; for the day will come, as Emerson predicted," "when no badge, uniform, or star will be worn."

This gives a new significance to Karl Marx's conception of the future society, which he threw out in passing in *Capital*, despite his own strict aversion to any kind of utopian prohecy. In this society, as Marx defined it, "the 'fragmentary man' would be replaced by the completely developed individual,' one for whom different social functions are but alternative forms of activity. Men would fish, hunt, or engage in literary criticism without becoming professional fishermen, hunters, or critics." That moment of insight, based chiefly on his admiration for the freedon and human balance of American culture during the Golden Day, offsets, indeed nullifies, the more characteristic absolutism of Marx's dialectic. To complete it, one should perhaps add his master Hegel's admirable definition of an educated man: One who can do what any other man can do.

One may say of One World man, then, that he is no longer the incarnation of his class, his trade, his profession, or his religious faith, any more than he is the incarnation of his exclusive national group. He is, in fact, just the opposite of the competent technician— the impersonal, neutral functionary, obedient only to science governing his métier, incurious about any process beyond his limited range: he whom Max Weber singled out as the type that would finally dominate the modern world. The bureaucrat and the technocrat are rather the ideal prototypes of post-historic man. One World man will gladly sacrifice his mechanical efficiency, along with his cocksureness and complacency, in order to enhance the quality of life itself.

The conquering hero, the suffering saint, the ardent lover, the reckless adventurer, the patient scientist, in short all the ideal types of previous cultures, took on their personalities for a whole lifetime. They were committed to their particular virtues, as soldiers, merchants, and craftsmen were dedicated to their single vocation. Each was imprisoned by his role in a cramped chamber and never had the run of the house. The saint could not remain a saint if he became a lover, nor the sage a sage if he became an adventurer. This fixation in permanent roles, vocational and moral, brought about an arrest of life itself; and its correction will be one of the happy tasks of One World personalities. While he is open to any of these possible roles, when the moment demands, a unified man would no more think of playing them throughout life than a capable actor would play only Hamlet. The historic function of these ideal images was to intensify and widen the capacities of man.

Though no single life can make use of all its opportunities or reveal all its potentialities, though restriction and concentration are in fact necessary for any creative expression, the openness of the One World self will widen the area of its transactions and energize all its activities. It was such a widening of medieval Christian culture, by contact with the ideal world of Greece and Rome and the actual world of China, India, Africa, and America, that made possible the brilliant achievements of the Renascence. Similarly, personal acquaintance has taught me, people like Patrick Geddes and Ananda Coomaraswamy, who actively participated in both Western and Eastern cultures, brought into the common human focus all that they touched. Even reading can do much to break through the parochialism of culture, as Emerson and Thoreau proved by their early use of Hindu texts; and when travel becomes more than mere sightseeing, when it brings about an interchange of experiences, it will mutiply the number of those who are capable of reaching full human stature.

This basic ideological change and personal transformation have long been under way. But the obstacles in the way of a world-wide emergence of unified man are formidable; for the energies that will make it possible cannot be brought to the surface by any purely rational means. As with the early Christians one must prayerfully watch and wait, making every possible conscious preparation, yet realizing that no cold act of will suffices. When the favorable moment comes and its challenge is accepted, thousands and tens of thousands will spontaneously respond to it, stirred by the sense of fellowship the moment will produce. In that act forces that were neutral or antagonistic to any larger plan or purpose will likewise undergo polarization and become actively helpful. Then a new self will be born.

Ripeness is the condition for any organic transformation. The change to One World man was not possible, certainly, at an earlier stage of human development. When the inner ripening had taken place, as it did more than once under the axial religions, the lack of technical facilities and organs of communication alone was enough to impose a veto on the most generous dreams. Again, when technical facilities had brought about physical intercourse on the widest scale, the lack of adequate moral ideas and social purposes largely emptied this intercourse of ideal content and kept it from contributing to the common development. Today, neither the technical means nor the relevant social pressures are absent: it is rather the inner readiness that is lacking. Our generations needs faith in the processes of life sufficient to bring about a willing surrender to life's new demands.

Yet in isolated persons, like Albert Schweitzer in the present day, like Peter Kropotkin or Patrick Geddes in an earlier day, and Goethe and Emerson even earlier, the kind of self that the moment demands has actually been incarnated. Schweitzer, for example, has transcended the specializations of vocation and nationality and religious faith. In deliberately choosing an uninviting region in Africa as the seat of his lifework, and the ministry of medicine as a means of translating his Christian ethic into practice, he sacrificed the opportunities that his special talents as theologian, musician, and philosopher seemed to demand. Seemingly under the most hostile conditions, he has demonstrated the possiblility of actualizing a unified personality; and the course of life he chose, which involved the heaviest of renunciations, has proved richer in its fruits than one that would have conformed to more orthodox patterns of Old World culture.

To reach full human stature, at the present stage of development, each of us must be ready, as opportunity offers, to assimilate the contributions of other cultures; and to develop, for the sake of wholeness, those parts of his personality that are weakest. Not least, he must renounce perfection in any single field for the sake of balance and continued growth. He who belongs exclusively to a single nation, a single party, a single religion, or a single vocation without any touch or admixture from the world beyond is not yet a full man, still less can he take part in this transformation. This is a fundamental lesson of human growth, always true—but now imperatively true. In its critical moment of integration, Christianity took in Persian and Egyptian myths, Greek philosophy, and Roman organization, just as Mohammedanism took in the lessons of Moses and Zoroaster and Jesus. So One World man will embrace an even wider circle; and the whole person so created will cast aside the series of masks, some weakly benign, some monstrous, that so long concealed the living features of man.

In his very completeness, One World man will seem ideologically and culturally naked, almost unidentifiable. He will be like the Jain saints of old, "clothed in space," his nakedness a sign that he does not belong exclusively to any nation, group, trade, sect, school, or community. He who has reached the level of world culture will be at home in any part of that culture: in its inner world no less than its outer world. Everything that he does or feels or makes will bear the imprint of the larger self he has made his own. Each person, no matter how poorly endowed or how humble, is eligible to take part in this effort, and indeed is indispensable; yet no matter how great any individual's talents may be, the results will always be incomplete; for the equilibrium we seek is a dynamic one and the balance we promote is not an end in itself but a means to further growth. "It is provided in the essence of things," as Walt Whitman said, "that from any fruition of success, no matter what, shall come forth something to make a greater struggle necessary."

7

So we stand on the brink of a new age: the age of an open world and of a self capable of playing its part in that larger sphere. An age of renewal, when work and leisure and learning and love will unite to produce a fresh form for every stage of life, and a higher trajectory for life as a whole. Archaic man, civilized man, axial man, mechanized man, achieved only a partial development of human potentialities; and though much of their work is still viable and useful as a basis for man's further development, no mere quarrying of stones from their now-dilapidated structures will provide material for building the fabric of world culture. No less important than the past forces that drive men on are the new forms, dimly emerging in man's unconscious, that begin to beckon him and hold before him the promise of creativity: a life that will not be at the mercy of chance or fettered to irrelevant necessities. He will begin to shape his whole existence in the forms of love as he once shaped the shadowy figments of his imagination—though, under the compulsions of his post-historic nihilism he now hardly dares thus to shape even purely aesthetic objects. But soon perhaps the dismembered bones will again knit together, clothed in flesh.

In carrying man's self-transformation to this further stage, world culture may bring about a fresh release of spiritual energy that will unveil new potentialities, no more visible in the human self today than radium was in the physical world a century ago, though always present. Even on its lowest terms, world culture will weld the nations and tribes together in a more meaningful network of relations and purposes. But unified man himself is no terminal point. For who can set bounds to man's emergence or to his power of surpassing his provisional achievements? So far we have found no limits to the imagination, nor yet to the sources on which it may draw. Every goal man reaches provides a new starting point, and the sum of all man's days is just a beginning.

Humanism and Futurism: Enemies or Allies?

IRVING H. BUCHEN

> Human life is reduced to real suffering, to hell, only when two
> ages, two cultures and religions overlap. A man of the Classical
> Age who had to live in medieval times would suffocate miserably
> just as a savage does in the midst of civilization. Now there are
> times when a whole generation is caught in this way between
> two ages, two modes of life, with the consequence it loses all
> power to understand itself and has no standard, no security, no
> simple acquiescence.
> —Hermann Hesse, *Steppenwolf*
>
> There is a miracle in every new beginning.
> —Hermann Hesse, *Steppenwolf*

One of the most cherished ideals of the humanistic tradition is the
notion of the whole man. And yet the moment one asks the perfectly
basic and big question, "What constitutes our wholeness as human
beings?" it is more often than not greeted with either a tolerance that
is patronizing or an impatience that is inhibiting. "Our wholeness as
human beings? Yes, well, it all depends whether the context is religious, philosophical, political, economic, cultural, psychological,
etc. Define your terms." Thus, in rapid fashion, the big question is
splintered and sorted out into various cages in which different expert
trainers put the now-tamed question through flaming hoops with as-
tounding and enviable dexterity. Result: the humanities train gener-
alists who are really professional fragments or specialists who are all
broken off in the same place.

Even humanities programs that officially seek interdisciplinary
convergences contain distortions, although perhaps of a higher order.
Many exclude the physical sciences or bewail the dehumanization of
man by technology. Frequently, those who cry the loudest against
the evils of technocracy consult concordances put together by computers, cite articles reproduced by Xerox, allude to manuscripts and
out-of-print books made available on microfilm, and play Hopi burial
chants on audio cassettes. Even more serious, their pejorative attitude toward technology often jeopardizes communication with their
students who already are quite comfortable with computers and
teaching machines, and are aware that the human element, namely
themselves, has not been mechanized.

Finally, even the best of humanities programs generally exist apart from any contact or relationship with programs in business, education, science and engineering, etc. As a result, liberal-arts and business students, for example, confront each other like two armed camps, and stake out a gulf that embodies the widest generational or cross-cultural gap imaginable. Such mutual and unnecessary opacity is not limited to education, but appears in almost every single collision between environmentalists and businessmen. Indeed, it might not be far-fetched to claim that the intransigence between such groups is due less to the inherent extremism of each postion (a decent environment versus a reasonable profit) than to the mutual self-defensive excesses each has forced upon the other (the purest of environments and the maximizing of profits) in the absence of any holistic frame that might move them toward an accommodating center.

I am not calling for a cessation to honest disagreement or legitimate differences, but I am maintaining that insofar as the humanities cut themselves off from an intercollege position, they directly and indirectly create the basis for a wasteful rather than an interactive confrontation of differences. Moreover, as a result, the humanistic tradition ironically has set up its students for the dreadful prospects of impotence on the one hand or fascism on the other, which are not so much alternatives as versions of each other.

How did this process of fragmentation occur? At what point and for what reasons did the great tradition of the whole man become parceled out? More important, what solutions are available to us in the future?

Over-Individualization

The twentieth century can be summed up quickly as the century that exceeded itself, that went to the moon before it was either comfortable or dispossessed from earth, that left the past further and faster behind than any previous age or perhaps all centuries combined, and above all that leaped into the twenty-first century without having the courtesy to allow the present one to come to its natural chronological end. Indeed, the overreaching appears to have reached such dislocating proportions that there is often a frantic search for mythic metaphors to comprehend the phenomena of changing change and exponential transcendence. Those who find humanistic prospects imperiled have revived Mary Shelley's *Frankenstein*. Others, more hopeful, base their metaphors on the oracle at Delphi, Prometheus, Faust, Conciousness III, or Jesus Christ, Superstar. But whether the future is seen as dark or rosy, we face the possibility of total generational discontinuity. It is one thing to bring forth a wave of the future, but quite another for that wave to break before one's own has crested. On raises children, but they are not supposed to raze parents; one expects human variations—not aliens from another planet.

The standard scapegoats trotted out by the humanists to explain such presumption are materialism and technology. Yet the condemnation of materialism is usually a refuge for those already comfortable. What would we have the Appalachian poor do? Retreat to Walden Pond to lead lives of noisy desperation? Contemplation and love will not fill empty stomachs; besides, the highest form of charity is to make recipients independent of such handouts. And so far as technology is concerned, nearly all the major problems of man antedated the industrial revolution, are still with us and are still not solvable through technology. The issues of war, racial relations, social justice, abortions, divorce, etc., cannot be blamed on the outer-space program. As Buckminster Fuller often has noted: If one dumps all the technology into the ocean, millions will starve; but if one dumps all the politicians into the ocean, no one will starve.

The major achievements of the modern world are not materialism or technology, but the supreme emergence of the individual and the rout of those classic reactionaries who insist that the "democratic dregs" or common man, given equal opportunity, would reduce or tarnish the quality of society, culture and civilization. But if individualism has triumphed, where are our men of genius? Individualism theoretically raises up saviors and superstars. We have had many of them in the past. Yet today, something is different. They are here and they are not. A Ralph Nader appears, but he is now a we— Nader's Raiders. A class-action suit on behalf of the schoolchildren of California is brought not by some lonely, starry-eyed or muckraking lawyer, but by a collectivity, a team of experts from many fields from all over the country. Why do we automatically despair when we discover that "It is just too much for any one man to do!" Perhaps it is a good thing—that so many of the tasks facing us exceed any individual's capacity. Perhaps the superstar system is not the only, or even the best, way to make something happen and to have it endure. Perhaps the persistent search for saviors has tyrannically tied us to an equally tenacious search for scapegoats. In short, a special and sometimes destructive psychology has accompanied the emergence of individuality in Western civilization through the reinforcing notion of a search for individual identity.

One basic reason why the humanities did not honor the past legacy of educating the whole man is that they turned, instead, to

educating the individual; and the concept of individuality and that of
the whole man are not synonymous. The individual man is stirred by
independence, autonomy and self-reliance; the holistic man by interdependence, collectivism and reliance. And if one views the history
of the presumptuous twentieth century as essentially the history of
individuality, then what perhaps becomes clear is that individuality
is the great overreacher, the lovely presumption. Indeed, we may
have reached a point in history when individuality, traditionally conceived, may have gone as far as it can go. What we need today is not
merely traditional means for multiplying or extending individuality,
but also nontraditional ways for surrendering part of it.

For the humanist the idea of "surrendering" even a fraction of
one's individuality will no doubt seem like heresy. Perhaps this
alarm can be reduced, however, if we dispose immediately of a misconception.

There may be a direct correlation between our present contemplation of the limits to industrial and economic growth and our
contemplation of the limits of individuality. But just as the concept
that growth has limits need not necessarily signify the end of growth,
so, too, the notion that individuality may have limits need not signify
the end of individuality. Understanding the limits of any system is
the first step toward expanding or transcending those limits. In short,
the real conflict we face now is a conflict not between the old and the
new, but between the new and the futuristic, between what is
known and what is emerging, between the individual and the new,
emerging image of what might be termed the collectivized individual. The whole person is not and cannot be totally individual; part of
the whole—today more than ever—must be nonindividualized, communal, or "collectivized." For we all live in a social environment
with others. And that social environment, explosive with change, by
continually impinging on us, becomes part of us.

The new focus of the humanities should be the collectivized individual as the futuristic image of the whole man. But what exactly is
a "collectivized individual" and how does one go about employing
humanistic studies to educate this hybrid man and woman of the future?

The Collectivized Individual

A collectivized individual is multiple rather than singular. If the
traditional notion in the West has been one God, one love, one job,
one identity, one country and one planet, the futuristic notion is
many gods, many jobs, many identities, many countries and many

planets. The collectivized individual may unexpectedly prove more responsive to and cooperative with overt and official planning of aspects of his life, partly because he will be better able to comprehend the communal imperatives for such overall planning, partly because he will be a participant in that planning, rather than a passive object of it, and partly because he will, in effect, be compensated by enjoying the greater personal freedoms granted by his multiplicity. He will be capable of sustaining many allegiances, without contradiction, on both a national and international scale, and be closer to being, especially through the concept of global perspectives, a world citizen. Work will neither tyrannically absorb nor determine his life; indeed, because no one component will ever dominate his reality frame, he will often be proficient, although perhaps not outstanding, in a remarkable number of areas. He will learn to make peace with incompletion. And, of course, he will recognize that he is not just a "he" but also a "she"—that wholeness includes not the elimination of sexual differences, but a recognition that the planet was not put here for the exclusive advantage of one sex.

But it is one thing to describe what the collectivized individual might or should be like and quite another matter to determine how he can be encouraged to develop his complex potential. We need to observe the educational process and to identify within it those built-in obstacles to educating collectivized individuals. (Throughout, I will discuss education at its best, so that any failures are fundamental to the process rather than our inability to realize it fully.)

It is not accidental that we speak of a "hunger" for knowledge, of cultivating a "taste" for art; and that many sociologists and psychologists use terms like impoverished environmental "diets" or "undernourished" social conditions to describe the plight of the educationally and culturally disadvantaged. A subject comprehends an object by claiming, encircling and ingesting it. Internalization—the term itself is revealing—takes the form of the now-grasped object being converted into an absorbable form of nourishment within the now-expanded and satisfied subject. Feeding and knowing are both ways of growing.

The ingestion of information is reflected psychologically in ego-building or identity-granting additions. Thus, we know; and we know that we know. The knowing of what we know constitutes both the identity of knowledge and the knowledge of identity. This dual process exists and should continue. Nevertheless, because it buttresses the individual self as a separate and perhaps even separatist activity, and because such a self sustains itself often in competition and as an ego-island, there is a serious question as to whether such an educational process is not inherently inimical to the goals of collective cooperation and to the possibilities of change. I am not suggesting that ego-identity as a basic building block of self-esteem be scrapped, any more than individuality as a basic strand be eliminated. What I would suggest is that a series of supplemental and extending processes be introduced to enlarge and extend the ego-centricity.

Extending the Ego

The first has to do with the rejection of the notion of the singular self, because that is ultimately as much an impoverishment of human potential as the complete denial of self. The truth is we are many selves. Singular selfhood is the egotistical attempt of a part of the whole to be self-sufficient and to subordinate other parts to its own desires and purposes. Culturally, it is reflected in the lie of the melting pot; internationally, in the self-sufficiency of isolationism; economically, in the unilateralism of being solely a consumer. Among the affluent, the self stands at the center and demands to have its individual needs satisfied. But surfeit soon comes, and, with it, the characteristic attitudes of boredom, loss of hunger or jaded appetite that preclude education and change. Far from supporting such further impoverishment or aggrandizement of the self, the educational process should instead focus on the image of multiple selves which simultaneously can serve as a maximum invitation to the underdeveloped self and as a strong antidote to the overdeveloped self.

Similarly, the temporal extension of self becomes important. As Benjamin Singer notes in the second chapter, the projected self or future-focused role image is a critical part of the present self, and the educational process that ignores it does so at its own risk. If we are many selves, we are also likely to become many future selves, and a humanist education will recognize and serve that inevitability.

Simultaneously, it will help call attention to those purposes that are not achievable by the individual alone. Educationally, this involves the interdependent rather than the independent learning model in which cooperation is structured to be as productive of results as competition and which involves the extensive use of games, simulations, and role-playing techniques that instruct through transactional means, i.e., through negotiation. The futurist emphasis on these forms of learning is truly a liberating one.

Futurist education also emphasizes the creative process, the mutual conversion of objects and subjects. From the creative point of view, the subject-object relationship is not a static but a transferable relationship. In other words, an object under investigation has, so to speak, the capacity to become a communicating subject or, to use the larger more meaningful term, an "alive" environment in its own right. The traditional analytical process is unilateral, one-directional and monolingual; the subject comprehends the object, tree. The creative process is mutual, two-directional and bilingual; the object, tree, communicates its own meaning even in its own language. The tree need not be regarded solely as a passive object with no identity other than that given to it by a comprehending subject. Rather, a tree ultimately has as much to say about human systems as it does about systems of tree-ness or ecology. In analytical thinking, the stress is on the discipline of control.

In creative thinking, the stress is on the discipline of surrender. Subjects and objects are thus interchangeable at crucial points of mutual understandings. André Gide rightly observed: "One imagines one possesses and in reality one is possessed. . . ." By striking a balance between possessing and being possessed, between subject and environment, the individual ego, i.e., the subject, can learn to "listen" to the object. The more we are capable of so doing, the more we may learn to listen to people from different cultures and, ultimately, perhaps, to those creatures from other planets who may some day confront us.

By extending the ego-building process in these lateral, interactive directions, it may be possible to overcome or minimize the obstacles to cooperative and collective ends within the traditional educational process. Subjects who can become objects, in turn establish the dynamic interplay of the collectivized individual and the multiplistic unity of the world citizen.

But even the best of educational processes needs direction and shape—needs a sense of what we are becoming and why. That perspective can revivify the humanities, and it can be found in the emerging field of futurism itself.

Futurism As Ally

Let me begin here by indicating what futurism is not, and disowning what has been put upon it. Futurism is neither supergadgetry nor salvationist ideology. It does not traffic in hysterics or lullabies. It does not seek to change human nature in manipulative fashion, but rather to encourage awareness of the rich changes inherent in its own multiplicity. Above all, futurism does not now, and never will, possess an assured or fixed body of content that exists apart from what it seeks to comprehend. Indeed, in the final analysis, what recommends futurism is its inclusiveness, its capacity to generate synthesizing and unifying ways of looking at man, mind and matter.

Futurism dovetails with the concept of the collectivized individual because it provides a synthesizing framework that does not violate, but rather interrelates, the separate disciplines. It provides them with a collectivized framework within which to nest their individuality.

And it is for this very reason that I believe futurism, in partnership with humanism, could stir a second renaissance.

A study of the next thirty years may appear puny in comparison with the humanist's traditional study of the last five thousand. Yet it is quite possible that change in the next three decades may equal in magnitude the change from an agrarian to an industrial society. Then, too, futurism is by no means at odds with the past. First, the past no longer is and the future is yet to be—and the imaginative bond necessary to sustain one carries over to the other. Second, in some respect the future may already have happened in the past. No one can read or write today's pessimistic science fiction without noting it is based on a solid understanding of primitive societies. Similarly, many of the proposed new international symbols gradually being introduced all over the world as a global sign language have their roots in the mythic imaginations of the ancients. And no futurist can ignore the past when he confronts the "leap-frog" concept that sees developing countries like Bolivia, in which 50 per cent of the people are regularly unemployed, conceivably spurting ahead of the economically advanced countries to become leisure societies sustained by guaranteed incomes.

Futurism also provides an excellent academic opportunity to test a student's true knowledge of what he has learned, for example, of the principles of sociology or economics, by asking him or her to design a new social institution or some new aspect of an economic system. Both history and futurism can be honored by reconvening the first Constitutional Assembly and drafting anew a portion of the Constitution. Or the entire enterprise can be projected on an international scale by creating a "Global Planning Council" manned by students representing different countries and ideologies and negotiating agreements on outer space, fishing rights, etc.; and that can be done before, during and even after such negotiations are completed in real life.

Futurism also offers the prospect of comprehensive research projects and curricula developments in all fields, for there is no subject in the humanities that does not have a futuristic dimension. For example, there is the lovely contradiction of doing research on a comprehensive history of attitudes toward futurism. Equally important, we are not the only age to experience cultural dislocation. How various cultures faced "Copernicus Shock," collapsing and then renewing themselves, is an area of legitimate interest for both specialist and generalist.

The need to examine resistances to change, the capacity for creative or nonlinear thinking, the development of a new psychology of multiplicity for the collectivized individual, are all potential benefits of looking ahead. Finally, we are oversaturated with war studies and not enough with peace studies, such as the thorough and rigorous programs already developed by the World Law Fund; and we are foolishly wasting our energies debating whether aggression is inborn or acquired when what we need are studies and courses on the conversion of aggression into creativity as models for both the individual and the society.

All the above examples—and there are many more—designate futurism in its supportive role, as an extender of traditional disciplines. But futurism can also serve as a comprehender in its own right and subsume a variety of existing disciplines. Imagine the design of new societies to be planted on Mars or Venus. And imagine the humanistic concerns involved in such an exercise. What values should be dominant? What might its conceptions of justice, beauty or time be? To be sure, initial designs might reveal the extent to which we are slaves of the past and obediently duplicate existing arrangements. But even if so, how often is that limitation exposed? Moreover, releasing that bias often opens the way for more imaginative possibilities.

In turn, imaginative excesses or wild fantasies are correctable through two indispensable futuristic controls. Futurists search for consequences, examining decisions for their unsuspected impacts. Such foresightedness, then, points to the real possibility that many of the major decisions in the future will be decisions *not* to do something. A second control lies in the necessity to engage in goal- and value-generating processes by those who have to live that futuristic design. In a democratic society, such communication is not just a crucial prelude to implementation, but is, in fact, a form of implementation itself.

Futurism is not an enemy of the past or of the tradition of solid and rigorous scholarship, but on the contrary an ally; it seeks not to supplant, but to extend, existing disciplines; and it offers precisely the kind of comprehensive and comprehending perspective that will enable faculty in the humanities to gracefully extricate themselves from excessively compartmentalized, isolationist structures.

Three accusations generally are directed against futurists. The first is that the entire enterprise is a fad, the latest form of swinging fun and games. That is a not-very-subtle assault on academic credibility. I can respond to this only on a very personal basis by saying there is no real way to defend yourself against snide and thoughtless criticism. But if you are a genuine futurist, the charge will not bother you or your students because you both will be engaged in one of the most difficult and comprehensive learning experiences of your entire lives, and you will never have read and thought so much in so many fields.

The second canard is favored by the professionally bored, in and out of the news media; it holds that futurists are elitists. This total misconception—almost, one might say, willful misconception—can be met frontally if the futurist builds into his model or design a participatory process for generating goals and values. Such correctives, however, will fail to satisfy the cynics, and they will assemble as their third line of attack a long list of previous predictions that have turned out to be false. Here, you can retaliate, for such a view completely misunderstands or distorts futurism.

Futurists are not prophets; they do not "predict" what will happen. They employ devices, ranging from extremely simple to highly sophisticated, to detect trends. However, their output is not a "final" projection but an array of possibilities—a multiple series of alternatives, not a fixed singularity. Besides, futurists are not so much interested in predicting as in creating desirable futures; the stress is not on what *will* be but what *can* or should be. Futurists leap ahead to the future not so that they may stay in an escapist never-never land, but so that they can lure that future into the present and negotiate with it while the options are to be chosen rather than imposed. If there is indeed the prospect of future shock, then dealing with it now may transform future shock into something less intimidating. Above all, futurists are keenly aware that if they do nothing about the future, it will come about for good or bad. Therefore, their commitment to do something about the future is a moral commitment.

And that brings us full circle to the humanist's concern with the whole man or woman. For that wholeness, as traditionally defined, has been, as I hope I have demonstrated, something considerably less than whole. The individual isolated from the surrounding social environment is not and cannot be whole. He, indeed, takes his individuality in part from it. But neither can the individual who is focused exclusively on past and present. Just as there is no wholeness without society, there is no wholeness without the future. Only through this recognition can the humanities themselves survive and serve the future.

Part II

Educational Contexts: Implications for Humanistic Change

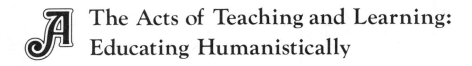

The Acts of Teaching and Learning: Educating Humanistically

Conventionally, teaching has been viewed as something a teacher does, whereas learning is something a student does. And the attitude that dichotomizes teaching and learning can be seen throughout the history of educational institutions. Philosophically and psychologically, of course, teaching and learning should be viewed as a continuous and interactive process, engaging both the student and the teacher alike as persons. On a sociological level, teaching has had at least two important functions that cannot be separated, experientially, from psychological and philosophical ideas about teaching and learning. They may be termed the *transmissive* and *transformative.*

The transmissive mode of teaching, which is the more traditionally established one, assumes, among other things, that the "teacher" has something to transmit or pass on to the "student." This mode of teaching is essentially constitutive of an active teacher-passive student relationship, in which the student has been viewed as a sponge soaking up the knowledge of the teacher. More critical observers of transmissive teaching have viewed such passivity in learning as the source of social conformity, obedience to authority, and the lack of creative thinking in students.

The transformative mode of teaching assumes that significant change can and does take place when both the teacher and the student act as persons rather than merely as role-players toward one another. Although the teacher's role may be authority-based in terms of the academic subject matter, that does not prevent an active, transformative experience from occurring for both teacher and student, an experience that contributes to

260

their mutual growth as persons, intellectually, emotionally, and ethically. In fact, in the transformative mode of teaching, which I think is the more humanistic one, knowledge of the academic subject matter is viewed as the active catalyst for significant change in both the teacher and the student as persons.

The selections for this section take into account both the transformative and the transmissive modes of teaching and learning, at least indirectly. They also reflect the recent tendency in the literature of humanistic education to emphasize learning rather than teaching as the most important condition for significant change in the schools and colleges. In addition, all of the writers of this section show a keen appreciation of the affective, or psychological and phenomenological,* nature of learning and teaching.

We have already encountered Carl R. Rogers in considering the psychological foundations of humanistic education. His essay, "The Interpersonal Relationship in the Facilitation of Learning," stresses one of the most crucially important themes in humanistic education. Indeed, if there is any one thing most characteristic of humanistic education as it has developed in the 1960s and 1970s in America, it is the significance attached to the interpersonal dimension of learning and teaching. And Carl R. Rogers has perhaps had the most influential voice on this theme in educational theory and practice. To be sure, there have been many other influences—psychological, philosophical, and social—that have set the scene for the goals and values of interpersonal learning. However, Rogers stands out, because he has worked closely with the problems of education for many years from his own professional viewpoint of psychotherapy. Furthermore, Rogers writes in a style that is personal, warmly objective and subjectively real. His style of writing reflects the values of his own philosophy of education: communication between persons; honesty toward self and others; realness in a role, whether it be the role of teacher, administrator, or whatever; and openness toward the world.

Rogers' view of learning shows the influence of the philosophy of pragmatism, which, among other things, posits that reality is characterized essentially by change. He states that if there is ". . . one truth about modern man, it is that he lives in an environment which is continually changing." And in seeking the humanization of education, *this* social and philosophical idea must be taken into account, if learning and teaching are to be based upon solid foundations.

Rogers shows a keen appreciation of the importance of the problem-solving attitude in learning. As he terms it, "a real contact with problems" along with an authentic contact with self are the twin prerequisites for real

* In this context, *phenomenological* means that which concerns the individual as a whole in terms of his personal consciousness and experience.

learning. He is also committed to the importance of caring on the part of the teacher and an atmosphere of trust in a classroom as other prerequisites for the humanization of education. Rogers' overall philosophy of teaching and learning is perhaps nowhere so well expressed as in his statement "that people count, that interpersonal relationships *are* important, that we know something about releasing human potential, that we could learn much more, and that unless we give strong positive attention to the human interpersonal side of our educational dilemma, our civilization is on its way down the drain."

"The Preparation of Humanistic Teachers," by C. H. Patterson, deals with a highly important dimension of humanistic education, namely teacher education. Like many before him, Patterson asserts that education in human relationships is the core of humanistic education. His essay cites—and offers possible solutions to—the problems of teacher education as they concern the interests of humanistic education.

Although it would probably be possible to perform an infinite regression in the task of finding humanistic persons, Patterson assumes that "somewhere there are humanistic persons to start with . . . ; " otherwise, we may all be doomed to an existence of only partial humanity. Patterson has many specific and explicit ideas about how teachers can be educated humanistically, beginning with teacher educators who are themselves humanistic and ending with an in-depth psychological training that is both experiential and theoretical. Like Rogers, Patterson assumes that the model for humanistic teaching is in counseling and psychotherapy. He believes that the basic encounter group and a "continuous, integrative seminar," meeting throughout the training period, should be required ingredients of a humanistic education for teachers.

Patterson's approach to humanistic education is basically compatible with that of the vast majority of humanists in education, who advocate ". . . an understanding of the observational process, [and] an attitude of critical inquiry towards self, others, and problems." Furthermore, his approach shows an appreciation of the need for balance between the didactic, or teacher-centered, classroom and the experiential, or student-centered, classroom for the realization of humanistic goals, values, and ends.

After some deliberation I have included an essay from John Dewey, the famous pragmatic philosopher, entitled "Thinking in Education." I have done so because I feel that the activity of thinking is too little emphasized and poorly understood by most practitioners of humanistic education; and, in my opinion, there can be no humanistic education, or education of any kind, without an understanding and appreciation of what thinking is and how it connects with significant learning and teaching, in the classroom and elsewhere.

Avoiding labels to justify the aim of thinking in education, Dewey goes right to the heart of the matter when he says "Thinking which is not connected with increase of efficiency in action, and with learning more about ourselves and the world in which we live, has something the matter with it. . . ." Thinking begins with experience; and it is fallacious to think that "we can begin with ready-made subject matter of arithmetic, or geography, or whatever, irrespective of some direct personal experience of a situation." A successful educational method for thinking refers students "back to the type of the situation which causes reflection out of school in ordinary life." In other words, the student should be aware of some explicit interconnections between the "problems" presented to him in school and his everyday life situations outside of school.

Thinking, to Dewey, is conditioned by data, or "actions, facts, events, and the relations of things"; by ideas, or "suggestions, inferences, conjectured meanings, suppositions, tentative explanations"; and by the testing and application of ideas to the situations of experience. Dewey's conception of mind as "the purposive and directive factor in the development of experience" puts him at odds with the traditional, non-humanistic theory of mind that separates thinking from feeling and the mind from the world.

Dewey's educational and supremely humanistic concept of intelligent action has probably not been rivalled in its richness and profundity. In this regard, Dewey may well be the most unsung hero and champion of humanistic education; like so many great thinkers, he will probably have to await future generations for complete discovery.

Finally, although I have not included an extract from his writing, I would urge the reader to consider the viewpoint of George Isaac Brown, a well-known practitioner of humanistic education. In *Human Teaching for Human Learning,* Brown focuses attention primarily upon affective or psychological techniques for learning intellectual subject matter. Brown's emphasis on the directive and manipulative side of teaching may raise some eyebrows among humanists in education, especially those who are influenced by non-directive and self-initiating theories of learning, such as those proposed by Carl Rogers, Sylvia Ashton-Warner, and others. Brown, however, shows a keen appreciation of and deep commitment toward the importance of involving the learner in the here-and-now through the learner's own actions, even though those actions may be suggested or triggered by the teacher. Because of the many techniques or ways to actualize the total self of the person, Brown assumes that we do know something about humanizing the educational process, enough to teach teachers how to humanize their classrooms.

Brown, like so many practitioners of humanistic education, shows the clear influence of Gestaltism upon his viewpoint. He draws on Gestalt therapy, for example, in stating that "hanging on to the past and anticipating the future are both illusionary conditions that can become substitutes for contact with what is real in both substance and process." Also, like many humanistic educators, Brown freely and imaginatively experiments with the grouping of persons for different educational goals and experiences.

DISCUSSION QUESTIONS

1. Carl R. Rogers is best known for his commitment to the interpersonal dimension of learning and teaching. What problems does the goal of interpersonal learning and teaching raise for education, in view of the way in which schools and colleges are presently structured? Do you feel that human relationships are important in the classroom or wherever learning takes place? Why? Do you think that there is any special significance in the fact that Rogers is both a psychotherapist by training and committed to the humanization of education? Are the values of dialogue in learning, honesty in feeling, openness in relating, and commitment in acting humanistic ones? Lastly, do you think that the ideal of freedom in education can be best achieved through self-initiated learning, as Rogers believes? If so, why?

2. C. H. Patterson deals with the problems and possibilities of teacher education as an integral part of humanistic education. Do you feel that his points about teacher education are well taken and his proposals for reform well conceived? Why, or why not? Drawing on your experience with teacher education, is there anything that you would recommend in the way of institutional or procedural reform? Do you agree that education in human relationships should be the core concern of humanistic education? Why, or why not? And finally, why does Patterson advocate an internal frame of reference rather than an external one in the teaching and learning process?

3. John Dewey's theory of thinking holds that thinking, to be significant, must begin with a personal sense of a problem or difficulty. Do you feel that his concept of thinking is an adequate one or that it leaves out something? Do you think that it is preferable to begin with ready-made subject matters, or with the personal and experiential approach that Dewey recommends? Do you think that learning through discovery is more important to the goal of thinking than the passive acquisition of facts and information? Why? Does Dewey's notion that the teacher is a learner and the learner is a teacher create any problems for you, either as a teacher or as a student? If so, what are they? Lastly, does the idea that mind is the

"purposive and directive factor in the development of experience"
contribute to the ideals of humanistic education? Explain.

FURTHER READING

Brown, George Isaac. *Human Teaching for Human Learning.* New York:
    The Viking Press, Inc., 1972.
Holt, John. *How Children Fail.* New York: A Delta Book, 1964.
James, William. *Talks to Teachers.* New York: The Norton Library, 1958.
Kohl, Herbert R. *The Open Classrooms.* New York: Vintage Books, 1970.
Lyon, Harold C., Jr. *Learning to Feel—Feeling to Learn.* Columbus, Ohio:
    Charles E. Merrill Publishing Company, 1971.
Nyquist, Ewald B., and Gene R. Hawes (editors). *Open Education.* New
    York: Bantam Books, 1972.
Phillips, Gerald M., David E. Butt, and Nancy Metzger. *Communication in
    Education.* New York: Holt, Rinehart and Winston, Inc., 1974.
Postman, Neil, and Charles Weingartner. *Teaching as a Subversive Activity.*
    New York: A Delta Book, 1969.
Raths, Louis E., Merrill Harmin, and Sidney B. Simon. *Values and Teaching.*
    Columbus, Ohio: Charles E. Merrill Publishing Company, 1966.
Richards, M. C. *Centering in Pottery, Poetry and the Person.* Middletown,
    Connecticut: Wesleyan University Press, 1972.

The Interpersonal Relationship
in the Facilitation of Learning

CARL R. ROGERS

I wish to begin this chapter with a statement which may seem surprising to some and perhaps offensive to others. It is simply this:
Teaching, in my estimation, is a vastly over-rated function.

Having made such a statement, I scurry to the dictionary to see if
I really mean what I say. Teaching means "to instruct." Personally I
am not much interested in instructing another in what he should
know or think. "To impart knowledge or skill." My reaction is, why
not be more efficient, using a book or programmed learning? "To
make to know." Here my hackles rise. I have no wish to *make* any-

one know something. "To show, guide, direct." As I see it, too many people have been shown, guided, directed. So I come to the conclusion that I *do* mean what I said. Teaching is, for me, a relatively unimportant and vastly overvalued activity.

But there is more in my attitude than this. I have a negative reaction to teaching. Why? I think it is because it raises all the wrong questions. As soon as we focus on teaching the question arises, what shall we teach? What, from our superior vantage point, does the other person need to know? I wonder if, in this modern world, we are justified in the presumption that we are wise about the future and the young are foolish. Are we *really* sure as to what they should know? Then there is the ridiculous question of coverage. What shall the course cover. This notion of coverage is based on the assumption that what is taught is what is learned; what is presented is what is assimilated. I know of no assumption so obviously untrue. One does not need research to provide evidence that this is false. One needs only to talk with a few students.

But I ask myself, "Am I so prejudiced against teaching that I find no situation in which it is worthwhile?" I immediately think of my experiences in Australia, not so long ago. I became much interested in the Australian aborigine. Here is a group which for more than 20,000 years has managed to live and exist in a desolate environment in which modern man would perish within a few days. The secret of the aborigine's survival has been teaching. He has passed on to the young every shred of knowledge about how to find water, about how to track game, about how to kill the kangaroo, about how to find his way through the trackless desert. Such knowledge is conveyed to the young as being *the* way to behave, and any innovation is frowned upon. It is clear that teaching has provided him the way to survive in a hostile and relatively unchanging environment.

Now I am closer to the nub of the question which excites me. Teaching and the imparting of knowledge make sense in an unchanging environment. This is why it has been an unquestioned function for centuries. But if there is one truth about modern man, it is that he lives in an environment which is *continually changing*. The one thing I can be sure of is that the physics which is taught to the present day student will be outdated in a decade. The teaching in psychology will certainly be out of date in 20 years. The so-called "facts of history" depend very largely upon the current mood and temper of the culture. Chemistry, biology, genetics, sociology, are in such flux that a firm statement made today will almost certainly be modified by the time the student gets around to using the knowledge.

We are, in my view, faced with an entirely new situation in education where the goal of education, if we are to survive, is the *facilitation of change and learning*. The only man who is educated is the man who has learned how to learn; the man who has learned how to adapt and change; the man who has realized that no knowledge is secure, that only the process of *seeking* knowledge gives a basis for security. Changingness, a reliance on *process* rather than upon static knowledge, is the only thing that makes any sense as a goal for education in the modern world.

So now with some relief I turn to an activity, a purpose, which really warms me—the facilitation of learning. When I have been able to transform a group—and here I mean all the members of a group, myself included—into a community of *learners*. then, the excitement has been almost beyond belief. To free curiosity; to permit individuals to go charging off in new directions dictated by their own interests; to unleash the sense of inquiry; to open everything to questioning and exploration; to recognize that everything is in process of change—here is an experience I can never forget. I cannot always achieve it in groups with which I am associated but when it is partially or largely achieved then it becomes a never-to-be-forgotten group experience. Out of such a context arise true students, real learners, creative scientists and scholars and practitioners, the kind of individuals who can live in a delicate but ever-changing balance between what is presently known and the flowing, moving, altering, problems and facts of the future.

Here then is a goal to which I can give myself wholeheartedly. I see *the facilitation of learning* as the *aim* of education, the way in which we might develop the learning man, the way in which we can learn to live as individuals in process. I see the facilitation of learning as the function which may hold constructive, tentative, changing, *process* answers to some of the deepest perplexities which beset man today.

But do we know how to achieve this new goal in education, or is it a will-o'-the-wisp which sometimes occurs, sometimes fails to occur, and thus offers little real hope? My answer is that we possess a very considerable knowledge of the conditions which encourage self-initiated, significant, experiential, "gut-level" learning by the whole person. We do not frequently see these conditions put into effect because they mean a real revolution in our approach to education and revolutions are not for the timid. But we do, as we have seen in the preceding chapters, find examples of this revolution in action.

We know—and I will briefly describe some of the evidence—that the initiation of such learning rests not upon the teaching skills of the leader, not upon his scholarly knowledge of the field, not upon his curricular planning, not upon his use of audiovisual aids, not upon the programmed learning he utilizes, not upon his lectures and presentations, not upon an abundance of books, though each of these might at one time or another be utilized as an important resource. No, the facilitation of significant learning rests upon certain attitudinal qualities which exist in the personal *relationship* between the facilitator and the learner.

We came upon such findings first in the field of psychotherapy, but increasingly there is evidence which shows that these findings apply in the classroom as well. We find it easier to think that the intensive relationship between therapist and client might possess these qualities, but we are also finding that they *may* exist in the countless interpersonal interactions (as many as 1,000 per day, as Jackson [1966] has shown) between the teacher and her pupils.

Qualities Which Facilitate Learning

What are these qualities, these attitudes, which facilitate learning? Let me describe them very briefly, drawing illustrations from the teaching field.

Realness in the Facilitator of Learning

Perhaps the most basic of these essential attitudes is realness or genuineness. When the facilitator is a real person, being what he is, entering into a relationship with the learner without presenting a front or a façade, he is much more likely to be effective. This means that the feelings which he is experiencing are available to him, available to his awareness, that he is able to live these feelings, be them, and able to communicate them if appropriate. It means that he comes into a direct personal encounter with the learner, meeting him on a person-to-person basis. It means that he is *being* himself, not denying himself.

Seen from this point of view it is suggested that the teacher can be a real person in his relationship with his students. He can be enthusiastic, he can be bored, he can be interested in students, he can be angry, he can be sensitive and sympathetic. Because he accepts these feelings as his own he has no need to impose them on his students. He can like or dislike a student product without implying that it is objectively good or bad or that the student is good or bad. He is simply expressing a feeling for the product, a feeling which exists within himself. Thus, he is a person to his students, not a faceless embodiment of a curricular requirement nor a sterile tube through which knowledge is passed from one generation to the next.

It is obvious that this attitudinal set, found to be effective in psychotherapy, is sharply in contrast with the tendency of most teachers to show themselves to their pupils simply as roles. It is quite customary for teachers rather consciously to put on the mask, the role, the façade, of being a teacher, and to wear this façade all day removing it only when they have left the school at night.

But not all teachers are like this. Take Sylvia Ashton-Warner, who took resistant, supposedly slow-learning primary school Maori children in New Zealand, and let them develop their own reading vocabulary. Each child could request one word—whatever word he wished—each day, and she would print it on a card and give it to him. "Kiss," "ghost," "bomb," "tiger," "fight," "love," "daddy"— these are samples. Soon they were building sentences, which they could also keep. "He'll get a licking." "Pussy's frightened." The children simply never forgot these self-initiated learnings. But it is not my purpose to tell you of her methods. I want instead to give you a glimpse of her attitude, of the passionate realness which must have been as evident to her tiny pupils as to her readers. An editor asked her some questions and she responded: "A few cool facts you asked me for . . . I don't know that there's a cool fact in me, or anything else cool for that matter, on this particular subject. I've got only hot long facts on the matter of Creative Teaching, scorching both the page and me" (Ashton-Warner, 1963, p. 26).

Here is no sterile façade. Here is a vital *person*, with convictions, with feelings. It is her transparent realness which was, I am sure, one of the elements that made her an exciting facilitator of learning. She doesn't fit into some neat educational formula. She *is*, and students grow by being in contact with someone who really and openly *is*.

Take another very different person, Barbara Shiel, whose exciting work in facilitating learning in sixth graders has been described earlier. She gave her pupils a great deal of responsible freedom, and I will mention some of the reactions of her students later. But here is an example of the way she shared herself with her pupils—not just sharing feelings of sweetness and light, but anger and frustration. She had made art materials freely available, and students often used these in creative ways, but the room frequently looked like a picture of chaos. Here is her report of her feelings and what she did with them.

I find it maddening to live with the mess—with a capital M! No one seems to care except me. Finally, one day I told the children . . . that I am a neat, orderly person by nature and that the mess was driving me to distraction. Did they have a solution? It was suggested there were some volunteers who could clean up . . . I said it didn't seem fair to me to have the same people clean up all the time for others—but it would solve it for me. "Well, some people like to clean," they replied. So that's the way it is (Shiel, 1966).

I hope this example puts some lively meaning into the phrases I used earlier, that the facilitator "is able to live these feelings, be them, and able to communicate them if appropriate." I have chosen an example of negative feelings, because I think it is more difficult for most of us to visualize what this would mean. In this instance, Miss Shiel is taking the risk of being transparent in her angry frustrations about the mess. And what happens? The same thing which, in my experience, nearly always happens. These young people accept and respect her feelings, take them into account, and work out a novel solution which none of us, I believe, would have suggested. Miss Shiel wisely comments, "I used to get upset and feel guilty when I became angry. I finally realized the children could accept *my* feelings too. And it is important for them to know when they've 'pushed me.' I have my limits, too" (Shiel, 1966).

Just to show that positive feelings, when they are real, are equally effective, let me quote briefly a college student's reaction, in a different course:

. . . Your sense of humor in the class was cheering; we all felt relaxed because you showed us your human self, not a mechanical teacher image. I feel as if I have more understanding and faith in my teachers now . . . I feel closer to the students too. . . .

Another says:

. . . You conducted the class on a personal level and therefore in my mind I was able to formulate a picture of you as a person and not as merely a walking textbook.

Another student in the same course:

. . . It wasn't as if there was a teacher in the class, but rather someone whom we could trust and identify as a "sharer." You were so perceptive and sensitive to our thoughts, and this made it all the more "authentic" for me. It was an "authentic" *experience*, not just a class (Bull, 1966).

I trust I am making it clear that to be real is not always easy, nor is it achieved all at once, but it is basic to the person who wants to become that revolutionary individual, a facilitator of learning.

Prizing, Acceptance, Trust

There is another attitude which stands out in those who are successful in facilitating learning. I have observed this attitude. I have experienced it. Yet, it is hard to know what term to put to it so I shall use several. I think of it as prizing the learner, prizing his feelings, his opinions, his person. It is a caring for the learner, but a non-possessive caring. It is an acceptance of this other individual as a separate person, having worth in his own right. It is a basic trust— a belief that this other person is somehow fundamentally trustworthy. Whether we call it prizing, acceptance, trust, or by some other term, it shows up in a variety of observable ways. The facilitator who has a considerable degree of this attitude can be fully acceptant of the fear and hesitation of the student as he approaches a new problem as well as acceptant of the pupil's satisfaction in achievement. Such a teacher can accept the student's occasional apathy, his erratic desires to explore by-roads of knowledge, as well as his disciplined efforts to achieve major goals. He can accept personal feelings which both disturb and promote learning—rivalry with a sibling, hatred of authority, concern about personal adequacy. What we are describing is a prizing of the learner as an imperfect human being with many feelings, many potentialities. The facilitator's prizing or acceptance of the learner is an operational expression of his essential confidence and trust in the capacity of the human organism.

I would like to give some examples of this attitude from the classroom situation. Here any teacher statements would be properly suspect, since many of us would like to feel we hold such attitudes, and might have a biased perception of our qualities. But let me indicate how this attitude of prizing, of accepting, of trusting, appears to the student who is fortunate enough to experience it.

Here is a statement from a college student in a class with Dr. Morey Appell:

Your way of being with us is a revelation to me. In your class I feel important, mature, and capable of doing things on my own. I want to think for myself and this need cannot be accomplished through textbooks and lectures alone, but through living. I think you see me as a person with real feelings and needs, an individual. What I say and do are significant expressions from me, and you recognize this (Appell, 1959).

One of Miss Shiel's sixth graders expresses much more briefly her misspelled appreciation of this attitude: "You are a wounderful teacher period!!!"

College students in a class with Dr. Patricia Bull describe not only these prizing, trusting attitudes, but the effect these have had on their other interactions.

. . . I feel that I can say things to you that I can't say to other professors. . . . Never before have I been so aware of the other students or their personalities. I have never had so much interaction in a college classroom with my classmates. The climate of the classroom has had a very profound effect on

me . . . the free atmosphere for discussion affected me . . . the general atmosphere of a particular session affected me. There have been many times
when I have carried the discussion out of the class with me and thought
about it for a long time.

*   *   *

. . . I still feel close to you, as though there were some tacit understanding
between us, almost a conspiracy. This adds to the in-class participation on
my part because I feel that at least one person in the group will react, even
when I am not sure of the others. It does not matter really whether your reaction is positive or negative, it just *IS*. Thank you.

*   *   *

. . . I appreciate the respect and concern you have for others, including
myself. . . . As a result of my experience in class, plus the influence of my
readings, I sincerely believe that the student-centered teaching method does
provide an ideal framework for learning; not just for the accumulation of
facts, but more important, for learning about ourselves in relation to others.
. . . When I think back to my shallow awareness in September compared to
the depth of my insights now, I know that this course has offered me a learning experience of great value which I couldn't have acquired in any other
way.

*   *   *

. . . Very few teachers would attempt this method because they would feel
that they would lose the students' respect. On the contrary. You gained our
respect, through your ability to speak to us on our level, instead of ten miles
above us. With the complete lack of communication we see in this school, it
was a wonderful experience to see people listening to each other and really
communicating on an adult, intelligent level. More classes should afford us
this experience (Bull, 1966).

As you might expect, college students are often suspicious that
these seeming attitudes are phony. One of Dr. Bull's students writes:

. . . Rather than observe my classmates for the first few weeks, I concentrated my observations on you, Dr. Bull. I tried to figure out your motivations
and purposes. I was convinced that you were a hypocrite. . . . I did change
my opinion, however. You are not a hypocrite, by any means. . . . I do wish
the course could continue. "Let each become all he is capable of being."
. . . (Bull, 1966).

I am sure these examples are more than enough to show that the
facilitator who cares, who prizes, who trusts the learner, creates a
climate for learning so different from the ordinary classroom that any
resemblance is "purely coincidental."

Empathic Understanding

A further element which establishes a climate for self-initiated,
experimental learning is empathic understanding. When the teacher

has the ability to understand the student's reactions from the inside, has a sensitive awareness of the way the process of education and learning seems *to the student,* then again the likelihood of significant learning is increased.

This kind of understanding is sharply different from the usual evaluative understanding, which follows the pattern of, "I understand what is wrong with you." When there is a sensitive empathy, however, the reaction in the learner follows something of this pattern, "At last someone understands how it feels and seems to be *me* without wanting to analyze me or judge me. Now I can blossom and grow and learn."

This attitude of standing in the other's shoes, of viewing the world through the student's eyes, is almost unheard of in the classroom. One could listen to thousands of ordinary classroom interactions without coming across one instance of clearly communicated, sensitively accurate, empathic understanding. But it has a tremendously releasing effect when it occurs.

Let me take an illustration from Virginia Axline, dealing with a second grade boy. Jay, age 7, has been aggressive, a trouble maker, slow of speech and learning. Because of his "cussing" he was taken to the principal, who paddled him, unknown to Miss Axline. During a free work period, he fashioned a man of clay, very carefully, down to a hat and a handkerchief in his pocket. "Who is that?" asked Miss Axline. "Dunno," replied Jay. "Maybe it is the principal. He has a handkerchief in his pocket like that." Jay glared at the clay figure. "Yes," he said. Then he began to tear the head off and looked up and smiled. Miss Axline said, "You sometimes feel like twisting his head off, don't you? You get so mad at him." Jay tore off one arm, another, then beat the figure to a pulp with his fists. Another boy, with the perception of the young, explained, "Jay is mad at Mr. X because he licked him this noon." "Then you must feel lots better now," Miss Axline commented. Jay grinned and began to rebuild Mr. X. (Adapted from Axline, 1944.)

The other examples I have cited also indicate how deeply appreciative students feel when they are simply *understood*—not evaluated, not judged, simply understood from their *own* point of view, not the teacher's. If any teacher set himself the task of endeavoring to make one non-evaluative, acceptant, empathic response per day to a student's demonstrated or verbalized feeling, I believe he would discover the potency of this currently almost non-existent kind of understanding.

What Are the Bases of Facilitative Attitudes?

A "Puzzlement"

It is natural that we do not always have the attitudes I have been describing. Some teachers raise the question, "But what if I am *not* feeling emphatic, do *not*, at this moment, prize or accept or like my students. What then?" My response is that realness is the most important of the attitudes mentioned, and it is not accidental that this attitude was described first. So if one has little understanding of the student's inner world, and a dislike for his students or their behavior, it is almost certainly more constructive to be *real* than to be pseudo-empathic, or to put on a façade of caring.

But this is not nearly as simple as it sounds. To be genuine, or honest, or congruent, or real, means to be this way about *oneself*. I cannot be real about another, because I do not *know* what is real for him. I can only tell—if I wish to be truly honest—what is going on in me.

Let me take an example. Early in this chapter I reported Miss Shiel's feelings about the "mess" created by the art work. Essentially she said, "I find it maddening to live with the mess! I'm neat and orderly and it is driving me to distraction." But suppose her feelings had come out somewhat differently, in the disguised way which is much more common in classrooms at all levels. She might have said, "You are the messiest children I've ever seen! You don't care about tidiness or cleanliness. You are just terrible!" This is most definitely *not* an example of genuineness or realness, in the sense in which I am using these terms. There is a profound distinction between the two statements which I should like to spell out.

In the second statement she is telling nothing of herself, sharing none of her feelings. Doubtless the children will *sense* that she is angry, but because children are perceptively shrewd they may be uncertain as to whether she is angry at them, or has just come from an argument with the principal. It has none of the honesty of the first statement in which she tells of her *own* upsetness, of her *own* feeling of being driven to distraction.

Another aspect of the second statement is that it is all made up of judgments or evaluations, and like most judgments, they are all arguable. Are these children messy, or are they simply excited and involved in what they are doing? Are they *all* messy, or are some as disturbed by the chaos as she? Do they care nothing about tidiness, or is it simply that they don't care about it every day? If a group of visitors were coming would their attitude be different? Are they terrible, or simply children? I trust it is evident that when we make judgments they are almost never fully accurate, and hence cause resentment and anger as well as guilt and apprehension. Had she used the second statement the response of the class would have been entirely different.

I am going to some lengths to clarify this point because I have found from experience that to stress the value of being real, of *being* one's feelings, is taken by some as a license to pass judgments on others, to project on others all the feelings which one should be "owning." Nothing could be further from my meaning.

Actually the achievement of realness is most difficult, and even when one wishes to be truly genuine, it occurs but rarely. Certainly it is not simply a matter of the *words* used, and if one is feeling judgmental the use of a verbal formula which sounds like the sharing of feelings will not help. It is just another instance of a façade, of a lack of genuineness. Only slowly can we learn to be truly real. For first of all, one must be close to one's feelings, capable of being aware of them. Then one must be willing to take the risk of sharing them as they are, inside, not disguising them as judgments, or attributing them to other people. This is why I so admire Miss Shiel's sharing of her anger and frustration, without in any way disguising it.

A Trust in the Human Organism

It would be most unlikely that one could hold the three attitudes I have described, or could commit himself to being a facilitator of learning, unless he has come to have a profound trust in the human organism and its potentialities. If I distrust the human being then I *must* cram him with information of my own choosing, lest he go his own mistaken way. But if I trust the capacity of the human individual for developing his own potentiality, then I can provide him with many opportunities and permit him to choose his own way and his own direction in his learning.

It is clear, I believe, that the three teachers whose work was described in the preceding chapters rely basically upon the tendency toward fulfilment, toward actualization, in their students. They are basing their work on the hypothesis that students who are in real contact with problems which are relevant to them wish to learn, want to grow, seek to discover, endeavor to master, desire to create, move toward self-discipline. The teacher is attempting to develop a quality of climate in the classroom, and a quality of personal relationship with his students, which will permit these natural tendencies to come to their fruition.

Living the Uncertainty of Discovery

I believe it should be said that this basically confident view of man, and the attitudes toward students which I have described, do not appear suddenly, in some miraculous manner, in the facilitator of learning. Instead, they come about through taking risks, through *acting* on tentative hypotheses. This is most obvious in the chapter describing Miss Shiel's work, where, acting on hypotheses of which she is unsure, risking herself uncertainly in new ways of relating to her students, she finds these new views confirmed by what happens in her class. I am sure Professor Faw went through the same type of uncertainty. As for me, I can only state that I started my career with the firm view that individuals must be manipulated for their own good; I only came to the attitudes I have described, and the trust in the individual which is implicit in them, because I found that these attitudes were so much more potent in producing learning and constructive change. Hence, I believe that it is only by risking himself in these new ways that the teacher can *discover*, for himself, whether or not they are effective, whether or not they are for him.

I will then draw a conclusion, based on the experiences of the several facilitators and their students which have been included up to this point. When a facilitator creates, even to a modest degree, a classroom climate characterized by all that he can achieve of realness, prizing, and empathy; when he trusts the constructive tendency of the individual and the group; then he discovers that he has inaugurated an educational revolution. Learning of a different quality, proceeding at a different pace, with a greater degree of pervasiveness, occurs. Feelings—positive, negative, confused—become a part of the classroom experience. Learning becomes life, and a very vital life at that. The student is on his way, sometimes excitedly, sometimes reluctantly, to becoming a learning, changing, being.

The Evidence

Already I can hear mutterings: "A very pretty picture—very touching. But where is the solid evidence? How do you know?" I would like to turn to this evidence. It is not overwhelming, but it is consistent. It is not perfect, but it is suggestive.

First of all, in the field of psychotherapy, Barrett-Lennard (1962) developed an instrument whereby he could measure these attitudinal qualities: genuineness or congruence, prizing or positive regard, empathy or understanding. This insturment was given to both client and therapist, so that we have the perception of the relationship both by the therapist and by the client whom he is trying to help. To state some of the findings very briefly it may be said that those clients who eventually showed more therapeutic change as measured by various instruments, perceived *more* of these qualities in their relationship with the therapist than did those who eventually showed less change. It is also significant that this difference in perceived relationships was evident as early as the fifth interview, and predicted later change or lack of change in therapy. Furthermore, it was found that the *client's* perception of the relationship, his experience of it, was a better predictor of ultimate outcome than was the perception of the relationship by the therapist. Barrett-Lennard's original study has been amplified and generally confirmed by other studies.

So we may say, cautiously, and with qualifications which would be too cumbersome for the present volume, that if, in therapy, the client perceives his therapist as real and genuine, as one who likes, prizes, and emphatically understands him, self-learning and therapeutic change are facilitated.

Now another thread of evidence, this time related more closely to education. Emmerling (1961) found that when high school teachers were asked to identify the problems they regarded as most urgent, they could be divided into two groups. Those who regarded their most serious problems, for example, as "Helping children think for themselves and be independent"; "Getting students to participate"; "Learning new ways of helping students develop their maximum potential"; "Helping students express individual needs and interests" fell into what he called the "open" or "positively oriented" group. When Barrett-Lennard's Relationship Inventory was administered to the students of these teachers, it was found that they were perceived as significantly more real, more acceptant, more empathic than the other group of teachers whom I shall now describe.

The second category of teachers were those who tended to see their most urgent problems in negative terms, and in terms of student deficiencies and inabilities. For them the urgent problems were such as these: "Trying to teach children who don't even have the ability to follow directions"; "Teaching children who lack a desire to learn"; "Students who are not able to do the work required for their grade"; "Getting children to listen." It probably will be no surprise that when the students of these teachers filled out the Relationship Inventory they saw their teachers as exhibiting relatively little genuineness, acceptance, trust, or empathic understanding.

Hence we may say that the teacher whose orientation is toward releasing the student's potential exhibits a high degree of these attitudinal qualities which facilitate learning. The teacher whose orientation is toward shortcomings of his students exhibits much less of these qualities.

A small pilot study by Bills (1961, 1966) extends the significance of these findings. A group of eight teachers were selected, four of them rated as adequate and effective by their superiors, and also showing this more positive orientation to their problems. The other four were rated as inadequate teachers and also had a more negative orientation to their problems, as described above. The students of these teachers were then asked to fill out the Barrett-Lennard Relationship Inventory, giving their perception of their teacher's relationship to them. This made the students very happy. Those who saw their relationship with the teacher as good were happy to describe this relationship. Those who had an unfavorable relationship were pleased to have, for the first time, an opportunity to specify the ways in which the relationship was unsatisfactory.

The more effective teachers were rated higher in every attitude measured by the Inventory: they were seen as more real, as having a higher level of regard for their students, were less conditional or judgmental in their attitudes, showed more emphatic understanding. Without going into details of the study it may be illuminating to mention that the total scores summing up these attitudes vary sharply. For example, the relationships of a group of clients with their therapists, as perceived by the clients, received an average score of 108. The relationship with the four most adequate high school teachers as seen by their students, received a score of 60. The relationship of the four less adequate teachers received a score of 34. The lowest rated teacher received an average score of 2 from her students on the Relationship Inventory.

This small study certainly suggests that the teacher regarded as effective displays in her attitudes those qualities I have described as facilitative of learning, while the inadequate teacher shows little of these qualities.

A more comprehensive study, by Macdonald and Zaret, studied the recorded interactions of nine teachers with their students. They found that both teacher and student behaviors could be reliably categorized. When teacher behaviors tended to be "open—clarifying, stimulating, accepting, facilitating—the student responses tended to be "productive"—discovering, exploring, experimenting, synthesizing, deriving implications. When teacher behaviors tended to be "closed"—judging, directing, reproving, ignoring, probing, or priming—the student responses tended to be "reproductive"—parroting, guessing, acquiescing, reproducing facts, reasoning from given or remembered data. The pairing of these two sets of teacher-student behaviors were significantly related (Macdonald & Zaret, 1966). Though they are careful to qualify their findings, it would appear that teachers who are interested in process, and facilitative in their interactions, produce self-initiated and creative responses in their students. Teachers who are interested in evaluation of students produce passive, memorized, "eager to please" responses from their students. This evidence fits in with the thesis I have been presenting.

Approaching the problem from a different angle, Schmuck (1963) has shown that in classrooms where pupils perceive their teachers as understanding them, there is likely to be a more diffuse liking structure among the pupils. This means that where the teacher is empathic, there are not a few students strongly liked and a few strongly disliked, but liking and affection are more evenly diffused throughout the group. In a later study he has shown that among students who are highly involved in their classroom peer group, "significant relationships exist between actual liking status on the one hand and utilization of abilities, attitude toward self, and attitude toward school on the other hand" (1966, pp. 357–358). This seems to lend confirmation to the other evidence by indicating that in an understanding classroom climate where the teacher is more emphatic, every student tends to feel liked by all the others, to have a more positive attitude toward himself and toward school. If he is highly involved with his peer group (and this appears probable in such a classroom climate), he also tends to utilize his abilities more fully in his school achievement.

But you may still ask, does the student actually *learn* more where these attitudes are present? Here an interesting study of third graders by Aspy (1965) helps to round out the suggestive evidence. He worked in six third-grade classes. The teachers tape-recorded two full weeks of their interaction with their students in the periods devoted to the teaching of reading. These recordings were done two months apart so as to obtain an adequate sampling of the teacher's interactions with her pupils. Four-minute segments of these recordings were randomly selected for rating. Three raters, working independently and "blind," rated each segment for the degree of congruence or genuineness shown by the teacher, the degree of her prizing or unconditional positive regard, and the degree of her empathic understanding.

The Reading Achievement Tests (Stanford Achievement) were used as the criterion. Again, omitting some of the details of a carefully and rigorously controlled study, it may be said that the children in the three classes with the highest degree of the attitudes described above showed a significantly greater gain in reading achievement than those students in the three classes with a lesser degree of these qualities.

So we may say, with a certain degree of assurance, that the attitudes I have endeavored to describe are not only effective in facilitating a deeper learning and understanding of self in a relationship such as psychotherapy, but that these attitudes characterize teachers who are regarded as effective teachers, and that the students of these teachers learn more, even of a conventional curriculum, than do students of teachers who are lacking in these attitudes.

The Evidence from Students

I am pleased that such evidence is accumulating. It may help to justify the revolution in education for which I am obviously hoping. But the most striking learnings of students exposed to such a climate are by no means restricted to greater achievement in the three R's. The significant learnings are the more personal ones—independence; self-initiated and responsible learning; release of creativity; a thendency to become more of a person. I can only illustrate this by picking, almost at random, statements from students whose teachers have endeavored to create a climate of trust, of prizing, of realness, of understanding, and above all, of freedom.

Again I must quote from Sylvia Ashton-Warner one of the central effects of such a climate. ". . . The drive is no longer the teacher's, but the childrens' own . . . the teacher is at last with the stream and not against it, the stream of childrens' inexorable creativeness" (Ashton-Warner, p. 93).

If you need verification of this, here is one of a number of statements made by students in a course on poetry lead (not taught) by Dr. Samuel Moon.

In retrospect, I find that I have actually enjoyed this course, both as a class and as an experiment, although it had me quite unsettled at times. This, in itself, made the course worthwhile since the majority of my courses this semester merely had me bored with them and the whole process of "higher education." Quite aside from anything else, due mostly to this course, I found myself devoting more time to writing poetry than to writing short stories, which temporarily interfered with my writing class.
. . . I should like to point out one thing very definite which I have gained from the course; this is an increased readiness on my part to listen to and to seriously consider the opinions of my fellow students. In view of my past attitude, this alone makes the course valuable. I suppose the real result of any course can be expressed in answer to the question, "Would you take it over again?" My answer would be an unqualified "Yes" (Moon, 1966, p. 227).

I should like to add to this several comments from Dr. Bull's sophomore students in a class in adolescent psychology. The first two are mid-semester comments.

This course is proving to be a vital and profound experience for me. . . . This unique learning situation is giving me a whole new conception of just what learning is. . . . I am experiencing a real growth in this atmosphere of constructive freedom . . . the whole experience is challenging.

* * *

I feel that the course had been of great value to me. . . . I'm glad to have had this experience because it has made me think. . . . I've never been so personally involved with a course before, especially *outside* the classroom. It has been frustrating, rewarding, enjoyable, and tiring!

The other comments are from the end of the course:

. . . This course is not ending with the close of the semester for me, but continuing. . . . I don't know of any greater benefit which can be gained from a course than this desire for further knowledge.

* * *

. . . I feel as though this type of class situation has stimulated me more in making me realize where my responsibilities lie, especially as far as doing required work on my own. I no longer feel as though a test date is the criterion for reading a book. I feel as though my future work will be done for what *I* will get out of it, not just for a test mark.

* * *

I have enjoyed the experience of being in this course. I guess that any dissatisfaction I feel at this point is a disappointment in myself, for not having taken full advantage of the opportunities the course offered.

* * *

I think that now I am acutely aware of the breakdown in communications that does exist in our society from seeing what happened in our class. . . . I've grown immensely. I know that I am a different person than I was when I came into that class. . . . It has done a great deal in helping me understand myself better . . . thank you for contributing to my growth.

* * *

My idea of education has been to gain information from the teacher by attending lectures. The emphasis and focus were on the teacher. . . . One of the biggest changes that I experienced in this class was my outlook on education. Learning is something more than a grade on a report card. No one can measure what you have learned because it's a personal thing. I was very confused between learning and memorization. I could memorize very well, but I doubt if I ever learned as much as I could have. I believe my attitude toward learning has changed from a grade-centered outlook to a more personal one.

* * *

I have learned a lot more about myself and adolescents in general. . . . I also gained more confidence in myself and my study habits by realizing that I could learn by myself without a teacher leading me by the hand. I have also learned a lot by listening to my classmates and evaluating their opinions and thoughts . . . this course has proved to be a most meaningful and worthwhile experience . . . (Bull, 1966).

If you wish to know what this type of course seems like to a sixth grader, let me give you a sampling of the reactions of Miss Shiel's youngsters, misspellings and all.

I feel that I am learning self abilty [*sic*]. I am learning not only school work but I am learning that you can learn on your own as well as someone can teach you.

*   *   *

I have a little trouble in Socail [*sic*] Studies finding things to do. I have a hard time working the exact amount of time. Sometimes I talk to [*sic*] much.

*   *   *

. . . My parents don't understand the program. My mother say's [*sic*] it will give me a responsibility and it will let me go at my own speed.

*   *   *

I like this plan because there is a lot of freedom. I also learn more this way than the other way you don't have to wate [*sic*] for others you can go at your own speed rate it also takes a lot of responsibility (Shiel, 1966).

Or let me take two more, from Dr. Appell's graduate class:

. . . I have been thinking about what happened through this experience. The only conclusion I come to is that if I try to measure what is going on, or what I was at the beginning, I have got to know what I was when I started— and I don't . . . so many things I did and feel are just lost . . . scrambled up inside. . . . They don't seem to come out in a nice little pattern or organization I can say or write. . . . There are so many things left unsaid. I know I have only scratched the surface, I guess. I can feel so many things almost ready to come out . . . maybe that's enough. *It seems all kinds of things have so much more meaning now than ever before.* . . . This experience has had meaning, has done things to me and I am not sure how much or how far just yet. I think I am going to be a better me in the fall. *That's one thing I think I am sure of* (Appell, 1963).

*   *   *

. . . You follow no plan, yet I'm learning. Since the term began I seem to feel more alive, more real to myself. I enjoy being alone as well as with other people. My relationships with children and other adults are becoming more emotional and involved. Eating an orange last week, I peeled the skin off each separate orange section and liked it better with the transparent shell off. It was juicier and fresher tasting that way. I began to think, that's how I feel sometimes, without a transparent wall around me, really communicating my feelings. I feel that I'm growing, how much, I don't know. I'm thinking, considering, pondering and learning (Appell, 1959).

I can't read these student statements—sixth grade, college, graduate level—without being deeply moved. Here are teachers, risking themselves, *being* themselves, *trusting* their students, adventuring into the existential unknown, taking the subjective leap. And what happens? Exciting, incredible *human* events. You can sense persons being created, learnings being initiated, future citizens rising to meet the challenge of unknown worlds. If only one teacher out of one hundred dared to risk, dared to be, dared to trust, dared to understand, we would have an infusion of a living spirit into education which would, in my estimation, be priceless.

The Effect upon the Instructor

Let me turn to another dimension which excites me. I have spoken of the effect upon the *student* of a climate which encourages significant, self-reliant, personal learning. But I have said nothing about the reciprocal effect upon the instructor. When he has been the agent for the release of such self-initiated learning, the faculty member finds *himself* changed as well as his students. One such says:

To say that I am overwhelmed by what happened only faintly reflects my feelings. I have taught for many years but I have never experienced anything remotely resembling what occurred. I, for my part, never found in a classroom so much of the whole person coming forth, so deeply involved, so deeply stirred. Further, I question if in the traditional setup, with its emphasis on subject matter, examinations, grades, there is, or there can be a place for the "becoming" person with his deep and manifold needs as he struggles to fulfill himself. But this is going far afield. I can only report to you what happened and to say that I am grateful and that I am also humbled by the experience. I would like you to know this for it has enriched my life and being (Tenenbaum in Rogers, 1961, p. 313).

Another faculty member reports as follows:

Rogers has said that relationships conducted on these assumptions mean "turning present day education upside down." I have found this to be true as I have tried to implement this way of living with students. The experiences I have had have plunged me into relationships which have been significant and challenging and beyond compare for me. They have inspired me and stimulated me and left me at times shaken and awed with their consequences for both me and the students. They have led me to the fact of what I can only call . . . the tragedy of education in our time—student after student who reports this to be his first experience with total trust, with freedom to be and to move in ways most consistent for the enhancement and maintenance of the core of dignity which somehow has survived humiliation, distortion, and corrosive cynicism (Appell, 1959).

Too Idealistic?

Some readers may feel that the whole approach of this chapter—the belief that teachers can relate as persons to their student—is hopelessly unrealistic and idealistic. They may see that in essence it is encouraging both teachers and students to be creative in their relationship to each other and in their relationship to subject matter, and feel that such a goal is quite impossible. They are not alone in this. I have heard scientists at leading schools of science and scholars in leading universities, arguing that it is absurd to try to encourage all students to be creative—we need hosts of mediocre technicians and workers and if a few creative scientists and artists and leaders emerge, that will be enough. That may be enough for them. It may be enough to suit you. I want to go on record as saying it is *not* enough to suit me. When I realize the incredible potential in the ordinary student, I want to try to release it. We are working hard to release the incredible energy in the atom and the nucleus of the atom. If we do not devote equal energy—yes, and equal money—to the release of the potential of the individual person then the enormous discrepancy between our level of physical energy resources and human energy resources will doom us to a deserved and universal destruction.

I'm sorry I can't be coolly scientific about this. The issue is too urgent. I can only be passionate in my statement that people count, that interpersonal relationships *are* important, that we know something about releasing human potential, that we could learn much more, and that unless we give strong positive attention to the human interpersonal side of our educational dilemma, our civilization is on its way down the drain. Better courses, better curricula, better coverage, better teaching machines, will never resolve our dilemma in a basic way. Only persons, acting like persons in their relationships with their students can even begin to make a dent on this most urgent problem of modern education.

Summary

Let me try to state, somewhat more calmly and soberly, what I have said with such feeling and passion.

I have said that it is most unfortunate that educators and the public think about, and focus on, *teaching.* It leads them into a host of questions which are either irrelevant or absurd so far as real education is concerned.

I have said that if we focused on the facilitation of *learning*—how, why, and when the student learns, and how learning seems and feels from the inside—we might be on a much more profitable track.

I have said that we have some knowledge, and could gain more, about the conditions which facilitate learning, and that one of the most important of these conditions is the attitudinal quality of the interpersonal relationship between facilitator and learner. (There are other conditions, too, which I will endeavor to spell out later.)

Those attitudes which appear effective in promoting learning can be described. First of all is a transparent realness in the facilitator, a willingness to be a person, to be and live the feelings and thoughts of the moment. When this realness includes a prizing, a caring, a trust and respect for the learner, the climate for learning is enhanced. When it includes a sensitive and accurate empathic listening, then indeed a freeing climate, stimulative of self-initiated learning and growth, exists. The student is *trusted* to develop.

I have tried to make plain that individuals who hold such attitudes, and are bold enough to act on them, do not simply modify classroom methods—they revolutionize them. They perform almost none of the functions of teachers. It is no longer accurate to call them teachers. They are catalyzers, facilitators, giving freedom and life and the opportunity to learn, to students.

I have brought in the cumulating research evidence which suggests that individuals who hold such attitudes are regarded as effective in the classroom; that the problems which concern them have to do with the release of potential, not the deficiencies of their students; that they seem to create classroom situations in which there are not admired children and disliked children, but in which affection and liking are a part of the life of every child; that in classrooms approaching such a psychological climate, children learn more of the conventional subjects.

But I have intentionally gone beyond the empirical findings to try to take you into the inner life of the student—elementary, college, and graduate—who is fortunate enough to live and learn in such an interpersonal relationship with a facilitator, in order to let you see what learning feels like when it is free, self-initiated and spontaneous. I have tried to indicate how it even changes the student-student relationship—making it more aware, more caring, more sensitive, as well as increasing the self-rated learning of significant material. I have spoken of the change it brings about in the faculty member.

Throughout, I have tried to indicate that if we are to have citizens who can live constructively in this kaleidoscopically changing world, we can *only* have them if we are willing for them to become self-starting, self-initiating learners. Finally, it has been my purpose to show that this kind of learner develops best, so far as we now know, in a growth-promoting, facilitative, relationship with a *person*.

REFERENCES

Appell, M. L. Selected Student Reactions to Student-centered Courses. Unpublished manuscript, Terre Haute, Indiana: State University of Ind., 1959.

Appell, M. L. Self-understanding for the Guidance Counselor. *Personnel & Guidance Journal*, October, 1963, 143–148.

Ashton-Warner, Sylvia. *Teacher.* New York: Simon and Schuster, 1963.

Aspy, D. N. A Study of Three Facilitative Conditions and Their Relationship to the Achievement of Third Grade Students. Unpublished doctoral dissertation, University of Kentucky, 1965.

Axline, Virginia M. Morale on the School Front. *Journal of Educational Research,* 1944, 521–533.

Barrett-Lennard, G. T. Dimensions of Therapist Response as Causal Factors in Therapeutic Change. *Psychological Monographs,* 1962, 76 (Whole No. 562).

Bills, R. E. Personal correspondence. 1961, 1966.

Bull, Patricia. Student Reactions, Fall, 1965. Unpublished manuscript, State University College, Cortland, New York, 1966.

Emmerling, F. C. A Study of the Relationships Between Personality Characteristics of Classroom Teachers and Pupil Perceptions. Unpublished doctoral dissertation, Auburn University, Auburn, Alabama, 1961.

Jackson, P. W. The Student's World. Unpublished manuscript, University of Chicago, 1966.

Macdonald, J. B., and Zaret, Esther. A Study of Openness in Classroom Interactions. Unpublished manuscript, Marquette University, 1966.

Moon, S. F. Teaching the Self. *Improving College and University Teaching,* 14, Autumn, 1966, 213–229.

Rogers, C. R. *On Becoming a Person.* Boston: Houghton Mifflin, 1961.

Schmuck, R. Some Relationships of Peer Liking Patterns in the Classroom to Pupil Attitudes and Achievement. *The School Review,* 1963, 71, 337–359.

Schmuck, R. Some Aspects of Classroom Social Climate. *Psychology in the Schools.* 1966, 3, 59–65.

Shiel, Barbara J. Evaluation: A Self-directed Curriculum, 1965. Unpublished manuscript, 1966.

The Preparation of Humanistic Teachers

C. H. PATTERSON

> I see the facilitation of learning as the aim of education. . . . We know . . . that the facilitation of such learning rests not upon the teaching skills of the leader, not upon his curricular planning, not upon his use of audio-visual aids, not upon the programmed learning he utilizes, not upon his lectures and presentations, not upon his lectures and presentations, not upon an abundance of books, though each of these might at one time or another be utilized as an important resource. No, the facilitation of signifi-

C. H. Patterson, *Humanistic Education,* © 1973, pp. 210–225. Reprinted by permission of Prentice-Hall, Inc., Englewood Cliffs, New Jersey.

cant learning rests upon certain attitudinal qualities which exist in the personal relationship between the facilitator and the learner.*
—Carl R. Rogers, *Freedom to Learn*

In Chapter 1 it was stated that preparation for teaching in the school of the future, the humanistic school, would consist of education in human relationships. It should be clear now why this is so. In Chapter 7 it was emphasized that it is not teaching methods which make a good teacher, but the person of the teacher. It is thus paradoxical, and difficult to understand, that the emphasis in teacher education has been on methods, as well as on subject matter.

Teacher education, along with education, has been the object of criticism. Coladarci states that "the contents and procedures of teacher education frequently have no demonstrable relevance to the actual teaching task." [1] Teachers have been highly critical of an dissatisfied with the preparation they have received. Silberman concludes: "That the preparation should be substantially different from what they now receive seems hardly open to debate; there is probably no aspect of contemporary education on which there is greater unanimity of opinion than that teacher education needs a vast overhaul. Virtually everyone is dissatisfied with the current state of teacher education: the students being educated, the teachers in the field, the principals, superintendents, and school board members who hire them, the liberal arts faculties, and the lay critics of education." [2]

Those who have been concerned about student achievement in subject matter areas have focused upon the inadequate preparation of teachers in subject matter content, as well as in the liberal arts in general. Changes have been made toward this end in many teacher education programs. Other than this, there has been very little change in the preparation of teachers for the last fifty years. Although knowledge of subject matter is clearly necessary, it is not sufficient to make a good teacher. More emphasis on methods courses does not seem to be the answer, since there are probably too many now, with much overlapping, and repetition. Yet these two alternatives appear to be the only solutions to the problem of teacher education which have been seriously considered. Neither Silberman nor the other

---

* (Columbus, Ohio: Merrill, 1967), pp. 105–106.

[1] Arthur P. Coladarci, in Foreword to Seymour B. Sarason, Kenneth S. Davidson & Burton Blatt, *The Preparation of Teachers: an Unstudied Problem in Education* (New York: Wiley, 1962).

[2] Charles E. Silberman, *Crisis in the Classroom* (New York: Random House, 1970), p. 413.

critics of education propose any approach to the preparation of humanistic teachers.

It might appear that the answer would be more courses in psychology, an area in which teachers certainly have too little background. A course in general psychology and one in educational psychology and/or child development is all that most teachers have, and experience with teachers who have just completed their undergraduate education leads one to conclude that they might as well have had none, as far as what they remember or have learned. It seems apparent that something is wrong with the courses.

If one looks at what is taught in these undergraduate courses, one quickly realizes what is wrong. The standard courses have nothing to do with people, with real students in real classrooms. They focus upon research done in laboratories (often with rats) or in special experimental situations. The courses consist of review of research study after research study which are irrelevant to teaching since no generalizations can be made to the real classroom situation. There is little attempt to teach principles, or a theory which can be applied in real life situations. To do this would be to depart from a rigorous approach to psychology as a science.

The Teacher As a Psychologist

The teacher works with human beings. Since teaching is a psychological relationship, a helping relationship, it should be apparent that teaching is applied psychology, and that the basic science of education, and the basic preparation of teachers, is, or should be, psychology. There has been some recognition of this: the psychology of learning has received increasing attention in education. But not without difficulties, however. First, the psychology of learning currently available is, as suggested above, essentially irrelevant to classroom teaching. Bruner and Skinner have attempted to remedy this situation, by working on a psychology (or technology) of teaching or instruction.

But this is not sufficient, because of the second difficulty. The psychology which has been applied to education and teaching is too *narrow* a psychology, being essentially a cognitive psychology of learning and teaching. If teacher education is inadequate to prepare teachers to facilitate cognitive learning, it has been nonexistent for the preparation of teachers to facilitate affective learning.

The psychology appropriate to teaching must then be broader. It must encompass the total behavior of the teacher in interaction with the student. It must focus upon those characteristics and behaviors of teachers which are most important in the teaching-learning relationship, upon those conditions of learning which are more important than subject matter knowledge, methods, or techniques.

These characteristics, as has been emphasized in this book, are the personal characteristics of the teacher—emphatic understanding, respect or warmth, and genuineness. It is the person of the teacher which is the most important factor in teaching and learning. It is therefore apparent that teacher education should focus upon the development of the person of the teacher. Teacher education must center upon the feelings, attitudes, and beliefs of the teacher, including attitudes toward himself, or the self-concept.

That good teachers differ from poor teachers in their attitudes and beliefs is shown in studies by Combs and his associates. It was found that good teachers, as compared to poor ones, perceived others as able rather than unable, as friendly rather than unfriendly, as worthy rather than unworthy, as internally rather than externally motivated or controlled, as dependable rather than undependable, and as helpful rather than hindering.[3] Good teachers also operated from an internal rather than from an external frame of reference; that is, they were sensitive to and concerned about how others saw and felt about things and reacted to people on this basis. In addition, good teachers were more concerned about people and their reactions than about things and events.[4]

These same studies also found that good teachers perceive themselves differently than poor teachers. Compared to poor teachers, good teachers see themselves as more adequate, trustworthy, worthy, wanted and identified with others. Their beliefs about themselves, their self-concepts, are different from, and more adequate than, those of poor teachers.

What does this imply for teacher education programs? It is not our purpose here to deal with the total teacher education program, but only with that part of it relevant to humanistic or affective education. We shall first propose a basis for the psychological preparation of teachers, and then consider some necessary aspects of a humanistic teacher education program.

Humanistic Psychology

It would seem logical that humanistic teaching should be based upon a humanistic psychology.

[3] Arthur W. Combs, Donald L. Avila, and William W. Purkey, *Helping Relationships: Basic Concepts for the Helping Professions* (Boston: Allyn & Bacon, 1971), pp. 12–13.

[4] Arthur W. Combs, *The Professional Education of Teachers: a Perceptual View of Teacher Education* (Boston: Allyn & Bacon, 1965), p. 55.

Humanistic psychology has been developing rapidly in America since World War II. Many prominent psychologists have participated in its development, including Gordon Allport, Sidney Jourard, Abraham Maslow, Clark Moustakas, and Carl Rogers. Although their influence is being felt throughout the field of psychology, it has not reached down to the teaching of undergraduate or, indeed, graduate courses in psychology. Thus, neither psychology nor teacher education students are exposed to this system or point of view, though it is the most relevant and practical approach to understanding human behavior. When the writer has presented this approach to beginning graduate students in education they have responded by asking why they hadn't learned about this theory of human behavior as undergraduates.

The basic characteristic of this humanistic or perceptual psychology is that it assumes an internal frame of reference rather than the external frame of reference of so-called scientific psychology. It is interesting that, as noted above, the best teachers were found to look at their students in this way, since they had not been taught this point of view. Combs writes: "Apparently, good teachers arrive at this frame of reference with respect to people as a consequence of their experience. If this is true, it is time we introduced it much more widely into our teacher-training programs." [5]

This systematic approach to human behavior provides the necessary theoretical base for a humanistic approach to education, which, as noted in the last chapter is lacking in the writings in humanistic and affective education.

In Chapter 5 we provided an introduction to this theory. The most complete and systematic presentation is found in the book by Combs and Snygg referred to in that chapter.[6] Every teacher education student should be familiar with this book.

A Humanistic Atmosphere

Teacher education is more than the teaching of subject matter, even the subject matter of a humanistic psychology. It must be concerned with the development of persons with humanistic beliefs about people and attitudes toward them. It must make it possible for the student to develop an adequate self concept. In short, it must foster the development of self-actualizing teachers.

We have been concerned in this book with the conditions for

[5] Ibid., p. 59.

[6] Arthur W. Combs and Donald Snygg, *Individual Behavior: a Perceptual Approach to Behavior*, Rev. Ed. (New York: Harper & Row, 1959).

facilitating the development of self-actualizing persons in our public schools. *These are the same conditions necessary for the development of self-actualizing teachers in teacher education programs. Thus, this book is not only a text for teachers, but for the teachers of teachers.* If we want teachers who are capable of fostering self-actualization in their students, they must be self-actualizing persons themselves, and they can become such persons only by experiencing the conditions which are necessary for the development of self-actualizing persons.

This, perhaps more than anything else, is the defect or lack in teacher preparation programs. We cannot *tell* teachers how to teach humanistically; we can teach them how only by teaching humanistically ourselves. Combs says this in referring to the saying among counselor educators that "students teach like they have been taught rather than the way we taught them to teach." [7] Teacher educators are models upon which teacher education students base their teaching. Unfortunately, too often they are not models of humanistic education.

Some More Specific Aspects of Teacher Education

Laboratory and Supervised Practice Experiences

A universal aspect of teacher education is practice teaching. Though it is necessary, practice teaching is far from adequate as it is presently conducted, as will be noted later. But in addition to necessary changes in practice teaching, teacher education students need some pre-practice teaching experiences, a graded sequence of experiences culminating in practice teaching. One of the reasons that practice teaching is not as effective as it could be is that students are not adequately prepared for it. Teacher education could benefit from examining the methods of preparing counselors or psychotherapists in graduate programs.

Laboratory experiences should begin with *observation*. Courses in child psychology, child development, and adolescent psychology should include experiences in observing children and adolescents—not only in classrooms, but in a variety of situations.

Now it is true that in many instances these courses do include some observation. Combs notes that:

Most teacher-education programs require students to spend many hours observing the behavior of students or teachers. Many instructors put great

[7] Op. cit., p. 40.

faith in this technique despite the fact that student teachers often find it distasteful and a waste of time . . .

Many of us have made such a fetish of objectivity in the making of observations that we have blinded students to the real meaning and values of observing. Because we want to develop in students "disciplined observation," to see what is *really* going on, we have insisted that they report exactly what occurred, precisely and in detail.[8]

The kind of report which results is illustrated by the following:

"Jimmy picked up his pencil, examined the end of it. He saw that it needed sharpening so he got out of his seat and walked to the back of the room. He sharpened his pencil, looked out the window for a moment and returned to his seat. On the way back to his seat, he tapped his friend, Joe, on the head with the pencil as he passed him. He sat down and straightened his paper. He looked at the board where the teacher had placed the problem. He read the problem to himself. He sucked on the end of his pencil. He twisted his feet around the bottom of his desk and then he started to write the answer. He worked very slowly and once in a while he would look up and around the room. Once he put his head down on his arm and wrote from that position . . ." [9]

Combs asks: "Is it any wonder that students often find this kind of reporting sheer drudgery?" But the major criticism is that this procedure directs the student's attention to the wrong things. It ignores feelings, attitudes, perceptions, goals and purposes—the meaning of behavior.

Observation should be directed toward these factors, towards trying to see things from the child's point of view. Combs has abandoned requiring "objective" observation and reports:

I now ask them to do what I myself do when I watch a child behaving or a teacher teaching—to get the "feel" of what's going on, to see if they can get inside the skin of the person being observed, to understand how things look from his point of view. I ask them "What do you think he is trying to do?" "How do you suppose he feels?" "How would you have to feel to behave like that?" "How does he see the other kids?" "What does he feel about the subject?" and so on.[10]

The point of view of humanistic psychology must be applied to the teaching of courses in child behavior, especially to the observation of behavior.

A second phase of laboratory experiences should include some practice in taking the internal frame of reference in interaction with individuals. Such training can or should include several aspects:

[8] Ibid., pp. 64–65.
[9] Ibid., p. 65.
[10] Ibid., p. 66.

The first stage of this phase can begin with learning to recognize the existence of various levels of the conditions of empathy, respect, and genuineness. Carkhuff's book provides materials for such training.[11] Collingwood reports a study of eight female junior high school teachers, whose teaching experience ranged from one to ten years. They received eight hours of training in a one week workshop, learning to discriminate and communicate the core conditions using taped stimulus expressions. Following this they spent five hours roleplaying with each other, and five hours discussing the application of the experience to teaching. They were tested before and after the workshop. A significant increase in facilitative functioning was found.[12] Collingwood suggests that the communication of the core conditions is a concrete, operational definition of being pupil-centered, a concept which is usually vague and relatively meaningless. This study by Collingwood supports the results of other studies which were referred to in Chapter 8.

The practice of the core conditions in roleplaying constitutes the second aspect of laboratory experience in developing the conditions. The third stage is actual supervised experience in talking with other people. The scales developed by Carkhuff can be applied to tape recordings of these interviews so that the level of the core conditions can be evaluated.

This kind of experience offers opportunity for the student to engage in self-exploration regarding his beliefs and attitudes, leading to a better understanding of himself and the possibility of change in himself and his self-concept.

A third phase of laboratory and supervised practice is the observation of the teaching situation. This phase should come relatively early in the student's education, so that he may re-evaluate his decision to go into teaching, but not before the student has had the opportunity to learn enough about teaching and human relationships to know what to look for. It could be concurrent with the laboratory experience in the core conditions. Sarason, Davidson and Blatt report on an interesting project of teaching students' observation of a teacher in which fifteen students beginning their junior year participated.[13] One of the things which they learned was that their perceptions, or their observations, were selective, being influenced by the student's own values. It is interesting that the teacher which the

[11] Robert R. Carkhuff, *Helping and Human Relations. Vol. I: Selection and Training* (New York: Holt, Rinehart, & Winston, 1969).

[12] Thomas R. Collingwood, "A Further Delineation of the Integrated Didacticexperiential Training Approach for Teachers," Discussion Papers, Arkansas Rehabilitation Research and Training Center, University of Arkansas, Vol. III, No. 8.

[13] Seymour B. Sarason, Kenneth S. Davidson, & Burton Blatt, op. cit.

group observed (an unusually good teacher) had no discipline problems. The students began to realize that this was related to the nature of her relations with the students. It was obvious to them that
she was warm, that she had consistent limits for student behavior,
and that she was available to help when needed. One student
seemed to sum it up when she said: "You get a lot of talk about how
you have to respect your pupils and that there is something about
each of them that you can develop. When you watch Miss ——— you
know she respects each one. It's as if she really respects each one
and is going to bring out the best in them." [14]

Students should have the opportunity to observe more than one
teacher, and for periods of time adequate to get to feel and understand the relationships between the teacher and the students. Such
observation should be accompanied by a seminar in which students
discuss their observations. Closed circuit TV would be useful to extend the range and variety of teachers and students observed.

A final method of laboratory instruction, which has been recently
developed, must be mentioned. This is micro-teaching. This involves the teacher education student practicing a specific method or
technique with a small group of four to six students. The brief "practice period"—five to ten minutes in length—is videotaped. The student and an instructor view the playback, analyzing and evaluating
the student's performance. The student may then engage in another
practice session, which is then evaluated. This can continue for as
many sessions as is desired.

This method of instruction would appear to be promising. Certainly the viewing of a videotape of one's performance can be instructive to a teacher. But the way in which this is done in micro-
teaching is not necessarily helpful, and indeed the evidence regarding its value is limited, and indicates that results are small and short-
lived.

Although it would appear that breaking complex behaviors into
simpler components for instruction would be useful, this is not necessarily the case. There are perhaps optimum amounts in which
things can be best learned, and micro-techniques such as asking
questions, reinforcing student responses, answering questions, or
similar small tasks may not be optimum for learning. In addition, one
faces the problem of putting these all together in a classroom period.

A further problem is one which plagues our whole teacher education program, one which we have raised before and will raise again
in connection with practice teaching. It concerns the basis on which
we break the teaching process down, or upon which we choose spe-

[14] Ibid., p. 86.

cific techniques for use in micro-teaching. Silberman puts it as follows:

Neither the techniques the student teachers practice nor their supervisors' analysis of their videotaped performance are related to any concept of education or any theories of teaching or learning. Thus there is no structure to the micro-teaching sessions themselves, no attempt to develop an hierarchy of skills. On the contrary, the education students are merely taught to use various techniques that are not related to one another, still less to any conception of what teaching is about or any notion of which strategies are most appropriate for which teaching objectives, or which kinds of students or which subject matters.[15]

The problem of the effectiveness of generalization to the real classroom is also present. It is not true that four to six students are similar to a group of thirty students, or that teaching in a specific way for five or ten minutes is similar in any real or fundamental respects to teaching for forty or fifty minutes. Moreover, the so-called "students" in the micro-teaching situation may bear no resemblance to students in the real classroom. In a research study, a student of mine utilized some micro-teaching classes. The "students" who constituted the micro-teaching group were paid college students, who could care less about the whole thing. One sat with his hat on throughout the session, paying not the least bit of attention to the student teacher.

Micro-teaching, in my opinion, is of little value in teacher education. Even if it were changed to eliminate the criticisms considered above, it would appear that there are better, more realistic and more relevant ways to use the teacher education student's time. In the discussion of modeling in the last chapter, it was noted that this means of teaching and learning was efficient, as well as effective, because it involved the learning of wholes, or of patterns and sequences as wholes, rather than of parts which then must be assembled into wholes.

Practice Teaching

Practice teaching, which is one of the most important experiences in teacher education, is one of its major problems. Though there is widespread dissatisfaction with the way it is conducted, nothing is being done to change it, and changes in the rest of teacher education are useless if practice teaching is not changed. In fact, if the rest of teacher education becomes humanistic in its orientation,

[15] Op. cit., p. 458.

and practice teaching continues as it now is, it can be a traumatic and damaging experience for the student. This experience is similar to the supervised practicum in counseling or psychotherapy and should receive as much attention and support.

The classroom teacher (supervising or critic teacher) with whom the student does his practice teaching is an important influence on the teacher education student, often becoming a model for the student. Yet such teachers are not carefully selected, and are often chosen on the recommendation of a principal or superintendent, whose essential concept of a good teacher may be one who maintains discipline and control. Thus, as Silberman notes, "practice teaching may do more harm than good, confirming students in bad teaching habits rather than training them in good ones." [16]

Not only are supervising or critic teachers not adequately selected, but they do little if any real supervising. They have had no training in supervision, and get little if any help from the college or university supervisor of student teaching. The teacher education student also gets little if any supervision or help from the college or university coordinator, who is responsible for too many students to be able to give each individual help.

Supervising or critic teachers vary tremendously in how much actual teaching they permit the student teacher to engage in. Too many give the student little opportunity to teach, but much opportunity to become a teacher aide—handing out materials and supplies, writing material on the blackboard, maintaining bulletin boards— and constructing innumerable lesson plans which he is never given the opportunity to use. Thus he never gets any real experience in teaching, and if he does, he

never experiences the 'real thing'—never gets the feel of what teaching is actually like. Because the regular classroom teacher remains responsible for everything that goes on in his room, the student teacher cannot feel the full impact of that responsibility. Neither can he experience the full responsibility of being a teacher. He is, after all, a visitor in someone else's classroom, and visitors are not welcome to rearrange their host's furniture, alter his schedule, revise his curriculum, or change the atmosphere he has labored to create. Nor is the student teacher likely to be able to make those kinds of changes if he wanted to.[17]

Not only do student teachers get little if any feedback from the supervising teacher or their college or university supervisor,[18] but they are not given adequate instruction prior to entering practice

[16] Ibid., p. 451.

[17] Ibid., p. 460.

[18] See Sarason, Davidson, and Blatt, op. cit., pp. 102–106, 110–114, for reactions of student teachers to their practice teaching.

teaching on what is expected of them in their assignment, or informed just what the criteria are on which they will be judged and evaluated. This is in part because the teacher education program and its instructors have no consistent theory of instruction or, more basically, theory of human behavior, in or out of the classroom. Silberman's indictment may be too harsh but it is not without substance. Referring to college and university supervisors of practice teaching he writes:

> Lacking any conception of teaching, and without having thought about the ends or means of education, supervisors of student teaching tend to focus on the minutiae of classroom life, e.g., the fact that a child in the third row was chewing gum, rather than on the degree to which the student teacher was able to achieve his teaching objective, or relate to students, or evoke their interests, or what have you. Without any conception of teaching, moreover, the supervisors frequently disagree among themselves as to what constitutes good or bad teaching. Indeed, individual supervisors are frequently unable to agree even with themselves, applying different criteria to different student teachers, or to the same student on different days.[19]

It is apparent that supervisors cannot tell students what the criteria are by which they are being evaluated if they are not clear what those criteria are themselves, or disagree on them. The need for a systematic theory becomes apparent again. If students know what they are supposed to do, they might be successful in doing it. They can then be aware of whether or not they are successful, or the degree or extent to which they are successful. They can, in effect, evaluate themselves, give themselves feedback, and change their behaviors.

If instructors and supervisors can agree upon a humanistic approach to education, then there are instruments which can be used in evaluating student teachers. . . .

It is possible that the concept of practice teaching as being a one-time experience is inadequate. Combs suggests a graded series of experiences in the classroom. The beginning student would function as a teacher-helper or aide a half day a week, and would progress to the place where he would be in full charge of a classroom for at least a four-month period.[20]

There is much that can be done to improve practice teaching and its supervision. Again, the model is to be found in the teaching of counseling or psychotherapy. The student must be given the opportunity to engage in practice teaching where he has responsibility for the teaching situation; one cannot learn to be responsible unless he

---

[19] Op. cit., pp. 453–454.
[20] Op. cit., p. 125.

has the opportunity. He must be adequately prepared, so that he knows what he should do and what he is expected to do by his supervisors. This involves more than a series of how-to-do-it rules; it must consist of a theory and a system of principles to be applied to specific situations. Given these things, the student is able to evaluate himself—with the aid of audiotapes, or videotapes, and instruments to obtain feedback from his students. The supervisor then can become a facilitator for the student's development, not simply an evaluator assigning a grade to the student.

Encounter Groups and Group Training in Teacher Education

If the essence of successful professional work with people is the effective use of the self as an instrument, then teacher education should focus on the development of the teacher as a person, and as a person who can offer the necessary conditions of learning and self-actualization to others. The discussion of teacher education so far has related to this concept of teacher education. People feel or see themselves as adequate or able, worthy, wanted, acceptable, etc., when they are treated that way. Thus, the general atmosphere of the teacher education program contributes to the development of an adequate and helping self. Individual counseling can and does help, though to make it available to, or to require it of, all students would be prohibitive. It should certainly be available for those who need and want it. But perhaps the most direct and most effective method for developing teachers who can facilitate the personal development of their students is the experience provided by the basic encounter group.

In Chapter 11 we emphasized the basic encounter group as a method of humanistic education in the schools. If such an approach is helpful to students below the college level, it should be helpful to college students, and particularly to teacher education students. It is a most effective way to help students to greater experiences of self-fulfillment, "to perceive themselves in more positive ways, to confront themselves and the world with openness and acceptance, and to develop a deep sense of identification with the human condition"—or in short, to become what Combs calls "adequate personalities." [21]

Borton suggests that "it is helpful for teachers to have had some experience in exploring their own feelings before working with stu-

[21] Op. cit., p. 73.

dents on a feeling level," and that this can be obtained through a group experience. He warns that teachers should be careful about the qualifications of the leader.[22] For teachers in the field, group experiences should be provided by qualified leaders in workshops or in-service training programs. But teacher education students should be provided with this experience, under competent leadership, as part of their preparation.

Several of the humanistic critics of education recommend a group experience for teachers in training. Rogers sees it as being as important as the classroom situation for the education of teachers and administrators.[23] Dennison supports the idea of group therapy for teacher education students.[24] Knoblock and Goldstein suggest that a group experience is not only useful for the personal development of the teacher education student, but as preparation for classroom management. They write:

It is our rather strong belief that guided experience in understanding one's own group behavior and the management of groups is a necessary prerequisite to effective functioning with groups. While there are texts written on dynamics of classroom groups, without a personal frame of reference for group participation the application of sound techniques remains elusive.[25]

Silberman, while warning against the potential dangers of sensitivity training, sees a place for a group experience for teachers.[26] Silberman apparently fails to recognize the difference between the active probing and cracking of defenses used by some extremists in the field and the encounter group experience described by Rogers and referred to in the last chapter.[27]

In addition to a group experience, teachers should also have some preparation in conducting groups. Experience in an encounter group, as Knoblock and Goldstein suggest, is helpful, even necessary, but not sufficient. Some understanding of the nature of groups and the group process, beyond that presented in Chapter 11, is necessary.

Goodman contends that "the only profitable training for teachers

---

[22] Terry Borton, *Reach, Touch and Teach* (New York: McGraw-Hill, 1970), p. 199.

[23] Carl R. Rogers, *Freedom to Learn* (Columbus, Ohio: Merrill, 1969), p. 141.

[24] George Dennison, *The Lives of Children* (New York: Vintage Books, 1969), p. 257.

[25] Peter Knoblock and Arnold P. Goldstein, *The Lonely Teacher* (Boston: Allyn & Bacon, 1971), p. 40.

[26] Op. cit., p. 502.

[27] Carl R. Rogers, *Carl Rogers on Encounter Groups* (New York: Harper & Row, 1970).

is a group therapy and, perhaps, a course in child development." [28]
He also writes: "I see little merit, for teaching this age]the first five
grades], in the usual teacher-training. . . . Since at this age one
teaches the child, not the subject, the relevant art is psychotherapy,
and the most useful course for a normal school is probably group
therapy.[29]

If teachers are to be involved in conducting the kinds of groups
discussed in the last chapter, whether classroom size groups of the
kind suggested by Glasser, Moustakas, and Seeley or the smaller
basic encounter grvups, they need preparation. Such preparation is
possible at the undergraduate level.

The Continuous Integrative Seminar

Encounter groups are concerned with personal development and
interpersonal relations. Students should also have the opportunity to
participate in seminars in which they can, with the instructor, and
with each other, consider, evaluate, and integrate their total experience in teacher education, including content, laboratory, and other
experiences, and their personal development in terms of ideas, beliefs and attitudes. This seminar should be a continuing one from the
beginning of their college education to its end, including the practice teaching experience. It need not consist of the same group of
students, or the same instructor. It shoud be small enough for discussion, say 15 to 20 students.

Combs proposes a continuous seminar of from 15 to 30 students,
remaining constant, and meeting 2 hours per week throughout the
student's education.[30] However, as students left the group for whatever reason, including differing rates of progress through the program, they would be replaced by beginning students, so there would
be students at differing levels.

Glasser also recommends a continuing four-year seminar for
teacher education students, which would include observation of
teachers at every level. Practicing teachers would be invited in for
discussions. With a full year of practice teaching, Glasser feels that
few other education courses would be necessary in teacher education.[31]

---

[28] Paul Goodman, "No Processing Whatever," in Beatrice Gross & Ronald Gross,
(Eds.) *Radical School Reform* (New York: Simon & Schuster, 1969), p. 100.

[29] Paul Goodman, quoted in George Dennison, op. cit., p. 266.

[30] Op. cit., pp. 119–121.

[31] William Glasser, *Schools Without Failure* (New York: Harper & Row, 1969),
p. 10.

The seminar provides an opportunity for students to think and talk about their observations, laboratory experiences, practicum, and their reading. The seminar described by Sarason, Davidson, and Blatt illustrates the value of such a seminar in conjunction with observation of classroom teaching.[32] One of the purposes of this seminar was to start the students thinking about the way children are usually taught in the schools and the way *they* were learning in the seminar and observation. These writers suggest a series of seminars, the first beginning as soon as students have decided on a teaching career. This seminar would not be professional in nature, but focused on an understanding of the observational process, and will develop an attitude of critical inquiry toward self, others, and problems. Child psychology courses would also have an observational seminar. A third kind of seminar would concern itself with what is covered in conventional methods courses.[33] Former students who have become teachers, or practicing teachers could be involved in these seminars.

Summary

In this chapter we have been concerned with the preparation of humanistic teachers. Such teachers will of course need some preparation in subject matter areas, but the emphasis in their preparation should be in human relations.

A major defect in the psychological preparation of teachers is that they are not provided with a systematic theoretical approach to human behavior. Such a theory, which is highly practical, is to be found in humanistic psychology, especially in the perceptual approach to behavior of Combs and Snygg. This should be the focus of the psychological preparation of teachers.

The importance of a humanistic atmosphere in teacher education is emphasized. It is essential that the methods of teacher education should exemplify the nature of what is being taught.

In addition to the didactic aspect of teacher education, an experiential aspect is necessary. This should include a graded series of laboratory experiences, beginning with observation. Practice teaching is also part of the experiential curriculum, but it must be modified and expanded if it is to be maximally effective. More adequate supervision is necessary.

A further aspect of the experiential curriculum is a group experience, which should exist in addition to a continuing seminar, to in-

[32] Op. cit.
[33] Ibid., pp. 107–108.

tegrate the total educational experience of the student. Finally, the teacher education student must be prepared for leading groups of the kind described in the last chapter. While the experience of being in an encounter group is necessary, some didactic or course work in group methods and procedures is also required.

Davis says that "it may be that humanistic education can only exist in a humanistic society." [34] But it might also be contended that we can only achieve a humanistic society by developing a humanistic educational system. We must start somewhere, and society is too large and pervasive a place. Essentially, we can only work with individuals in developing humanistic—or self-actualizing—persons. It would appear that the most effective place to start is with the education of teachers. This, of course, assumes that the educators of teachers are themselves humanistic, which is perhaps unrealistic. But we must assume that somewhere there are humanistic persons to start with, and hopefully we are more likely to find them among educators than in most other groups. Perhaps this book can help to facilitate the development of humanistic educators—including administrators—as well as humanistic teachers.

[34] David C. Davis, *Model for Humanistic Education: the Danish Folk Highschool* (Columbus, Ohio: Merrill, 1971), p. 105.

Thinking in Education

JOHN DEWEY

The Essentials of Method

No one doubts, theoretically, the importance of fostering in school good habits of thinking. But apart from the fact that the acknowledgement is not so great in practice as in theory, there is not adequate theoretical recognition that all which the school can or need do for pupils, so far as their *minds* are concerned (that is, leaving out certain specialized muscular abilities), is to develop their ability to think. The parceling out of instruction among various ends such as acquisition of skill (in reading, spelling, writing, drawing, reciting); acquiring information (in history and geography), *and* training of thinking is a measure of the ineffective way in which we accomplish all three. Thinking which is not connected with increase of efficiency in action, and with learning more about ourselves and the world in which we live, has something the matter wtith it just as thought. And skill obtained apart from thinking is not connected with any sense of the purposes for which it is to be used. It consequently leaves a man at the mercy of his routine habits and of the authoritative control of others, who know what they are about and who are not especially scrupulous as to their means of achievement. And information severed from thoughtful action is dead, a mind-crushing load. Since it simulates knowledge and thereby develops the poison of conceit, it is a most powerful obstacle to further growth in the grace of intelligence. The sole direct path to enduring improvement in the methods of instruction and learning consists in centering upon the conditions which exact, promote, and test thinking. Thinking *is* the method of intelligent learning, of learning that employs and rewards mind. We speak, legitimately enough, about the method of thinking, but the important thing to bear in mind about method is that thinking is method, the method of intelligent experience in the course which it takes.

I. The initial stage of that developing experience which is called thinking is *experience*. This remark may sound like a silly truism. It ought to be one; but unfortunately it is not. On the contrary, thinking is often regarded both in philosophic theory and in educational practice as something cut off from experience, and capable of being cultivated in isolation. In fact, the inherent limitations of experience are often urged as the sufficient ground for attention to thinking. Experience is then thought to be confined to the senses and appetites; to a mere material world, while thinking proceeds from a higher faculty (of reason), and is occupied with spiritual or at least literary things. So, oftentimes, a sharp distinction is made between pure mathematics as a peculiarly fit subject matter of thought (since it has nothing to do with physical existences) and applied mathematics, which has utilitarian but not mental value.

Speaking generally, the fundamental fallacy in methods of instruction lies in supposing that experience on the part of pupils may be assumed. What is here insisted upon is the necessity of an actual empirical situation as the initiating phase of thought. Experience is here taken as previously defined: trying to do something and having the thing perceptibly do something to one in return. (The fallacy consists in supposing that we can begin with ready-made subject matter of arithmetic, or geography, or whatever, irrespective of some direct personal experience of a situation. Even the kindergarten and Montessori techniques are so anxious to get at intellectual distinc-

tions, without "waste of time," that they tend to ignore—or reduce—
the immediate crude handling of the familiar material of experience,
and to introduce pupils at once to material which expresses the intellectual distinctions which adults have made. But the first stage of
contact with any new material, at whatever age of maturity, must
inevitably be of the trial and error sort. An individual must actually
try, in play or work, to do something with material in carrying out his
own impulsive activity, and then note the interaction of his energy
and that of the material employed. This is what happens when a
child at first begins to build with blocks, and it is equally what happens when a scientific man in his laboratory begins to experiment
with unfamiliar objects.

Hence the first approach to any subject in school, if thought is to
be aroused and not words acquired, should be as unscholastic as possible. To realize what an experience, or empirical situation, means,
we have to call to mind the sort of situation that presents itself outside of school; the sort of occupations that interest and engage activity in ordinary life. And careful inspection of methods which are permanently successful in formal education, whether in arithmetic or
learning to read, or studying geography, or learning physics or a
foreign language, will reveal that they depend for their efficiency
upon the fact that they go back to the type of the situation which
causes reflection out of school in ordinary life. They give the pupils
something to do, not something to learn; and the doing is of such a
nature as to demand thinking, or the intentional noting of connections; learning naturally results.

That the situation should be of such a nature as to arouse thinking means of course that it should suggest something to do which is
not either routine or capricious—something, in other words, presenting what is new (and hence uncertain or problematic) and yet sufficiently connected with existing habits to call out an effective response. An effective response means one which accomplishes a
perceptible result, in distinction from a purely haphazard activity,
where the consequences cannot be mentally connected with what is
done. The most significant question which can be asked, accordingly, about any situation or experience proposed to induce learning
is what quality of problem it involves.

At first thought, it might seem as if usual school methods measured well up to the standard here set. The giving of problems, the
putting of questions, the assigning of tasks, the magnifying of difficulties, is a large part of school work. But it is indispensable to discriminate between genuine and simulated or mock problems. The
following questions may aid in making such discrimination. (a) Is
there anything but a problem? Does the question naturally suggest

itself within some situation or personal experience? Or is it an aloof thing, a problem only for the purposes of conveying instruction in some school topic? Is it the sort of trying that would arouse observation and engage experimentation outside of school? (b) Is it the pupil's own problem, or is it the teacher's or textbook's problem, made a problem for the pupil only because he cannot get the required mark or be promoted or win the teacher's approval, unless he deals with it? Obviously, these two questions overlap. They are two ways of getting at the same point: Is the experience a personal thing of such a nature as inherently to stimulate and direct observation of the connections involved, and to lead to inference and its testing? Or is it imposed from without, and is the pupil's problem simply to meet the external requirement?

Such questions may give us pause in deciding upon the extent to which current practices are adapted to develop reflective habits. The physical equipment and arrangements of the average schoolroom are hostile to the existence of real situations of experience. What is there similar to the conditions of everyday life which will generate difficulties? Almost everything testifies to the great premium put upon listening, reading, and the reproduction of what is told and read. It is hardly possible to overstate the contrast between such conditions and the situations of active contact with things and persons in the home, on the playground, in fulfilling of ordinary responsibilities of life. Much of it is not even comparable with the questions which may arise in the mind of a boy or girl in conversing with others or in reading books outside of the school. No one has ever explained why children are so full of questions outside of the school (so that they pester grown-up persons if they get any encouragement), and the conspicuous absence of display of curiosity about the subject matter of school lessons. Reflection on this striking contrast will throw light upon the question of how far customary school conditions supply a context of experience in which problems naturally suggest themselves. No amount of improvement in the personal technique of the instructor will wholly remedy this state of things. There must be more actual material, more *stuff*, more appliances, and more opportunities for doing things, before the gap can be overcome. And where children are engaged in doing things and in discussing what arises in the course of their doing, it is found, even with comparatively indifferent modes of instruction, that children's inquiries are spontaneous and numerous, and the proposals of solution advanced, varied, and ingenious.

As a consequence of the absence of the materials and occupations which generate real problems, the pupil's problems are not his; or, rather, they are his *only as* a pupil, not as a human being. Hence the lamentable waste in carrying over such expertness as is achieved in dealing with them to the affairs of life beyond the schoolroom. A pupil has a problem, but it is the problem of meeting the peculiar requirements set by the teacher. His problem becomes that of finding out what the teacher wants, what will satisfy the teacher in recitation and examination and outward deportment. Relationship to subject matter is no longer direct. The occasions and material of thought are not found in the arithmetic or the history or geography itself, but in skillfully adapting that material to the teacher's requirements. The pupil studies, but unconsciously to himself the objects of his study are the conventions and standards of the school system and school authority, not the nominal "studies." The thinking thus evoked is artificially one-sided at the best. At its worst, the problem of the pupil is not how to meet the requirements of school life, but how to *seem* to meet them—or, how to come near enough to meeting them to slide along without an undue amount of friction. The type of judgment formed by these devices is not a desirable addition to character. If these statements give too highly colored a picture of usual school methods, the exaggeration may at least serve to illustrate the point: the need of active pursuits, involving the use of material to accomplish purposes, if there are to be situations which normally generate problems occasioning thoughtful inquiry.

II. There must be *data* at command to supply the considerations required in dealing with the specific difficulty which has presented itself. Teachers following a "developing" method sometimes tell children to think things out for themselves as if they could spin them out of their own heads. The material of thinking is not thoughts, but actions, facts, events, and the relations of things. In other words, to think effectively one must have had, or now have, experiences which will furnish him resources for coping with the difficulty at hand. A difficulty is an indispensable stimulus to thinking, but not all difficulties call out thinking. Sometimes they overwhelm and submerge and discourage. The perplexing situation must be sufficiently like situations which have already been dealt with so that pupils will have some control of the meanings of handling it. A large part of the art of instruction lies in making the difficulty of new problems large enough to challenge thought, and small enough so that, in addition to the confusion naturally attending the novel elements, there shall be luminous familiar spots from which helpful suggestions may spring.

In one sense, it is a matter of indifference by what psychological means that subject matter for reflection is provided. Memory, observation, reading, communication, are all avenues for supplying data. The relative proportion to be obtained from each is a matter of the specific features of the particular problem in hand. It is foolish to in-

sist upon observation of objects presented to the senses if the student
is so familiar with the objects that he could just as well recall the
facts independently. It is possible to induce undue and crippling
dependence upon sense-presentations. No one can carry around with
him a museum of all the things whose properties will assist the conduct of thought. A well-trained mind is one that has a maximum of
resources behind it, so to speak, and that is accustomed to go over its
past experiences to see what they yield. On the other hand, a quality
or relation of even a familiar object may previously have been passed
over, and be just the fact that is helpful in dealing with the question.
In this case direct observation is called for. The same principle applies to the use to be made of observation on one hand and of reading and "telling" on the other. Direct observation is naturally more
vivid and vital. But it has its limitations; and in any case it is a necessary part of education that one should acquire the ability to supple-
ment the narrowness of his immediately personal experiences by
utilizing the experiences of others. Excessive reliance upon others
for data (whether got from reading or listening) is to be depreciated.
Most objectionable of all is the probability that others, the book or
the teacher, will supply solutions ready-made, instead of giving material that the student has to adapt and apply to the question in hand
for himself.

There is no inconsistency in saying that in schools there is
usually both too much and too little information supplied by others.
The accumulation and acquisition of information for purposes of reproduction in recitation and examination is made too much of.
"Knowledge," in the sense of information, means the working capital, the indispensable resources, of further inquiry; of finding out, or
learning, more things. Frequently it is treated as an end itself, and
then the goal becomes to heap it up and display it when called for.
This static, cold-storage ideal of knowledge is inimical to educative
development. It not only lets occasions for thinking go unused, but it
swamps thinking. No one could construct a house on ground clut-
tered with miscellaneous junk. Pupils who have stored their "minds"
with all kinds of material which they have never put to intellectual
uses are sure to be hampered when they try to think. They have no
practice in selecting what is appropriate, and no criterion to go by;
everything is on the same dead static level. On the other hand, it is
quite open to question whether, if information actually functioned in
experience through use in application to the student's own purposes,
there would not be need of more varied resources in books, pictures,
and talks than are usually at command.

III. The correlate in thinking of facts, data, knowledge already
acquired is suggestions, inferences, conjectured meanings, supposi-

tions, tentative explanations:—*ideas,* in short. Careful observation and recollection determine what is given, what is already there and hence assured. They cannot furnish what is lacking. They define, clarify, and locate the question; they cannot supply its answer. Projection, invention, ingenuity, devising come in for that purpose. The data *arouse* suggestions, and only by reference to the specific data can we pass upon the appropriateness of the suggestions. But the suggestions run beyond what is, as yet, actually *given* in experience. They forecast possible results, things *to* do, not facts (things already done). Inference is always an invasion of the unknown, a leap from the known.

In this sense, a thought (what a thing suggests but is not as it is presented) is creative,—an incursion into the novel. It involves some inventiveness. What is suggested must, indeed, be familiar in *some* context; the novelty, the inventive devising, clings to the new light in which it is seen, the different use to which it is put. When Newton thought of his theory of gravitation, the creative aspect of his thought was not found in its materials. They were familiar; many of them commonplaces—sun, moon, planets, weight, distance, mass, square of numbers. These were not original ideas; they were established facts. His originality lay in the *use* to which these familiar acquaintances were put by introduction into an unfamiliar context. The same is true of every striking scientific discovery, every great invention, every admirable artistic production. Only silly folk identify creative originality with the extraordinary and fanciful; others recognize that its measure lies in putting everyday things to uses which had not occurred to others. The operation is novel, not the materials out of which it is constructed.

The educational conclusion which follows is that *all* thinking is original in a projection of considerations which have not been previously apprehended. The child of three who discovers what can be done with blocks, or of six who finds out what he can make by putting five cents and five cents together, is really a discoverer, even though everybody else in the world knows it. There is a genuine increment of experience; not another item mechanically added on, but enrichment by a new quality. The charm which the spontaneity of little children has for sympathetic observers is due to perception of this intellectual originality. The joy which children themselves experience is the joy of intellectual constructiveness—of creativeness, if the word may be used without misunderstanding.

The educational moral I am chiefly concerned to draw is not, however, that teachers would find their own work less of a grind and strain if school conditions favored learning in the sense of discovery and not in that of storing away what others pour into them; nor that it would be possible to give even children and youth the delights of personal intellectual productiveness—true and important as are these things. It is that no thought, no idea, can possibly be conveyed as an idea from one person to another. When it is told, it is, to the one to whom it is told, another given fact, not an idea. The communication may stimulate the other person to realize the question for himself and to think out a like idea, or it may smother his intellectual interest and suppress his dawning effort at thought.But what he *directly* gets cannot be an idea. Only by wrestling with the conditions of the problem at first hand, seeking and finding his own way out, does he think. When the parent or teacher has provided the conditions which stimulate thinking and has taken a sympathetic attitude toward the activities of the learner by entering into a common or conjoint experience, all has been done which a second party can do to instigate learning. The rest lies with the one directly concerned. If he cannot devise his own solution (not of course in isolation, but in correspondence with the teacher and other pupils) and find his own way out he will not learn, not even if he can recite some correct answer with one hundred per cent accuracy. We can and do supply ready-made "ideas" by the thousand; we do not usually take much pains to see that the one learning engages in significant situations where his own activities generate, support, and clinch ideas—that is, perceived meanings or connections. This does not mean that the teacher is to stand off and look on; the alternative to furnishing ready-made subject matter and listening to the accuracy with which it is reproduced is not quiescence, but participation, sharing, in an activity. In such shared activity, the teacher is a learner, and the learner is, without knowing it, a teacher—and upon the whole, the less consciousness there is, on either side, of either giving or receiving instruction, the better.

IV. Ideas, as we have seen, whether they be humble guesses or dignified theories, are anticipations of possible solutions. They are anticipations of some continuity or connection of an activity and a consequence which has not as yet shown itself. They are therefore tested by the operation of acting upon them. They are to guide and organize further observations, recollections, and experiments. They are intermediate in learning, not final. All educational reformers, as we have had occasion to remark, are given to attacking the passivity of traditional education. They have opposed pouring in from without, and absorbing like a sponge; they have attacked drilling in material as into hard and resisting rock. But it is not easy to secure conditions which will make the getting of an idea identical with having an experience which widens and makes more precise our contact with the environment. Activity, even self-activity, is too easily thought of as something merely mental, cooped up within the head, or finding expression only through the vocal organs.

While the need of application of ideas gained in study is acknowledged by all the more successful methods of instruction, the exercises in application are sometimes treated as devices for *fixing* what has already been learned and for getting greater practical skill in its manipulation. These results are genuine and not to be despised. But practice in applying what has been gained in study ought primarily to have an intellectual quality. As we have already seen, thoughts just as thoughts are incomplete. At best they are tentative; they are suggestions, indications. They are standpoints and methods for dealing with situations of experience. Till they are applied in these situations they lack full point and reality. Only application tests them, and only testing confers full meaning and a sense of their reality. Short of use made of them, they tend to segregate into a peculiar world of their own. It may be seriously questioned whether the philosophies which isolate mind and set it over against the world did not have their origin in the fact that the reflective or theoretical class of men elaborated a large stock of ideas which social conditions did not allow them to act upon and test. Consequently men were thrown back into their own thoughts as ends in themselves.

However this may be, there can be no doubt that a peculiar artificiality attaches to much of what is learned in schools. It can hardly be said that many students consciously think of the subject matter as unreal; but it assuredly does not possess for them the kind of reality which the subject matter of their vital experiences possesses. They learn not to expect that sort of reality of it; they become habituated to treating it as having reality for the purposes of recitations, lessons, and examinations. That it should remain inert for the experiences of daily life is more or less a matter of course. The bad effects are twofold. Ordinary experience does not receive the enrichment which it should; it is not fertilized by school learning. And the attitudes which spring from getting used to and accepting half-understood and ill-digested material weaken vigor and efficiency of thought.

If we have dwelt especially on the negative side, it is for the sake of suggesting positive masures adapted to the effectual development of thought. Where schools are equipped with laboratories, shops, and gardens, where dramatizations, plays, and games are freely used, opportunities exist for reproducing situations of life, and for acquiring and applying information and ideas in the carrying forward of progressive experiences. Ideas are not segregated, they do not form an isolated island. They animate and enrich the ordinary course of life. Information is vitalized by its function; by the place it occupies in direction of action.

The phrase "opportunities exist" is used purposely. They may not be taken advantage of; it is possible to employ manual and constructive activities in a physical way, as means of getting just bodily skill; or they may be used almost exclusively for "utilitarian," *i.e.*, pecuniary, ends. But the disposition on the part of upholders of "cultural" education to assume that such activities are merely physical or professional in quality, is itself a product of the philosophies which isolate mind from direction of the course of experience and hence from action upon and with things. When the "mental" is regarded as a self-contained separate realm, a counterpart fate befalls bodily activity and movements. They are regarded as at the best mere external annexes to mind. They may be necessary for the satisfaction of bodily needs and the attainment of external decency and comfort, but they do not occupy a necessary place in mind nor enact an indispensable rôle in the completion of thought. Hence they have no place in a liberal education—*i.e.*, one which is concerned with the interests of intelligence. If they come in at all, it is as a concession to the material needs of the masses. That they should be allowed to invade the education of the élite is unspeakable. This conclusion follows irresistibly from the isolated conception of mind, but by the same logic it disappears when we perceive what mind really is—namely, the purposive and directive factor in the development of experience.

While it is desirable that all educational institutions should be equipped so as to give students an opportunity for acquiring and testing ideas and information in active pursuits typifying important social situations, it will, doubtless, be a long time before all of them are thus furnished. But this state of affairs does not afford instructors an excuse for folding their hands and persisting in methods which segregate school knowledge. Every recitation in every subject gives an opportunity for establishing cross connections between the subject matter of the lesson and the wider and more direct experiences of everyday life. Classroom instruction falls into three kinds. The least desirable treats each lesson as an independent whole. It does not put upon the student the responsibility of finding points of contact between it and other lessons in the same subject, or other subjects of study. Wiser teachers see to it that the student is systematically led to utilize his earlier lessons to help understand the present one, and also to use the present to throw additional light upon what has already been acquired. Results are better, but school subject matter is still isolated. Save by accident, out-of-school experience is left in its crude and comparatively irreflective state. It is not subject to the refining and expanding influences of the more accurate and comprehensive material of direct instruction. The latter is not motivated and impregnated with a sense of reality by being intermingled with the realities of everyday life. The best type of teaching bears in mind the desirability of affecting this interconnection. It puts the student in the habitual attitude of finding points of contact and mutual bearings.

SUMMARY. Processes of instruction are unified in the degree in which they center in the production of good habits of thinking. While we may speak, without error, of the method of thought, the important thing is that thinking is the method of an educative experience. The essentials of method are therefore identical with the essentials of reflection. They are first that the pupil have a genuine situation of experience—that there be a continuous activity in which he is interested for its own sake; secondly, that a genuine problem develop within this situation as a stimulus to thought; third, that he possess the information and make the observations needed to deal with it; fourth, that suggested solutions occur to him which he shall be responsible for developing in an orderly way; fifth, that he have opportunity and occasion to test his ideas by application, to make their meaning clear and to discover for himself their validity.

The Ends and the Means
of the Curriculum:
Humanistic Knowledge

In view of the way education is usually conducted, it may not be an etymological coincidence that in Latin the word *curriculum* meant a running or a racecourse. Now, of course, the term is usually used to denote a program of studies offered by an educational institution and leading to some kind of diploma or degree.

It may be valuable to contemplate some of the goals that have been a part of the history of the curriculum. Traditionally, the development of the mind or intellect has always been high on the list of conventional, academic goals. The goal of spiritual development for the purposes of enlightenment and salvation has also been important, especially in curriculums that are religiously oriented. In recent decades a sometimes bewildering plethora of educational goals has been visible. For example, the social behaviorists advocate curriculum goals that are "relevant" to the so-called real world, such as career development and consumer education, while the social reconstructionists call for a curriculum that could transform society through development of a critically informed sense of culture or the world. In addition there has been the burgeoning of interest in educational goals connected with the psychological and affective development of the individual. On a public level, because of the state of our economic world in the mid 1970s, i.e., high inflation and unemployment, there has been increasing demand for programs that are "practical." And on a methodological level, the behavioral analysts and positivists have been concerned with the conceptual and behavioral clarification of educational purposes, through statements that everybody can publicly agree to or verify.

313

I think that it makes some sense to picture the curriculum as a many-layered cake. For this "cake" the goals, the resources, the knowledge, and the roles of education, are mixed according to a particular recipe or course of studies. To follow our metaphor through, the mixture for the cake is not put into baking pans or baked until the persons for whom it is intended, i.e., students, actually appear in the kitchen or school. When the school opens, the students, together with their teachers, begin to prepare the mixture in their own way for the oven. In the process, some discover that they do not like the mixture prepared for them and want to start over again from scratch, while others discover that they do not know how to turn the "oven" on. But since both the ingredients and the oven were provided by the state, they have to follow the guidelines of the state in creating new recipes or curriculums or even in using their ovens.

My extended metaphor is intended to imply, among other things, that most public school curriculums are pre-planned and carefully controlled. The student usually has no really meaningful choice either in what he is supposed to learn or about the conditions under which he will learn. Consequently, the typical public school or college curriculum is, by most standards, dehumanizing for the learner. And the overall psychological and intellectual effect upon the learner has been the encouragement of low motivation, underachievement, and educational apathy. On these grounds alone, the typical curriculum is existentially absurd, since it separates the ends of teaching and learning from the necessary psychological, emotional, aesthetic, and intellectual means or conditions for achieving them.

The selections of this section are intended to offer a balanced and broadly based view of the curriculum, giving consideration to the child, the adult, the nature of knowledge, humanism, and the possible goals of education. It makes no pretense that it is exhaustive of all the possible problems and values of the humanistic study of the curriculum. However, it does attempt to offer a wide spectrum of readings that are provocative, suggestive (rather than prescriptive), and philosophically oriented. At the same time, I hope that this section throws additional light upon the general ideal of educating humanistically.

The first selection by Colonel Francis W. Parker, entitled "The Child," views the fundamental biological nature of the child and how the child grows. Through song, story, and myth, the child develops a sense of the world that becomes the experiential basis for grasping all knowledge in later life. The child, for example, "studies" zoology through the animals and insects that he meets; and his encounter with vegetable and plant life form the basis of his understanding of botany. "The child," says Parker, "begins every subject spontaneously and unconsciously." Fundamentally, this is due to the fact that "the child itself is a central energy, or complex of energies, upon which and through which certain external energies act," educating him, as it were, through the things and events of the environment. And not only are learning to walk and learning to talk automatic and natural, but they are according to Parker in strict conformity to the laws of God; as teachers, "we are here to find and present the conditions adapted to the divine nature of the child." Parker's somewhat romantic and theistic view of the child discloses, with philosophical depth, the extent to which internal, biological energies are tied developmentally to purely sensory experience. His entire position may be summed up in the statement: "The child instinctively begins all subjects known in the curriculum of the university."

In "The Child and the Curriculum," the redoubtable John Dewey gives us the benefit of his philosophic vision in saying that education must be seen as a whole, instead of as a series of conflicting terms, such as "the child vs. the curriculum" and "individual nature vs. social culture." In this extract from his famous essay Dewey states that "the child and the curriculum are simply two limits which define a single process." Even though the child lives in a "somewhat narrow world of personal contacts," school subjects fractionalize and divide experience for the child. The "studies as classified are the product . . . of the science of the ages, not of the experience of the child." The problem, therefore, for the teacher as well as the curriculum planner, is to see how the experience of the child "contains within itself elements, facts and truths of just the same sort as those entering the formulated study" of the curriculum. Dewey's observation is that the child exists psychologically while the curriculum exists logically. This makes it necessary for the teacher to psychologize the logical. And this is done by "inducing a vital and personal experience" for the learner.

In "Physical and Social Studies: Naturalism and Humanism," the second selection from John Dewey in this section, he traces the extent to which the study of man and nature, or of humanism and naturalism, were interrelated, particularly in the philosophies of Socrates, Plato, and Aristotle. Later forces, however, caused man to lose sight of the unity of man and nature and of the literary and physical studies. Among them were the rise of medieval scholasticism and its reliance upon authority and acquisition rather than discovery and inquiry; a one-sided literary humanism; an aristocratic disdain for the material, sensory world; the Protestant Reformation, in which both sides appealed to literary documents; the corruption of Francis Bacon's ideal of science that knowledge be used to serve the interests of mankind rather than a select class; dualistic philosophies, separating mind and matter; and the new science that was exclusively quantitative, seeking a mathematical formula to explain the whole universe.

To Dewey, humanism "means at bottom being imbued with an intelligent sense of human interests"; "any study producing greater sensitiveness to social well-being and greater ability or promote that well-being is humane study." Thus, although Dewey has great esteem for Greek philosophy, he criticizes the humanism that derived from it because it was the product of an elitist culture, based upon an economic system of slavery and antagonistic to all outsiders, "the barbarians." Furthermore, the "older humanism" carried over this narrow outlook into the modern world, preserving an aristocratic cast and ignoring the economic and industrial conditions of society. The consequence of this for education was the tendency "to treat the sciences as a separate body of studies consisting of technical information regarding the physical world, and to reserve the older literary studies as distinctively humanistic."

Once again we see Dewey's profound understanding of the forces, cultural and intellectual, that have tended to separate man from nature and from his deeply humanistic hunger for all knowledge and experience. And although Dewey's essay deals only tangentially with the problem of the curriculum, its focus upon the problem of divided knowledge throws light upon the problems that have prevented the humanization of knowledge in the schools and colleges and the solutions that seem required.

In "Education on the Nonverbal Level," Aldous Huxley uncovers one of the most important dimensions of humanistic education, i.e., the nonverbal, the nameless, and the unique. His primary assumption is that man is a "multiple amphibian," meaning that we live in many worlds simultaneously, the rational and the animal, the symbolic and the psychophysical, and so on. Education must take cognizance of all worlds that people live in to be completely adequate or good.

Huxley is critical of the humanities in that they have been excessively verbal. He therefore advocates what he calls nonverbal humanities, beginning with training in Eastern philosophy, centering, internal awareness techniques, and psychophysical education in general, to counterbalance the one-sidedness of verbal and symbolic education. Huxley also posits the need for "physical safety values for reducing the pressure of our negative emotions," or training in "the indispensable art of letting off steam." Despite Huxley's emphasis upon nonverbal education, he also advocates "a thorough education in language; its uses and abuses" as the obverse side of an education and a curriculum designed to enable people to live freely and fully in society, actualizing more of their desirable psychophysical potentialities.

The last essay, entitled "Curriculum and Humanistic Education: Monolism vs. Pluralism," by Bruce Joyce, is a somewhat abridged version of the original. Joyce posits two main goals for a humanistic curriculum: (1) environments for self-actualization, and (2) a shared consciousness that respects traditional values while questing and reaching for new ones. He perceives a critical and vital balance existing between education and society, giving education the opportunity to solve major social problems, because it is a "major agent in the transmission of culture." The task of the humanist in curriculum design is a straightforward one: to free himself from the bureaucratic school and from the sorting function that it performs for the status system and to "actualize a pluralistic education." This can be done by identifying the various domains of the learner, such as the personal, the social, and the academic, and designing programs that effectively enter into the life of the learner, changing his responses to living in the world. "In practice," Joyce asserts, such a curriculum will enable students to "create their own school by selecting from a wide offering of planned educational programs."

This last selection not only makes explicit many of the themes and ideas explored in this section, but anticipates the final section of this anthology in showing the interconnection that exists, at least in theory, between the freedom of the learner, the curriculum, and the school environment.

Finally, I would like the reader to consider the viewpoint of Claudio Naranjo, although I have not included an extract from his writings. In his book, *The One Quest*, Naranjo, the Chilean psychiatrist, stresses that the quest of man, namely for the unity of Being, is the truest basis for actualizing the curriculum goals of education. The studies of education, psychotherapy, and religion, even though they are concerned with the apparently separate goals of growth, health, and enlightenment respectively, are actually taking different paths toward the same end, the discovery of *I* or the center of Being. All three approaches toward knowledge of the person imply a positive, self-actualizing image of man, but they are in conflict with each other due to the institutional ills of the culture. Hence, Naranjo's injunction (quoting Idries Shah, a savant of Eastern religions) that "you have to teach people how to learn. And before that you have to teach them that there is still something to be learned . . ." which goes against the romantic concept of learning, namely that we are born already knowing how to learn.

Discussion Questions

1. Colonel Francis W. Parker contends that "the child instinctively begins all subjects known in the curriculum of the university." Assuming that this is true, at what age do you think the process of formal, conscious education should begin? Or is there, in your opinion, any strict separation between the conscious and the subconscious, or instinctive, processes of learning and growing? Also, do you agree with Parker's view that the child is a center of energy "upon which and through which certain external energies act"? What implications in general do you think Parker's view of the child

has for thinking creatively about the design of a curriculum? Do you feel, for example, that we can ignore the nature of the child in planning a curriculum for adults? Do you think that Parker's emphasis upon external, sensory experience in the learning process of the child can be ignored at any level of education? Finally, do you feel that Parker's view of the child is humanistic? Why?

2. In "The Child and the Curriculum," John Dewey emphasized the need to adapt the logical structure of academic subject matter to the psychological needs of the student. Is this a valid contention? Why? If you were planning a curriculum, what ways would you devise to achieve this end? Also, of what significance is the student-teacher relationship in actualizing the logical and the psychological dimensions of knowledge?

3. John Dewey believes that humanism points to "an intelligent sense of human interests." Do you think that his definition of humanism is broad and general enough to justify almost any educational goal or value? What implications does Dewey's overall view of humanism in relation to naturalism have for planning a curriculum? Do you agree with Dewey's concern for connecting all knowledge with social issues and problems in the educational process? Why, or why not? Finally, in what ways do you think Dewey qualifies as a humanistic educator?

4. Aldous Huxley advocates "Education on the Nonverbal Level" to complement education on the verbal and symbolic level. Why? Are there, in your opinion, great difficulties in planning a curriculum that would allow education on the nonverbal level? Also, do you think that it is necessary to conduct education on the nonverbal level when much of learning takes place nonverbally or beyond words at subconscious levels anyway? What knowledge and experience do you possess that would enable you to plan for education at the nonverbal level? Finally, do you feel that your education has been too verbal, too cognitive, and too much at head-level? Do you think that the curriculum, any curriculum for whatever goals or ends, should be concerned with the psychophysical dimension of man as it relates to the world of the learner? Why, or why not?

5. Bruce Joyce asserts that the task of the humanist in curriculum design is to "actualize a pluralistic education." What difficulties stand in the way of achieving a wide variety of educational programs for the learner in the typical school or college? Do you think that it is desirable for students to create their own school by choosing from an offering of planned educational programs? Is there a significant difference, in your opinion, between a program that is pre-planned and one that the learner participates in the planning of? Explain. What kind of curriculum do you envision to maximize the freedom and re-

sponsibility of the learner, to himself and to others, and enable him to live fully in the world?

FURTHER READING

Dewey, John. *Experience and Education*. New York: Collier Books, 1963.

Harmin, Merrill, Howard Kirschenbaum, and Sidney B. Simon. *Clarifying Values Through Subject Matter*. Minneapolis: Winston Press, Inc., 1973.

Leeper, Robert B. (ed.). *Humanizing Education: The Person in the Process*. Washington, D.C.: Association for Supervision and Curriculum Development, NEA, 1967.

Naranjo, Claudio. *The One Quest*. New York: Ballantine Books, 1973.

Van Til, William (ed.). *Curriculum: Quest for Relevance*. Boston: Houghton Mifflin Company, 1974.

Weinstein, Gerald, and Mario D. Fantini. *Toward Humanistic Education*. New York: Praeger Publishers, Inc., 1973.

White, Lloyd W. *Education and the Personal Quest*. Columbus, Ohio: Charles E. Merrill Publishing Company, 1971.

Wilson, L. Craig. *The Open Access Curriculum*. Boston: Allyn and Bacon, Inc., 1972.

The Child

COLONEL FRANCIS W. PARKER

I propose . . . to present a general exposition of the theory of Concentration.

The least that can be said for this theory is that it presents to some extent an outline of a rounded educational doctrine for the study and criticism of teachers.

In the beginning of these discussions, the question of all questions, and indeed the everlasting question, is: what is the being to be educated? What is the child? What is this little lump of flesh, breathing life and singing the song of immortality? The wisdom and philosophy of ages upon ages have asked this question, and still it remains unanswered. It is the central problem of the universe. The child is the climax and culmination of all God's creations, and to answer the question, "What is the child?" is to approach nearer the still greater question, What is the Creator and Giver of Life?

"The Child" is from Col. Francis W. Parker, "The Child", *Talks on Pedagogics: An Outline of the Theory of Concentration*, E. L. Kellog & Co., 1894. Reprinted by Arno Press Inc., 1970.

I can answer the question tentatively. It is a question for you and for me, and for the teachers of the present and the future, to answer; and still it will ever remain the unanswered question. We should study the child, as we study all phenomena, by its actions, and by its tendencies to act. The child is born, we are told by scientists, deaf, dumb, and blind, yet, in design, possessing marvellous possibilities for development. It is well for us to stand by the cradle of a little child who has drawn his first breath, and is ready to be acted upon by the external energies which surround him.

One hypothesis we can accept as true: the inherited organism of bone, muscle and brain determines exactly the limits or boundaries of the baby's development. Each nerve-fibre or convolution of the brain says: "Thus far shalt thou go and no farther;" and it is well to say in the same breath that no human being ever had the external conditions for growth by which the full possibilities, predetermined and fixed by the organism, have been realized. The organism itself determines the external conditions for development. Every muscle, every nerve, every fibre, every convolution of the brain, their nature and power, are in themselves possibilities for the reception of those external energies which act upon the body of the child, and make their way to the brain through the sensorium. The child itself is a central energy, or complex of energies, upon which and through which certain external energies act. No simple energy can enter a child's brain except by first touching the child's body (the end organs), and countless energies touch the child's body which do not enter the brain at all; others enter, but lie below the plane of consciousness.

Forms or waves of light touch the eye and create elementary ideas of color in the brain, but just what colors there shall be in the brain is determined by the passive power and delicacy of the organism itself. Vibrations of air touch and enter the brain through the ear. Strongest and most effective of all is the contact and resistance of the body to objects more dense than waves of air or waves of ether. The great giant sense of touch begins its creative power in the brain at the birth of the child, and even before birth. It is well for us to understand thoroughly that the child, an organic complex of energies, is acted upon and through by external energies, and, whatever matter may be in itself, the mind is conscious of nothing but pure energy, and is primarily developed by external energies which, we infer, act through forms and qualities of matter. Stimuli come from all the surroundings of the child. The products of the stimuli create in the child's mind concepts corresponding to external objects. These concepts are activities in themselves, or phases of differentiated energy. Units of elementary ideas, individual concepts, enable the mind to react upon externality. The child begins to move under the stimulus created by external activities, to smile, to laugh, to stretch out its hands, to see, to hear, to touch, to taste, and to smell.

It is not possible for me to state the exact order of the succession of the arousing to action of the different senses. Our questions here are: What are the spontaneous activities of the child? In other words, what must the child do from the nature of its being, the nature of the stimulus acting through its body and in its mind, and the potentialities of the ego? What are the tendencies of these spontaneous activities? The child's consciousness begins in obscurity, weakness, and vagueness, and still in this very obscurity and vagueness there is great activity. The very few weak and obscure ideas of color and sound and form set the whole being into motion. Before there is any consciousness, before the child has the most obscure feeling of itself, music affects it in a wonderful way. Lullaby songs will soothe it to sleep, changing vague pain into vague pleasure. The whole being is sensitive to the rhythm of music. Not only can it be soothed and lulled to sleep with music, but its first dawning consciousness of life is marked by a smile aroused by a song. The first spiritual breath of external life comes with musical cadences. One of the first sounds that it makes is an imitation of rhythm. What is this marvellous gift that makes the child so sensitive to musical cadence? The whole universe moves in rhythm: the avalanche thunders from the mountain side in deep cadences; the ocean surf roars in musical cadence. The rippling of the brook and the soughing of the breeze in the foliage are the simple music of nature. The little child is the centre of all this rhythm, and the feeling of this rhythm is the truth of the universe whispering its sweet songs to the child's soul.

Perhaps the most marked mental action of the little child is the fanciful creation of new ideas and images. A little vague color and sound, and a few percepts of touch, are sufficient to set the little being into most vigorous action. External objects act upon the child and produce their correspondences, individual concepts, in its mind. As I have already said, these concepts are very vague, obscure, and indistinct. Notwithstanding all this, creation is the moving, central power and delight of the child. The baby creates out of its meagre store of ideas a new world, its own world, in which it lives and moves and has its being. Let us pause a moment, and look at the marvellous meaning of this wonderful power of the child in the creations of fancy. If the little human being were limited to actuality, that is, to the vague reflex of external objects, if it were bound by its own meagre store of so-called facts, it would indeed live in a dark and dismal prison; but it bursts the bands of reality and goes out into a higher world to the invisible life. It lives over again the childhood of the race in the myth. It revels in fanciful forms of its own weak but vivid creations; it spontaneously seeks the invisible.

Next to the cradle song is the cradle story. You know very well how eager a child is for stories that arouse its love for rhythm and excite its fancy. The child most delights in fairy tales, the mythical treasures of the ages. The cruel bonds of stern reality are broken, and it enters a beautiful and invisible world, peopled by creations of its own fancy. If a child were limited in its early stages to the world of reality, if it could not go out into the unknown world, the invisible world, it would lead the life of a brute. The human animal differs from the brute in its faith in an invisible world. The self-created, invisible world, to the child, is the fire-mist heaven; it is the chaos that precedes the spiritual life. Banish myth from the child, and you take away that beauty which is the essence of truth. Parents who forbid the myth because they conceive, forsooth, it is not the truth, limit the child to the baldest materialism, or prepare the way for fancy to run riot to ruin.

What is the myth? The record of the human race is full of myths. Myth comes from the imperfect answer which nature gives to the childish soul of man. The answers are not false, but they are imperfect and partial, and are, to childish souls, the solution of their great problems. Every answer given to a spontaneous and innocent question contains a golden kernel of intrinsic truth. It is that truth which a child can bear in its early years. It cannot grasp precepts and logic, but it can understand the truth, like those who crowded around the Saviour,—in parables. The myth is common to all tribes and nations on the face of the earth. All myths have a wonderful similarity, proving that the human spirit in every stage of growth, and in every clime, and under all environments, has the same strong everlasting tendency upward. Every myth contains a lesson to man. Out of the ignorance of the nature of the child, and from the spirit of dogmatism and bigotry, there has come the falsehood that says the myth does not contain the whole truth, and therefore must be rejected. Who knows the whole truth? Shall the child be robbed of that which delights its soul and lays the foundation of true religious life? No greater mistake can be made in regard to the spontaneous activities of the child, for the myth is the true fire-mist of character, it contains golden symbols that point upward to God and to heaven. The myth is the foundation of faith in the future life, the foundation of all spiritual growth. The fairies and trolls change, as the soul changes, to real folks and real life.

The myth is the beginning of history. The creatures of fancy foreshadow the real people with whom the child must live. It is, indeed, the child seeing through a glass darkly, but that obscurity of truth and tendency towards it are absolutely essential to its growth. Myth, I say, is the beginning of history. The myths presented to the child should contain in themselves the guiding stars of life and immortality.

The myth is the beginning of science. The human race began, we are told, with a firm belief that every object in the universe was animated, life-like, human-like. This was the childish study of science, but it sustained a great truth. The stone and the mountain are not organisms for life, it is true, but there breathes through them an irresistible energy, which comes from the Giver of all Life. The myth of the early ages points towards the marvellous revelations of the scientific truth of the present. The myth is an imperfect and partial apprehension of truth. The myth clears away under the steady light of the ever-moving mind; it is essential to the weak state of the child. "The night veileth the morning."

Just as the human race arose in its development from the myths of antiquity, so the child must rise from the myths of childhood. The lack of ideality, the failure in spiritual growth, in true religious life, are caused more by the failure of the parents to recognize the true nature of the child and his inborn love for myth than any other cause whatever. The rankest materialism in its worst form has never struck harder blows at true spiritual life than the ignorance of misguided parents, who keep their child from fairy life and fairy land. Fairy land is over the border of the present, into the future, and the truest tendency of the human life is to live in the ideal of the future, to reach forward towards the invisible and the unknown. Slowly the human beings have arisen—guided by a glimmering light—and have climbed spiritually from the earth and the clod, from the shrub and tree up the broad walls of the arched sky, to stars, and moon, and sun, and then beyond the sun, for the divinity seeking and striving imagination stretches away to the invisible, all-powerful, all-controlling, all-loving, One who permeates the universe, lives in it, and breathes His life through it, the eternal life to be taken into the human soul. The myth is the obscure image, in the child's soul, of God Himself. There are many parents who shudder at the myth of Santa Claus, an invisible being that brings the child gifts; but that invisible being, to the child's weak apprehension, is the foreshadowing of the All-Giver, the forerunner of the One who came to man on the blessed Christmas night. No rough voice and no ignorant soul should ever tell the little child that Santa Claus does not exist, for Santa Claus is the foreshadowing of the All-Giver, All-Lover, and One who gives because He loves.

It is impossible to take a child into history, science, ethics, and religion without the continued exercise of these spontaneous fanciful tendencies. You may reply that a child may live in myth and fancy all its life. I admit that this is possible. Many people do live in myth all their lives just because myth is not put into the crucible of highest reason; just because the conditions are not presented for myth to change to history, to science, to ethics, and to religion. This is no proof that the strongest spontaneous tendency of the child is wrong; it is only a proof of neglect to build upon it. I think we can take it for granted that, as God, the loving Creator of the child, made the child His highest creation, He put into that child Himself, His divinity, and that this divinity manifests itself in the seeking for truth through the visible and tangible.

The child is brought into direct contact with its mother, its father, and the whole family, and who will dare to say that the child is not, above all, a student of human nature? Who will say that its eyes, when they touch one's face, cannot read the soul better than older people? The child looks at you with the innocence and purity of childhood, and no hypocrisy, no dissimulation, though it may veil the truth from older eyes, can keep it from the little ones. It studies the relation of being to being, father to mother, parents to children. It may be that I use too strong a word when I say it "studies," but still it is something very like study. The study of family life is the child's beginning of the study of anthropology and of history. The child is not only a student of individual life, but of community life, the life of the family, the life of the neighbors, of the children he meets at play, in the house, in the yard, in the street; and the measure of the child's judgment of community life is the measure in its after study of history. It may study history in school or the university, but in all life the judgments formed at home, in the nursery, in the parlor, in the kitchen, in the street, are the strongest, ever-enduring measures in all his after-judgments of the record of the human life taught by experience and in history. Every human being with whom he comes in contact is a new study to him. The looks, the manners, the dress, the attitude, and the facial expression lead him to make his childish inferences. Then comes the kindergarten and the school, the first step in a broader community life than that which home furnishes. Here, the study, not only of history, but of civics, begins. The true foundation of civics is community life. The child's home measure of life, the government of his home, give him democratic, monarchical, or socialistic principles. Whatever the rule of the home or school may be, that rule is ever afterwards either loved or hated by the child. Thus the child spontaneously begins the study of anthropology, ethnology, and history, and in these studies he has a profound, abiding interest, in these studies he forms habits of judgment which to a great extent are fixed and permanent.

It needs no argument to prove that the child studies or, at least, is exceedingly interested in zoology. Few beings, except, perhaps, the father and mother, can interest a child more deeply than the brute life which surrounds him. The cat is "a thing of beauty and a joy forever"; the dog is its particular friend. It stretches out its little hands before it can speak, and its first utterances follow the attempts of its original ancestors in imitating the voice of the dog. The child delights in birds, butterflies, and bees. Place any moving, living thing before the child, and it moves towards it with an excited interest. It wants to touch it, to stroke it, to know more about it. Endowed with the original idea of animism, it no doubt believes every brute that it sees to have a mind like its own. It will imitate the dog, the cat, and the birds, and will talk to them as to its own companions. He studies zoology in that he becomes acquainted with the animals he meets: every insect, every animal, wild or tame, the grasshopper, the locust, bugs that scurry away when he lifts a stone, the fish-worms which he digs for bait, are objects of intense interest. He knows the difference between the white grub and the common earthworm. The animals in the woods are his friends. The birds, their habits, their nests, their little ones, and their songs fill him with joy. He can take a lesson from the timid partridge, who is ever ready to give her life for her children. He knows the sly habits of the crows, studies the psychology of their reasoning. The horses, and oxen, and sheep are all his friends. What farm-boy has not cried over the loss of a favorite sheep, taken away by the cruel butcher?

The child has a great love for vegetable life. There never was a child that lived who did not worship flowers, reach out for them, desire to hold them in its hands, gaze at them, and smell them. Of course, the spontaneous activities of the child are governed to a great degree by its environment. Take a little boy with the environment of a farm,—such an instance comes to me,—a boy upon a rocky farm in New England. He studies spontaneously his entire environment. It is safe to say that he knows every plant upon the farm, every kind of grass, every weed. He comes in direct contact with worm-wood, sorrel, rag-weed. He can tell all the the kinds of grass from the graceful silver grass to the stately timothy. He knows the mosses and lichens that cling to the rocks and carpet the marshy land. He knows the shrubs and bushes; the huckleberry-bush is his delight. The strawberry in the rich meadow he watches from blossom to fruit with a keen sense of the joy which is to follow. Every tree he knows—the magnificent pine, the stately maple, the spreading chestnut in the pasture. He can tell you the shape of the tree; its trunk, its foliage: its fruit he spontaneously classifies. Thus, every child is an earnest, indefatigable lover of botany. In his future life, the farm-boy carries his botany of the farm with him wherever he goes. He compares all other plants and classifies them according to the spontaneous classifications made on the farm. He says: "This was on the old farm; this was not." "This is something new." "This is like something I've seen before." "This bush is like the lilac; this rose is like the rose in the old garden."

Not only is the boy on the farm a student of life, but he extends his study to the forces of earth, and air, and water. The earth touches him, heaven bends down to him and asks him questions. The clouds he knows, from the rounded thunderhead to the mackerel sky. He knows also the winds; he can foretell the weather. He looks with intense joy to the next rainy day; that will bring him rest, or, something better, fishing. He watches the sun with a deep interest. It will be a very stupid boy who cannot tell exactly the noon hour by the sun, aided by that internal monitor, his stomach. Winds, clouds, air, and heat, everything that influences vegetation, come within the mental range of the farm-boy.

Mineralogy, especially upon a rocky farm, comes very close to the boy in clearing the ground, in picking stones, in building stone walls, in quarrying ledges. Watch a crowd of children upon the beach gathering pebbles and curious stones. They are interested in the color and form of the pebbles, and may be made exceedingly interested in the origin of the different forms, if some kind, observant friend is there to continue the questions which the stones themselves ask. Children naturally take to playing in the dirt as ducks to water. The different kinds of soils attract their attention—sand, gravel, and clay. They never tire of playing in the sand, or expressing crude fancies by modelling in the clay. The changes which natural forces bring about on the earth's surface are of deep interest to children, especially the changes brought about by running water, after a rain, or the wind swirling the sand into piles. They never tire of damming up a temporary stream or changing its current, and of watching its effects when it spreads out silt, or the cuts it makes in the soft earth. The brooks and rivers are never-ceasing sources of delight to children; they watch them at flood-time, when the water spreads out over the meadows; they notice the caving in of banks, the carrying of earth by water and its deposition on the shelving shores.

Real geography, or the appearance of the earth's surface, is a subject of intense, though unconscious, interest on the part of the child. Let a boy hunt stray cows or sheep over a large farm; he soon learns to know every crook, every turn and corner in the whole farm, every hiding-place. He knows the hills, valleys, springs, and meadows. Of all the mental pictures that remain vivid through life and are recalled with ever-renewed pleasure, are the pictures of the country surrounding the birthplace, or the house in which we lived when children. The house itself, the fireplace, paper on the wall, furniture,—everything is distinct in our minds when other pictures fade or are blurred by time. The country round about, every hillock, every depression, brook, and rivulet are never-fading images in the brain.

To sum up, the subjects of the child's spontaneous study and persistent interest include all the central subjects of study— geography, geology, mineralogy, botany, zoology, anthropology, etc. In fact, the child begins every subject spontaneously and unconsciously. He must begin these subjects, because he lives, and because his environment acts upon him and educates him. Of course, the difference in environment makes a great difference in the child's mental action, the child's individual concepts; still, in all children there are the same spontaneous tendencies. The boy, for instance, on a farm may have a large range of vegetation to study, and the poor little child in the dark city may worship with his whole soul some potted plant and from it draw lessons of inspiration and love. The child studies the clouds, the sky, the stars, the earth, vegetation, animal life, history, every hour of the day. To be sure, he may have more interest in one subject than another, but to him all these subjects are related one to the other, as the cloud is related to rain, and the rain is related to vegetation and soil. It is the tendency of pedantry to search in the far distance for facts and mysteries, but the truth is that the marvellous is close to us, that miracles are of the most common occurrence.

I wish to call your attention to the wonderful powers acquired by the child in the first three years of its life, and the wonderful persistence there is in such acquirement. Take, for instance, the art of locomotion, the creeping and walking. Watch the face of the child standing for the first time upon its little legs, attracted by the outstretched arms of its mother, who stands across the room; look at the mingled courage and fear in the baby's face. He has a great ambition to move, as he has seen others move, upon his two feet. He stretches out his arms, he fears, he takes courage, he moves one foot and is successful, and then the other; he looks at his mother's encouraging smile, takes another step, and then another, until the great feat of walking across the room is accomplished. From the time he first stands upon his feet to the time he runs around with perfect unconsciousness of his power of movement, there takes place a succession of experiments, of trials, and of failures and successes, all guided and controlled by his desire to walk.

More wonderful than learning to walk is the learning to hear language and to talk. In the beginning the child creates his own language of gesture by means of his own body. He hears language, words that are in themselves complex. Oral words act upon his consciousness and are associated by a fixed and everlasting law of the mind. Idioms are acquired by hearing and association, and with it all comes an intense desire to express thought. With his voice he creates at first his own language, which consists of crudely articulate sounds, and then follows the acquisition of the vernacular which he hears. It is well for us to consider carefully the processes of learning to talk. The child must learn to hear first; that is, the words must act upon consciousness and their correspondences must be associated with the appropriate activities in consciousness. The idioms must act in the same way and be associated with their appropriate activities or relations of ideas. Then follows the making of oral words. He learns enunciation, or the utterance of single sounds. He learns articulation, or the unity of sounds in words. He learns accent, pronunciation, and syntax, all by hearing language and under the one controlling motive of expressing his own thought. He begins, it is true, with crude utterances, but these utterances are to him the best possible expression of his thought. He learns any language and every language that he hears. If we could understand the psychological mechanical processes by which a child learns his own vernacular from the first step of hearing to the last step by which the sentence is in his power, we should understand the whole theory of learning any language. Those who have tried to speak a foreign language will readily understand something of the struggle the child goes through in order to master one single phonic element. You see that he does all this unconsciously, that all these efforts are natural and to a great degree automatic. He never for a moment thinks of a single sound by itself unless that sound is a whole word. He knows nothing at all of the complex elements of a language, nothing of slow pronunciation, nothing of syntax, still he masters the language by a natural process. This word natural is variously interpreted. It is exceedingly ambiguous, almost as ambiguous as the word "abstract." Still I believe that we can find a scientific definition of the word natural. If the word natural means anything, it means strict conformity to God's laws. That is, a child learns every oral word by the same law under which every oral or written word in any and every language must be learned. The child does not know the law, but he obeys the law by instinct. If the child makes these marvellous acquisitions naturally, in conformity to law, why not have him continue that conformity to law in all his after-acquisitions?

Learning to write is far easier in itself, if we follow the law, than learning to hear language or learning to speak. The great lesson to teachers is, find the law, follow the law; give the child conditions in learning to write like those he has had in learning to speak. Indeed, the conditions can be made far better, for learning to speak is left very much to accident and to desultory instruction, while learning to write may be under the most careful guidance.

It goes without saying that the child is a student of form and color. Everything that enters his brain, as I have already said, must touch the end-organs, and these attributes or objects which touch the end-organs are forms of matter. Froebel who had such divine insight, understood the great value of the tactual sense. Color is representative in its power. It brings into consciousness the correspondences to forms of external objects.

Not only does the child study form, but he makes intuitively a systematic preparation for the study of number. The child begins with no idea of distance. He grasps for the moon with the same confidence as he does for an object near at hand. The ideas of distance, size, weight, are preparations for number. The child first learns to measure by constantly reaching out his hands, creeping and walking, and after that it measures distance by sight. Not only does it begin to measure and estimate distances, but it judges area and bulk, and compares different sizes, areas, weights, and bulks. The study of weight to him also has its charms, the difference of pressure upon his hand, his own weight in the effort of other children to lift him. He measures force and time in the same unconscious way, the time of sleeping, the time between a promised pleasure and its anticipated realization, and soon he learns to look at the clock to help him out in his judgment. He estimates very carefully the value of a cent and a stick of candy. All these spontaneous activities are in the direction of number study, are mingled with all his activities and are absolutely necessary to his mental and physical action. It is true these measures are very inadequate and imperfect, but they are the beginnings of the power of accurate measuring, that mode of judgment which will end, if he continues to have the right conditions, in exact measuring and weighing, and in accurate knowledge of values.

There is at first a perfect unity of thought and action. Hear the voice and watch the movements of a little child! No dancing teacher, no teacher of elocution, no actor, can ever successfully imitate the voice of the child, or the perfectly unconscious beauty and grace of its movements. Indeed it is the highest aim of artists in acting and elocution to acquire the unconscious grace and power of a child. Listen to the voice of the child,—melodious, harmonious, perfect in emphasis, it is the immediate pulsations of his soul, the instantaneous reflex of his consciousness, with unconsciousness of his body, his organs of expression, his forms of speech. The child, until education intervenes, is a unit of action and expression, and that unity is ac-

quired and maintained by action under a motive with no overpowering consciousness of the means or forms of expression. Must that
beautiful unity be broken? Can it be perpetuated and strengthened?

There never was such a thing as a lazy child born on earth.
Childhood is full of activities of every kind, stimulated by external
energies and shaped by internal power. The child experiments continually until it gains its ends. It will reach hundreds of times for an
object, and at last succeed. What modes of expression, excepting
speech, does a child acquire in the first years of its life? I should say
that all children love music, though there is a vast difference in individual organisms in this as in all other modes of expression. Most
children strive to imitate that which they hear in rhythm. Making, or
manual work, is really the natural element of the child. I think I can
say, without fear of dispute, that a child tries to make everything that
he sees made. The little girl wishes to use the scissors, needle and
thread. In the kitchen, unless repressed by the mother, she makes
cakes and bread. In fact, the whole round of housekeeping in the
beginning furnishes countless objects for activity and a desire to imitate. Boys in the shop, or on the farm, strive to do what they see
done. They harness each other in teams, they drive the dog and the
goat, they make mill-wheels and dams. The tendency to imitate, the
desire to make the objects they see made, is intensely strong in every
child.

Every child has the artist element born in him; he loves to
model objects out of sand and clay. Paint is a perfect delight to children, bright colors charm them. Give the child a paint-brush, and
though his expression of thought will be exceedingly crude, it will
be very satisfactory to him; he will paint any object with the greatest
confidence. It is very interesting to watch the crowd of little children
near Lake Chautauqua, as busy as bees and as happy as angels. Let
us look at the forms the children make out of the pliable sand. Here
are caves where the fairies dwell, mountains, volcanoes, houses
where the giants live. All these fantastic forms spring from the brain
of the child and are expressed by means of this plastic material. See
that little three-year-old girl with the model of a house in her brain:
she is now wheeling a wheelbarrow, assisted by a little companion;
in the barrow is the wood, and in her brain is the house. Energetic,
persistent, happy,—in what direction? In the direction of true
growth! The little girl in the kitchen is not happy until she can
mould and change the flour into dough, and dough into forms for
baking; and here begin her first lessons in chemistry, the wonderful
changes which heat brings about. She will dress her doll, working
patiently for hours. Inexpert beholders may not know what the crude
forms mean, but the child knows and is satisfied,—nay, delighted.

Give a child a piece of chalk, and its fancy runs riot: people, horses, houses, sheep, trees, birds, spring up in the brave confidence of childhood. In fact, all the modes of expression are spontaneously and persistently exercised by the child from the beginning except writing. It sings, it makes, it moulds, it paints, it draws, it expresses thought in all the forms of thought expression, with the one exception.

I have very imperfectly presented, in this brief outline, some of the spontaneous activities of the little child. The more I strive to present them, the more imperfect seems the result, so much lies beyond in the interpretation of the child's instinctive activities, so much seem to exceed all present discovery. The question, my fellow-teachers, is, what should these lessons teach us? The child instinctively begins all subjects known in the curriculum of the university. He begins them because he cannot help it; his very nature impels him. These tendencies, these spontaneous activities of the child spring from the depths of its being, spring from all the past, for the child is the fruit of all the past, and the seed of all the future. These quiet, persistent, powerful tendencies we must examine and continue with the greatest care. The child overcomes great obstacles by persistent energy, always acting with great confidence of himself and his powers. He overcomes these obstacles because his whole being is a unit of action, controlled by one motive. The spontaneous tendencies of the child are the records of inborn divinity; we are here, my fellow-teachers, for one purpose, and that purpose is to understand these tendencies and continue them in all these directions, following nature. First of all, we should recognize the great dignity of the child, the child's divine power and divine possibilities, and then we are to present the conditions for their complete outworking. We are here that the child may take one step higher; we are here to find and present the conditions adapted to the divine nature of the child.

I have tried to show that the whole round of knowledge is begun by the child, and begun because it breathes, because it lives. If the child loves science and history, and studies or attends to them instinctively, then he should go on, and we must know the conditions or subjects and means which should be presented to him for each new demand or need.

I grant that in the past of education attention has been directed too much to dead forms of thought, and for one good reason at least: the sciences are a modern creation of man and have not yet reached the child. Now we have these marvellous subjects presented to us, worked out by great thinkers of the present, and we are to choose whether we will continue the dead formalism that too often leads to pedantry and bigotry, or whether we are to lead the child's soul in that direction which God designed in His creation of the human being.

In conclusion I commend to you, in the words of our greatest American philosopher [Ralph Waldo Emerson, although he is generally considered an essayist rather than a philosopher, ed.]:

> A babe by its mother lies, bathed in joy;
> Glide the hours uncounted; the sun is its toy;
> Shines the peace of all being without cloud in its eyes,
> And the sum of the world in soft miniature lies.

I commend to you the "sum of the world" for your study, for in this direction lies all the future progress of humanity.

The Child and the Curriculum

JOHN DEWEY

Profound differences in theory are never gratuitous or invented. They grow out of conflicting elements in a genuine problem—a problem which is genuine just because the elements, taken as they stand, are conflicting. Any significant problem involves conditions that for the moment contradict each other. Solution comes only by getting away from the meaning of terms that is already fixed upon and coming to see the conditions from another point of view, and hence in a fresh light. But this reconstruction means travail of thought. Easier than thinking with surrender of already formed ideas and detachment from facts already learned is just to stick by what is already said, looking about for something with which to buttress it against attack.

Thus sects arise: schools of opinion. Each selects that set of conditions that appeals to it; and then erects them into a complete and independent truth, instead of treating them as a factor in a problem, needing adjustment.

The fundamental factors in the educative process are an immature, undeveloped being; and certain social aims, meanings, values incarnate in the matured experience of the adult. The educative process is the due interaction of these forces. Such a conception of each in relation to the other as facilitates completest and freest interaction is the essence of educational theory.

But here comes the effort of thought. It is easier to see the conditions in their separateness, to insist upon one at the expense of the other, to make antagonists of them, than to discover a reality to which each belongs. The easy thing is to seize upon something in the nature of the child, or upon something in the developed consciousness of the adult, and insist upon *that* as the key to the whole problem. When this happens a really serious practical problem—that of interaction—is transformed into an unreal, and hence insoluble, theoretic problem. Instead of seeing the educative steadily and as a whole, we see conflicting terms. We get the case of the child *vs.* the curriculum; of the individual nature *vs.* social culture. Below all other divisions in pedagogic opinion lies this opposition.

The child lives in a somewhat narrow world of personal contacts. Things hardly come within his experience unless they touch, intimately and obviously, his own well-being, or that of his family and friends. His world is a world of persons with their personal interests, rather than a realm of facts and laws. Not truth, in the sense of conformity to external fact, but affection and sympathy, is its keynote. As against this, the course of study met in the school presents material stretching back indefinitely in time, and extending outward indefinitely into space. The child is taken out of his familiar physical environment, hardly more than a square mile or so in area, into the wide world—yes, and even to the bounds of the solar system. His little span of personal memory and tradition is overlaid with the long centuries of the history of all peoples.

Again, the child's life is an integral, a total one. He passes quickly and readily from one topic to another, as from one spot to another, but is not conscious of transition or break. There is no conscious isolation, hardly conscious distinction. The things that occupy him are held together by the unity of the personal and social interests which his life carries along. Whatever is uppermost in his mind constitutes to him, for the time being, the whole universe. That universe is fluid and fluent; its contents dissolve and re-form with amazing rapidity. But, after all, it is the child's own world. It has the unity and completeness of his own life. He goes to school, and various studies divide and fractionize the world for him. Geography selects, it abstracts and analyzes one set of facts, and from one particular point of view. Arithmetic is another division, grammar another department, and so on indefinitely.

Again, in school each of these subjects is classified. Facts are torn away from their original place in experience and rearranged with reference to some general principle. Classification is not a matter of child experience; things do not come to the individual pigeonholed. The vital ties of affection, the connecting bonds of activity, hold together the variety of his personal experiences. The adult mind is so familiar with the notion of logically ordered facts that it does not recognize—it cannot realize—the amount of separating and reformu-

lating which the facts of direct experience have to undergo before
they can appear as a "study," or branch lf learning. A principle, for
the intellect, has had to be distinguished and defined; facts have had
to be interpreted in relation to this principle, not as they are in themselves. They have had to be regathered about a new center which is
wholly abstract and ideal. All this means a development of a special
intellectual interest. It means ability to view facts impartially and objectively; that is, without reference to their place and meaning in
one's own experience. It means capacity to analyze and to synthesize. It means highly matured intellectual habits and the command of
a definite technique and apparatus of scientific inquiry. The studies
as classified are the product, in a word, of the science of the ages, not
of the experience of the child.

These apparent deviations and differences between child and
curriculum might be almost indefinitely widened. But we have here
sufficiently fundamental divergences: first, the narrow but personal
world of the child against the impersonal but infinitely extended
world of space and time; second, the unity, the single whole-
heartedness of the child's life, and the specializations and divisions
of the curriculum; third, an abstract principle of logical classification
and arrangement, and the practical and emotional bonds of child life.

From these elements of conflict grow up different educational
sects. One school fixes its attention upon the importance of the subject-matter of the curriculum as compared with the contents of the
child's own experience. It is as if they said: Is life petty, narrow, and
crude? Then studies reveal the great, wide universe with all its
fulness and complexity of meaning. Is the life of the child egoistic,
self-centered, impulsive? Then in these studies is found an objective
universe of truth, law, and order. Is his experience confused, vague,
uncertain, at the mercy of the moment's caprice and circumstance?
Then studies introduce a world arranged on the basis of eternal and
general truth; a world where all is measured and defined. Hence the
moral: ignore and minimize the child's individual peculiarities,
whims, and experiences. They are what we need to get away from.
They are to be obscured or eliminated. As educators our work is
precisely to substitute for these superficial and casual affairs stable
and well-ordered realities; and these are found in studies and lessons.

Subdivide each topic into studies; each study into lessons; each
lesson into specific facts and formulae. Let the child proceed step by
step to master each one of these separate parts, and at last he will
have covered the entire ground. The road which looks so long when
viewed in its entirety is easily traveled, considered as a series of particular steps. Thus emphasis is put upon the logical subdivisions and
consecutions of the subject-matter. Problems of instruction are prob-

lems of procuring texts giving logical parts and sequences, and of presenting these portions in class in a similar definite and graded way. Subject-matter furnishes the end, and it determines method. The child is simply the immature being who is to be matured; he is the superficial being who is to be deepened; his is narrow experience which is to be widened. It is his to receive, to accept. His part is fulfilled when he is ductile and docile.

Not so, says the other sect. The child is the starting-point, the center, and the end. His development, his growth, is the ideal. It alone furnishes the standard. To the growth of the child all studies are subservient; they are instruments valued as they serve the needs of growth. Personality, character, is more than subject-matter. Not knowledge or information, but self-realization, is the goal. To possess all the world of knowledge and lose one's own self is as awful a fate in education as in religion. Moreover, subject-matter never can be got into the child from without. Learning is active. It involves reaching out of the mind. It involves organic assimilation starting from within. Literally, we must take our stand with the child and our departure from him. It is he and not the subject-matter which determines both quality and quantity of learning.

The only significant method is the method of the mind as it reaches out and assimilates. Subject-matter is but spiritual food, possible nutritive material. It cannot digest itself; it cannot of its own accord turn into bone and muscle and blood. The source of whatever is dead, mechanical, and formal in schools is found precisely in the subordination of the life and experience of the child to the curriculum. It is because of this that "study" has become a synonym for what is irksome, and a lesson identical with a task.

This fundamental opposition of child and curriculum set up by these two modes of doctrine can be duplicated in a series of other terms. "Discipline" is the watchword of those who magnify the course of study; "interest" that of those who blazon "The Child" upon their banner. The standpoint of the former is logical; that of the latter psychological. The first emphasizes the necessity of adequate training and scholarship on the part of the teacher; the latter that of need of sympathy with the child, and knowledge of his natural instincts. "Guidance and control" are the catchwords of one school; "freedom and initiative" of the other. Law is asserted here; spontaneity proclaimed there. The old, the conservation of what has been achieved in the pain and toil of the ages, is dear to the one; the new, change, progress, wins the affection of the other. Inertness and routine, chaos and anarchism, are accusations bandied back and forth. Neglect of the sacred authority of duty is charged by one side, only to be met by counter-charges of suppression of individuality through tyrannical despotism.

Such oppositions are rarely carried to their logical conclusion. Common-sense recoils at the extreme character of these results. They are left to theorists, while common-sense vibrates back and forward in a maze of inconsistent compromise. The need of getting theory and practical common-sense into closer connection suggests a return to our original thesis: that we have here conditions which are necessarily related to each other in the educative process, since this is precisely one of interaction and adjustment.

What, then, is the problem? It is just to get rid of the prejudicial notion that there is some gap in kind (as distinct from degree) between the child's experience and the various forms of subject-matter that make up the course of study. From the side of the child, it is a question of seeing how his experience already contains within itself elements—facts and truths—of just the same sort as those entering into the formulated study; and, what is of more importance, of how it contains within itself the attitudes, the motives, and the interests which have operated in developing and organizing the subject-matter to the plane which it now occupies. From the side of the studies, it is a question of interpreting them as outgrowths of forces operating in the child's life, and of discovering the steps that intervene between the child's present experience and their richer maturity.

Abandon the notion of subject-matter as something fixed and ready-made in itself, outside the child's experience; cease thinking of the child's experience as also something hard and fast; see it as something fluent, embryonic, vital; and we realize that the child and the curriculum are simply two limits which define a single process. Just as two points define a straight line, so the present standpoint of the child and the facts and truths of studies define instruction. It is continuous reconstruction, moving from the child's present experience out into that represented by the organized bodies of truth that we call studies.

Physical and Social Studies: Naturalism and Humanism

JOHN DEWEY

Allusion has already been made to the conflict of natural science with literary studies for a place in the curriculum. The solution thus far reached consists essentially in a somewhat mechanical compromise whereby the field is divided between studies having nature and studies having man as their theme. The situation thus presents us with another instance of the external adjustment of educational values, and focuses attention upon the philosophy of the connection of nature with human affairs. In general, it may be said that the educational division finds a reflection in the dualistic philosophies. Mind and the world are regarded as two independent realms of existence having certain points of contact with each other. From this point of view it is natural that each sphere of existence should have its own separate group of studies connected with it; it is even natural that the growth of scientific studies should be viewed with suspicion as marking a tendency of materialistic philosophy to encroach upon the domain of spirit. Any theory of education which contemplates a more unified scheme of education than now exists is under the necessity of facing the question of the relation of man to nature.

1. THE HISTORIC BACKGROUND OF HUMANISTIC STUDY. It is noteworthy that classic Greek philosophy does not present the problem in its modern form. Socrates indeed appears to have thought that science of nature was not attainable and not very important. The chief thing to know is the nature and end of man. Upon that knowledge hangs all that is of deep significance—all moral and social achievement. Plato, however, makes right knowledge of man and society depend upon knowledge of the essential features of nature. His chief treatise, entitled the Republic, is at once a treatise on morals, on social organization, and on the metaphysics and science of nature. Since he accepts the Socratic doctrine that right achievement in the former depends upon rational knowledge, he is compelled to discuss the nature of knowledge. Since he accepts the idea that the ultimate object of knowledge is the discovery of the good or end of man, and is discontented with the Socratic conviction that all we know is our own ignorance, he connects the discussion of the good of man with consideration of the essential good or end of nature itself. To attempt to determine the end of man apart from a knowledge of the ruling end which gives law and unity to nature is impossible. It is thus quite consistent with his philosophy that he subordinates literary studies (under the name of music) to mathematics and to physics as well as to logic and metaphysics. But on the other hand, knowledge of nature is not an end in itself; it is a necessary stage in bringing the mind to a realization of the supreme purpose of existence as the law of human action, corporate and individual. To use the modern phraseology, naturalistic studies are indispensable, but they are in the interests of humanistic and ideal ends.

Aristotle goes even farther, if anything, in the direction of naturalistic studies. He subordinates civic relations to the purely cognitive life. The highest end of man is not human but divine—participation in pure knowing which constitutes the divine life. Such knowing deals with what is universal and necessary, and finds, therefore, a more adequate subject matter in nature at its best than in the transient things of man. If we take what the philosophers stood for in Greek life, rather than the details of what they say, we might summarize by saying that the Greeks were too much interested in free inquiry into natural fact and in the aesthetic enjoyment of nature, and were too deeply conscious of the extent in which society is rooted in nature and subject to its laws, to think of bringing man and nature into conflict. Two factors conspire in the later period of ancient life, however, to exalt literary and humanistic studies. One is the increasingly reminiscent and borrowed character of culture; the other is the political and rhetorical bent of Roman life.

Greek achievement in civilization was native; the civilization of the Alexandrians and Romans was inherited from alien sources. Consequently it looked back to the records upon which it drew, instead of looking out directly upon nature and society, for material and inspiration. We cannot do better than quote the words of Hatch to indicate the consequences for educational theory and practice. "Greece on one hand had lost political power, and on the other possessed in her splendid literature an inalienable heritage. . . . It was natural that she should turn to letters. It was natural also that the study of letters should be reflected upon speech. . . . The mass of men in the Greek world tended to lay stress on that acquaintance with the literature of bygone generations, and that habit of cultivated speech, which has ever since been commonly spoken of as education. . . . Our own comes by direct tradition from it. It set a fashion which until recently has uniformly prevailed over the entire civilized world. We study literature rather than nature because the Greeks did so, and because when the Romans and the Roman provincials resolved to educate their sons, they employed Greek teachers and followed in Greek paths." [1]

The so-called practical bent of the Romans worked in the same direction. In falling back upon the recorded ideas of the Greeks, they not only took the short path to attaining a cultural development, but they procured just the kind of material and method suited to their administrative talents. For their practical genius was not directed to the conquest and control of nature but to the conquest and control of men.

Mr. Hatch, in the passage quoted, takes a good deal of history for granted in saying that we have studied literature rather than nature

[1] Edwin Hatch, *The Influence of Greek Ideas and Usages upon the Christian Church*, pp. 43–44.

because the Greeks, and the Romans whom they taught, did so. What is the link that spans the intervening centuries? The question suggests that barbarian Europe but repeated on a larger scale and with increased intensity the Roman situation. It had to go to school to Greco-Roman civilization; it also borrowed rather than evolved its culture. Not merely for its general ideas and their artistic presentation but for its models of laws it went to the records of alien peoples. And its dependence upon tradition was increased by the dominant theological interests of the period. For the authorities to which the Church appealed were literatures composed in foreign tongues. Everything converged to identify learning with linguistic training and to make the language of the learned a literary language instead of the mother speech.

The full scope of this fact escapes us, moreover, until we recognize that this subject matter compelled recourse to a *dialectical* method. Scholasticism frequently has been used since the time of the revival of learning as a term of reproach. But all that it means is the method of The Schools, or of the School Men. In its essence, it is nothing but a highly effective systematization of the methods of teaching and learning which are appropriate to transmit an authoritative body of truths. Where literature rather than contemporary nature and society furnishes material of study, methods must be adapted to defining, expounding, and interpreting the received material, rather than to inquiry, discovery, and invention. And at bottom what is called Scholasticism is the whole-hearted and consistent formulation and application of the methods which are suited to instruction when the material of instruction is taken ready-made, rather than as something which students are to find out for themselves. So far as schools still teach from textbooks and rely upon the principle of authority and acquisition rather than upon that of discovery and inquiry, their methods are Scholastic—minus the logical accuracy and system of Scholasticism at its best. Aside from laxity of method and statement, the only difference is that geographies and histories and botanies and astronomies are now part of the authoritative literature which is to be mastered.

As a consequence, the Greek tradition was lost in which a humanistic interest was used as a basis of interest in nature, and a knowledge of nature used to support the distinctively human aims of man. Life found its support in authority, not in nature. The latter was moreover an object of considerable suspicion. Contemplation of it was dangerous, for it tended to draw man away from reliance upon the documents in which the rules of living were already contained. Moreover nature could be known only through observation; it appealed to the senses—which were merely material as opposed to a purely immaterial mind. Furthermore, the utilities of a knowledge of nature were purely physical and secular; they connected with the bodily and temporal welfare of man, while the literary tradition concerned his spiritual and eternal well-being.

2. THE MODERN SCIENTIFIC INTEREST IN NATURE. The movement of the fifteenth century which is variously termed the revival of learning and the renascence was characterized by a new interest in man's present life, and accordingly by a new interest in his relationships with nature. It was naturalistic, in the sense that it turned against the dominant supernaturalistic interest. It is possible that the influence of a return to classic Greek pagan literature in bringing about this changed mind has been overestimated. Undoubtedly the change was mainly a product of contemporary conditions. But there can be no doubt that educated men, filled with the new point of view, turned eagerly to Greek literature for congenial sustenance and reënforcement. And to a considerable extent, this interest in Greek thought was not in literature for its own sake, but in the spirit it expressed. The mental freedom, the sense of the order and beauty of nature, which animated Greek expression, aroused men to think and observe in a similar untrammeled fashion. The history of science in the sixteenth century shows that the dawning sciences of physical nature largely borrowed their points of departure from the new interest in Greek literature. As Windelband [2] has said, the new science of nature was the daughter of humanism. The favorite notion of the time was that man was in microcosm that which the universe was in macrocosm.

This fact raises anew the question of how it was that nature and man were later separated and a sharp division made between language and literature and the physical sciences. Four reasons may be suggested. (a) The old tradition was firmly intrenched in institutions. Politics, law, and diplomacy remained of necessity branches of authoritative literature, for the social sciences did not develop until the methods of the sciences of physics and chemistry, to say nothing of biology, were much further advanced. The same is largely true of history. Moreover, the methods used for effective teaching of the languages were well developed; the inertia of academic custom was on their side. Just as the new interest in literature, especially Greek, had not been allowed at first to find lodgment in the scholastically organized universities, so when it found its way into them it joined hands with the older learning to minimize the influence of experi-

---

[2] Wilhelm Windelband, 1848–1915, was a German philosopher. He was interested more in the cultural and historical problems of philosophy, as opposed to strictly scientific ones. Editor.]

mental science. The men who taught were rarely trained in science; the men who were scientifically competent worked in private laboratories and through the medium of academies which promoted research, but which were not organized as teaching bodies. Finally, the aristocratic tradition which looked down upon material things and upon the senses and the hands was still mighty.

(b) The protestant revolt brought with it an immense increase of interest in theological discussion and controversies. The appeal on both sides was to literary documents. Each side had to train men in ability to study and expound the records which were relied upon. The demand for training men who could defend the chosen faith against the other side, who were able to propagandize and to prevent the encroachments of the other side, was such that it is not too much to say that by the middle of the seventeenth century the linguistic training of gymnasia and universities had been captured by the revived theological interest, and used as a tool of religious education and ecclesiastical controversy. Thus the educational descent of the languages as they are found in education to-day is not direct from the revival of learning, but from its adaptation to theological ends.

(c) The natural sciences were themselves conceived in a way which sharpened the opposition of man and nature. Francis Bacon presents an almost perfect example of the union of naturalistic and humanistic interest. Science, adopting the methods of observation and experimentation, was to give up the attempt to "anticipate" nature—to impose preconceived notions upon her—and was to become her humble interpreter. In obeying nature intellectually, man would learn to command her practically. "Knowledge is power." This aphorism meant that through science man is to control nature and turn her energies to the execution of his own ends. Bacon attacked the old learning and logic as purely controversial, having to do with victory in argument, not with discovery of the unknown. Through the new method of thought which was set forth in his new logic an era of expansive discoveries was to emerge, and these discoveries were to bear fruit in inventions for the service of man. Men were to give up their futile, never-finished effort to dominate one another to engage in the coöperative task of dominating nature in the interests of humanity.

In the main, Bacon prophesied the direction of subsequent progress. But he "anticipated" the advance. He did not see that the new science was for a long time to be worked in the interest of old ends of human exploitation. He thought that it would rapidly give man new ends. Instead, it put at the disposal of a class the means to secure their old ends of aggrandizement at the expense of another class. The industrial revolution followed, as he foresaw, upon a revolution in scientific method. But it is taking the revolution many centuries to produce a new mind. Feudalism was doomed by the applications of the new science, for they transferred power from the landed nobility to the manufacturing centers. But capitalism rather than a social humanism took its place. Production and commerce were carried on as if the new science had no moral lesson, but only technical lessons as to economies in production and utilization of saving in self-interest. Naturally, this application of physical science (which was the most conspicuously perceptible one) strengthened the claims of professed humanists that science was materialistic in its tendencies. It left a void as to man's distinctively human interests which go beyond making, saving, and expending money; and languages and literature put in their claim to represent the moral and ideal interests of humanity.

(d) Moreover, the philosophy which professed itself based upon science, which gave itself out as the accredited representative of the net significance of science, was either dualistic in character, marked by a sharp division between mind (characterizing man) and matter, constituting nature; or else it was openly mechanical, reducing the signal features of human life to illusion. In the former case, it allowed the claims of certain studies to be peculiar consignees of mental values, and indirectly strengthened their claim to superiority, since human beings would incline to regard human affairs as of chief importance at least to themselves. In the latter case, it called out a reaction which threw doubt and suspicion upon the value of physical science, giving occasion for treating it as an enemy to man's higher interests.

Greek and medieval knowledge accepted the world in its qualitative variety, and regarded nature's processes as having ends, or in technical phrase as teleological. New science was expounded so as to deny the reality of all qualities in real, or objective, existence. Sounds, colors, ends, as well as goods and bads, were regarded as purely subjective—as mere impressions in the mind. Objective existence was then treated as having only quantitative aspects—as so much mass in motion, its only differences being that at one point in space there was a larger aggregate mass than at another, and that in some spots there were greater rates of motion than at others. Lacking qualitative distinctions, nature lacked significant variety. Uniformities were emphasized, not diversities; the ideal was supposed to be the discovery of a single mathematical formula applying to the whole universe at once from which all the seeming variety of phenomena could be derived. This is what a mechanical *philosophy* means.

Such a philosophy does not represent the genuine purport of science. It takes the technique for the thing itself; the apparatus and the terminology for reality, the method for its subject matter. Science does confine its statements to conditions which enable us to predict and control the happening of events, ignoring the qualities of the events. Hence its mechanical and quantitative character. But in leaving them out of account, it does not exclude them from reality, nor relegate them to a purely mental region; it only furnishes means utilizable for ends. Thus while in fact the progress of science was increasing man's power over nature, enabling him to place his cherished ends on a firmer basis than ever before, and also to diversify his activities almost at will, the philosophy which professed to formulate its accomplishments reduced the world to a barren and monotonous redistribution of matter in space. Thus the immediate effect of modern science was to accentuate the dualism of matter and mind, and thereby to establish the physical and the humanistic studies as two disconnected groups. Since the difference between better and worse is bound up with the *qualities* of experience, any philosophy of science which excludes them from the genuine content of reality is bound to leave out what is most interesting and most important to mankind.

3. THE PRESENT EDUCATIONAL PROBLEM. In truth, experience knows no division between human concerns and a purely mechanical physical world. Man's home is nature; his purposes and aims are dependent for execution upon natural conditions. Separated from such conditions they become empty dreams and idle indulgences of fancy. From the standpoint of human experience, and hence of educational endeavor, any distinction which can be justly made between nature and man is a distinction between the conditions which have to be reckoned with in the formation and execution of our practical aims, and the aims themselves. This philosophy is vouched for by the doctrine of biological development which shows that man is continuous with nature, not an alien entering her processes from without. It is reënforced by the experimental method of science which shows that knowledge accrues in virtue of an attempt to direct physical energies in accord with ideas suggested in dealing with natural objects in behalf of social uses. Every step forward in the social sciences—the studies termed history, economics, politics, sociology—shows that social questions are capable of being intelligently coped with only in the degree in which we employ the method of collected data, forming hypotheses, and testing them in action which is characteristic of natural science, and in the degree in which we utilize in behalf of the promotion of social welfare the technical knowledge ascertained by physics and chemistry. Advanced methods of dealing with such perplexing problems as insanity, intemperance,

poverty, public sanitation, city planning, the conservation of natural resources, the constructive use of governmental agencies for furthering the public good without weakening personal initiative, all illustrate the direct dependence of our important social concerns upon the methods and results of natural science.

With respect then to both humanistic and naturalistic studies, education should take its departure from this close interdependence. It should aim not at keeping science as a study of nature apart from literature as a record of human interests, but at cross-fertilizing both the natural sciences and the various human disciplines such as history, literature, economics, and politics. Pedagogically, the problem is simpler than the attempt to teach the sciences as mere technical bodies of information and technical forms of physical manipulation, on one side; and to teach humanistic studies as isolated subjects, on the other. For the latter procedure institutes an artificial separation in the pupils' experience. Outside of school pupils meet with natural facts and principles in connection with various modes of human action. In all the social activities in which they have shared they have had to understand the material and processes involved. To start them in school with a rupture of this intimate association breaks the continuity of mental development, makes the student feel an indescribable unreality in his studies, and deprives him of the normal motive for interest in them.

There is no doubt, of course, that the opportunities of education should be such that all should have a chance who have the disposition to advance to specialized ability in science, and thus devote themselves to its pursuit as their particular occupation in life. But at present, the pupil too often has a choice only between beginning with a study of the results of prior specialization where the material is isolated from his daily experiences, or with miscellaneous nature study, where material is presented at haphazard and does not lead anywhere in particular. The habit of introducing college pupils into segregated scientific subject matter, such as is appropriate to the man who wishes to become an expert in a given field, is carried back into the high schools. Pupils in the latter simply get a more elementary treatment of the same thing, with difficulties smoothed over and topics reduced to the level of their supposed ability. The cause of this procedure lies in following tradition, rather than in conscious adherence to a dualistic philosophy. But the effect is the same as if the purpose were to inculcate an idea that the sciences which deal with nature have nothing to do with man, and *vice versa*. A large part of the comparative ineffectiveness of the teaching of the sciences, for those who never become scientific specialists, is the result of a separation which is unavoidable when one begins with technically organized subject matter. Even if all students were embryonic scientific specialists, it is questionable whether this is the most effective procedure. Considering that the great majority are concerned with the study of sciences only for its effect upon their mental habits—in making them more alert, more open-minded, more inclined to tentative acceptance and to testing of ideas propounded or suggested,—and for achieving a better understanding of their daily environment, it is certainly ill-advised. Too often the pupil comes out with a smattering which is too superficial to be scientific and too technical to be applicable to ordinary affairs.

The utilization of ordinary experience to secure an advance into scientific material and method, while keeping the latter connected with familiar human interests, is easier to-day than it ever was before. The usual experience of all persons in civilized communities to-day is intimately associated with industrial processes and results. These in turn are so many cases of science in action. The stationary and traction steam engine, gasoline engine, automobile, telegraph and telephone, the electric motor enter directly into the lives of most individuals. Pupils at an early age are practically acquainted with these things. Not only does the business occupation of their parents depend upon scientific applications, but household pursuits, the maintenance of health, the sights seen upon the streets, embody scientific principles. The obvious pedagogical starting point of scientific instruction is not to teach things labeled science, but to utilize the familiar occupations and appliances to direct observation and experiment, until pupils have arrived at a knowledge of some fundamental principles by understanding them in their familiar practical workings.

The opinion sometimes advanced that it is a derogation from the "purity" of science to study it in its active incarnation, instead of in theoretical abstraction, rests upon a misunderstanding. As matter of fact, any subject is cultural in the degree in which it is apprehended in its widest possible range of meanings. Perception of meanings depends upon perception of connections, of context. To see a scientific fact or law in its human as well as in its physical and technical context is to enlarge its significance and give it increased cultural value. Its direct economic application, if by economic is meant something having money worth, is incidental and secondary, but a part of its actual connections. The important thing is that the fact be grasped in its social connections—its function in life.

On the other hand, "humanism" means at bottom being imbued with an intelligent sense of human interests. The social interest, identical in its deepest meaning with a moral interest, is necessarily supreme with man. Knowledge *about* man, information as to his past, familiarity with his documented records of literature, may be as technical a possession as the accumulation of physical details. Men may keep busy in a variety of ways, making money, acquiring facility in laboratory manipulation, or in amassing a store of facts about linguistic matters, or the chronology of literary productions. Unless such activity reacts to enlarge the imaginative vision of life, it is on a level with the busy work of children. It has the letter without the spirit of activity. It readily degenerates itself into a miser's accumulation, and a man prides himself on what he has, and not on the meaning he finds in the affairs of life, any study producing greater sensitiveness to social well-being and greater ability to promote that well-being is humane study.

The humanistic spirit of the Greeks was native and intense but it was narrow in scope. Everybody outside the Hellenic circle was a barbarian, and negligible save as a possible enemy. Acute as were the social observations and speculations of Greeks thinkers, there is not a word in their writings to indicate that Greek civilization was not self-inclosed and self-sufficient. There was, apparently, no suspicion that its future was at the mercy of the despised outsider. Within the Greek community, the intense social spirit was limited by the fact that higher culture was based on a substratum of slavery and economic serfdom—classes necessary to the existence of the state, as Aristotle declared, and yet not genuine parts of it. The development of science has produced an industrial revolution which has brought different peoples in such close contact with one another through colonization and commerce that no matter how some nations may still look down upon others, no country can harbor the illusion that its career is decided wholly within itself. The same revolution has abolished agricultural serfdom, and created a class of more or less organized factory laborers with recognized political rights, and who make claims for a responsible rôle in the control of industry—claims which receive sympathetic attention from many among the well-to-do, since they have been brought into closer connections with the less fortunate classes through the breaking down of class barriers.

This state of affairs may be formulated by saying that the older humanism omitted economic and industrial conditions from its purview. Consequently, it was one sided. Culture, under such circumstances, inevitably represented the intellectual and moral outlook of the class which was in direct social control. Such a tradition as to culture is, as we have seen . . . , aristocratic; it emphasizes what marks off one class from another, rather than fundamental common interests. Its standards are in the past; for the aim is to preserve what has been gained rather than widely to extend the range of culture.

The modifications which spring from taking greater account of industry and of whatever has to do with making a living are frequently condemned as attacks upon the culture derived from the past. But a wider educational outlook would conceive industrial activities as agencies for making intellectual resources more accessible to the masses, and giving greater solidity to the culture of those having superior resources. In short, when we consider the close connection between science and industrial development on the one hand, and between literary and æsthetic cultivation and an aristocratic social organization on the other, we get light on the opposition between technical scientific studies and refining literary studies. We have before us the need of overcoming this separation in education if society is to be truly democratic.

SUMMARY. The philosophic dualism between man and nature is reflected in the division of studies between the naturalistic and the humanistic with a tendency to reduce the latter to the literary records of the past. This dualism is not characteristic (as were the others which we have noted) of Greek thought. It arose partly because of the fact that the culture of Rome and of barbarian Europe was not a native product, being borrowed directly or indirectly from Greece, and partly because political and ecclesiastic conditions emphasized dependence upon the authority of past knowledge as that was transmitted in literary documents.

At the outset, the rise of modern science prophesied a restoration of the intimate connection of nature and humanity, for it viewed knowledge of nature as the means of securing human progress and well-being. But the more immediate applications of science were in the interests of a class rather than of men in common; and the received philosophic formulations of scientific doctrine tended either to mark it off as merely material from man as spiritual and immaterial, or else to reduce mind to a subjective illusion. In education, accordingly, the tendency was to treat the sciences as a separate body of studies, consisting of technical information regarding the physical world, and to reserve the older literary studies as distinctively humanistic. The account previously given of the evolution of knowledge, and of the educational scheme of studies based upon it, are designed to overcome the separation, and to secure recognition of the place occupied by the subject matter of the natural sciences in human affairs.

Education on the Nonverbal Level

ALDOUS HUXLEY

Early in the mid-Victorian period the Reverend Thomas Binney, a Congregationalist divine, published a book with the alluring title, *Is It Possible to Make the Best of Both Worlds?* His conclusion was that perhaps it might be possible. In spite of its unorthodox message, or perhaps because of it, the book was a best seller, which only showed, said the more evangelical of Mr. Binney's Nonconformist colleagues and Anglican opponents, how inexpressibly wicked Victorian England really was.

What Mr. Binney's critics had done (and their mistake is repeated by all those who use the old phrase disapprovingly) was to equate "making the best of both worlds" with "serving two masters." It is most certainly difficult, perhaps quite impossible, to serve Mammon and God simultaneously—to pursue the most sordid interests while aspiring to realize the highest ideals. This is obvious. Only a little less obvious, however, is the fact that it is very hard, perhaps quite impossible, to serve God while failing to make the best of both worlds—of *all* the worlds of which, as human beings, we are the inhabitants.

Man is a multiple amphibian and exists at one and the same time in a number of universes, dissimilar to the point, very nearly, of complete incompatibility. He is at once an animal and a rational intellect; a product of evolution closely related to the apes and a spirit capable of self-transcendence; a sentient being in contact with the brute data of his own nervous system and the physical environment and at the same time the creator of a home-made universe of words and other symbols, in which he lives and moves and has anything from thirty to eighty percent of his being. He is a self-conscious and self-centered ego who is also a member of a moderately gregarious species, an individual compelled by the population explosion to live at ever closer quarters, and in ever tighter organizations, with millions of other egos as self-centered and as poorly socialized as himself. Neurologically, he is a lately evolved Jekyll-cortex associated with an immensely ancient brain-stem-Hyde. Physiologically, he is a creature whose endocrine system is perfectly adapted to the conditions prevailing in the lower Paleolithic, but living in a metropolis and spending eight hours a day sitting at a desk in an air-conditioned office. Psychologically, he is a highly educated product of twentieth-

Reprinted by permission of *Daedalus*, Journal of The American Academy of Arts and Sciences, Boston, Massachusetts. Spring 1972, *Intellectuals and Tradition*.

century civilization, chained, in a state of uneasy and hostile symbiosis, to a disturbingly dynamic unconscious, a wild phantasy and an unpredictable id—and yet capable of falling in love, writing string quartets, and having mystical experiences.

Living amphibiously in all these incommensurable worlds at once, human beings (it is hardly surprising) find themselves painfully confused, uncertain where they stand or who they really are. To provide themselves with a recognizable identity, a niche in the scheme of things that they can call "home," they will give assent to the unlikeliest dogmas, conform to the most absurd and even harmful rules of thought, feeling, and conduct, put on the most extravagant fancy dress and identify themselves with masks that bear almost no resemblance to the faces they cover. "Bovarism" (as Jules de Gaultier calls it) is the urge to pretend that one is something that in fact one is not. It is an urge that manifests itself, sometimes weakly, sometimes with overpowering strength, in all human beings, and one of the conditions of its manifestation is precisely our uncertainty about where we stand or who we are. To explore our multiple amphibiousness with a view to doing something constructive about it is a most laborious process. Our minds are congenitally lazy, and the original sin of the intellect is oversimplification. Dogmatism and bovaristic identification with a stereotype are closely related manifestations of the same kind of intellectual delinquency. "Know thyself." From time immemorial this has been the advice of all the seers and philosophers. The self that they urge us to know is not, of course, the stylized persona with which, bovaristically, we try to become identified; it is the multiple amphibian, the inhabitant of all those incompatible worlds that we must somehow learn to make the best of.

A good education may be defined as one which helps the boys and girls subjected to it to make the best of all the worlds in which, as human beings, they are compelled, willy-nilly, to live. An education that prepares them to make the best of only one of their worlds, or of only a few of them, is inadequate. This is a point on which, in principle, all educators have always agreed. *Mens sana in corpore sano* is an ancient educational ideal and a very good one. Unfortunately, good ideals are never enough. Unless they are accompanied by full instructions regarding the methods by which they may be realized, they are almost useless. Hell is paved with good intentions, and whole periods of history have been made hideous or grotesque by enthusiastic idealists who failed to elaborate the means whereby their lofty aspirations might be effectively, and above all harmlessly, implemented.

Just how good is modern education? How successful is it in helping young people to make the best of all the worlds which, as multiple amphibians, they have to live in? In a center of advanced scientific and technical study this question gets asked inevitably in terms of what may be called the paradox of specialization. In science and technology specialization is unavoidable and indeed absolutely necessary. But training for this unavoidable and necessary specialization does nothing to help young amphibians to make the best of their many worlds. Indeed, it pretty obviously prevents them from doing anything of the kind. What then is to be done? At the Massachusetts Institute of Technology and in other schools where similar problems have arisen, the answer to this question has found expression in a renewed interest in the humanities. Excessive scientific specialization is tempered by courses in philosophy, history, literature, and social studies. All this is excellent so far as it goes. But does it go far enough? Do courses in the humanities provide a sufficient antidote for excessive scientific and technical specialization? Do they, in the terminology we have been using, help young multiple amphibians to make the best of a substantially greater number of their worlds?

Science is the reduction of the bewildering diversity of unique events to manageable uniformity within one of a number of symbol systems, and technology is the art of using these symbol systems so as to control and organize unique events. Scientific observation is always a viewing of things through the refracting medium of a symbol system, and technological praxis is always the handling of things in ways that some symbol system has dictated. Education in science and technology is essentially education on the symbolic level.

Turning to the humanities, what do we find? Courses in philosophy, literature, history, and social studies are exclusively verbal. Observation of and experimentation with nonverbal events have no place in these fields. Training in the sciences is largely on the symbolic level; training in the liberal arts is wholly and all the time on that level. When courses in the humanities are used as the only antidote to too much science and technology, excessive specialization in one kind of symbolic education is being tempered by excessive specialization in another kind of symbolic education. The young amphibians are taught to make the best, not of all their worlds, but only of two varieties of the same world—the world of symbols. But this world of symbols is only one of the worlds in which human beings do their living and their learning. They also inhabit the nonsymbolic world of unconceptualized or only slightly conceptualized experience. However, effective it may be on the conceptual level, an education that fails to help young amphibians to make the best of the inner and outer universes on the hither side of symbols is an inadequate education. And however much we may delight in Homer or Gibbon, however illuminating in their different ways Pareto and

William Law, Hui-neng and Bertrand Russell may strike us as being, the fact remains that the reading of their works will not be of much help to us in our efforts to make the best of our worlds of unconceptualized, nonverbal experience.

And here, before I embark on a discussion of these nonverbal worlds, let me add parenthetically that even on the verbal level, where they are most at home, educators have done a good deal less than they might reasonably have been expected to do in explaining to young people the nature, the limitations, the huge potentialities for evil as well as for good, of that greatest of all human inventions, language. Children should be taught that words are indispensable but also can be fatal—the only begetters of all civilization, all science, all consistency of high purpose, all angelic goodness, and the only begetters at the same time of all superstition, all collective madness and stupidity, all worse-than-bestial diabolism, all the dismal historical succession of crimes in the name of God, King, Nation, Party, Dogma. Never before, thanks to the techniques of mass communication, have so many listeners been so completely at the mercy of so few speakers. Never have misused words—those hideously efficient tools of all the tyrants, war-mongers, persecutors, and heresy-hunters—been so widely and so disastrously influential as they are today. Generals, clergymen, advertisers, and the rulers of totalitarian states—all have good reasons for disliking the idea of universal education in the rational use of language. To the military, clerical, propagandist, and authoritarian mind such training seems (and rightly seems) profoundly subversive. To those who think that liberty is a good thing, and who hope that it may some day become possible for more people to realize more of their desirable potentialities in a society fit for free, fully human individuals to live in, a thorough education in the nature of language, in its uses and abuses, seems indispensable. Whether in fact the mounting pressures of overpopulation and overorganization in a world still enthusiastically dedicated to nationalistic idolatry will permit this kind of subversive linguistic education to be adopted by even the more democratic nations remains to be seen.

And now, after this brief digression, let us return to our main theme, the education of multiple amphibians on levels other than the verbal and the symbolic. "Make the body capable of doing many things," wrote Spinoza. "This will help you to perfect the mind and come to the intellectual love of God." Substitute "psychophysical organism" for "body," and you have here the summary of a program for universal education on the nonsymbolic level, supplemented by a statement of the reasons why such an education is desirable and indeed, if the child is to grow into a fully-human being, absolutely necessary. The detailed curriculum for an education in what may be called the nonverbal humanities has still to be worked out. All I can do at this time is to drop a few fragmentary hints.

Two points, to begin with, must be emphatically stressed. First, education in the nonverbal humanities is not just a matter of gymnastics and football, of lessons in singing and folk dancing. All these, of course, are good, but by themselves not good enough. Such traditional methods of training young people in vonverbal skills need to be supplemented, if they are to yield their best results, by other kinds of training, beginning with a thorough training in elementary awareness. And the second point to be remembered is that education in the nonverbal humanities is a process that should be started in the kindergarten and continued through all the years of school and college—and thereafter, as self-education, throughout the rest of life.

At the end of a delightful anthology entitled *Zen Flesh, Zen Bones*, its editor, Mr. Paul Reps, has printed an English version of an ancient Tantrik text in which Shiva, in response to Parvati's questions about the nature of enlightened consciousness, gives a list of one hundred and twelve exercises in the art of being aware of inner and outer reality on its nonsymbolic levels. *Gnosce Teipsum.*[1] But how? From the vast majority of our pastors and masters no answer is forthcoming. Here, for a blessed change, is a philosophical treatise that speaks of means as well as of ends, of concrete experience as well as of high abstractions. The intelligent and systematic practice of any half-dozen of these hundred and twelve exercises will take one further towards the realization of the ancient ideal of self-knowledge than all the roaring or pathetic eloquence of generations of philosophers, theologians, and moralists. (Let me add, in passing, that whereas Western philosophy tends to be concerned with the manipulation of abstract symbols for the benefit of the speculative and moralizing intellect, oriental philosophy is almost always essentially operational. "Perform such and such psychophysical operations," the exponents of this philosophy say, "and you will probably find yourself in a state of mind which, like all those who have achieved it in the past, you will regard as self-evidently and supremely valuable. In the context of this state of mind, speculation about man and the universe leads us, as it led earlier thinkers, to the metaphysical doctrine of *Tat tvam asi* [thou art That], and to its ethical corollary—universal compassion. In this philosophy it is the experiential element that is important. Its speculative superstructure is a thing of words, and words, though useful and necessary, should never be taken too seriously.")

[1] Meaning "know thyself" (editor).

Education in elementary awareness will have to include techniques for improving awareness of internal events and techniques for improving awareness of external events as these are revealed by our organs of sense. In his introductions to several of F. M. Alexander's books, John Dewey insisted upon the importance of a properly directed training in the awareness of internal events. It was Dewey's opinion that the training methods developed by Alexander were to education what education is to life in general—and indispensable condition for any kind of improvement. Dewey had himself undergone this training and so knew what he was talking about. And yet in spite of this high praise bestowed by one of the most influential of modern philosophers and educational reformers, Alexander's methods have been ignored, and schoolchildren still receive no training in the kind of internal awareness that can lead to what Alexander described as "creative conscious control."

The educational and therapeutic values of training aimed at heightening awareness of internal events was empirically demonstrated during the first quarter of the present century by the eminently successful Swiss psychiatrist, Dr. Roger Vittoz. And in recent years methods similar to those of Vittoz and to the Tantrik exercises attributed many centuries ago to Shiva have been developed and successfully used both in the treatment of neurotics and for the enrichment of the lives of the normal by the authors of Gestalt Therapy, Drs. Frederick F. Perls, Ralph F. Hefferline, and Paul Goodman.

All our mental processes depend upon perception. Inadequate perceiving results in poor thinking, inappropriate feeling, diminished interest in and enjoyment of life. Systematic training of perception should be an essential element in all education.

Our amphibiousness is clearly illustrated in the two modes of our awareness of external events. There is a receptive, more or less unconceptualized, aesthetic and "spiritual" mode of perceiving; and there is also a highly conceptualized, stereotyped, utilitarian, and even scientific mode. In his "Expostulation and Reply" and "The Tables Turned," Wordsworth has perfectly described these two modes of awareness and has assigned to each its special significance and value for the human being who aspires to make the best of both worlds and so, by teaching his psychophysical organism to "do many things," to "perfect the mind and come to the intellectual love of God."

> "Why, William, on that old grey stone,
> Thus for the length of half a day,
> Why William, sit you thus alone,
> And dream your time away?

Where are your books?—that light bequeathed
To beings else forlorn and blind?
Up! Up! and drink the spirit breathed
From dead men to their kind.

You look round on your Mother Earth,
As if she for no purpose bore you;
As if you were her first-born birth,
And none had lived before you."

One morning thus, by Esthwaite lake,
When life was sweet, I knew not why,
To me my good friend Matthew spake,
And thus I made reply.

"The eye it cannot choose but see;
We cannot bid the ear be still;
Our bodies feel, where'er they be,
Against or with our will.

Nor less I deem that there are Powers
Which of themselves our minds impress;
That we can feed this mind of ours
In a wise passiveness.

Think you, 'mid all this mighty sum
Of things for ever speaking,
That nothing of itself will come,
But we must still be seeking?

Then ask not wherefore, here, alone,
Conversing as I may,
I sit upon this old grey stone
And dream my time away."

In "The Tables Turned" it is the poet who takes the offensive
against his studious friend. "Up! Up! my Friend," he calls, "and quit
your books." And then, "Books!" he continues impatiently,

Books! 'tis a dull and endless strife;
Come, hear the woodland linnet;
How sweet his music! on my life,
There's more of wisdom in it.

And hark how blithe the throstle sings!
He too is no mean preacher.
Come forth into the light of things,
Let Nature be your teacher.

One impulse from a vernal wood
May teach you more of man,
Of moral evil and of good
Than all the sages can.

> Sweet is the lore which Nature brings;
> Our meddling intellect
> Mis-shapes the beauteous forms of things—
> We murder to dissect.
>
> Enough of Science and of Art;
> Close up those barren leaves;
> Come forth and bring with you a heart
> That watches and receives.

Matthew and William—two aspects of the multiple amphibian that was Wordsworth, that is each of us. To be fully human, we must learn to make the best of William's world as well as of Matthew's. Matthew's is the world of books, of the social heredity of steadily accumulating knowledge, of science and technics and business, of words and the stock of second-hand notions which we project upon external reality as a frame of reference, in terms of which we may explain, to our own satisfaction, the enigma, moment by moment, of ongoing existence. Over against it stands William's world—the world of sheer mystery, the world as an endless succession of unique events, the world as we perceive it in a state of alert receptiveness with no thought of explaining it, using it, exploiting it for our biological or cultural purposes. As things now stand, we teach young people to make the best only of Matthew's world of familiar words, accepted notions, and useful techniques. We temper a too exclusive concentration on scientific symbols, not with a training in the art of what William calls "wise passiveness," not with lessons in watching and receiving, but with the injunction to concentrate on philosophical and sociological symbols, to read the books that are reputed to contain a high concentration of "the spirit breathed from dead men to their kind." (Alas, dead men do not always breathe a spirit; quite often they merely emit a bad smell.)

It is related in one of the Sutras that on a certain occasion the Buddha preached a wordless sermon to his disciples. Instead of saying anything, he picked a flower and held it up for them to look at. The disciples gaped uncomprehendingly. Only Mahakasyapa understood what the Tathagata was driving at, and all that he did was to smile. Gautama smiled back at him, and when the wordless sermon was over, he made a little speech for the benefit of those who had failed to comprehend his silence. "This treasure of the unquestionable teaching, this Mind of Nirvana, this true form that is without forms, this most subtle Dharma beyond words, this instruction that is to be given and received outside the pale of all doctrines—this I have now handed on to Mahakasyapa." Perceived not as a botanical specimen, not as the analyzed and labeled illustration of a pre-exis-

tent symbol system, but as a nameless, unique event, in which all the
beauty and the mystery of existence are manifest, a flower can become the means to enlightenment. And what is true of a flower is
true, needless to say, of any other event in the inner or outer world—
from a toothache to Mount Everest, from a tapeworm to *The Well-
Tempered Clavichord*—to which we choose to pay attention in a
state of wise passiveness. And wise passiveness is the condition not
only of spiritual insight. ("In prayer," wrote St. Jeanne Chantal, "I
always want to *do* something, wherein I do very wrong. . . . By
wishing to accomplish something myself, I spoil it all.") In another
context, wise passiveness, followed in due course by wise hard work,
is the condition of creativity. We do not fabricate our best ideas; they
"occur to us," they "come into our heads." Colloquial speech re-
minds us that, unless we give our subliminal mind a chance, we shall
get nowhere. And it is by allowing ourselves at frequent intervals to
be wisely passive that we can most effectively help the subliminal
mind to do its work. The *cogito* of Descartes should be emended,
said von Baader, to *cogitor*. In order to actualize our potentialities, in
order to become fully human and completely ourselves, we must not
merely think; we must also permit ourselves to be thought. In
Gardner Murphy's words, "Both the historical record of creative
thought and the laboratory report of its appearance today, indicate
clearly that creative intelligence can spring from the mind that is not
strained to its highest pitch, but is utterly at ease." Watching and
receiving in a state of perfect ease or wise passiveness is an art
which can be cultivated and should be taught on every educational
level from the most elementary to the most advanced.

Creativity and spiritual insight—these are the highest rewards of
wise passiveness. But those who know how to watch and receive are
rewarded in other and hardly less important ways. Receptivity can
be a source of innocent and completely harmless happiness. A man
or woman who knows how to make the best of both worlds—the
world revealed by wise passiveness and the world created by wise
activity—tends to find life enjoyable and interesting. Ours is a civilization in which vast numbers of children and adults are so chroni-
cally bored that they have to resort during their leisure hours to a
regimen of nonstop distractions. Any method which promises to
make life seem enjoyable and the commonplaces of everyday experience more interesting should be welcomed as a major contribution to
culture and morality.

In *Modern Painters* there is a remarkable chapter on "the Open
Sky"—a chapter which even by those who find Ruskin's theology absurd and his aesthetics frequently perverse may still be read with
profit and admiring pleasure. "It is a strange thing," Ruskin writes,
"how little in general people know about the sky. It is the part of cre-

ation in which nature has done more for the sake of pleasing man, more for the sake and evident purpose of talking to him and teaching him, than in any of her works, and it is just the part in which we least attend to her. . . . There is not a moment in any day of our lives in which nature is not producing (in the sky) scene after scene, picture after picture, glory after glory, and working always upon such exquisite and constant principles of the most perfect beauty, that it is quite certain it is all done for us and intended for our perpetual pleasure." But, in point of fact, does the sky produce in most people the perpetual pleasure which its beauty is so eminently capable of giving? The answer, of course, is No. "We never attend to it, we never make it a subject of thought. . . . We look upon it . . . only as a succession of monotonous and meaningless accidents, too common or too vain to be worthy of a moment of watchfulness or a glance of admiration. . . . Who, among the chattering crowd, can tell me of the forms and the precipices of the chain of tall white mountains that girded the horizon at noon yesterday? Who saw the narrow sunbeam that came out of the south and smote their summits until they melted and mouldered away in a dust of blue rain? . . . All has passed unregretted as unseen; or if the apathy be ever shaken off, if even for an instant, it is only by what is gross or what is extraordinary." A habit of wise passiveness in relation to the everyday drama of the clouds and mist and sunshine can become a source, as Ruskin insists, of endless pleasure. But most of the products of our educational system prefer Westerns and alcohol.

In the art of watching and receiving Ruskin was self-educated. But there seems to be no reason why children should not be taught that wise passiveness which gave this victim of a traumatic childhood so much pleasure and kept him, in spite of everything, reasonably sane for the greater part of a long and productive life. A training in watching and receiving will not turn every child into a great stylist but, within the limits imposed by constitution, temperament, and the circumambient culture, it will make him more sensitive, more intelligent, more capable of innocent enjoyment and, in consequence, more virtuous and more useful to society.

In the United States life, liberty, and the pursuit of happiness are constitutionally guaranteed. But if life hardly seems worth living, if liberty is used for subhuman purposes, if the pursuers of happiness know nothing about the nature of their quarry or the elementary techniques of hunting, these constitutional rights will not be very meaningful. An education in that wise passiveness recommended by the saints and the poets, by all who have lived fully and worked creatively, might help us to transform the paper promises of a democratic constitution into concrete contemporary fact.

Let us now consider very briefly two other areas in which an ed-

ucation in the art of making the best of all our seemingly incommensurable worlds would certainly be helpful and might also turn out to
be practicable within the system now prevailing in our schools and
colleges. It is a matter of observable fact that all of us inhabit a world
of phantasy as well as a world of first-order experience and a world of
words and concepts. In most children and in some adults this world
of phantasy is astonishingly vivid. These people are the visualizers
of Galton's classical dichotomy. For them the world presented to
their consciousness by their story-telling, image-making phantasy is
as real as, sometimes more real than, the given world of sense impressions and the projected world of words and explanatory concepts. Even in nonvisualizers the world of phantasy, though somewhat shadowy, is still real enough to be retreated into or shrunk
from, tormented by or voluptuously enjoyed. The mentally ill are the
victims of their phantasy, and even more or less normal people find
themselves tempted into folly, or inhibited from behaving as they
know they ought to behave, by what goes on in the superreal but
unrealistic world of their imagination. How can we make the best of
this odd, alien, almost autonomous universe that we carry about with
us inside our skulls?

The question has been partially answered by the apostles of
those numerous religious movements stemming from "New
Thought." Using a vaguely theological language and interpreting the
Bible to suit themselves, they have given a religious form to a
number of useful and practical methods for harnessing imagination
and its suggestive power in the service of individual well-being and
social stability. For about a quarter or perhaps a third of the population their methods work remarkably well. This is an important fact,
of which professional educators should take notice and from whose
implications they should not be ashamed to learn. Unfortunately,
men and women in high academic positions tend to be intellectually
snobbish. They turn up their noses at the nonscientific, distressingly
"inspirational" but still astute and experienced psychologists of the
modern heretical churches. This is deplorable. Truth lives, prover-
bially, at the bottom of a well, and wells are often muddy. No genuinely scientific investigator has any right to be squeamish about
anything.

And here is another truth-containing well abhorred by academic
scientists of the stricter sort. Excellent techniques for teaching children and adults to make the best of the chaotic world of their phantasy have been worked out by the Dianeticists and their successors,
the Scientologists. Their Imagination Games deserve to be incorpo-
rated into every curriculum. Boys and girls, and even grown men and
women, find these games amusing and, what is more important,
helpful. Made the worst of, our imagination will destroy us; made

the best of, it can be used to break up long-establshed habits of undesirable feeling, to dissipate obsessive fears, to provide symbolic
outlets for anger and fictional amends for real frustrations.

In the course of the last three thousand years how many sermons
have been preached, how many homilies delivered and commands
roared out, how many promises of heaven and threats of hell-fire
solemnly pronounced, how many good-conduct prizes awarded and
how many childish buttocks lacerated with whips and canes? And
what has been the result of all this incalculable sum of moralistic
words, and of the rewards and savage punishments by which the verbiage has been accompanied? The result has been history—the suc-
cessive generations of human beings comporting themselves vir-
tuously and rationally enough for the race to survive, but badly
enough and madly enough for it to be unceasingly in trouble. Can
we do better in the future than we are doing today, or than our fathers did in the past? Can we develop methods more effective than
pious talk and Pavlovian conditioning?

For an answer to these questions—or at least for some hints as to
the nature of a possible answer—we must turn to history and anthropology. Like many primitive societies today, many highly civilized
societies of the past provided their members with realistically am-
phibious methods for dealing with negative emotions and the instinctive drives that are incompatible with communal living. In these
societies morality and rational behavior were not merely preached
and rewarded; they were made easier by the provision of religiously
sanctioned safety valves, through which the angry, the frustrated,
and the anxiously neurotic could release their aggressive or self-des-
tructive tendencies in a satisfyingly violent and yet harmless and
socially acceptable way. In Ancient Greece, for example, the orgies
of Dionysus and, at a somewhat later date, the Corybantic dances,
sacred to the Great Mother, were safety valves through which rage
and resentment found an innocuous outlet, while the paralyzing inhibitions of anxiety were swept away in a wild rush of nervous,
muscular, and hormonal activity. In this ethical and therapeutic context Dionysus was known as Lusios, the Liberator. His orgies delivered the participants from the dismal necessity of running amok, or
retreating into catatonia, or stoically bottling up their feelings and so
giving themselves a psychosomatic illness. Corybantic dancing was
regarded as a form of medical treatment and at the same time as a
religious rite, cathartic to the soul no less than to the adrenalin-
charged body. Which did most for morality and rational behavior—
the dialogues of Plato or the orgies of Dionysus, Aristotle's *Ethics* or
the Corybantic dances? My guess is that, in this competition, Lusios
and the Great Mother would be found to have won hands down.

In a society like ours it would doubtless be impracticable to revive Maenadism or the congregational antics of the Dionysian orgies. But the problem of what multiple amphibians should do about their frustrations and their tendencies to aggression remains acute and still unsolved. Sixty years ago William James wrote an essay entitled *The Moral Equivalent of War*. It is an excellent essay as far as it goes; but it does not, unfortunately, go far enough. Moral equivalents must be found not only for war but also for delinquency, family squabbles, bullying, puritanical censoriousness, and all the assorted beastliness of daily life. Preaching and conditioning will never of themselves solve these problems. It is obvious that we must take a hint from the Greeks and provide ourselves with physical safety valves for reducing the pressure of our negative emotions. No ethical system which fails to provide such physical safety valves, and which fails to teach children and their elders how to use them, is likely to be effective. It will be the business of psychologists, physiologists, and sociologists to devise acceptable safety valves, of moralists and clergymen to provide rationalizations in terms of the local value systems and theologists, and for educators to find a place in the curriculum for courses in the indispensable art of letting off steam.

And there is another art that merits the educator's closest attention—the art of controlling physical pain. Pain, as recent studies have made abundantly clear, is not simply a mechanical affair of peripheral receptors and special centers in the brain, and its intensity is not directly proportional to the extent of the injury which is its cause. Pain may be aggravated or inhibited by numerous psychological and even cultural factors. Which means, of course, that to some extent at least pain is controllable. This fact, needless to say, has been known from time immemorial, and for the last century and a half (from the days of Elliotson and Esdaile) has been systematically exploited in hypnotic anesthesia. Neurological research is now discovering the organic and functional reasons for these old observations and empirical practices; a somewhat disreputable "wild" phenomenon is in process of being turned into a domesticated scientific fact, consonant with other well-known facts and safely caged within a familiar symbol-system. Taking advantage of the newfound respectability of hypnosis and suggestion, educators should now include elementary pain control in the curriculum of physical training. Control of pain through suggestion and auto-suggestion is an art which, as every good dentist knows, can be learned by most children with the greatest of ease. Along with singing and calisthenics, it should be taught to every little boy and little girl who can learn it.

Training in a closely similar art may prove to be very useful as a part of ethical education. In his book *Auto-Conditioning* Professor Hornell Hart has outlined simple and thoroughly practical methods for changing moods, intensifying motivations, and implementing good intentions. There are no educational panaceas, no techniques that work perfectly in every case. But if auto-conditioning produces good results in only twenty or thirty percent of those who have been instructed in the art, it deserves to take its place in every educator's armamentarium.

That we are multiple amphibians is self-evident, and the corollary of this self-evident truth is that we must attack our problems on every front where they arise—on the mental front and on the physiological front, on the front of concepts and symbols and on the front of wordless experience, on the rational front and on the irrational front, the individual front and the social front. But what should be our strategy? How are we to learn and successfully practice the art of attacking on all the fronts simultaneously? Many valuable discoveries were made by the amphibians of earlier times and alien cultures, and many discoveries are being made within our own culture today. These empirical findings of the past and the present should be studied, tested, related to the best scientific knowledge now available, and finally adapted for practical use within our educational systems. Ten million dollars from the coffers of one of the great foundations would pay for the necessary research and largescale experimentation. Out of such research and experimentation might come, within a few years, a radical improvement in the methods currently used to prepare young people to meet the challenges of their anifold amphibiousness and to make the best of all the strangely assorted worlds in which, as human beings, they are predestined to live.

Curriculum and Humanistic Education: Monolism vs. Pluralism

BRUCE JOYCE

To plan for humanism at all may seem to be a paradox; at first blush deliberate unplanning or "decivilizing" may seem a more likely avenue to create an environment in which gentle self-actualization can take place.

Not to plan for humanistic growth, however, is to give the field to the philistines on one hand and the accidents of "natural" societal forces on the other. I do not know which is worse. The philistines would regiment children to economic purpose—and they *will* plan, and powerfully, a social system which reduces man to an economic entity and cultivate in children a utilitarian philosophy which will emasculate their humanitarian potential. The "natural" forces of society would mindlessly overpopulate the world and gather men into inward-looking social groups, national and tribal, unable to cope with the scale of problems generated by worldwide social forces. The resulting crises would force men into a collective materialism which might preserve life but would eschew humanistic development.

So plan we must, and in education it is the curriculum planner whose task it is to generate a field of humanistic planning. Although most curriculum theorists of this century would classify themselves as humanists and many are well aware of the forces mitigating against humanistic curriculum planning, such a field has not emerged to become a powerful force in education. Hence this paper will present an analysis of the reasons why the curriculum field has not succeeded in humanizing itself and will present a platform which, I believe, offers realistic humanistic direction to the field. A simple-minded definition of the humanists' objectives will be assumed throughout as the focus of the work of the humanist in curriculum. This definition sees humanism in terms of two interacting, mutually dependent dimensions. Stated as goals of curriculum planning these are:

a. To create environments which enable individuals to actualize themselves on their own terms—emotionally, intellectually, and socially.

b. To create environments which help people reach each other and live with an expanding common consciousness—one which not only embraces the traditional liberal values of mutual respect and protection of the rights of others, but also reaches out to explore the development of expanded human experiences through new dimensions of relationships with others.

Both of these objectives assume that the child will have to learn to help shape a new type of human society that embraces possibilities of personal and social development rarely achieved in our present human community.

The possibility that curriculum planning can actually relate to such goals derives from the critical relationship between education and society. A human culture can be described as an elaborate set of problem solutions.[1] Some of these solutions are addressed to physi-

---

[1] This is a common anthropological definition. See Ina Corinne Brown, *Understanding Other Cultures* (Englewood Cliffs, N.J.: Prentice-Hall, 1962).

cal problems (such as hunger and cold) and it is toward these that our economic and technological systems were originally developed. Other problems consist of meeting emotional needs, and some aspects of families and some modes of interpersonal interaction help to solve these for us. For each of us the culture largely defines the way we see problems and solutions, and also enables us to share reality with other humans. That is, those of us who share the same culture tend to see things in similar ways and to respond similarly to other human beings, although there is of course a wide individual variation within any cultural pattern.[2]

A culture is never complete. It is in continuous need for regeneration and reorganization. Within every culture there are certain problems that have never been defined adequately, and certain others for which there are no solutions, even though there are definitions. Within complex cultures such as ours, there is at all times a multitude of problems begging for help. Formal education systems have a potentially dynamic social role as a direct result of the incomplete and imperfect nature of the existing culture—the existing solutions to problems.

This opportunity exists, obviously, because education is a major agent in the transmission of culture. It fulfills the exceedingly important function (shared with other socializing agencies) of giving us humaneness, and transmitting to us a technology on which we can stand as we face the problems of human existence. Our present bureaucratic educational institution bids well to become increasingly effective at transmitting the general-purpose skills of the culture (especially reading and mathematics) and this is a role I would not want to undersell under any circumstances. (I am not *against* using the existing culture, although I do not believe it is perfect.) *However, the great dynamic challenge of the future is to develop entirely new modes of education, designed to help people create new solutions to problems, and to define problems that were not perceived before at all. Equally important, in a time when culture is growing ever stronger and more powerful and society is more urbanized and alienated, is to produce modes of education which can help people make contact with each other in new and stronger ways, and can help individuals to create lives which are unique, uniquely fulfilling, and socially productive—even transcendentally cooperative.*

Since the most visible and theoretically powerful leaders of the education community (John Dewey is the classic example) are well

---

[2] Leslie White's *A Science of Culture: A Study of Man and Civilization* (New York: Farrar, Straus & Giroux, 1949) presents the extreme technocratic view, but in so doing clearly defines the dimensions of dependence each of us has with respect to his culture.

aware of the possibility of such goals and have been committed to some form of them, we have to ask ourselves why the field has not learned to create schools devoted to humanistic goals on any wide scale.

.   .   .   .

Humanization of Curricular Technology

The task of the humanist in curriculum is to free himself from the confines of the bureaucratic school and the sorting functions it performs for the status system, and develop instead the capacity to design and actualize a pluralistic education—the educational aspects of a pluralistic society.

The task is to move from educational routes which are largely characterized by bureaucratic procedures that sort students into the channels of the technical-industrial system into an educational panorama providing many avenues toward many kinds of personal and social development and which, through its pluralism, leads the other aspects of the society toward a world of alternatives and commitment to social improvement.

Thus:

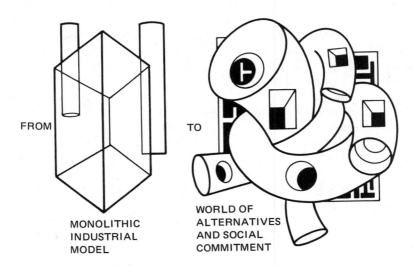

FROM   TO

MONOLITHIC
INDUSTRIAL
MODEL

WORLD OF
ALTERNATIVES
AND SOCIAL
COMMITMENT

Because we have worked so long within the confines of the school as an institution and the teacher role as usually defined, this task will not be easy, for most existing curriculum theory and subtheories are straitjacketed by the existing structure of the school and that ubiquitous teacher role. What we need to erect are sets of engineering propositions which can be used to bring about a wide variety of educational environments, including the institutional forms which can nurture them.

The Spectrum of Educational Missions [26]

The pluralistic world of education will be composed of many kinds of educational programs designed to further a large number of educational missions. The missions of the present school are tied to ascendency and survival in the technical-economic system. In place of this, a vast variety of missions must emerge.

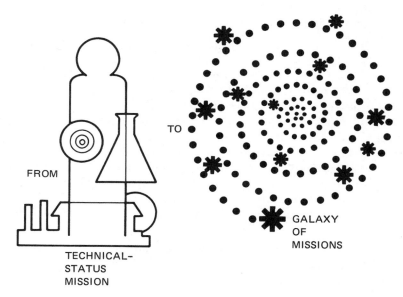

Monolithic to Humanistic Education: the Problem of Missions

The mission of an educational program can be defined in terms of the domains through which it (the program) enters into the life of the student. Since education is an attempt to enter one's life and change it or assist one in changing oneself, the product of education can be described as a developed capacity to respond to reality in

[26] This description of educational missions has been amplified in Bruce R. Joyce, *Alternative Models for Elementary Education* (Waltham, Mass.: Blaisdell, 1969).

new ways. The primary task in selecting an educational mission is to identify the domains through which the program will enter the life of the learner in order to change his responses to living in the world. The pluralistic education should represent many domains of possible development.

The possible domains of missions can be divided into three, with the caution that the categories overlap somewhat:

1. We can attempt to improve the capacity of the learner through direct intervention in the personal domain (as through a direct attempt to improve his intelligence or to give him greater control over directing his own destiny);
2. We can attempt to enter the social domain, to assist him at a point where he is in interaction with his fellow man (as when we attempt to teach him social or economic skills); or
3. We can attempt to reach him through an academic domain, by teaching him academic skills and ways of dealing intellectually with complexity (as when we attempt to teach him the social sciences).

We can use these three categories—the personal, the social, and the academic—to sort out some of the possible direction of education. Then, for each type of mission we can learn what kinds of environments are likely to promote development in that domain. To assist us, we can turn to those educators who have specialized in creating environments appropriate to specific domains. For example, Rogers,[27] Maslow,[28] and others have developed approaches for achieving missions in the personal domain. The National Training Laboratory [29] among others, has developed principles to apply to the interpersonal domain. Psychologists like Ausubel,[30] Piaget,[31] and others have developed theoretical structures from which engineering propositions in the academic domain can be developed and devel-

---

[27] Carl Rogers, *Client Centered Therapy* (Boston: Houghton Mifflin, 1951).

[28] Abraham Maslow, *Toward a Psychology of Being* (Princeton, N.J.: Van Nostrand, 1962).

[29] Leland R. Bradford; Jack Gibb; and Kenneth Benne, eds., *T-Group Theory and Laboratory Method* (New York: John Wiley, 1964).

[30] David Ausubel, *The Psychology of Meaningful Verbal Learning* (New York: Grune and Stratton, 1963).

[31] For curriculum strategies built on Piaget's work see: (a) Edmund Sullivan, "Piaget and the School Curriculum: A Critical Appraisal," Bulletin no. 2 of the Ontario Institute for Studies in Education, 1967.   (b) Irving Siegel, "The Piagetian System and the World of Education," in David Elkind and John Flavell, eds., *Studies in Cognitive Development: Essays in Honor of Jean Piaget* (New York: Oxford University Press, 1969).   (c) Hanne Sonquist, Constance Kamii, and Louise Derman, "A Piaget-Derived Preschool Curriculum," to be published in *Educational Implications of Piaget's Theory: A Book of Readings*, ed. I. J. Athey and D. O. Rubadeau (Waltham, Mass.: Blaisdell, in press).

opers like Schwab,[32] Taba,[33] and Suchman,[34] have developed engineering propositions with which academic missions can be approached.

The result of this work is an array of potential curriculum theories which can be applied to the creation of alternative educational environments. The figure below displays the theoretical model of such an enterprise:

MEANS

		1	2	3	4	ETC.
	1					
	2					
MISSIONS	3					
	4					
	ETC.					

Missions-Means Matrix

Just as missions can be categorized into the personal, the social, and the academic, so it is with approaches to the creation of educational environments. Approaches vary according to which view of reality is emphasized. The *personalists* view reality from an individual perspective, and concentrate on environments which *help* the individual create his reality and his worldview. The *interaction-oriented* emphasize the social negotiation of reality and focus on environments which facilitate social processes. A third category is that of the *information-oriented,* who emphasize the symbolization of knowl-

[32] Joseph Schwab, ed., *The Biology Teachers Handbook* (New York: John Wiley, 1965).

[33] Hilda Taba, *Teaching Strategies and Cognitive Functioning in Elementary School Children,* Cooperative Research Project no. 2404 (San Francisco: San Francisco State College, 1961).

[34] J. Richard Suchman, *The Elementary School Training Program in Scientific Inquiry,* Report of U.S. Office of Education Project Title VIII, Project no. 216 (Urbana: University of Illinois, 1962).

edge and concentrate on environments which improve our symbolic capacity to process information. A fourth approach focuses on how culture shapes behavior, and concentrates on the manipulation of the social environment to shape external behavior.

Hence, four types of approaches to the creation of educational environments can be related to three categories of educational mission.

The family of "personalists" includes those theoreticians and practitioners who focus primarily on the individual's construction of his own reality. Thus they focus on the development of the individual, and speculate on the environments which might affect his personality or his general ways of relating to the world. Therapists especially tend to share a concern with the distinctive ways each person constructs his world; they see human nature in terms of individuals.

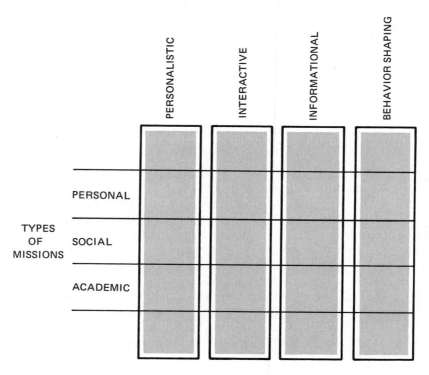

Types of Environments

The second family, those educational theorists and practitioners who focus on the processes by which groups and societies negotiate rules and construct social reality, see education as a process of improving the society. Many in this group have suggested an ideal model for society and procedures for creating an education which can help bring that model to a wider audience.

Others who emphasize social behavior concentrate on interpersonal relations and the dynamics of improving them. The approaches to education in either case have a distinctly social character.

The *information-processing* category consists of educational theoreticians and practitioners who are concerned with affecting the information processing system of the student. It includes those who have developed educational procedures designed to increase general thinking capacity (that is, the capacity to think abstractly or to think inductively). It also includes those who focus on ways of teaching

Table 1. A List of Educational Approaches, Grouped by Orientation and Domain of Mission

APPROACH	MAJOR THEORIST	ORIENTATION (PERSON, SOCIAL INTERACTION, INFORMATION- PROCESSING, OR BEHAVIOR- MODIFICATION)	MISSIONS FOR WHICH APPLICABLE
Non-Directive	Carl Rogers [35]	Person	Development into "fully-functioning" individual (however, broad applicability is suggested, for personal development includes all aspects of growth).
Awareness Training	Schutz,[36] Perls [37]	Person	Increasing personal capacity. Much emphasis on interpersonal development.
Group Investigation	Dewey,[38] Thelen [39]	Social-Interests	Social relations are permanent, but personal development and academic rigor are included.

[35] Rogers, *Client Centered Therapy.*

[36] See William Schutz, *Joy: Expanding Human Awareness* (New York: Grove Press, 1967).

[37] Fritz Perls, *Gestalt Therapy: Excitement and Growth in Human Personality* (New York: Dell Publishing, 1965).

[38] Dewey, *Democracy and Education.*

[39] Herbert Thelen, *Education and the Human Quest* (New York: Harper & Row, 1960).

Table 1. *(Continued)*

APPROACH	MAJOR THEORIST	ORIENTATION (PERSON, SOCIAL INTERACTION, INFORMATION-PROCESSING, OR BEHAVIOR-MODIFICATION)	MISSIONS FOR WHICH APPLICABLE
Reflective Thinking and Social Inquiry	Hullfish and Smith,[40] Massialas and Cox [41]	Social Interaction	Improvement of democratic process is central, with more effective thinking the primary route.
Inductive Reasoning	Taba,[42] Suchmann [43] and others	Information-Processing	Primarily designed to teach academic reasoning, but used for social and personal goals as well.
Logical Reasoning	Extrapolations from Piaget (See Siegel, Sullivan) [44]	Information-Processing	Programs are designed to increase thinking, but also are applied to moral development and other areas. (See Koblberg)
Psychoanalytic	See L. Tyler [45] and others	Person	Personal emotional development is primary and would take precedence.
Creative Reasoning	Torrance,[46] Gordon	Person	Personal development of creativity in problem-solving has priority, but creative problem solving in social and academic domains is also emphasized.

[40] H. Gordon Hullfish and Phillip Smith, *Reflective Thinking: The Method of Education* (New York: Dodd, Mead, 1961).

[41] Cox and Massialas, "The Inquiry Potential of the Social Studies."

[42] Taba, *Teaching Strategies and Cognitive Functioning.*

[43] Suchmann, *The Elementary School Training Program.*

[44] Siegel, "The Piagetian System . . ." and Sullivan, "Piaget and the School Curriculum."

[45] Louise Tyler, "A Case History: Foundation of Objectives from a Psychoanalytic Framework," *Instructional Objectives*, AERA Monograph no. 3 (Washington, D.C.: National Education Association, 1969).

[46] E. Paul Torrance, *Guiding Creative Behavior* (Englewood Cliffs, N.J.: Prentice-Hall, 1962).

Table 1. (*Continued*)

APPROACH	MAJOR THEORIST	ORIENTATION (PERSON, SOCIAL INTERACTION, INFORMATION-PROCESSING, OR BEHAVIOR-MODIFICATION)	MISSIONS FOR WHICH APPLICABLE
Academic Modes	Much of the Curriculum Reform Movement (See especially Schwab and Bruner for rationales)	Information-Processing	Designed to teach the research system of the disciplines, but also expected to have effect in other domains (e.g., sociological methods may be taught in order to increase social understanding and problem-solving).
Programmed Instruction	Skinner [47]	Behavior Modification & Theory	General applicability; domains of objectives.
Conceptual Systems Matching Model	D. E. Hunt [48]	Person	An approach designed to increase personal complexity and flexibility.

students to process information about specific aspects of life. For example, many educational theorists believe that a major mission of education is to develop approaches to the teaching of the academic disciplines, so that the student learns to process information the way the academic scholar processes it and thereby achieve the intellectual power of scholarship.

The fourth group focuses on the processes by which human behavior is externally shaped and reinforced. Their major efforts have been devoted to understanding the shaping of human behavior and how education can be built on an understanding of processes. The major theorist in this area is B. F. Skinner.[49]

It is to these four families that curriculum workers can turn for ideas about educational missions and means. The following is a list

---

[47] B. F. Skinner, *Verbal Behavior* (New York: Appleton-Century-Crofts, 1957).

[48] David E. Hunt, "A Conceptual Level Matching Model for Coordinating Learner Characteristics with Educational Approaches," *Interchange* 1, no. 2 (June 1970).

[49] Individually Prescribed Instruction, Learning Research and Development Center, University of Pittsburgh, Pittsburgh, Pa.

of some educational theorists and approaches from each of the four
categories, grouped according to the domain of mission that each one
favors.

*The purpose of the curriculum field is to develop general knowl-
edge about how to bring educational missions and means together
in the real world. It is the creation of pluralistic educational environments that is our business. We need the ability to specify alternative missions, to create the environments that will accomplish those
missions, and to carry out the engineering necessary to create the
material, the social systems, and the instructional systems that will
actuate them.*

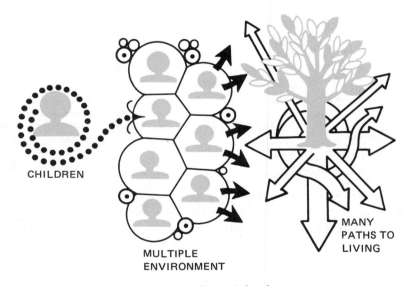

CHILDREN

MULTIPLE
ENVIRONMENT

MANY
PATHS TO
LIVING

The Pluralistic School

The result will be an array of environments, each serving students in
a particular kind of way.

In practice, students will create their own school by selecting
from a wide offering of planned educational programs.

The Environments of Humanistic Education: The School

The Greek and Latin words from which the word *school* is derived originally meant a place where learning takes place in an atmosphere of leisure. There is considerable question whether modern schools are places of either leisure or learning in any significant sense. In fact, in the last fifteen years or so the attack upon the schools of America has been so vehement and hostile that it is a wonder that any of them are still standing and conducting business as usual. But social institutions, as the anthropologists tell us, are very slow to change, especially when they are charged with the task of socializing the young and transmitting the knowledge and values of the past.

The schools, of course, perform many functions, although almost everyone has raised at least some questions as to the extent to which the schools truly educate. The truth of the matter is that the vast majority of the public schools of America are very confused about their purposes or ends. Consequently, it should not be surprising to find many persons who are confused as to the purpose of their membership in them. It is not of purely philosophic concern that most schools lack any overall guiding philosophy of education, whereby rationally felt purposes for human activity might be divined. In fact, a good case could probably be made for the lack of an adequate philosophy of education being the chief cause for the confusion and discontent that is rampant in some schools and colleges.

True education, of course, whether it takes place in a school building or far away from one, is always something more than can be planned for and intellectualized about. Careful planning and intelligently projected goals or

373

"ends-in-view," in Dewey's words, will always remain important dimensions of any truly humanistic education. However, in the schools the administrative, strictly bureaucratic, and political nature of decision-making tends to be emphasized at the expense of the truly humanizing values of education. For example, crucially important decisions about the possible subject matter of education may be made not with a view to the educational benefits of an intellectual, psychological, and scientific encounter with, say, a social problem of man, but rather in terms of whether or not the subject will be too controversial and against the established values of the middle class. Consequently, it could be argued that the problems of war, poverty, racism, sexism, and the like are too controversial, politically, for the public schools of America.

The purpose of this section is to focus attention upon the importance of thinking institutionally about humanistic education. And by implication, at least, the history, philosophy, psychology, and sociology of educating humanistically, find their most complete synthesis in the school. Now, what do I mean by this assertion? Briefly, like any other social institution, the school exists as the product of historical development. In the course of that development it has undergone deeply controversial, philosophical changes, reflective of changing images about man, knowledge, society, and human values. The so-called philosophy of the school, which always issues in part from the historical context of a given society, is intimately related to the psychological and existential make-up of the individual, who lives through his own subjective historical consciousness. In this sense, the psychology of the individual, which is a basic constituent of the philosophical and social values that the individual holds, is the most powerful and important determinant in the possible synthesis of knowledge and experience that the school could embody. Freedom, creativity, and all of the acts and experiences that lead toward the greater humanization and development of the individual as a person, are grounded in the sense of identity that the individual potentially can achieve through the educational situations of the school. Lastly, the school in its sociological aspect presents the viewpoints and values of society at large, where the individual must live out his own subjective beliefs and values. And provided the individual is actualizing his or her full self in the continuous creation of a personally sensed and valued social existence, contributed to most essentially by other persons in their respective social roles and identities, the school represents the most dynamically infused environment for this re-enactment.

To throw light on the goal of creating a humanistic consciousness in the school I have chosen an article by an internationally famous educator A. S. Neill, entitled "I Hate My School—Can I Come to Summerhill?" In his typical hard-hitting but good-humored style, Neill writes about his school, Summerhill, and the philosophy that underlies it. Although Neill rejects the word *humanism,* many people have seen his school as being humanistic and Neill himself as a great humanist. Neill's philosophy of the school shows the extent to which his views about religion, politics, sex, morality, war, child-rearing, knowledge, learning, and freedom are interrelated with education. Basically, the belief behind Summerhill is that "man is originally good," but he "kills his own life and the lives of his children by harsh and anti-life laws and morals and taboos." The theme of Summerhill is freedom, "real freedom, not the sham thing so often called democracy." And Neill has found that when children are free to govern themselves and are free to choose what they want to study or do, and under what conditions, they are happier, more well-balanced, and pro-life. Neill's main assumption that the freedom of the learner is the highest value in school life has had a significant influence in American education, notably in the recent rise of the largely privately backed free school movement.

In the extract from his book *Free Schools,* Jonathan Kozol distinguishes between the different kinds of schools that make up the free school or alternative school movement. On the one hand, there is the urban, "public-school-connected, neighborhood-created, and politically controversial" type, such as the Parkway School of Philadelphia, Pennsylvania. On the other hand, there are the physically isolated, all-white, high-tuition, and politically noncontroversial schools, such as those found in the mountains of Vermont or New Hampshire. While schools of the former type may serve noble, educational ends, such as the responsibility and freedom of the learner, Kozol believes that they suffer from their accountability to the "flag and to the power and to the values which it represents." Schools of the latter type, Kozol feels, dodge real responsibility for the problems of the world, especially those associated with classism and racism, and are "a perfect way to sidetrack ethical men from dangerous behavior." Kozol's own type of free school enjoys some of the advantages, while avoiding the abuses, of both the other types. Basically, Kozol's concept of the ideal free school is that it should be private, nonelitist, urban, social problem-solving, small, and as little known as possible.

Although the free schools of America have not directly affected the great majority of the students, who still attend state-controlled, highly bureaucratized, and standardized schools, they appear to have had a subtle, subliminal influence upon the well-established, middle-class system of public education. This is hard to measure but perhaps discernible in flexible scheduling plans, independent study time, work-study programs, individualized and personalized learning, and other such innovations in the public school system. Changes at a deeper level are only now beginning to be discussed; they would require, in one instance, a constitutional amendment to change compulsory school laws. Any changes in public school education that would increase the sense of freedom and responsibility of the learner for his or her own education would, in my opinion, be a humanizing one.

The selection "E $= SA^2$," extracted from the book *Bodies in Revolt,* by Thomas Hanna, focuses upon what has been called somatology, or the philosophical study of the body. Hanna concludes that "our present educational institutions directly reflect the defunct and now ludicrous policies of the traditional culture, our schools and universities are both corrupt and corrupting." Basically, E $= SA^2$ means that the Energy that is potentially available for the education of man is equal to the Soma, or the bodily me of the self, multiplied by Adaptability to the technological, sensual environment of the twentieth century, squared. Although this is admittedly only play upon the famous Einstein formula, E $= MC^2$, it effectively stresses the significance of energy in the context of an educational institution. At one point Hanna says, "To speak of an educational institution as a way of life organically related to our immediate social and physical environment—and not as a place apart and a time apart—is a radically different conception of an educational institution." Somatic education, to Hanna, includes training in perception, adaptational education, expressive behavioral training, and, in general, new ways of releasing the long pent-up energy within the soma of man. Hanna's bountiful optimism and Nietzschean spirit are visible in his concept of education (or "adaptation") as a "gay science of existence" and the conclusion that "we cannot help but become healthy, happy and powerful" if we are somatically oriented toward the world and life. He calls for the development of a "radically humanistic culture" that can realign us with the world and ourselves.

The last article in this anthology is "First Street School" by George Dennison. It focuses upon one of the most important qualities of humanistic education, love. Dennison asserts that "in humane affairs—and education is *par excellence* a humane pursuit—there is no such thing as competence without love." And not only is love an essential ingredient of educational competence, but "communication, in its true sense of communion and change, is inconceivable apart from this background of love." Dennison holds that the "generalized love that I have been describing is a criterion of wholeness." And wholeness, particularly the wholeness of man, is the fundamental problem as well as experience that unites us all, humanistically, in education.

Dennison's writing on the subject of love is probably the most profound basis upon which to end this anthology. For although he shows sensitivity to the necessity for balance in the educational process, such as that between the carefully guided, informed thought and the affective giving of a Leo Tolstoy, he believes that "a failure of mind is, at bottom, a failure of love." And, as he and many others have indicated, the anonymous, impersonal, bureaucratic rigidity of educational institutions can be the greatest enemy not only of true thought and feeling but also of the very spirit and life of humanistic education.

DISCUSSION QUESTIONS

1. A. S. Neill's Summerhill is known mainly as a school based upon the ideal of freedom in learning. Is there anything else, in your opinion, that is more important in the process of learning than freedom? What is the relationship between freedom and responsibility? Can freedom and responsibility be separate in practice, even though they may be in theory? To what extent is school life or the learning and living atmosphere of an educational institution dependent upon the real freedom of the persons within it? For example, can the political, emotional, sexual, social, and economic realities of school life be separated from intellectual and academic goals? Should they be? Explain. Finally, in what ways would A. S. Neill qualify as a humanistic educator, even though he rejects the term "humanism"?

2. One of Jonathan Kozol's basic assumptions about free schools is that they must fight against "bigness, growth and constant expansion." Do you agree that it is a characteristic of our culture that size is valued more than quality, and that this tendency has influenced the development of our educational institutions? What are the advantages in having a school that has only eighty to one hundred children, as Kozol recommends? Do you think that small size alone will ensure a worthwhile humanistic educational institution? Do you agree with Kozol's criticism of free schools that they are isolated from the problems of the disadvantaged? Do you feel that an alternative or free school that is supported by the public school system must necessarily be "accountable to the flag"? What, in your opinion, would be the ideal form for the free school, one with the characteristics Kozol recommends or something different altogether? Finally, what makes a free school humanistic?

3. Thomas Hanna's main criticism of the schools and colleges appears to be that they are places set apart, both in time and in space, and that they are not "organically related to our immediate social-physical environment. . . ." Do you feel that this is true? If so, of what significance is it to realizing the "radically humanistic culture" that Hanna calls for? Do you think that the schools and colleges should become places where new "ways of living of an experimental nature" are tried out? Why, or why not? What significance could Hanna's concept of energy have for humanizing educational institutions? Do you think, for example, that a new concept of moral-

ity could develop from somatic education? Do you share Hanna's optimism that "we cannot help but become healthy, happy and powerful" through the process of somatic involvement in the twentieth century? Which conditions would hinder and which promote the development of a radically humanistic culture in the schools, colleges, and universities?

4. George Dennison believes that without a "background of love," true communication and a humane use of the mind is not possible. Do you personally place such a high value upon love, and if so, why? What is the significance of human love to educational institutions? Do you think, for example, that an educational institution can be humanistic without a background of love and caring? Do you think that the rigidity and dehumanization of bureaucratic institutions is due to the absence of a background of love and caring? Do you agree with Dennison that any solution to our present educational problems is "doomed to failure" if it perpetuates the existing authoritarian bureaucracy? How can we transform the authoritarian structure of our educational institutions so that schools may be places of true human concern, as Dennison recommends? Can this be done by love alone? Is more required? What?

FURTHER READING

Bremer, John, and Michael von Moschzisker. *The School Without Walls.* New York: Holt, Rinehart and Winston, Inc., 1971.

Goodman, Paul. *Compulsory Mis-education and the Community of Scholars.* New York: Vintage Books, 1966.

Gross, Ronald and Beatrice. *Radical School Reform.* New York: A Clarion Book, 1969.

Heath, Douglas H. *Humanizing Schools.* New York: Hayden Book Company, Inc., 1971.

Katz, Michael B. *The Irony of Early School Reform.* Boston: Beacon Press, 1968.

Leonard, George B. *Education and Ecstasy.* New York: A Delta Book, 1968.

Neill, A. S. *Summerhill: A Radical Approach to Child Rearing.* New York: Hart Publishing Company, 1960.

Sarason, Seymour B. *The Culture of the School and the Problem of Change.* Boston: Allyn and Bacon, Inc., 1971.

I Hate My School—Can I Come to Summerhill?

A. S. NEILL

Just over 20 years ago I had two books published in New York, *The Problem Teacher* and *The Problem Family*. So far as I could make out each issue sold a few hundred copies and the rest were sold as remainders at a few dimes each. The press notices I got were either luke-warm or hostile. One called the books old hat. "We have lived through this in the States and there is nothing new for us." Twenty years later the book *Summerhill* became a best seller in the States. Why? I have no idea. I like to think that the U.S.A. has come up to date rather than that I have gone out of date. I do not know why I get so large a mail from the U.S.A. It is mostly from young people and in the seven years since the book was published I can recall only two hostile letters. Many are from school children. "Can I come to Summerhill? I hate my school. It is all pressurization. The teachers make every lesson dull and dead and originality is frowned upon." Oddly enough, although our British education is all wrong, I never get letters from home children.

The mystery to me is this: Why has America become conscious that its education is not good enough? Why now and not 20 years ago? Surely the schools have not changed all that much. But is it a case of a change of society? Is society sicker than it was a couple of decades ago? I fancy that that is the deep reason. In all countries youth is rebelling. Alas, too often rebelling against all that does not matter. The hippies, the flower merchants show their protests, not against war, not against race discrimination, not against the stupid learning we call education; no, all the challenge is the right to wear long hair and leather jackets and blue jeans. That is the impression I get in this country, but from what I hear and read about America the young, especially in the universities, are challenging real evils—the insane dollar values, the dead uniformity of the people who have been molded and indoctrinated so much that they are automatic slaves to any ideas thrown out by the press and the TV screens. In Britain I think that the average TV program is geared to a nation of 10-year-olds. Our B.B.C. refused to put on *The War Game* because it told of the horrors of an atomic war and it might upset the nice folks who want to think that God is in his Heaven and all is right with the world. The young feel that they have been cheated by the old, lied to, castrated by their parents and teachers. They no longer accept glib answers—in Vietnam we are saving the world from Communism; in South Africa we are preserving the God-given rights of the superior whites; in the U.S.A. we are battling to preserve the white civilization. It is significant that all these reasons involve hate and war and possibly ultimate death to humanity. Youth sees a world full of savagery. Hitler's six million Jews paved the way for a world that accepted torture and death as almost commonplace factors in our modern life. In short, the world is very very sick, and youth feels it but, alas, cannot do much about it. Summerhill's good friend Joan Baez, recently in prison, has no power over the hate merchants; all she can do is to march in protest and then be carted to prison. It is the helplessness of youth that so often brings despair.

In this American *Stimmung* the book *Summerhill* was launched in 1960. It caught on because it was voicing what so many of the young had felt but had not intellectualized, had not made conscious. For its theme was freedom—real freedom, not the sham thing so often called democracy. Freedom for all to grow at their own pace; freedom from all indoctrination, religious, political, moral; freedom for children to live in their own community, making their own social laws. To many a youth Summerhill became synonymous with Paradise. I hasten to say that it isn't—*Gott set dank!* Most of the rebellion stems from home, from what Wilhelm Reich called the compulsive family, the family that strangles youth, fears youth, often hates youth. From my mail I am led to believe that the American family is more dangerous than the British one. I never get the sort of letter I had two days ago from New York. "I am 17 and I am allowed no freedom at all. I have to be in at certain hours and if I am late my father hits me. I hate my parents." A girl of a middle-class family. I have had scores of similar letters. A boy of 15 writes, "I hate school and cannot concentrate on my work and my parents bully me all the time because they say that I must go to college and get a good job." I have no idea how much truth is in Vance Packard's *The Status Seekers* but even if a 10th is true it gives a terrible picture of American civilization. A Cadillac-civilization with its sequel, dope and drugs and misery for those who cannot accept the god of cars and furs and wealth.

This looks like an attack on a country by an outsider and it may well be resented by some readers, but I do not mean it as an attack; it is a case of trying to think aloud the answer to the question: Why did the Summerhill book catch on in the U.S.A.? At home we have our own miseries and troubles. The growing race hate due to the immigration from Jamaica. The futility of a culture that gives the cheap sensational press millions of readers while the more cultured papers—*The New Statesman,* the *Observer,* the *Sunday Times*—too often struggle to keep themselves alive. World sickness is not confined to North America. Russia has its teen-age gangsters also.

One reason why Summerhill appealed to the U.S.A. may be that it is, so to say, anti-education. The great American educationists, Dewey, Kilpatrick and their kind, were mostly pre-Freudian in their outlook. They kept linking education to learning, and today in all countries educational journals concentrate on the learning process. I escaped that trap. I was and I am ill-versed on what the educationists did. I never read Rousseau or Pestalozzi or Froebel; what I read in Montessori I did not like, partly because it made play the mate of learning. Learning what? Summerhill is not a seat of learning; it is a seat of living. We are not so proud of David who became a professor of mathematics as we are of Jimmy who was hateful and antisocial and is now a warm-hearted engineer with much charity and love to give out. Summerhill puts learning in its own place. I have more than once written that if the emotions are free the intellect will look after itself. What a waste it all is! Sixty years ago I could read some Latin and Greek. Today I can't decipher the Latin words on a tombstone. Our schools teach children to read Shakespeare and Hardy and Tennyson and when they leave school the vast majority never read anything better than a crime story. For my part I'd abolish nearly every school subject, making geography and history matters for the school library, and quadratic equations a luxury for the few boys and girls who loved maths. Abolish exams and my school will have only creative teachers—art, music, drama, handwork, etc.

Every man has a bee in his bonnet. It was comforting to read in Erich Fromm that Freud had to be in the station an hour before his train was due. My original bee was psychology. In the 1920s my home was Vienna and my associates the psychoanalysts. Like all young fools I thought that Utopia was just 'round the corner. Make the unconscious conscious and you have a world full of love and fellowship with no hate. I grew out of that phase but did retain the belief that education must primarily deal with the emotions. Working for many years with problem children made my belief stronger. I saw that the aim of all education must be to produce happy, balanced, pro-life children, and I knew that all the exams and books in a million classrooms could not do a thing to make children balanced. A B.A. could be a hopeless neurotic—I am an M.A. myself. A professor could remain at the age of 10 emotionally. What the emotional level of the British Cabinet or the American Pentagon is is anyone's guess; my own guess is a low one. Today in any school anywhere it is the head that is educated; every exam paper proves the point.

Now one cannot flee from reality. I could not say to prospective parents, "Exams and school subjects are not education and I refuse to teach the ordinary school subjects." That is what the Americans would call flunking out, and, by the way, I get too many letters from students in the U.S.A. saying, "I can't go on with my college career. The teaching is too dull; I am flunking out. I want to be a child psychologist." I answer that they won't let one be a child psychologist unless one accepts their qualification demands. I wrote to the last man who had flunked out, "If you haven't the guts to walk through the muck heaps, how can you ever except to smell the roses you value so much?"

I do not find this flunking-out element in old Summerhill pupils. One of my first pupils spent two years standing at a mechanical belt in a car factory. He is now a successful engineer with his own business. His brother who wanted to be a doctor had to pass an exam in Latin. In just over a year he passed the matriculation exam in Latin. "I hated the stuff but it was in my way and I had to master it." That was over 40 years ago when students did not as a rule flunk out. I do not think that youth has become defeatist; rather it is that society has reached a point of futility and cheapness and danger where youth, frustrated by the mundane standard of success, simply gives up in despair. "Make Love not War" is a most appropriate motto for youth even if youth feels it is a hopeless cry, and it is a hopeless cry; the hate men who make wars force youth to die for country but when the young demand freedom to have a sex life, holy hypocritical hands are held up in horror. Youth is free to die but not to live and love.

I fear I am rambling, not sticking to the point. My consolation— too many who stick to the point make it a blunt one. I ramble because I am trying to evaluate Summerhill as a factor in the sick world, really asking what value freedom has for youth. One is naturally apt to think that one's geese are swans; one tends to forget or ignore the outside world, so that when a lecturer in education in an American college wrote and told me that over 70 percent of his students thought that Summerhill was all wrong it came as a shock. I had repressed the idea that when the young are conditioned and indoctrinated from cradle days, it is almost impossible for them to break away, to challenge. Few can stand alone without a supporting crowd behind them. "The strongest man is he who stands most alone." Ibsen.

I like to think that freedom helps one to stand outside the maddening crowd. Symbolically one sees differences. The conventional suburban office-goer with his striped trousers and his neat tie and his neater mind on one side. On the other, the creator, the artist to whom exterior things mean but little. Compare the tailoring of L. B. J. with that of a film director or a Picasso. Symbols, but characteristic. Put it this way: Summerhill gets hundreds of visitors but I do not think that any visitor ever notices that my staff never wear ties. Summerhill hasn't got to the Old-School-Tie stage. But one cannot carry such phantasying too far; my old friend Bertrand Russell wears a tie, and no one would claim that he is a crowd man.

I think that one aspect of Summerhill is that it, rightly or wrongly, gives pupils an anti-crowd psychology. I could not imagine any old pupil following a Hitler or for that matter a Kennedy or a Reagan. This sounds incongruous because the chief feature of Summerhill is the self-government, the making of laws by one and all from the age of five to 84. Pupils become ego-conscious and at the same time community-conscious. Bill can do what he likes all day long as long as he does not interfere with the freedom of anyone else; he can sleep all day if he wants to but he is not allowed to play a trumpet when others want to talk or sleep. It is as near democracy as one can get; every child is a member of parliament able to speak "in the house." No doubt because this democracy is real and honest our old pupils cannot tolerate the sham we name politics. Because politicians have to rely on votes nearly every urgent reform is delayed for two generations. In England an M.P. has—say—a predominantly Catholic constituency or a Baptist one. How can he act honestly when faced with some reform—a bill to abolish punishment for homosexuality, a much-needed reform of the divorce and abortion laws? Was any great man a politician? Any Darwin, any Freud, any Einstein, any Beethoven? Was any big man ever a crowd-compeller, a demagogue?

When children are free they become wonderfully sincere. They cannot act a part; they cannot stand up in the presence of a school inspector because they will not countenance insincerity and make-believe. Tact forces them to make minor adaptations as it does with you and me. I dutifully doff my hat to a lady although I realize that it is a meaningless, even dishonest, gesture, hiding the fact that in a patriarchal society a woman is inferior in status, in pay, in power. To tell a social white lie is often a necessity but to live a lie is something that free people cannot do. And my pupils feel that to be a member of a crowd must involve living a lie.

This crowd psychology angle is important. It is at the root of the sickness of the world. A neighboring country insults your flag and many thousands of young men die for the honor and glory of their fatherland. National hatreds everywhere, Greek v. Turkey; Israel v. Arabs; Rhodesian white v. Black. And it is not only the nationalism crowd. Our football grounds are full of irrational, partisan hate and violence. Gang warfare is not confined to Chicago. Yet in a way violence is minor. It is the violence that a crowd inflicts on its members that frightens, the violence of intimidating, of molding. A school uniform means: We are members of a crowd, a crowd that will not tolerate opposition. We must all dress alike, think alike, act alike. For the great law of any crowd is: Thou shalt conform. The world is sick because its crowds are sick.

Education therefore should aim at abolishing crowd psychology. It can do this only by allowing the individual to face life and its choices freely. Such an education cannot lead to egocentricity and utter selfishness, not if the individual is free within the confines of the social order, an order made by himself. The slogan "All the way with L. B. J." shows the iniquity of the crowd, a system that makes crowd members sheep who can feel the most elementary emotions without having the intellectual capacity to connect such emotions with reason. Today our schools educate the head and leave the emotions to the crowd-compellers—the press, the radio, the TV, the churches, the commercial exploiters with their lying advertisements. Our pop heroes and film stars have become our leading schoolmasters, dealing with real emotions. What teacher in what school could have a few hundred hysterical females screaming their heads off when he appeared?

The danger today is undeveloped emotion, perverted emotion, infantile emotion. Millions scream in Britain every Saturday afternoon when their favorite football teams take the field. If the evening paper had a front page in big lettering "Atom War Very Near," most of the spectators would turn to the back page to see the latest scores. Crowd emotions are not touched by news of starvation in India or China. It is this same unattached unrealized emotion that makes the crowd numb to any realization of a likely atomic war. Crowd emotion is not shocked by our inhuman and un-Christlike treatment of criminals in prison; it does not even realize that the inhumanity is there. And none of us is guiltless. I do not cut down my tobacco and give the savings to the starving nations. We are all in the trap and only the more aware of us try to find a way out. My own way is Summerhill or rather the idea behind Summerhill, the belief that man is originally good, that, for reasons no one so far knows, man kills his own life and the lives of his children by harsh and anti-life laws and morals and taboos. It is so easy to cry, "Man is a sinner and he must be redeemed by religion" or what not. God and the Devil were comfortable explanations of good and evil. One thing I think Summerhill has proved is that man does not need to become a "sinner," that man does not naturally hate and kill. The crowd in Summerhill is a humane one. In 47 years I have never seen a jury punish a child for stealing; all it demanded was that the value of the theft be paid back. When children are free they are not cruel. Freedom and aggression do not go together, that is, without fear and outside discipline and imposed morality. They seem to have much less aggression than most children have, suggesting to me that the Freudians with their emphasis on aggression must have studied the wrong children.

Even in Summerhill, where very few pupils were self-regulated, there is a peacefulness, a minimum of criticism, a tolerance that is quite uncommon. When a Negress pupil came from the States not even the youngest child seemed to notice her color. Our TV showed white faces full of hatred when black pupils were being stoned in the Deep South. This is alarming. We can condition children to hate and kill by giving them a hate environment. But we can also give them another sort of environment—were I a Christian I'd call it a love-your-neighbor environment. But then, what is a Christian? Catholics and Protestants beat children in home and school—didn't Jesus say suffer the little children? The Christians see that they suffer, all right. But to narrow the life negation to religion is wrong. A humanist can hate life and children; he can be as anti-sex as any Calvinist.

Summerhill has not answered many questions, the biggest one being: Why does humanity kill the life of children, why does it take more easily to hate than to love? Why did jackboot Fascism conquer a nation of 60 million?

One answer to the question of world sickness is sex repression. Make sex a sin and you get perversions, crime, hates, wars. Approve of children's sex as the Trobriand Islanders did under a matriarchal system and a Malinowski will fail to find any trace of sex crime or homosexuality before the missionaries came and segregated the sexes. Wilhelm Reich, to me the greatest psychologist since Freud, dwelt on the necessity for a full natural orgastic life as a cure for the sickness of an anti-life society. Then came the new American Interpersonal Relationship school of Sullivan and Horney, with long case histories of patients who seemed to have no sex at all. I have a book on problem children written by an Adlerian; I failed to find the word sex in it. And in all this divergence of views on sex, what can one believe? One can make the guess that the torturers of German Jews were sex perverts, but can one safely conclude that the men in the Pentagon are Hawks because of their sex repressions?

I have gone through many phases in the last 50 years, the most exciting my long friendship with Homer Lane and then with Reich. Now, at 84, I simply do not know the truth about sex. Is a teacher who canes a boy's bottom a repressed homosexual or a sadist or simply a man who has never been conscious of what he is doing? I ask because my father in his village school tawsed children with a leather strap and when I became a teacher I automatically did likewise without ever once wondering if it were good or bad. Looking back now I see that one motive was fear, fear of losing one's dignity, one's power; fear that any slackness would lead to anarchy. I cannot see anything sexual in my tawsing.

Summerhill society is a sex-approving society. Every child soon learns that there is no moral feeling about masturbation or nudism or sex-play. But every adolescent is conscious of the fact that if approval meant the sharing of bedrooms by adolescents the school would be closed by the Establishment. One old boy once said to me: "The fear of closing the school if pregnancies occurred gave us a new form of sex repression." The difficulty was and is this: How far can a school go in being pro-sex in an anti-sex society? Not very far, I fear. Yet one factor is of moment; the pupils are conscious of our attitude of approval. They have had no indoctrination about sin or shame, no moralizing from Mrs. Grundy. Their free attitude shows itself in minor ways. In our local cinema a film showed a chamber pot. The audience went into fits of obscene laughter but our pupils did not even smile; one or two asked me later why the people laughed. Free children cannot be shocked—by cruelty, yes, but by sex, never.

Summerhill products are often said to be quiet, unaggressive, tolerant citizens, and I wonder how much their rational attitude on sex has to do with their calmness of life. They prove that censorship is the product of a life-hating civilization. I never see our adolescents taking from the school library *Lady Chatterley* or *Fanny Hill*. A girl of 16 said they were boring.

Most of our old pupils are pacific. They do not march with banners against the H-bomb or against racial discrimination. I cannot imagine any of them ever supporting warmongers or religious revivalists or play censors. But how much this has to do with a free attitude to sex I cannot know. Certainly sex is the most repressed of all emotions. Most of us were made anti-sex when in our cradles our hands were taken from our genitals, and it is an arresting thought that the men who have the power to begin a nuclear war are men who were made sex-negative long ago. Anglo-Saxon four-letter words are still taboo in most circles, maybe partly for class reasons; a navvy says fuck while a gentleman says sexual intercourse.

I confess to being muddled about the whole affair of sex. I do not know if we all experienced Reich's perfect orgasm there would be an end to war and crime and hate. *I hae ma doots.* Yet it is true that people who have a pro-sex attitude to life are the ones most likely to be charitable, to be tolerant, to be creative. Those who do not consider themselves sinners do not cast the first stone. For charity I would go to Bertrand Russell rather than to Billy Graham.

Billy naturally leads to religion. Summerhill has no religion. I fancy that very few religionists approve of it. A leading Church of England priest once called it the most religious school in the world, but few parsons would agree with him. It is interesting to note that I have had many letters of approval from Unitarians in the U.S.A. I asked one Unitarian minister what his religion was. Did he believe in God? No, he said. In eternal life? "Good heavens, no. Our religion is giving out love in this life," and I guess that is exactly what the Church of England priest meant. It is our being on the side of the child (Homer Lane's phrase) that has aroused so much antagonism among religionists. The other day a Catholic school inspector told a meeting of Catholics that corporal punishment was practiced much more in their schools than in Protestant ones. "We beat the body to save the soul." In the days of that life-hater John Knox I would have been burned at the stake. The widening interest in the freedom that Summerhill stands for fits in with the lessening belief in religion. Most young people, outside the R. C. faith, have no interest in religion. To them God is dead. God to them was father, molder, punisher, a fearful figure. The gods and fathers were always on the side of the suppressors. In Britain the enemies of youth, those who call for the return of beating with the cat, those who want to censor plays and films and language, those who demand strict punishment for the teen-age delinquents, they are not the young; they are the old, the old who have forgotten their teen-age period.

I am sure that the growing interest in freedom for children coincides with modern youth's rejection of a joyless, repressive religion. A religion that has become perverted. Christ's "love your neighbor as yourself" has become: Okay, so long as he isn't a Jew or a Black. "Let him who is without sin among you cast the first stone" has become: Censor plays and novels and measure bathing costumes. Owing to the threat of universal incineration youth today is possibly more pro-life than it has ever been. Juvenile crime is really at bottom an attempt to find the joy of life killed by morals and discipline and punishment. In the days when Summerhill had many delinquents they went out cured simply because they were free from adult standards of behavior. Religion must be rejected because it tells the young how to live, but it does not need to be religion; I have known humanists who gave their children sex repression; I know agnostics who believe in beating children. Really what one believes does not matter, it is what one is that matters. After all religion is geographical; had I been born in Arabia I'd have had three wives and, alas, no whisky.

There is a comic element in religion even if there isn't a joke in the Bible or the Prayer Book. The true believer must know that Bertrand Russell will roast in hell for eternity while Billy Graham sits at the right hand of God. With Russell to look after, the familiar words "poor Devil" will have a real significance.

What is the outlook for freedom? Will the minority ever take over from the majority? And if it does, will it retain its belief in freedom? Doesn't Ibsen say somewhere that a truth remains a truth for 20 years, then the majority takes it up and it becomes a lie? Summerhill has 64 children who are free from molding: the world has millions of children who have little or no freedom, millions of adults who frankly are sheep. One tragedy of life is that men have followers. Men who remain disciples are always inferiors. The Pharisee who thanked God that he was not as other men may have been a conceited ass but on the other hand he may have got hold of something. There is something wrong when millions who praise the Beatles never heard of Milton or Freud or Cézanne, when millions kill the life of their babies, when thousands of young men die in a battle for they know not what. Anti-life is all around us, and I wish I knew why. I wish I knew why mankind kills what it loves. I do not know the answer; all I know is that when children are free they do not kill life; they do not condemn their fellow men. They do not want to tell others how to live. It is significant that old pupils do not seek jobs where they will boss others; few have gone into business. I used to daydream of one's becoming a tycoon and endowing the school, knowing all the time that he would be so hard-boiled that he would not endow anything.

I am not trying to sell Summerhill. I am trying to say that the cure for the sickness of man does not lie in politics or religion or humanism; nay, the cure is freedom for children to be themselves. Like many others I once thought that the Russian Revolution would bring Utopia to youth, for it began with freedom for children, self-government in the schools. Then, according to Reich, the psychologists took charge and youth became sacrificed to political anti-life, so that today communism has no connection with individual freedom to grow naturally. Indeed I often wonder why the Americans are so scared of communism. Both systems believe in the terror of the bomb; both discipline and castrate children; both believe that education means subjects and exams and acquired knowledge. The only difference I can see is who takes the profit? The Russian Revolution proved that the sickness of the world cannot be cured by politics.

The only answer that I can think of is freedom for children, individual freedom, social freedom, sexual freedom as in a small way practiced in Summerhill.

I said that I thought Wilhelm Reich the greatest psychologist since Freud. His diagnosis of man's sickness is deep and wise. Man flees from natural sex by armoring himself against joy in life, stiffening his body, fearing any signs of genitality, changing good emotions into "emotional plague," in short, becoming anti-life, hence wars and many diseases and child-beating. Even if one accepts Reich's diagnosis the question arises: What can be done about it? How can we prevent folks from becoming anti-sex and anti-life? Analysis of any school is not the answer. What effect on humanity have all the case histories ever published? Do all the things Melanie Klein found in babies have any bearing on the education of children? So far psychology has been a matter of diagnosing without any salient suggestions for a cure. Ah, yes, some cases of cures of individual neurotics, but the cure for a sick world, none. A Scientologist has just told me that he could cure any problem child in my school in 10 days.

Are we all fakers? Self-deluders? Do the hundreds of books on psychology published every year have any effect at all? I am inclined to say none, but I am biased, for I cannot read a book on psychology now.

The psychologists have narrowed the science—or is it an art? The doctors have limited psychology to the consulting room and the rich and those with time to spare. How many psychoanalysts have opened schools? A few—Anna Freud, Susan Isaacs, e.g., but the main body of Freudians has done nothing in the way of prophylaxis. The Summerhill Society of New York issues a list of schools claiming to have self-regulation and self-government. Some may be excellent but, as I have not seen any of them, I cannot give an opinion pro or anti. I do not think that they belong to any special schools of psychology and I sincerely hope that they don't. I am sure that the list does not contain the name of the school that claimed to be Summerhillian and washed out a boy's mouth with soap and water when he swore.

The future of psychology should lie not in the consulting room or the hospital for neurosis but in the infant bedroom and the infant school. Mr. Brown's phobia of spiders may fascinate his analyst but his phobia is as nothing in a world of millions of half-alive children.

To return to Summerhill, it went through the stages of the Century—the faith in analysis, the futile attempt to find the original trauma in a young thief. I read them all—Freud, Jung, Adler, Rank, Stekel, Reich—and got more and more confused by their psychological jargon. I never learned the meaning of words like manic-depression, compulsive neurosis, hysteria, etc. Never knew how specialists could draw the line between one and another. Oh, so many were brilliant in their diagnosis and treatment, but in the end what did one learn? And today I feel as confused about the Interpersonal Relationship folks, for, if men like Stekel seemed to overemphasize sex, they seem to denigrate it altogether. So I left schools of thought and concentrated on Summerhill, forgetting theory and avoiding words like complex. "Everyone is right in some way," Reich used to say, the corollary being that everyone is wrong in some way.

Let us face the truth, that we are all little men, even the greatest among us. We do not know how and why the super Rolls Royce, the human body, ticks. We know nothing about life and how it began, nor can we account for the universe. We do not know why Brown dies of cancer and his brother of diabetes. In the psychological realm we can not account for a Bach or a Milton or a Hitler. We know little about heredity or the origins of love and hate. A doctor does not know what causes a headache. So that we should be wary of panaceas of all kinds—Zen Buddhism, Scientology, Theosophy, psychoanalysis, Moral Rearmament, and a few score of other isms and ologies. We must go on enquiring, searching for the truth, but if we follow a creed, if we label ourselves Freudian or Reichian or Hubbardian or any other ian we have stopped growing, stopped enquiring; we become "yes" men. It worries me to hear of schools in the U.S.A. that call themselves Summerhills. One should take from others what one feels is good. No one should accept any creed, religious or political or psychological. I got much from Homer Lane; later I got much from Reich. But in both men were views that I could not accept, and thus I escaped discipline. If a teacher claims that Summerhill inspired him, good, I wish him luck, but if a school claims to be a new Summerhill I fear it will fail. There is a pioneer in each of us, an explorer, a visionary. As in sport we pay others to play the game for us, so in pioneering; we find it easy to look for a leader and be content to be a humble follower of Billy Graham, Sigmund Freud, Barry Goldwater, Karl Marx. Fans are arrested creators, arrested pioneers. And the big question is: in a world in which the vast majority are fans, how can a few independent people set about "curing" the Establishment?

We must remember that the Establishment has the ultimate power. A bureaucratic Ministry of Education could close my school on material grounds alone: not enough lavatories, not enough cubic feet per child in a bedroom. But, to be fair, the Ministry has not interfered with me in the 44 years Summerhill has been in England. But now that the National Union of Teachers and many Labor M.P.'s demand the closing of all private schools, pioneering in education is going to have a bad time. Had there been no private schools there could not have been a Summerhill; the State, the Establishment will allow new methods of teaching history or maths but it is unlikely to tolerate new methods of living in a school. Really I should vote Tory, for the Tories will not lightly give up their Etons and Harrows, and as long as we have the public schools like Rugby the smaller private schools will be protected. Alas, the private school is I fear doomed by lack of finance alone. Summerhill would have died seven years ago had not the publication of *Summerhill* in the U.S.A. brought a flood of American pupils. Today people in England do not have the money to support private schools. Those who do, select the established schools, the public schools and the big co-ed schools with their well-equipped libraries, labs, etc. Parents, like teachers, still look on education as learning in all countries East and West. Educational journals seldom mention the child or freedom or creation. When I write a letter about the teaching of English I get quite a few replies, but when I write an article on the psychology of the child no teacher answers.

I want to claim that Summerhill has for 47 years demanded that character is of more moment than the ability to learn subjects. I have never denigrated learning; all I have done is to put it in its second or 10th place. But what effect the school has had on education I cannot judge. Some say that the permissiveness of some schools stems from Summerhill. Who can know? I like to think that it isn't Summerhill, that it is the *Zeitgeist*, the longing of youth for freedom. Maybe some *History of Education* in the year 2000 will have a footnote about a school called Summerfield run by a mad Scot called S. A. Neale. Sorry I won't be there to laugh at the footnote.

Free School as a Term Meaning Too Many Different Things: What Other People Mean— What I Mean—What I Do Not Mean

JONATHAN KOZOL

The term "Free School" is used very often, in a cheerful but unthinking way, to mean entirely different kinds of things and to define the dreams and yearnings of entirely disparate and even antagonistic individuals and groups. It is honest, then, to say, right from the start, that I am speaking mainly of one type of Free School and that many of the ventures which go under the name of Free School will not be likely to find much of their own experience reflected here.

At one end of the spectrum, there is the large, public-school-connected, neighborhood-created, and politically controversial operation best exemplified perhaps by I.S. 201, in its initial phase, or later by Ocean Hill-Brownsville in New York. Somewhat smaller, but still involving some of the same factors, and still tied in with the public-education apparatus, is the Morgan School in Washington, D.C. At the opposite extreme is a rather familiar type of physically isolated, politically noncontroversial, and generally all-white, high-tuition Free School. This kind of school is often tied in with a commune or with what is described as an "intentional community," attracts people frequently who, if not rich, have parents who are wealthy, and is often associated with a certain kind of media-promoted counterculture.

Neither of the two descriptions just preceding would apply directly to the kind of Free School I have tended to be most intensively involved with, though certainly I have been a great deal closer to the first than to the second. There is also a considerable difference in the way I feel about the two. The large, political, and public-school-associated ventures like Ocean Hill-Brownsville are, in my opinion, brave, significant, and in many ways heroic struggles for survival on the part of those who constitute the most despised and brutalized and properly embittered victims of North American racism and class exploitation. While these are not the kinds of schools that I am writing about here, they seem to me to be of vast importance, and I look upon the people who are active in them with immense respect.

The other end of the spectrum does not seem to me to be especially courageous or heroic. In certain ways it appears to me to be a dangerous and disheartening phenomenon—the radical version of benign neglect. I know, of course, that very persuasive arguments can be presented for the idea of escaping from the turmoil and the human desperation of the cities, and for finding a place of physical isolation in the mountains of Vermont or in the hills of Southern California. Like many people here in Boston and New York, I have often felt the urge to run away, especially when I see a picture or read something in a magazine about these pastoral and isolated Free Schools in their gentle and attractive settings of hillside, farmland, and warm country meadow. When I am the most weary, the inclination to escape is almost overwhelming.

Despite this inclination, which I feel so often, I believe we have an obligation to stay here and fight these battles and work out these problems in the cities, where there is the greatest need, and where, moreover, we cannot so easily be led into a mood of falsified euphoria. If a man should feel, as many people do, that whites should not be working in black neighborhoods, then there are plenty of poor white neighborhoods in major cities, or neighborhoods of the marginal lower-middle class along the edges of the major cities, as well as in several of the rural neighborhoods of Appalachia and the Deep South and Southwest, areas of need, of pain and devastation—in which we might establish roots and settle down to try to build our Free Schools and to develop those communities of struggle which so frequently grow up around them. I know it is very appealing, and for people who are weary from a long, long period of fruitless struggle and rebellion, it is almost irresistible to get away from everything. I don't believe, however, that we should give in to this yearning, even if it is very appealing and even if we are very, very weary. In any case, I am addressing this book primarily to those who do not plan to run away.

There is one point about the exodus of rich people to the woods and hills which is, to me, particularly disturbing. Some of the most conscientious and reflective of the people in the upper-class Free Schools will often seek to justify their manner of escape by pointing out that they, and their young children with them, have in a sense "retired" from the North American system as a whole, and especially from its agencies of devastation, power, and oppression. Though earnestly presented, this argument does not seem honest. Whether they like it or not, or whether they wish to speak of it or not, the beautiful children of the rich and powerful within this nation are going to be condemned to wield that power also. This power, which will be theirs if they are cognizant of it, and even if they aren't, will be the power to affect the lives of millions of poor men and women in this nation, to do so often in the gravest ways, often indeed to grant or to deny life to these people. It will be the power, as well, to influence the lives of several hundred million people who are now subject to North American domination in far distant lands. Even in the idealistic ritual of formal abdication of that power, as, for example, by going out into the isolated hills of western Massachusetts or into the mountains of Vermont to start a Free School, they will still be profiting from the consequences of that power and from the direct profits and extractions of a structure of oppression.

Free Schools, then, cannot, with sanity, with candor, or with truth, endeavor to exist within a moral vacuum. However far the journey and however many turnpike tolls we pay, however high the spruce or pine that grow around the sunny meadows in which we live and dream and seek to educate our children, it is still one nation. It is not one thing in Lebanon, New Hampshire: one thing in the heart of Harlem. No more is it one thing in Roxbury or Watts, one thing in Williamsburg or Canyon, California. The passive, tranquil, and protected lives white people lead depend on strongly armed police, well-demarcated ghettos. While children starve and others walk the city streets in fear on Monday afternoon, the privileged young people in the Free Schools of Vermont shuttle their hand-looms back and forth and speak of love and of "organic processes." They do "their thing." Their thing is sun and good food and fresh water and good doctors and delightful, old, and battered eighteenth-century houses, and a box of baby turtles; somebody else's thing may be starvation, broken glass, unheated rooms, and rats inside the bed with newborn children. The beautiful children do not *wish* cold rooms or broken glass, starvation, rats, or fear for anybody; nor will they stake their lives, or put their bodies on the line, or interrupt one hour of the sunlit morning, or sacrifice one moment of the golden af-ternoon, to take a hand in altering the unjust terms of a society in which these things are possible.

I know that I will antagonize many people by the tenor of these statements; yet I believe them deeply and cannot keep faith with the people I respect, and who show loyalty to me, if I put forward a piece of writing of this kind and do not say these things. In my belief, an isolated upper-class Free School for the children of the white and rich within a land like the United States and in a time of torment such as 1972 is a great deal too much like a sandbox for the children of the S.S. guards at Auschwitz. If today in our history books, or in our common conversation, we were to hear of a network of exquisite, idealistic little country schools operated with a large degree of personal freedom, but within the bounds of ideological isolation, in the beautiful sloping woodlands outside of Munich and Berlin in 1939 or 1940, and if we were to read or to be told that those who ran these schools were operating by all innovative methods and enlightened notions and that they had above their desks or on their walls large poster-photographs of people like Maria Montessori and Tolstoi and Gandhi, and that they somehow kept beyond the notice of the Nazi government and of the military and of the police and S.S. guards, but kept right on somehow throughout the war with no expe-rience of rage or need for intervention in the live of those defined by the German press and media as less than human, but kept right on with water play and "innovative" games while smoke rose over Da-chau . . . I think that we would look upon those people now as some very fine and terrifying breed of alienated human beings.

It is not a handsome or a comfortable parallel; yet, in my judg-ment it is not entirely different from the situation of a number of the country communes and the segregated Summerhills that we now see in certain sections of this nation. A best, these schools are obviating pain and etherizing evil; at worst, they constitute a registered escape valve for political rebellion. Least conscionable is when the people who are laboring and living in these schools describe themselves as revolutionaries. If this is revolution, then the men who have elected Richard Nixon do not have a lot to fear. They would do well in fact to subsidize these schools and to covertly channel resources to their benefactors and supporters, for they are an ideal drain on activism and the perfect way to sidetrack ethical men from dangerous behavior.

Size and Relationship to Public Schools

The direct opposite of the all-white, nonpolitical Free School for rich children may logically appear to be the large, controversial, public-school-affiliated venture such as I.S. 201 or Ocean Hill-Brownsville. These schools, for sure, have been two of the most important prototypes of strong and serious urban struggle in the eastern section of the nation in the past ten years. They also are two centers—or "complexes"—in which some of the most productive work has taken place in the creation and the evolution of a deep sense of black consciousness, of neighborhood participation, and of neighborhood control. It is, above all, in the reconstruction of the metaphor and symbolism of the *school itself* as something other than a walled and formidable bunker of archaic data and depersonalized people in the midst of living truth—it is, above all, in the labor of creative repossession of the "marketplace" by its own clientele—that many of us now view ourselves as the direct inheritors of men like Preston Wilcox and Charles Wilson.

There are, however, a number of important reasons for which I need to draw a clear and definite line of demarcation between large ventures of this shape and character and those within which I have tried to take my place and to invest my energies. It seems—to begin with—more than apparent to us all that, in such areas as New York, Washington, Cleveland, Boston, and St. Louis, there cannot be much serious role for white men and white women in the genesis of these operations. They constitute, in almost every situation, an important portion of the black and Spanish process of self-liberation and of self-determination. Their function is as much political as pedagogic. They are enormously significant in community organization. They are not, however, a sound or reasonable context for active and conspicuous participation on the part of white men.

There is a second reason why I have not chosen to participate in—or write about—these kinds of large, political "subsystems." The kinds of public-school-affiliated operations I now have in mind, no matter how inventive or how passionate or how immediately provocative, constitute nonetheless a basic extension of the ideology of

public school. They cannot, for reasons of immediate operation, finance and survival, raise serious doubts about the indoctrinational
and custodial function of the public-education apparatus. No matter
how sophisticated or how inventive these "alternatives within the
system" may contrive to be, they nonetheless must continue to provide, within a single package: custodial functions, indoctrinational
functions, credentializing, labeling and grading services, along with
more purely educational functions such as skill training. The public-
school-affiliated ventures such as those that I have named above, or
such as Parkway School in Philadelphia or Morgan School in Washington, D.C., may constantly run skirmishes on the edges of the functions and priorities of domestication; in the long run, however, they
cannot undermine them. The school that flies the flag is, in the long
run, no matter what the handsome community leader in the startling
Afro likes to say, *accountable to that flag* and to the power and to the
values which it represents. This is, and must remain, the ultimate
hang-up of all ventures which aspire to constitute, in one way or
another, a radical alternative "within the system."

There is a third reason, also, why I am not involved with public-
school-associated ventures. This reason has to do with size. It has
been my experience that something bad happens often to good people when they go into programs that involve large numbers of young
people and a correspondingly extended political constituency. The
most gentle and least manipulative of people often prove to be intol-
erable "operators" once they are faced with something like two thousand children and four thousand angry parents. Even those people
who care the most about the personal well-being of young children
turn easily into political performers once they are confronted with
the possibilities for political machinations that are created by a venture that involves so many people and so much publicity. There are
those, I think, who have been able to resist it to a large degree. Kenneth Haskins is one of several important leaders in the Washington
and New York area who seem to have been able to maintain a comfortable balance between politics and education in the face of formidable odds. The point, however, is that those odds are *there*—and
they are also very much against us.

Then, too, and possibly the most important, the likelihood of
going through deep transformations and significant alterations of our
own original ideas (by this I mean the possibilities for growth and for
upheaval in our consciousness of what "school" is about) is seriously
circumscribed when we become accountable to fifteen city blocks
and to ten thousand human beings. This is perhaps a somewhat im-
practical position. I just think many more remarkable things can happen to good people if they happen in small places and in a multiple

of good ways. Even a school of five hundred children and two thousand parents, friends, teachers, hangers-on, and teacher-aides seems much too large. The Free Schools that seem to have the greatest chance of real success, not just in terms of publishable statistics, but in deep human terms as well, are those in which there are not more than eighty to one hundred children.

Education writing is, of course, to some degree, disguised confessional. It may well be that I am only justifying my own inclinations. I know that I feel far more comfortable and can be more in touch with my own instincts and with my own sense of justice in a Free School that remains as small, non-formidable, and non-spectacular as possible. When I first read Paul Goodman's essay about "mini-schools," I felt it sounded coy and unrealistic. Today I believe that Goodman is correct in arguing for a limited size and for a modest scale of operations. It is not easy in this nation to resist the emphasis on bigness, growth, constant expansion. It is, however, something well worth fighting to resist, if it is in our power to do so.

I am, then, speaking for the most part about Free Schools (1) outside the public education apparatus, (2) outside the white man's counterculture, (3) inside the cities, (4) in direct contact with the needs and urgencies of those among the poor, the black, the dispossessed, who have been the most clearly victimized by public education, (5) as small, "decentralized," and "localized" as we can manage, (6) as little publicized as possible.

E = SA²

THOMAS HANNA

I have taken the history of the human soma and, in its recounting, allowed the story to run past the present and into the twenty-first century. This projection into the next century may not be quite correct—the plots of all stories have a way of suddenly veering and changing as new dramatic elements emerge from out of the plot's own development—but it is a fairly drawn historical index of what is portended by somatic thought and by contemporary proto-mutation.

With one eye held fast to this historical index, it is unavoidable that we should devote this last discussion of bodies in revolt to the question of what we shall do in carrying out this somatic revolt and in fulfilling this mutational task. To a large extent this has finally to do with what can best be called education, although the preparatory groundwork during the next generation will be laid, as we have mentioned, by the resolute constructive activities of revolutionary protomutants. With these factors in mind, let us now end this primer in somatic thinking with a few remarks about the policy of mutation.

From this point onward in the technological society of America (and those of Europe within a short period of time), the key word is *adaptation,* and the central human task will be to achieve a *somatic state of optimal adaptability.* During the first few generations of training ourselves in the art of adaptability, the emphasis will primarily be on the accommodative adaptation which takes place under the aegis of our sensual hungers. A technological society makes it invitingly easy to explore the uncharted labyrinth of our sensual hungers, but—far more significantly—this possibility is an invitation to human beings to discover the nature and extent of human wanting, so that men will at last live with their environment, knowing what they, as individual somas, *want* and *need* in their environmental intercourse. This is the only possible manner in which human beings will ever attain independence and, thus, personal freedom: by knowing that they, as somas, are the unique source and unique authority for determining what they want, what they need and what they shall do.

To attain this independence is to achieve the somatic state of optimal adaptability to one's constantly shifting environmental situation. And it is certain that, in order to attain this independent state of knowing one's own adaptational needs, the human being must learn to read his soma.

The educational goal of the traditional culture has been to learn to read the environment. The educational goal of the mutational culture is to learn to read oneself as soma.

Within our cultural tradition, the aim of educational policies has increasingly become apparent as we have neared our goal of constructing a technological society: the educational goal was to train the human for effective aggression against the environment. Just as surely as the newborn Aztec infant of any rank had his umbilical cord symbolically buried with a shield and sheath of arrows while his elders pronounced that he had come into this world to fight, so have the children of the West been born to combat their environment. And they *have* combatted it. And they have conquered it.

The traditional educational policy is clear in its intention to train the human being for a role or vocation or profession which fits somewhere into the whole panorama of societal aggression against the earthly environment. The training method has, typically, been the transplanting of a pre-established program of serial, mechanical procedures which the trainee was then to apply methodically in his effective vocational attack on his environment. In this respect, traditional education is exactly like traditional Western morality in its ill-adaptive, mechanical approach to adaptation: morality has been a pre-packaged program of behavioral procedures implanted in the conscious behavior of young humans. Living and confident adaptation is immensely more efficient than a programmed set of rules. The new educational policy is the training of humans for optimal somatic adaptability; the old educational policy has become easy and will painlessly preserve our technological machinery.

Now that we have entered into the full technological period, this mechanical training becomes precise and matter-of-fact. The guesswork is largely a thing of the past: we need to train so many people for this industrial area, so many for that, this number of physicians, this number of electrical engineers, that number of teachers, and they will be deployed in this section of the country or that segment of the business world. With this situation the traditional culture has fulfilled itself: surviving and prevailing over the environment have now become child's play. The manipulations are simple and anyone can learn: like the army, the business and technological worlds require neither talent nor vision—but only the staple items of the Western world, a minimal intelligence and an acceptance of the work-mentality.

We have now entered into the extraordinary paradise where everything has become easy and where little is demanded. We have won the battle and the challenge has vanished. We could continue for a protracted period of time within this beehive paradise, except for the fact that there is less and less to do and fewer and fewer needed vocations and jobs to be trained for. Quite literally we have entered the epoch when we *don't know what to do*. We do not know *what* to do, because there is little left in the environment *to do*.

Put simply, the traditional culture has rested solidly on the ancient fact that *human need was supplied by the environment*. Formerly, men knew what to do because the environment required it of them if they were to survive. But, with the achievement of a technological environment, we have created an environment which no longer compels us to do anything; it does not create our needs for us, and we therefore discover that we live in a world where we don't *have to* do anything. And, consequently, there is nothing to do: we don't know *what* to do, because factually there is hardly anything left to do.

It is without question that the achievement of a technological environment is, simultaneously, the fulfillment and the destruction of the traditional culture of the West. By fulfilling the needs imposed by the environing earth, this culture destroyed the needs of the environment. In the most exact sense, *our present environment no longer needs our traditional culture.*

And when the salt has lost its savor, wherewith shall it be salted?—this describes the situation of our ancient culture: when we no longer discover our wants and needs from within our environment, where can we discover them? At this moment, what is a man needed for? What is his purpose and function? Does he any longer have a reason for being?

It is to just this extremity of human self-questioning which the traditional culture has led us, and it is totally incapable of grappling with or even comprehending the nature of the question which it has raised.

Let me say this as emphatically as possible: for anyone who has eyes to see, our traditional culture is dead. It is not "sick," it is not "in trouble," it is not suffering momentary "adjustment" problems: it is dead. It is adaptationally irrelevant and ludicrous. And those who remain embroiled within it are enmeshed in a somatic circumstance of sickness, blindness, madness and semi-humanity.

And with equal emphasis I must announce that the only option left open for the survival of mankind is the rapid development of a radically different relationship to our environing world—the development of a radically humanistic culture.

When we have, after so many centuries, so contrived it that the imperatives of the natural world no longer are the sources of our needs and wants, the only option remaining is simultaneously the most obvious option: namely, that we, as individuals, can be the absolute source of our wants and needs. It is not merely that we *can* be this source; rather, the beginning of this radically humanistic culture is the insight that we have *always* been the source of our wants, except that we have, through the centuries, strayed from the light and must learn again to adjust our eyes, blinkingly, to the unaccustomed immediacy and dazzle of our needing self.

If this primer in somatic thinking has shown nothing else, it has at least made clear that we human beings are the bearers of ancient and accomplished somas whose phylogenetic patterns of adaptational wisdom are already part of our very being. It is solely a question of allowing that somatic wisdom free play in expressing itself in adaptive response to our world.

Over three centuries ago, Sir Francis Bacon put the final trim on the sails to Western culture for its rush toward its fulfillment in technology. He enjoined humanity—if it were to understand and conquer the environment—to undergo a "humiliation of the spirit" before the natural world. Humanity responded to this injunction and surrendered to the imperatives of nature. Now that it has achieved this goal, a new and radically different surrender is required of mankind: a surrender to one's own somatic being.

Surrendering to one's own somatic being and learning the patterns of its own imperatives is the educational task as of this moment. The immediate achievement of optimally adaptive human beings is the only meaningful task before men in a technological society—any other tasks are not genuine and without issue. This is what the evolution-revolution is all about, and this is where the action is, as the proto-mutants resolutely or militantly challenge the rules of our society in favor of what must come.

Because our present educational institutions directly reflect the defunct and now ludicrous policies of the traditional culture, our schools and universities are both corrupt and corrupting. It is not that they are "in need of reform," or that the curricula and teaching techniques should be "thoroughly reviewed"; rather, they very concept of education must be revolutionized or there will simply not be any education taking place. Instead, there will be beehive activities which will merely mark time until the bees and the hive are destroyed. It is quite conceivable that, as of this very moment, *no* educational institutions of *any* kind would be better in the long run than our current futile pretense at education. Young Americans are *not* being guided in becoming strong, adaptable, independent human beings. They are being trained to be curtailed, functional semi-human beings who are presumably dependent upon a technological society for their motivation, their self-definition and their *raison d'être*.

The universities of the United States are whistling in the dark, naïvely trying to persuade themselves that these strange currents that seem to be flowing amongst the younger American will somehow go away—that all they need to do is ride out the storm and all will be well. But these educational traditionalists do not have the slightest conception of what the storm is all about, and as long as they continue to cajole themselves into *not* accepting the possibility that something radically new is afoot and into *not* seriously responding to this situation, they can mark down each day on their calendars as being a day of loss, of waste, of stupidity and of betrayal to the future of man.

Certainly there is a paucity of authentic teachers for the proto-mutants of America but, with our technological capacities, even a few are enough to begin the task of educating ourselves for our environment and of creating the mutant culture that must be created.

Many of these teachers are young—very young. Many of them are completely outside of universities or have been forced out of universities. Many of them are older and are within universities, and you can spot them by the fact that their positive attraction of students is matched by their negative repulsion of administrators who finger their tenure papers and mutter that they just don't seem quite right for "our" university. They are correct.

But the teachers, the leaders are here, about us within our society, sharing the same fundamental understanding of what is transpiring and what is the educational goal before us. The first attempt is naturally that of trying to compel the schools, colleges and universities to become transformed into a vehicle of environmental relevance. There is perhaps only the slimmest of chances that this can happen. It is more than likely that absolutely unique and separate institutions will need to be created by deliberate action in order to implement the policies of an absolutely unique educational goal.

The specific manner in which mutational education will be conducted waits, in large part, upon the results of experimentations now taking place both informally, in the strategy planning of militant groups or the innovations within commune societies, and formally, in the scattered humanistic institutes and retreat centers which are burgeoning throughout the country. The general nature of these educational institutions is, however, obvious. The new schools and universities cannot be defined as *places* which are separate from the environing world, places where time is taken *out* of society while the "education" is being injected into the docile student. Rather than being places, the new schools and universities have no option but to be *ways of living* of an experimental nature. One cannot *stop* living and adapting to one's social and physical environment during education, but one must, instead, learn to live and adapt more intensely, more fluidly, more fully and efficiently.

In the same fashion that mutational education is not a *place apart,* it cannot conceivably be a *time apart;* that is, such an education cannot be limited artificially to a certain time of day or of night or to a certain age of life. It should fluidly begin and continue as long as its adaptational training is needed by some human being; when the human ceases to need it (and he may never cease to or he may never begin to) then he leaves off from the training and continues his own adaptive activities.

To speak of an educational institution as a way of life organically related to our immediate social-physical environment—and not as a place apart and a time apart—is a radically different conception of an educational institution. After all, say the traditionalists, it has to be some *place*—doesn't it?—and it has to take place at some *time*.

And of course, the answer is no. Education that has adapted to the nature and resources of a technological environment need not be *any* place or *any* time, inasmuch as it could be taking place *every-where* and *all* the time within the society. I am not in the least invoking the tawdry vision of a world of teaching machines and "canned" televised lectures, which is the final educational achievement of the traditional culture in its stultified, mechanical response to its technology; mechanized training will continue as a necessary but minor aspect of the mutant culture, producing as many technically trained persons as wish to pursue vocations within the shrinking domain of the technological professions which support all of society through the activity of only a small segment of that society. There will always be those whose genius and greatest delight will be in the exploration of further fields of mathematics, computer science, electronics, automation, cybernetics and practical engineering. The continued presence of this technological segment of our society will be guaranteed not by what I call "education" but by the simpler, mechanical learning process of *vocational* training. In evoking the possibility of truly adaptational education, I am referring to the kind of education made possible by the living immediacy of our technological systems of communication and transportation. The "where" and the "when" of educational institutions is no longer a matter of importance; the single matter of importance is the "how" of education. And this "how" is the process of training in somatic adaptation—a training which cannot be given to the student but which can only be acquired by the student himself in the active process itself of adaptation.

Necessarily, training in perception is central to this mutant educational process. Human beings must finally learn what it is to really see and hear and touch without editing and monitoring these perceptions through the constrictions of conscious focusing or unconscious fear. Very few persons know *how* to relax and surrender to the entire inflooding panorama of the environment world. To do so, just once, is a revelatory and never-to-be recovered-from experience—this is the profound effect of psychedelic drugs. But one does not need drugs in order to perceive; all that one needs is one's self and some guiding fellow human being or beings who can explain how they have learned to perceive in a sensual-accommodative manner and what this feels like to them. The whole literature of Indian Yoga is filled with similes and metaphors coined by gurus who were trying to describe "what it feels like" to experience certain somatic patterns: one is guided by being told to look for a certain "color" or a unique, soft-pitched "sound" or to feel a "snake uncoiling at the pit of one's abdomen." This is somatic talk. It doesn't refer to environmental events; it refers to very real and structured somatic patterns which cannot be "seen" or "heard" or "felt" in a consciously assimilative way but can only be perceived by surrender to the soma as it moves and fluidly restructures itself in subtle, immediate communication with its environment.

The gurus and teachers of adaptational education will devise their own methods for such perceptual training, as well as their own contemporary technological, metaphorical and somatic vocabulary for describing the experiences obtained.

In a fairly exact sense, this kind of training can be designated as "consciousness expanding," in that it is an expansion of perception beyond the limitations of traditional conscious perception. Somatic science and philosophy have made it obvious that human "consciousness" is a highly limited and inefficient form of perception; it is aggressively practical, rationally constricted and has a memory bank of auditory and visual atoms which are broken off pieces of reality. The goal of adaptational education is to train the human in the arts of trans-conscious perception, discovering the patterns of this kind of perception, the techniques of its deployment, the noting of the persistent forms of the environment and the consequent construction of a memory-bank of non-verbal, non-imagistic somatic and envirnnmental memory patterns. In its simplest sense this is "somatic education."

But because such education is taking place within the context of this living world and this immediate task of adaptation, training of perception cannot be separated from expressive behavioral training. To behave is to move the soma. To behave adaptively is to move the soma in concert with all aspects of one's shifting environment, responding through assimilative as well as accommodative adaptations, as well as with combinations of both.

This is to say that, unlike traditional education, the educational experience of mutational education must involve real fear, real anger, real sensual acuteness and real sexuality. Otherwise it cannot be educational; it would not be training for environmental adaptability. Full behavioral expression as well as full perceptual experience are, in this instance, a common educational goal. And in recognizing this, we simultaneously recognize that future education is a positive, universalized fulfillment of what in the past has been vaguely designated as "therapy."

What will be the effects of educating human beings as optimally adaptive somas? An obvious effect will be that we will have produced incorrigibly healthy human beings. Another effect will be that such men and women will be totally autonomous units of moral responsibility: i.e., they immediately and intimately know their own somatic nature (this was traditionally referred to as knowing or discovering one's self: as knowing "who" one is) and have learned to give it free vent in adapting to any and evey environmental event. Because they have learned to accept their whole soma as their all-sufficient adaptive source, they have no other thought nor option than to do "what is right." To behave "wrongly" has no meaning for them other than to be unhealthy, inefficient and inadaptable.

But the most explosive effect of somatic education for a mutational culture is that it is a releasor of human energy. Energy and power have always been the most profoundly fascinating and desired possessions of the human creature. The passion for energy, for fire and light, sent the mystics to the powerful godhead, it sent Prometheus to steal power from the gods, and it sent Icarus soaring upward toward the sun to merge with the source of that effulgence. And men have finally captured that power. Once they had ceased to seek it in the heavens, they began to find it within the earth; and during the last centuries we have focused all our effort upon discovering and opening up these energy conduits within the natural environment. And the ultimate and incredible expression of that power which we had finally traced to its lair was that within any quantity of matter there was as much energy as there was implied by squaring the speed of light and multiplying it by that given quantity of matter. The formula $E = MC^2$ was the ultimate and more-than-fulfilling discovery to be made by our traditional culture.

But this rational formula for grappling with the fantastic energy content of our environment was a discovery which was not an end in itself; rather than closing and completing a colossal pilgrimage of man toward controlling and wresting energy from the very bosom of his environment, this new discovery is, indeed, the yearning, beckoning vision that lay behind all the deeply felt myths of those men who had discovered and seized titanic power from legendary empyrean realms. Once men had fully and finally learned to open the conduits of energy in their natural environment, they had thereby freed man from the distracting tyranny of the earth and had made possible the pursuit of the only human goal that has ever finally mattered: the discovery of a way of releasing the energy which for aeons has been pent up within the soma of man.

I am being only moderately facetious when I ape Einstein's formula with a formula in a similar vein: $E = SA^2$—the energy within a human being is equal to the square of the amount of adaptability achieved by any given soma. This formula cannot exactly fit the human situation, inasmuch as the speed of light is a known constant but the amount of human adaptability is unlimited and inconstant.

A somatically balanced and fluidly adaptive human individual is a controlled releasor of living energy whose upward limits are totally unknown. What is known is that, throughout history, man has never been able to release his energies; he has always been a restricted, crimped container of his energies, never giving full expression to his assimilative energies any more than he was able to express his accommodative drives. But even in this distracted, crimped somatic state, men have been able not merely to dominate their earthly environment but they have succeeded in the incomparable achievement of discovering and using the final energy secret of the entire physical cosmos. If a crippled human soma could achieve this, how much more will a balanced and fully adaptive human soma achieve? The energy which one single, balanced soma can now generate within a technological environment has no upward limits. And any attempt to estimate the effects of an entire society of balanced human mutants existing within a technological environment can only conjure up the vague, almost mythically explosive vision of a civilization where anything is possible.

Fully understood and fully learned, adaptation is a game: the gay science of existence. The only way in which the pent-up energies of the human soma can be fully released is through the explosive abandon of play. And this release is now possible: against the supporting background of our technological society, men can now play with their environment. It is too late, now, for work and for seriousness; we have destroyed it along with our ancient culture. It is no longer possible for us to be crimped, pent-up, suffering and serious: we are condemned—through our children—to be healthy, explosive and gay. The result of centuries of work has been the discovery that work is inefficient; it is a dismal waste of energies which remain unused as they either are blocked or are channeled through the narrow apertures of rational, serious effort.

If we are to further transform ourselves and further transform our human environment, we must play, we must be powerful, we must be balanced and adaptive to the least winds of challenge and change. And, already, we are becoming refreshed with keen noses and sharp eyes and agile movements for the adaptational dance that we call life. Eventually we shall be happily startled to realize that the evolution-revolution is not a transient event which will someday be over as we settle into a new cultural routine; rather, evolution-revolution describes our future state of constant, fluid, never-ending adaptation which is the playful manner in which a technologized race finally learns to live.

How amazing it is that, after so many aeons of groping and blundering, we have placed ourselves in the situation where we cannot help but become healthy, happy and powerful: it is our fate. And once that fate is fulfilled and a new human culture has become established, on that day there will be but one sadness: in achieving what we will have achieved, we will have lost all of our gods; which is a pity, because men are thus robbed of the ultimate human triumph of seeing their old gods look down upon them with envy.

So, then, nothing finally is perfect. That, after all, is why it's so much fun.

First Street School

GEORGE DENNISON

I would like to close . . . with a word to parents and teachers, for we are not faced today by simple choices among methods of mass instruction—as if any of them were working—but by the Biblical question in all its severity: *If the salt hath lost its savour, wherewith shall it be salted?* This is as much as to say that any hope for a new spirit in education lies quite outside the present establishment. It lies among parents themselves, and in revitalized communities, and among younger teachers. I would like to say why this is so, why our school professionals, taken as a class, an institutionalized center of power, are fundamentally incompetent and must be displaced. My purpose is not to castigate the bureaucrats, but to recall parents and teachers to an awareness of one crucial truth, a truth that should be, but is not, the gut-wisdom of everyone: that in humane affairs—and education is *par excellence* a humane pursuit—there is no such thing as competence without love. This is the sort of statement that strikes many people, and especially our technocrats, as being sentimental, and so I would like to speak of it in some detail and make clear its truth. And I want to stress that I am not speaking here of excellence of performance, but of mere competence. Let me stress, too— because the question of competence comes down in the end to the characteristics of individuals—that I am not saying that among our fifty thousand bureaucrats there are no persons of real worth. The issue is precisely that of the effect of the institution upon the individual. The institution, the educational system in all its branches, is corrupting to the individual, and though the corruption may in many cases take the form of considerable expertise, the fact remains that competence is destroyed.

In naming love as the necessary base of competence in humane affairs, I am referring not only to the emotion of love, nor just to the moral actions and feelings that belong to caring, but to loving and caring in the very generalized, primitive sense in which they constitute a background condition of life, as we say of young children that they live "as if in love," and as adults, when they are simplified by disasters and extreme demands, reveal a constructive energy and compassion which are obviously generalized and basic.

There is nothing in this background of generalized love that is inimical to speculative thought or formalized research. On the contrary, where the issues are humane, where the field of attention is living persons, as in philosophy, psychology, and education in all its branches, we are more than ever aware of this background of love, and especially when we encounter excellence. The reason is obvious: the events of the field—which are often of the most subtle and elusive kind—cannot even be discerned unless there is a responding sensitivity in the observer. This sensitivity, if we are to speak of competence, must span a considerable range; and a range of any magnitude cannot be sustained except on some active principle of concern, attraction, care. What we call curiosity is no mere matter of the intellect, but is itself a generalized form of love. Einstein called it "holy." Often, in reading humane studies, we infer the background of love from the number of things observed, from the finesse of observation, and the unwavering insistence upon values. Quite simply, these are the qualities of one who cares. Sometimes, as in the pages of Darwin, Kant, Whitehead, or Freud, one feels a positive glow of benignity, or the flush of enchantment with the host of real events which form our lives. Dewey, in his knotty way, writes with love; and what else but this deep, ineradicable caring can give such sharpness to the eye, such patience, integrity, and persistence to the whole labor of a life? It does not matter, then, whether love is *expressed,* or whether it be a love of causes and meanings and not of individual persons. We are aware of it as a background, a source, the condition of the writer vis-à-vis his world. We are aware of more than this, however, for we also see that this generalized caring is the meaning of the speaker's very presence before us. It is the motive of his address. It is the justification of his words. Communication, in its true sense of communion and change, is inconceivable apart from this background of love. One might also speak of the sensual elements that belong to caring. The world is attractive in its sensual forms. Our knowledge of its forms begins in response (which soon becomes creative), and we cannot respond except with our senses. We cannot know feelings by analysis, but only by feelings. When it is diminished, we progressively lose our world, and as our world is fragmented, so are we. One might put it this way: that there is no other path except this original ground of attracted care by which the events and forms of the world can reach fruition as mind. When this background is corrupted, or held inoperative, true mind, true thought, is not to be attained. What we see instead is mere intellection. In Goethe's words: "All the thinking in the world will not bring us to thought. We must be right by nature, then thoughts present themselves to us like the children of God, they jump up and cry, 'Here we are!' " Thomas Mann calls this harmony the joy of the artist: "thought that can become feeling, feeling that can become thought."

It is in this sense, then, that failure of mind is, at bottom, a failure of love. The conditions which nullify caring as the vital breath of being in the world are ruinous to thought, and render competence in humane affairs quite unattainable. There is no need to point out that the deathly rigidity of bureaucratic institutions nullifies the organic demands of attracted care. If is enough to say that scientists, artists, professionals of all kinds (provided they have integrity), men of independent spirit, and all children are profoundly unwilling to surrender sensibility and will to the demands of the bureaucrat.

I have given three examples of the speech of our educationists. Let me refer to them now in order to contrast briefly the characteristics of the philosopher and the Expert, the scientist and the technocrat.

What is the social action of jargon? I have said that true communication is communion and change. Jargon is not innocent. The man who speak it, who prates in front of us of roles and reciprocally operative groups, and evaluative maps, and the aims of the curriculum, and better fits, and superordinate and subordinate persons means to hold us at a distance; he means to preserve his specialty— his little piece of an essentially indivisible whole—precisely as a specialty. He does not mean to draw near to us, or to empower us, but to stand over us and manipulate us. He wishes, in short, to remain an Expert. The philosopher, by contrast, wishes all men to be philosophers. His speech creates equality. He means to draw near to us and empower us to think and do for ourselves. He does not isolate little specialties and cling to them, but reconstitutes large forms, forms toward which he is modest and toward which he teaches modesty. He is *of* the community, and neither he nor we can escape it.

And how does the technocrat differ from the scientist? We need mention but one fundamental way, for it is decisive. Where the scientist recognizes no authority but nature, or truth, and will not accept premises at the hands of government, class, or superiors, the technocrat reverses this essential attitude of free thought and accepts precisely his premises at the hands of others. It matters very little if he calls himself a scientist, and makes a lesser divinity of Research, and a greater one of Basic Research. His methods, in the last analysis, are not serious. His objectivity is not objective. It is without gravity or risk. It is objective, for instance, to say that we must change our schools, *but only within the framework of existing authority?* Scientists in our time have discovered that the very act of observation influences the phenomena. They include themselves in their equations. Our technocrats have not yet, and never will, take that decisive step.

Now what is the point of all this? For one might say simply, "Our educators have failed. They have done nothing but fail. They are incompetent."

I have put it in this form in order to say that any solution which perpetuates the existing authoritarian bureaucracy is doomed to failure. And I have wanted very much to say that competence is impossible without love, for in this centralized, technological, Expert-ridden age of ours it needs desperately to be said. To say it indicates, too, the direction of the essential change. We must transfer authority to where concern already exists. We must place it where there is nothing in the environment which will *inevitably* destroy the vital breath of concern. Authority must reside in the community. It must be local, homely, modest, sensitive. And it must be tied, once and for all, to the persons who not only *do* care, but will go on caring. In my opinion, there is no other hope but this.

Community, of course, is a much-abused word, and often a vague one. It does not mean neighborhood, though neighborhood is indispensable to community. I have tried to make clear why I believe that parents and teachers, "laymen," "ordinary persons," possess the potential—and many the actuality—of true competence in the education of young children; and why the technocrat, isolated in his cubicle, does not and cannot possess it. But in fact no community need want for wisdom. The greatest of minds are, in effect, its permanent residents. Just as some men are of the bureaucracy, of the state, others are of the community. All philosophers are of the community. All scientists are. All artists are. It does not matter how difficult or elevated their work may be; its action is to create peers. And so the authority that needs to guide the educational function, in being local and close to home, need not forfeit one jot of its resources. Or put it this way: a community is not a true community unless, in principle, it is universal.

Let me close with the words of two men who are of the community. Between them they provide both largeness of conception and the vital breath that animates.

I see at bottom but two alternatives between which education must choose if it is not to drift aimlessly. One of them is expressed by the attempt to induce educators to return to the intellectual methods and ideals that arose centuries before scientific method was developed. The appeal may be temporarily successful in a period when general insecurity, emotional and intellectual as well as economic, is rife. For under these conditions the desire to lean on fixed authority is active. Nevertheless, it is so out of touch with all the conditions of modern life that I believe it is folly to seek salvation in this direction. The other alternative is systematic utilization of scientific method as the pattern and ideal of intelligent exploration and exploitation of the potentialities inherent in experience.

The words are Dewey's, in *Experience and Education*. Tolstoy is the other man, though these are not his words, but the words of a former pupil, recalling in his old age the school at Yásnaya Polyána.

We would surround Leo Nikoláievich, catch hold of him before and behind, try to trip him up, snowball him, and rush in and climb on his back, eager to overthrow him. But he was even more determined than we, and like a strong ox would carry us on his back. After a while from weariness, or more often for fun, he would fall into the snow. Then our ecstasy was indescribable! We at once began to cover him with snow and threw ourselves on him in a heap, crying, "The heap's too small! The heap's too small!"

We enjoyed school and worked eagerly. But Leo Nikoláievich worked yet more eagerly than we. He worked with us so eagerly that he often missed his lunch. In school his appearance was serious. He demanded of us cleanliness, care with the school things, and truthfulness. . . . He never punished anyone for pranks, disobedience, or idleness; and if we became too noisy he only said, "Quieter, please!" . . . In such pleasures and merriment, and with rapid progress in learning, we grew as close to Leo Nikoláievich as a cobbler's thread is to wax. . . . We spent the day in school and passed the evening at games, sitting on his balcony till late at night. He would tell us tales about the war, or of how a man-cook cut his aunt's throat in Moscow, and how he went hunting and a bear bit him, and he showed us the scar near his eye. There was no end to our talking. We told him terrible things—about wizards and wood demons. . . . He told us tales, terrible or funny, sang songs, suiting the words to us. . . . He was in general a great jester and never missed a chance to have a laugh. . . .

Fifty years have passed since then. I am already an old man. But my recollections of Leo Nikoláievich's school and of himself are still clear. They always cheer me, especially when I am in trouble. . . . The love of Leo Nikoláievich then kindled burns brightly in my soul and lights my whole life; and the recollection of those bright and happy days I have never lost, and never shall lose.

—Aylmer Maude's *The Life of Tolstoy*

Perhaps the emblem for our American primary schools should be a medallion without words, showing Tolstoy with the children on his back.

A Personal Note

Randomly thumbing through a half-dozen or so anthologies, I have discovered that there appears to be no preordained way of ending one. Therefore I am taking the liberty of checking into the consciousness and hopefully, the heart of the reader, before he assigns this book to the bookshelf of oblivion.

The root problems of man, Being, the person, the world, teaching and learning, the curriculum and the school, should raise some searching questions about education and the meaning of life. The metaphorical meaning of a "root" problem implies that the questions generated by the problems should take one underground, below the surface of reality, to the deeper ground where one's sense of identity exists. Such questions should enable one to penetrate the surface meanings and realities of any institution or situation, educational or otherwise. In fact, if the deeper meaning of one's self and, by implication, life is fully felt, sensed, and experienced, then the process of education will be encountered everywhere, all the time, and in every situation. In my opinion it makes no sense to isolate the process of education, as we have done in schools, colleges, and universities; and then to expect, after subjecting millions of children and young adults to frequently barbarous and inhumane conditions for learning about the subject matter of life, that we should not have the social and personal problems that we do. Most educational institutions, because of the conditions and attitudes that usually prevail in them, are in no position to solve the outstanding personal and social problems that are brought to them from the outside world. A few have tried, however, only to find that powerful pressures to desist are generated by the communities and institutions that they serve. So most educational institutions are in the same position as that anonymous but famous person who was "damned if he did and damned if he didn't."

Education as a formal, institutional phenomenon is not without hope, however. Some really good things are happening in some schools, due to the heroic, individual efforts of students, teachers, and even some administrators. But there is hardly a mass movement toward radical reform in the schools and institutions of so-called higher learning, nor is there one visible on the horizon. We are still rather romantically and adolescently "doing our own thing" in education and foolishly expecting that it may be enough. I sincerely and deeply believe that future generations of mankind will see much more clearly than we do the extent to which each individual is inextricably involved in both the deepest and the most superficial problems and values of his fellow man. I think that future generations will have much greater knowledge and sensitivity about the so-called interdependence of the individual with other people, nature, and the world at large. Much of what we now only very dimly perceive as being humanizing and deepening to our sense of life and self will become common knowledge and form a basis for universal human experiencing. In short, my critical view of present educational institutions and the greater world society to which they are inextricably tied does not prevent me from having optimism and good feelings for the future of humankind. Each of us, however, must do all that he or she can to know and to encounter personal freedom and the love of life, and by so doing, to fulfill our responsibility to humanity in the deepest and most meaningful of ways possible.